BEYOND THE COLD WAR

RESEARCH SERIES / NUMBER 80

BEYOND
THE COLD WAR

CONFLICT AND COOPERATION IN THE THIRD WORLD

George W. Breslauer, Harry Kreisler,
& Benjamin Ward, Editors

INSTITUTE OF INTERNATIONAL STUDIES
MacArthur Interdisciplinary Group on International Security Studies
UNIVERSITY OF CALIFORNIA AT BERKELEY

Library of Congress Cataloging-in-Publication Data

Beyond the cold war : conflict and cooperation in the Third World /
  George W. Breslauer, Harry Kreisler & Benjamin Ward, editors.
      p. cm. — (Research series ; no. 80)
    Includes bibliographical references.
    ISBN 0-87725-180-0 (pbk.)
    1. Developing countries—Politics and government. I. Breslauer,
George W. II. Kreisler, Harry. III. Ward, Benjamin (Benjamin N.)
IV. University of California, Berkeley. International and Area Studies.
V. Series: Research series (University of California, Berkeley. Institute
of International Studies) ; no. 80.
D883.B49 1991   91-31527
909′.09724—dc20   CIP

CONTENTS

PREFACE

In 1987 the MacArthur Foundation gave a major grant to an inter-disciplinary faculty committee of the Institute of International Studies at the University of California, Berkeley, to foster security studies on the Berkeley campus. Drawing on the Berkeley campus' strengths in international, comparative, and area studies, the MacArthur Interdisciplinary Group on International Security Studies (MIGISS) sought to help shape a new definition of international security studies for a post–Cold War world.

This collection of papers resulted from a conference on "Super-power Conflict and Cooperation in the Third World," held at Berkeley 4–6 October 1990. The stimulus for the conference was a recognition of the changing nature of power in the international system and its im-plications for the Soviet Union and the United States. By the end of the 1980s both superpowers were experiencing major resource constraints; both were becoming aware of their growing inability to control clients and allies; both were coming to terms with the emergence of a multipolar world in which economic power was becoming more important, even as military power retained its important role. These changes had their concrete manifestation in the end of the Cold War and a movement toward settlement of a number of regional conflicts in the Third World. At the end of the 1980s, violent conflicts in Southeast Asia, southern Africa, Afghanistan, and Central America, which had dominated U.S.-USSR relations for the better part of a decade, moved toward resolution with varying degrees of success. In the Middle East the 1991 war against Iraq, precipitated by Iraq's invasion of Kuwait, provided a compelling example of the complex nature of the international system after the demise of the Cold War.

The Berkeley conference examined regional conflicts in the five areas of the Third World noted above and the role of the superpowers in their initiation and resolution. The conference focused on the follow-ing questions: Under what conditions did the superpowers decide to disengage from regional conflicts? What are the implications of such disengagement for the region? With the end of Cold War competition, what forms of superpower involvement are likely to occur in the Third World? Does the end of the Cold War lessen or increase the likelihood of regional military conflict?

For each of the five regions examined, papers were presented on regional dynamics, U.S. policy, and Soviet policy. Summary papers by George Breslauer, Benjamin Ward, and Steve Weber suggest some general and comparative insights into superpower relations and the emerging international order in light of the conference papers presented and in light of lessons of the Gulf War.

We would like to acknowledge the John D. and Catherine T. MacArthur Foundation for its generous support of security studies on the Berkeley campus. The MacArthur Interdisciplinary Group on International Security Studies has greatly benefited from the administrative support provided by the Institute of International Studies. The details of the 1990 conference were deftly handled by the conscientious efforts of Letitia Carper, and this volume has benefited significantly from the skillful editing of Paul Gilchrist and Bojana Ristich and the meticulous typesetting of Stephen Pitcher.

G. B.
H. K.
B. W.

NOTES ON CONTRIBUTORS

GEORGE W. BRESLAUER is Professor of Political Science and Chairman of the Center for Slavic and East European Studies at the University of California, Berkeley.

HARRY KREISLER is Executive Director of the Institute of International Studies, University of California, Berkeley.

BENJAMIN WARD is Professor of Economics at the University of California, Berkeley.

FREDERICK Z. BROWN is Professorial Lecturer at the Johns Hopkins University School of Advanced International Studies.

GENNADY I. CHUFRIN is Deputy Director of the Institute of Oriental Studies, USSR Academy of Sciences.

MICHAEL CLOUGH is Senior Fellow for Africa at the Council on Foreign Relations.

GALIA GOLAN is Professor of Political Science and Director of the Mayrock Center for Research on the Soviet Union and Eastern Europe at the Hebrew University of Jerusalem.

SELIG S. HARRISON is Senior Associate at the Carnegie Endowment for International Peace.

TERRY LYNN KARL is Associate Professor of Political Science and Director of the Center for Latin American Studies at Stanford University.

BEN KIERNAN is Associate Professor of History at Yale University.

WINRICH KÜHNE is with the Africa Group of the Stiftung Wissenschaft und Politik in Ebenhausen, Germany.

ROBERT LITWAK is Director of International Studies at the Woodrow Wilson International Center for Scholars.

S. NEIL MacFARLANE is Professor of Politics at Queen's University, Kingston, Canada.

ROBERT PASTOR is Professor of Political Science at Emory University and Director of the Latin American and Caribbean Program at Emory's Carter Center.

WILLIAM B. QUANDT is a Senior Fellow in the Foreign Policy Studies Program at the Brookings Institution.

SHIBLEY TELHAMI is Professor of Government at Cornell University.

STEVE WEBER is Assistant Professor of Political Science at the University of California, Berkeley.

NIKOLAI G. ZAITSEV is Deputy Director of the Latin American Institute, USSR Academy of Sciences.

INTRODUCTION

COMPARING REGIONAL CONFLICTS

Benjamin Ward

This paper elicits some possible inductions from the conflicts considered by the MacArthur Conference on Superpower Conflict and Cooperation in the Third World. The aim is, first, to develop a list of factors suggested by a reading of the conference papers as being interesting aspects of regional conflict, and then to provide a brief appraisal of their more general relevance. The list is developed by means of a comparative look at four of the conflicts—Afghanistan, Angola, Cambodia, and Nicaragua—which possess a certain similarity of structure and for which the conference provided the most systematic treatment. Some twenty-nine factors end up on the list, which also contains a statement regarding their relevance for each of the four conflicts. These factors are displayed in Table 1, while the appraisal of their relevance follows in the text.

Appraisal is carried out in two steps. In the first, the question is asked: Do the commonalties among these conflicts suggest that they constitute a specific type of conflict upon which one might build a theory of the conditions under which conflicts of this type might be settled, and the properties of the settlement? After some discussion of the four conflicts and their settings, the question is answered with a reluctant negative. In the second step, the factors are used to characterize the conflicts in El Salvador and Lebanon and to discuss a few aspects of the overall Middle East situation. This leads, I believe, to a positive answer to the question: Can this set of traits be of help in analyzing other conflicts with a view to generating not models but insights into their structure and tendencies?

The conference focussed on the later stages of conflicts that were underway during the late 1980s and seemed to be moving toward some

---

The author would like to thank Ashok Bardhan and Xu Pingyi for research assistance, and the MacArthur Interdisciplinary Group for International Security Studies for support in preparing this paper.

sort of settlement. That is the portion of the conflicts that is being appraised here; attention is not given to their origin or early history. These conflicts were moving toward settlement during a time of dramatic change in Soviet-American relations, and during a particular moment in the world's movement toward increasing interaction among nations. These specific features of all the conflicts under consideration should be borne in mind when appraising the relevance of the factors for other times and places.

COMPARATIVE STRUCTURE AND TENDENCIES
OF THE FOUR CONFLICTS

A. NATURE OF THE FIGHTING

Stalemates. Before serious negotiation got underway, some stabilization of the strategic environment had occurred in all four of the conflicts.Tests of the benefits of escalation had been made in offensives by the Sandinistas, the Soviet-Afghan forces, UNITA-South African forces, and the Cambodian government forces. None was decisive, either because the opposing forces could not be destroyed, as was the case with Cambodia, or because of successful counter-escalation, as with the insertion of additional Cuban troops into Angola. With the prospects for decisive victory thus either excluded or delayed, peace, or at least some downgrading of the level of conflict, became a relatively more attractive option on at least one side of the lines.

Sanctuaries. External sanctuaries were essential to the continuation of the conflict in Nicaragua and Cambodia, and substantially increased the power of the guerrilla forces in Afghanistan. They were not a major factor in Angola, though external forces were involved on the guerrilla side. From the point of view of the fighting, sanctuaries permitted relatively weak forces to maintain their status as a "force in being," which greatly magnified their military significance. Only in Angola were the guerrillas and their terrain such that sanctuaries were not essential to continued conflict.

Foreign Military Units Engaged in the Fighting. This occurred in Cambodia (Vietnamese), Afghanistan (Soviet), and Angola (South African). In Nicaragua there were numerous military advisors (Cubans and Americans), but no organized fighting units from abroad were engaged. In the first three cases, the foreign units were necessary to prevent defeat

Table 1

Comparative Structure and Tendencies of the Four Conflicts: Afghanistan, Angola, Cambodia, Nicaragua

A. *Nature of the Fighting*

"Fighting stalemates"
Role of sanctuaries
Foreign military units engaged in the fighting?
Collateral wars
Were domestic forces decisively defeated?
Were there changes in the correlation of forces?
Post-settlement fighting?

B. *Economic and Social Factors in the Conflicts*

Domestic economic problems
External trade and the economy
Ethnic and regional rivalries
Class as a complicating factor
Nationalism/anti-imperialism

C. *Role of Regional Powers*

The provision of sanctuaries
Border disputes
Did regional powers feel threatened by the conflict?
Large increases in regional military forces?
Regional powers' economies substantially affected?
Regional powers as spoilers
Regional powers as dealers

D. *Role of the Superpowers*

Were they more spoilers or dealers?
Were economic instruments important levers in getting to serious negotiation?
Did domestically mandated policy shifts affect the settlement process?
How helpful was reduced superpower interest to:
    (1) controlling conflict escalation, or
    (2) the coming of peace?

E. *The Settlement Negotiation Process*

Does holding an international conference help?
How important was "piecemeal negotiation"?
Were basic issues compromised by negotiation?
Did the negotiations have a "climacteric"?

of the government forces or to establish a friendly government (Cambodia); probably neither was the case in Nicaragua.

Collateral Wars. The Sino-Vietnamese war was initiated by the Chinese to "punish" Vietnam. It succeeded in imposing a high price on the Vietnamese for continuing their occupation of Cambodia. In South Africa the black revolt has had some of the dimensions of a collateral war, raising the price of continuing involvement in Angola and in destabilizing efforts elsewhere.

Were any of the domestic fighting forces decisively defeated? The disarming of the Contras as part of the settlement suggests the answer is "yes" for Nicaragua; at any rate the Contras' ability to stage disruptive raids had become substantially reduced by the time of the formal settlement. On the other hand, in both Nicaragua and Cambodia the guerrilla forces have been rather weak throughout most of their history, relying more on attrition than on the prospect of conquering the governments they fought. Perhaps most important is that in all four conflicts the guerrillas maintained a force in being throughout the relevant period.

Changes in the Correlation of Forces. These were important in the later phases of all four conflicts. Most striking were the effects of the introduction of Stinger missiles in Afghanistan, the increase in Cuban forces to prevent the defeat of government forces around Cuito Canavale in Angola, and the unilateral withdrawal of Vietnamese forces from Cambodia. Also of significance was the prospect of a substantial reduction in external military support for the Sandinistas. All four served the interests of relative balance, reducing at least the short-run prospects of decisive victories by the more powerful sides in the conflicts.

Post-Settlement Fighting. At the present time there is some fighting in all four of the "host" countries. In Afghanistan the fighting continues at a moderate but reduced level. In Angola something similar seems to be happening despite post-settlement negotiated cease-fires. In Nicaragua there are only isolated small-group clashes so far, but the situation appears to be deteriorating. Guerrilla activity continues in Cambodia, where of course no formal settlement has been achieved.

B. ECONOMIC AND SOCIAL FACTORS IN THE CONFLICTS

Domestic Economic Problems. The Nicaraguan economy was in deep trouble by the late 1980s and was moving into a real depression. This was an important factor in Sandinista calculations. Much less is known about the other three economies. Clearly the economic costs of the fighting were catastrophic in Afghanistan. Famine has been intermittent in parts of Angola, partly due to wartime disruption; on the other hand, oil has continued to be pumped and sold in Western markets. In the case of Cambodia, the situation may have been just the opposite. The Cambodian economy appears to have improved considerably under the Heng Samrin government, and this may have served as a legitimizer of the government, and been a factor in the Vietnamese decision to remove most of its forces from Cambodia. However, there has been an economic downturn in the last two years. One might argue that only in Nicaragua did the domestic economic situation play a major (maybe even a decisive) role in the move toward settlement, though it was important in Cambodia. In the other two countries, the economic situation does not seem to have had a noticeable effect on the positions of the major actors.

External Trade and the Economy. The primitive nature of three of the four economies kept this factor from being of major significance. The Angolan government was of course helped by its oil production, which was the dominant factor in Angolan foreign trade (with, ironically, the United States as its major trading partner). Only in Nicaragua were external economic relations crucial to the domestic economy. The American boycott cut Nicaragua off from its major export markets (though there were international commodity markets on which sales of coffee and cotton could be made) and from direct connection with its major supplier of many capital goods and durables. These effects, which were clearly important, are additional to the effect on Nicaragua of the general halt to economic progress in most of Latin America as a result of the debt crisis, in which Nicaragua was a full participant.

Ethnic and Regional Rivalries. These two factors go together, and they are central in both Afghanistan and Angola. The Afghan situation is very nicely discussed in Selig Harrison's paper. In Angola, Savimbi's forces and support base are predominantly Ovimbundu, while the MPLA originally had distinct ethnic roots but has now added an urban and mestizo base which gives the government a broader, but by no means universal, base. Ethnic rivalry does not seem to be a major factor in Nicaragua (except the Misquito Indians, which represent a small and localized portion of the population) or Cambodia (except for the putative settlement of Vietnamese in eastern Cambodia). Ethnic tensions tend to be durable, and where they are powerful, settlements will tend to be more tenuous.

Class as a Complicating Factor. Urban-rural and secular-traditional differences are important in Afghanistan, but may not be in Angola, though urban interests there seem to be firmly on the side of the government. In Cambodia the Khmer Rouge is violently anti-urban, but it is not clear what effects with respect to class interests the looser economic policies of the Heng Samrin regime may create. Nicaragua is complicated with respect to class: the Chamorro government and its supporters seem strongly urban and middle class; the Contra supporters are probably mostly rural-lumpen and Sandinista-dissident elements (though the size and intensity of Contra support in the countryside is unknown); Sandinista support now comes largely from the government bureaucracy, the military, and the portion of the peasantry that benefitted from Sandinista land reform. This muting of class in three of the four conflicts is surprising. It may reflect the very low level of modernization in their economies and societies, or simply our ignorance of the working of this factor in such societies.

Nationalism/Anti-Imperialism. This is a factor in Nicaragua (anti–United States), Cambodia (anti-Vietnam), and Afghanistan (anti–Soviet Union), but apparently not in Angola. This is a murky phenomenon, which may or may not be of substantial importance in the post-settlement period. The role of both class and nationalism in the last three of these conflicts is in striking contrast to that which tended to predominate in the decolonization wars of the first three post–World War II decades.

C. ROLE OF REGIONAL POWERS

The Provision of Sanctuaries. Motives were varied for the three providers (Costa Rica was an additional and reluctant provider, but its role had ended by the later phases of the Central American conflict). Pakistan played an active role in influencing the course of the Afghan conflict and sought to ensure at least a friendly orientation in any future Afghan government. Thailand's primary aim in Cambodia was to control the power not of the Cambodian but of the Vietnamese government. Early in the Nicaraguan conflict, Honduras had aims somewhat like those of Pakistan, but toward the end seemed more interested in achieving a settlement than in its provisions. So two of the providers were prepared to continue support for the guerrilla forces for an extended period of time, and of course this role was central for those forces.

Border Disputes. In all four conflicts there was considerable permeability of borders of the civil war hosts. There was a long-standing border conflict between Nicaragua and Honduras over the Gulf of Fonseca; however, this was not a major factor in the Nicaraguan conflict, though it did serve to amplify predispositions. Namibia's existence became closely linked to the settlement process for Angola, and that was a complicating factor. But generally speaking, irredentism was not important in any of these conflicts.

Did the surrounding regional powers feel threatened by the conflict? The answers are complicated, because several motives combined to produce the resulting force levels. For example, in South Asia Pakistan felt threatened, but also welcomed the opportunity for more U.S. aid, which would enhance its position vis-à-vis India, which consequently felt threatened; Iran seems not to have been much affected. In Central America the dramatic increase in Sandinista forces, combined with their offensive potential, was certainly viewed with alarm. That fear was combined with the Salvadoran government's fear of Sandinista support for Salvador's guerrillas, and with Costa Rica's fear of the Contras (who made a sanctuary of army-less Costa Rica during part of the conflict). The Honduran government faced opposing fears—first, of the potential threat of the Sandinistas to its survival, and then, increasingly, of the domestic effects of the Contras, the refugees, and the American presence. In Southeast Asia, fear of the Cambodian conflict spreading seems to have been slight, and was not even large in Thailand, where border skirmishing with Vietnamese troops seems to have occurred occasionally. In southern Africa the contiguous black African states do not seem to have felt threatened by the Angolan conflict; Namibia may be an exception, though it had something to gain from the ending of the conflict. The big fear was presumably South Africa's—that apartheid protests might be turned into a combined internal and foreign war. No easy generalizations emerge, except that regional security structures are quite diverse.

Did the conflicts lead to large increases in military forces of the surrounding regional powers? The answer is clearly "yes" for Central America and South Asia. It was also true for the Sino-Vietnam border, where border forces far exceeded normal security needs (Vietnam's forces numbered 700,000 and China's, 250,000). Forcing this deployment by the Vietnamese was an instrument of Chinese policy toward the Cambodian civil war and a major factor of attrition working against the Vietnamese. Aside from modest changes in Thailand, it is not clear that much militarization occurred among the ASEAN powers. South Africa's policy of destabilization, combined with the revolt at home, substantially increased that government's security requirements. So in all cases, at least some of the surrounding regional powers substantially increased the forces committed to fight or deter various actions associated with the civil wars.

Were the surrounding regional powers' economies substantially affected by the conflict? Pakistan's growth rate was higher during 1980–87 than 1965–80, which is partly attributable to conflict-related U.S. aid. The economies surrounding Indochina thrived during the Cambodian conflict, which was irrelevant to their economic progress. South Africa's economic troubles resulted partly from apartheid, but destabilization must have been a fairly expensive policy to implement. The other Central American economies do not seem to have been much affected,* though there may have been a significant impact in the last couple of years before the settlement, which would have provided a bit more impetus to the

*Terry Karl disagrees with this statement, but I believe she is mistaken (see her contribution to this volume).

Economic Indicators

Countries	Annual Growth Rates				
	1965–80	1980–87	1980–87		1987/1980
	GDP	GDP	Exports	Imports	Terms of Trade
Latin America	6.0%	1.4%	3.0%	-5.6%	- -
Mexico	6.5	0.5	6.6	-8.1	.73
5 Central American	4.8	0.34	- -	- -	- -
4 Central American	5.2	0.28	-.1	-1.8	.80

Note: Data are from 1989 World Bank Development Report. The "5 Central American" countries are Karl's five; "4 Central American" omits Nicaragua.

The above data do not suggest "economic devastation" associated with the conflict. Like other countries at similar levels of per capita GNP around the world, growth slowed substantially around 1980 for other reasons (oil, debt, U.S. recession).

Gonzalez estimates "approximately $30 billion in economic losses since the outbreak of regional conflicts" (cited in Karl, p. 232 below). I assume he means 1980–87 losses. That is about 20 percent of the total GDP generated by the five economies over the seven years, which is not very plausible.

Assume that the Central American economies would have grown at the Latin American growth rates of 1965–80 (6 percent) if the conflict had not started in 1979. Then you get a seven-year GDP loss in the $30 billion neighborhood. Given the other problems faced by Latin and Central America, attributing this "loss" entirely to the war is implausible.

Assume that the relative reduction in Central American growth rates between 1965–80 and 1980–87, as compared to the Latin American reduction, is attributable to the conflict. That puts the loss at $2 billion or so. More plausible, I would say, though still pretty crude. If absolute differences in reductions are used, there is no dollar loss attributable to the four countries.

later phases of the negotiation. In sum, regional economic effects do not seem to have been substantial.

Regional Powers as Spoilers. To what extent did regional powers serve as spoilers, hindering the settlement process? The major spoilers were South Africa, with its destabilization policy; Pakistan, with its attempts to maintain dominant influence over some guerrilla groups; Vietnam, with its occupation of Cambodia; and China, with its continuing material support for the guerrillas and its military threat to Vietnam. Thailand's providing of sanctuary to the Cambodian guerrillas was also essentially a spoiler policy. South Africa's policy could not be successful over the long run; presumably destabilization was designed to provide breathing room while the black domestic revolt was brought under control. Pakistan's motives were not so defensive: Pakistan was in competition with India for hegemonic influence in South Asia and sought to bring as much of Afghanistan as possible under its political influence. Vietnam wished to maintain its influence on the Cambodian government, and to prevent a return of the Khmer Rouge to power, while China and Thailand were interested in containing Vietnamese influence. In each of these cases, using instruments such as fighting, armed threat, the granting of sanctuary to guerrillas, and military aid, neighboring governments sought to extend the conflicts until their own goals were met. In Central America one might think of El Salvador, Honduras, and Guatemala as potential spoilers, in terms of the political interests of their governments. However, the civil war in El Salvador weakened that government enough to substantially inhibit its policies; to a lesser extent, the same may have been true of Guatemala. As noted already, Honduran interests were changing from an active spoiling role to a serious interest in dealing. Spoiling interests are thus present in all four of the conflicts, though not to the same degree. This suggests that reliance on "regional solutions to regional problems" is a policy that will often fail.

Regional Powers as Dealers. To what extent did regional powers serve as dealers, actively supporting the settlement process? Dealers did not exist in South Asia, nor did effective ones in southern Africa. The ASEAN countries switched from satisfaction with the stalemate (and the isolation of Vietnam) to dealing only when it became clear that the Vietnamese were withdrawing, and perhaps also with the emerging signs that the expansion of Soviet military power into Southeast Asia was being ended. In Central America, Costa Rica was an early dealer: the threat to Costa Rica's borders, together with President Arias's situation and personality, played an important role in the rise of interest in dealing. Honduras and

Guatemala were perhaps never enthusiastic dealers, but may have shifted in part because they saw the United States losing interest in the conflict.

D. ROLE OF THE SUPERPOWERS

Given the rather common characterization of Soviet-American relations during the Cold War as that of a Soviet expansionist challenge to a more status quo–oriented United States, there is an odd feature to our four-conflict sample: in each of them the Soviet Union has been defending the existing government against American-supported guerrillas. No doubt this makes our sample unrepresentative in important respects, particularly with respect to an appraisal of superpower behavior in the Third World over the entire course of the Cold War. But aside from the Middle East, these *are* the major conflicts of the later 1980s and so come close to being not a sample but the universe of discourse for the present era. Even so, the question of representativeness of superpower behavior in these conflicts deserves some attention, which it will receive toward the end of the paper.

To what extent were the United States and Soviet Union spoilers and to what extent dealers in the later phases of the four conflicts? This question is complicated by the many changes that have occurred in each conflict over the last half dozen years. The United States was a rather consistent dealer with respect to Angola and Afghanistan, at least in the sense that basic features of the settlements ended up being fairly close to long-held U.S. proposals. The United States was a spoiler in Nicaragua in that it was holding out for victory, and in Cambodia in that U.S. diplomacy was directed toward preserving the continuation of the conflict at least until the Vietnamese army withdrew.

The Soviet role as spoiler or dealer is harder to appraise. Since in the "middle" of each of the four conflicts its aim was simply to maintain the existing government in power, one might think of it as a dealer. But that ignores the existing power structure, which in each case included a civil war as well as considerable international involvement in its course. In this context, one might argue that the Soviet Union was a spoiler with respect to all four conflicts as late as the mid-1980s, at least in the sense that it was insisting that each of the four governments be recognized as the only legitimate rulers of the countries. However, it then changed to become a dealer in all four. The policy shifts associated with this change included informal pressures toward settlement in the case of Vietnam (aid reductions), Nicaragua (pro-election), and Afghanistan (troop withdrawal). Oddly enough, in Angola the dealer posture entailed supporting a further buildup of Cuban forces in order to stabilize the fighting stalemate in the face of a South African invasion.

Were economic instruments important in moving the parties toward serious negotiation? The U.S. boycott of Nicaragua had an important impact; perhaps that is the only example. Frederick Brown claims the American boycott hurt Vietnam substantially; I doubt it, given the economic policies of the Vietnamese leadership. However, we probably both agree that it did not influence Vietnamese behavior significantly before the late 1980s. The international boycott of South Africa hurt that economy, but linkages to Angola are dubious. Nicaragua is a special case of dependence on trade with the United States. So the general feeling that boycotts are not very effective international policy instruments is not seriously challenged by the events of these conflicts. As for the Soviet Union, it had only modest potential economic leverage, though its economic support for Vietnam and Cuba certainly was influential in permitting those countries to continue their support for the Cambodian and Angolan governments.

Did domestically mandated policy shifts affect the settlement process? The most obvious candidate is the declining American political support for the Nicaraguan Contras. Karl suggests that positions were moderating within Nicaragua before the superpower shifts became evident, so that the latter changes were only supportive, not decisive. In Cambodia, the Soviet shift may have played a role in Vietnamese policy (though this is unclear, given other pressures on the Vietnamese); American policy shifts were trivial. In Angola, the key change seems to have occurred in South Africa rather than within either superpower. In Afghanistan, however, the changes in the Soviet Union appear to have been central, though even there you can tell a not too implausible story about an Andropov deciding to get out. So domestic superpower changes seem to have been moderately important with respect to two of the conflicts, and in those cases they were pushing in the direction of settlement.

How helpful has the reduction in superpower interest in the conflicts been in controlling the escalation of conflict? Prima facie this is the factor with respect to which the big gains might be expected to be made: in the era of New Thinking, regional conflict should be far less likely to escalate into a superpower confrontation. However, there is a problem with respect to these conflicts, since something approaching a fighting stalemate had been reached in all four. This stabilization of conflict implies that there probably would not have been escalation even without the New Thinking in the Soviet Union and the United States. This vital aspect of foreign policy simply cannot be appraised in our context.

How helpful has the reduction in superpower interest in the conflicts been to the coming of peace? In Nicaragua, it seems important (with Karl's qualifications), though the peace remains fragile. In Afghanistan peace has not come with settlement. During the 1980s the superpowers did not consider the Cambodia and Angola conflicts to be central foreign policy issues, so there was not much room for reduction. Unfortunately, reduction in superpower interest seems to go with a reduction in concern about whether or not peace is achieved.

E. THE SETTLEMENT NEGOTIATION PROCESS

Does holding an international conference help? The Esquipulas process provides evidence that a conference limited to the regional powers can be important in getting to a settlement. Something similar to Esquipulas has been happening in Cambodia, and probably has helped define the zone of possible agreement somewhat better. An international conference played no role in Angola or Afghanistan, and a regional-power conference would probably have been counter-productive in the latter. Except for Nicaragua, piecemeal negotiation seems a better characterization of the negotiation structures. In the Nicaraguan case the various regional meetings served to define feasible elements of a settlement and to keep public pressure on the negotiators.

Is piecemeal negotiation by relevant actors effective? It was clearly essential in all four conflicts. On the one hand, an international conference is a public forum, and there were items on the settlement agenda that could not be effectively negotiated in public, with the various constituencies in the United States that were concerned with the Nicaraguan issue serving as a prime exemplar of the difficulties. On the other hand, tacit agreement could not have stabilized the situations—for example, where some fairly specific programs of mutual withdrawal were key elements to a settlement. Also, the roles of the relevant parties cannot be fully anticipated, and at times agreement may require nonparticipation in a formal sense, as with Pakistan's role in the Afghan settlement. What remains, then, is piecemeal negotiation—a mixture of two-sided private talks, multi-sided public and private talks, and tacit agreement, adapted on an ad hoc basis to the specific state and prospects of the settlement process. This is a worthy topic for further study.

Did the negotiations lead to compromises on basic issues? In Nicaragua, paired compromises were the general elections and the disarming of the Contras. In Angola, Namibian independence and the withdrawal of Cuban troops qualify as basic paired or mutual compromises. The withdrawal of Soviet troops from Afghanistan and of Vietnamese troops from Cambodia might be thought of as basic compromises, but they were not really paired with anything basic on the other side. Both were more or less unilateral responses to the burdens that continued substantial military involvement in the civil wars entailed, though in each case there were some expectations of further deescalation linked to the withdrawals. Thus even though there is a stalemate, it does not follow that a settlement could only occur as the result of a carefully balanced set of mutual concessions.

Did the negotiations have a "climacteric"? The idea of the climacteric is that after the negotiating parties discover that there is a not too narrow zone of possible agreement and have moved close to a deal, one or both sides will decide to try and improve the deal by threatening to defect. This did occur in the Afghan negotiations, and probably also in the Nicaraguan case. Cambodia is not that far along yet. In Angola, the fighting intensified as negotiations moved closer to settlement, and so one might think of the South African attack and the Cuban counterattack as a form of tacit endgame bargaining for de facto advantage.

COMMONALTIES IN THE FOUR CONFLICTS

The four conflicts share several traits that might reasonably be considered as necessary conditions for a settlement. Let us state them as such: (1) a fighting stalemate had to be achieved before serious negotiations could begin; (2) some change in the correlation of forces was necessary before the stalemate could be stabilized; (3) the absence of serious border disputes reduced, *ceteris paribus*, the intensity of any spoiling operations by regional powers; and (4) at least one of the superpowers had to become an active dealer before a settlement could become a serious prospect.

There are also several properties of the settlement and the process by which it was achieved that might be considered as traits that must be accepted if settlement is to be achieved: (1) piecemeal negotiation is essential, with private negotiation by pairs and larger sets of the actors each being necessary to generate the final publicly agreed settlement; (2) basic compromises by at least one side are essential; (3) a settlement in which some fighting continues, though at a reduced level, must be considered acceptable; and (4) the post-settlement environment is rather fragile, requiring continuing effort by outsiders to sustain its structure.

In addition, there are some features not shared by all four of the conflicts that are of some interest for testing the extent to which these conflicts can provide guidance in understanding other similar conflicts: (1) holding an international conference is certainly not a necessary condition for conflict resolution, and in none of these settlements was a public international conference held in which all the interested parties participated; (2) the structure of interests of regional powers is quite diverse and may vary over the course of the conflict; (3) "regional solutions to regional conflicts" is thus a program that does not generalize, its promise varying with the extent to which some regional actors are spoilers; (4) domestic economic conditions are not decisive influences on the settlement process, and an improving economy may help the process sometimes, a deteriorating one at other times; (5) class conflict was not a simple matter of haves vs. have-nots, and domestic coalitions may have diverse structures; (6) basic compromises may be required of both sides, or they may be required only unilaterally.

CAN THE COMMONALTIES BE GENERALIZED?

Generalization from our set of facts to conditions for achieving the settlement of other conflicts may occur in two directions: one might seek the necessary or sufficient conditions for settlement of conflicts of the type to which the four conflicts belong, or one might seek conditions that are likely to be important in most regional conflicts without claiming either necessity or sufficiency. An effort to carry out the first of these two programs requires a specification of type for the four conflicts, which also serves as a test as to whether the type is of much interest to students of regional conflict.

One trait of these conflicts suggests a rather serious uncertainty with respect to extended relevance—namely, that in each case the Soviet Union was the supporter of the government in power, the United States of the guerrillas. This is almost unheard of in the history of the Cold War, if one restricts one's vision to countries in which a significant civil war was in progress. Thus history suggests that this set of conflicts represents a clutch of special cases.

On the other hand, there has been no lack of countries whose governments were supported by the Soviet Union and which had successfully squelched considerable dissent. As the Soviet Union's and the satellite government's abilities to squelch dissent have declined, perhaps we will have more of "our" type of conflict in the future. The dramatic shifts in Eastern Europe have for the time being at least ended this prospect for that part of the world, but if the Soviet Union is regarded as an empire in the early stages of decolonization, there may yet be more guerrillas for the United States to support.

A second aspect of great power relations with the Third World also complicates the issue of relevance. Roughly speaking, Third World countries tend to be most leery of the great power nearest them. Thus, in Latin America, the United States is far more feared than is the Soviet Union; in East Asia, Japan is more feared than the United States; and around its lengthy borders, the Soviet Union tends to be more feared than the United States. This "backyard" phenomenon means that generalizations that are not specific to the location of the region are somewhat suspect, though one might at least argue that, other things equal, regional powers will tend to be more wary of the nearest great power.

Finally, there is the obvious *zeitgeist* question. These four conflicts have entered and proceeded through much of the process of conflict resolution during a period of dramatic change in Soviet-American relations. Even though those changes do not appear to have been decisive to the settlement processes, they clearly affected them, and whatever the future brings, it will not bring a process of change in Soviet-American relations like that of the past five years.

When these qualifications are combined with the necessary traits listed in the section just above, it would seem that, despite their commonalties, we have a quite special type of conflict here. Another example may occur in the future, and if it does, and the qualifications of this section do not change the conflict's nature substantially, "our" type of conflict may provide a good deal of guidance. But then again it may not, and I am not even inclined to give it a name. This conference has just not provided a firm base of stylized facts for model-building with respect to regional conflict.

A FUZZY-RELEVANCE TEST

What remains, then, is the second program: an open-ended and less deterministic search for relevance in the later history of these conflicts. In fact, that has been the procedure we have followed in developing the factors in the main body of this paper. We finish off now with an ad hoc test of relevance in the form of a brief appraisal of the regional conflicts in El Salvador, Lebanon, and the broader Middle East region, testing the variables that have appeared to be most relevant in appraising the four conflicts.

A. EL SALVADOR

El Salvador has reached the fighting stalemate stage, but if serious negotiations have begun (February 1991), they are still in their early stages. The Salvadoran conflict is unequivocally a social class–based civil war, with ethnic and regional differences playing at best a modest role. Though the economy is in bad shape and probably deteriorating, it does not yet appear to be a factor pushing the government toward making compromises on basics. The guerrillas are not sustained by external sanctuaries, and direct regional power involvement in the conflict has been limited to modest supply and training of guerrilla forces by Nicaragua and Cuba. However, the regional group that played an important role in the Nicaraguan settlement is in place and exerting pressure on the parties to settle. Also, no regional actor is serving as a spoiler (Nicaraguan support for the guerrillas appears not to be substantial but may be having the effect of stabilizing a fighting stalemate). American pressure has substantially inhibited aid by outsiders to the guerrillas. Direct superpower involvement is limited to the United States, which has supplied substantial economic and military aid, training, and some advisors to the Salvadoran army. The Soviets' interest in the conflict was barely perceptible five years ago and is even less so today.

Not all the factors in our list are relevant for the Salvadoran conflict—especially those that relate to superpower involvement, which is quite one-sided, and the negotiation process, which is not very far along. However, with respect to the factors that *are* relevant, El Salvador's situation is quite different from that of any of the four conflicts. Class is central to this civil war, which is a classic case of rich against poor, with regional or white-against-Indian aspects of relatively little significance. The guerrillas do not enjoy sanctuaries, though the terrain and their support base provide them with a reasonably good domestic substitute, as in the Angolan case; their viability does not appear to be threatened, even without external support. Quite possibly the only effective compromise would involve a substantial land reform, which threatens the power of the government's principal support base.

The Salvadoran conflict is closer in its structure to the Nicaraguan conflict of the 1970s when the Sandinistas were the guerrillas.

The last-mentioned similarity points to the fact that domestic social and economic structure is central to all these conflicts. Of course that is not to say that foreign intervention cannot be decisive: U.S.-Pakistani intervention in Afghanistan, the 1988 Cuban troop escalation in Angola, and the U.S. boycott of Nicaragua are all candidates for decisiveness as policy instruments of external powers. Their effect was to make a compromise settlement more attractive. But given the more intense—"purer," if you will—quality of the domestic Salvadoran conflict, it becomes harder to perceive a way out based on a fighting stalemate–induced set of basic compromises.

An interesting and speculative cognitive issue arises with respect to the guerrilla coalition—the FMLN. The worldwide collapse of confidence in statist solutions to many economic problems (central planning and collective farming in the Soviet Union and Eastern Europe, worker management in Yugoslavia, privatization in the more successful Third World countries) might be thought to pose a threat to guerrilla ideology. As Karl says, they are "fighting for peasant rights," but rights to what? The next-door example of Nicaragua's collective farms must have some effect on peasant political aims. Can a program shift toward more "liberal" policies sustain support among both the leadership and its support base? This problem was not faced by the guerrilla movements in the four conflicts (unless possibly by the Khmer Rouge, about which we have no information).

B. LEBANON

The Lebanese civil war has been going on for fifteen years, and "fighting stalemate" has been a reasonable characterization of it. Domestic economic problems do not seem to have had much influence on the behavior of the major groups involved in the war. Ethnic and religious rivalries are very important, and among these, the Christian-Moslem conflict has been central from its inception.The war started when the Quota Government collapsed as the (mainly poor) Moslems became a rapidly increasing majority of the population compared to the (mainly urban and more affluent) Christians. There have been important variations in the list of key actors in the conflict—a distinctive trait. The United States came and went. Israel invaded southern Lebanon and threatened Beirut, which triggered a substantial Syrian invasion. The

Israelis then inflicted a decisive defeat on the PLO forces in the south before being defeated themselves (by attrition) and withdrawing. The Syrians then decisively defeated the PLO forces in the north and occupied central Lebanon.

The ensuing stalemate lasted until the Kuwait crisis, when a major change seems to have occurred. Iraq (together with France) had supported both the Christian fascists and some Moslem forces. The Kuwait crisis gave Syria the opportunity to score a decisive victory. Syrian forces defeated the Christians and have now taken control of Beirut, organized a pro-Syrian government, and begun training a Lebanese army. If this victory is decisive, the next steps will involve gaining control of Tyre, Sidon, and much of southern Lebanon up to the Israeli-occupied southern strip of the country. Thus this conflict, unlike the others, appears to be ending with a decisive victory—both by Syria and its Lebanese Moslem supporters.

Some noteworthy features of the Lebanese conflict are as follows:

(1) It went from a fighting stalemate to victory by one side. A key to this victory was a collateral war—that is, Syria's participation in the Kuwait war—which has the effects of providing Syria with a much freer hand in Lebanon. Defeat of the pro-Iraqi groups and a certain amount of cooperation by the pro-Iranian groups has been the result.

(2) The Syrian-Lebanese victory probably means predominant domestic power by one side in the struggle, combined with strong external influence (and perhaps dominance) by an external regional power.

(3) Even victory does not mean an end to the fighting, since conflict in the south still goes on, and there is no immediate prospect of a settlement with Israel.

(4) Both class and religion were basic issues in the civil war, but because of the overlap, religion could be used as a surrogate for class, and vice versa.

(5) Sanctuaries have positively proliferated, with Israel, Syria, and PLO-supporting governments playing an important role. However, the borders themselves did not serve to define the sanctuaries; they were rather autonomous enclaves established in Lebanon by foreign armies.

(6) Regional powers were centrally involved in the conflict, with major forces from two countries occupying parts of the country simultaneously. This is obviously a dangerous situation, but escalation was

avoided, probably because it was not in the interest of either Syria or Israel.

(7) Spoiling was the watchword for the regional powers. Israel, Syria, and other countries preferred the conflict to continue rather than make a settlement involving compromise on basics. Basically the civil war continued until an external power acquired the ability to end it forcibly.

(8) The Soviet Union's interest in Lebanon has seemed minimal; the United States found 250 dead marines already too high a cost to pay for direct involvement, aside from local diplomatic mediation of various attempts to form a compromise government. All in all, the superpower influence was exercised indirectly, perhaps mostly by massive military aid to Syria and Israel. The resulting power of the two opposing armies may actually have been a factor in inhibiting direct conflict.

(9) Negotiation aimed at a settlement of the basic conflict was unsuccessful. If the issue is now settled, it has been by the test of arms in the context of an externally generated opportunity—the American blockade of Iraq.

One of the most interesting aspects of the Lebanon conflict is the extent to which it was successfully isolated from superpower competition despite the fact that it was closely linked to vital American interests (Israel and oil) and that Syria was the Soviet Union's major ally in the region.

The four conflicts are examples of civil wars in which there is substantial external, including superpower, involvement. El Salvador and Lebanon represent extremes on this dimension: there is *less* external involvement in the Salvadoran civil war and rather *more* external involvement in Lebanon than in any of the four conflicts. Even so, the list of relevant factors generated by study of the four conflicts, combined with some intuitive sense of relative importance, constitutes a reasonably comprehensive checklist that helps provide at least an initial basis for analyzing these two conflicts. I think it reasonable to say that one would not want to omit these factors from consideration when thinking about moving toward settlement in El Salvador and Lebanon. But there is not any firm basis for forecasting, and the greater complexity of interaction and threat in the Lebanese case suggests that the checklist may need some expansion in order to gain a comparable level of understanding of the Lebanese situation.

C. THE MIDDLE EAST

There are, of course, a number of interdependent conflicts in the Middle East. In addition to the Lebanese civil war, there is the general Arab-Israeli conflict, the de facto civil war in Israel (*intifada*), the Iran-Iraq conflict's aftermath, the intermittent Kurdish rebellion, and now the war between Iraq and allied (mostly American) forces under United Nations auspices. It is far too late in this paper to try to characterize the structure and tendency of this lengthy conflict. But in order to appraise the transfer value of our checklist, it seems worthwhile to take a brief look at a few of the factors that may provide some comparative insight into this much more complex environment.

(1) *Border Conflicts.* Border conflicts were not of much significance for any of the four conflicts, or for El Salvador. In the case of Lebanon, the legal borders are not seriously in question, but the Israeli occupation of a portion of southern Lebanon, and the relevance of that area for the Syrian and Israeli strategic posture with respect to the Golan Heights, mean that a border question will probably be important in any settlement process. Border issues were a central part of the Iran-Iraq war, and Iraq's and Kuwait's and Israel's borders are continuing and central aspects of conflict in the region. The political problem that irredentism usually poses means that the Middle East conflicts are, ceteris paribus, going to be more difficult to resolve than any of the four.

(2) *Collateral Wars.* With respect to the Arab-Israel conflict, the Kuwait war is collateral; its effect is to enhance Israeli security (1) by reducing the military threat from a major rejectionist state, (2) by creating an incipient alliance between Egypt and the Gulf states, and (3) by establishing a strong and explicitly sanctioned American presence in the region. Of course, on the other side of the equation there were the risks of war, together with the possible stability threats to several governments in the region.

(3) *Toward a Settlement Negotiation.* The stricture that piecemeal negotiation is the central necessary (but of course not sufficient) procedure seems to apply in this region. There are too many spoilers with respect to each of the interdependent conflicts to expect the regional powers to reach a settlement on their own. Public opinions are too diverse and intense for a public negotiation to be an effective settlement device. In this environment an international conference is more an instrument of public opinion manipulation. This tends generally to be more true the more complex the situation, and the more

powerful some single-issue constituencies may be (in this case both Arab and Jewish).

(4) *Economic Issues.* In the Middle East, economic issues are dominated by oil. This ultimate monoculture economy has, as a consequence, unique implications for regional conflict. Oil means that, for many of the countries, foreign exchange is not a major constraint on military buildups or recoveries from war losses. It means that the outside world will continue to have a deep and abiding interest in the affairs of the region. It means that there is a natural trade-off between haves and have-nots in the region in the form of oil revenues and jobs for security guarantees. And it means that (unlike Vietnam's Cambodia occupation) the wherewithal for continued confrontation with Israel should be available for decades to come. In such a situation, a stalemate punctuated by occasional wars may be hard to avoid.

(5) *End of the Cold War.* The "ending" of the Cold War has had a dramatic effect on current superpower involvement in the region. The Soviet Union's joining of the United Nations coalition against Iraq represents a truly surprising turn in Soviet-American relations. Of perhaps comparable significance, if less surprising, is the massive emigration of Jews from the Soviet Union to Israel. Unfortunately, in the longer run this cooperation may be hard to sustain. The Soviet Union borders Turkey and Iran, is only 150 miles from Iraq, and contains a large Moslem population. Before many years have passed, the Soviet Union (or some of its constituent parts) may become net importers of oil. The Middle East, with its Israel, its Soviet borders, its Moslems, and its oil, is a major security issue for both the United States and the Soviet Union, and there remains a powerful competitive dimension to that issue. In this case, the ending of the Cold War does not necessarily imply a lessening of superpower interest in the conflict. Nevertheless, with respect to the prospects for some forms of settlement in the region, the change in Soviet attitudes and capabilities is a very positive step.

CONCLUSION

In this paper we have collected some twenty-nine factors which a reading of the conference papers suggests are important in understanding the later stages of at least one of the regional conflicts that have occurred as part of the civil wars in Afghanistan, Angola, Cambodia, and Nicaragua. These factors were then used in making thumbnail characterizations of the civil wars in El Salvador and Lebanon, and in discussing several aspects of the broadly ranging set of conflicts in the Middle East. What conclusions might one draw from this exercise? I suggest the following:

The modelling of wars as social phenomena has begun in earnest in the national security field, though it is still a controversial procedure. It is possible that this paper offers some help to potential modellers in the form of some stylized facts about one class of civil wars. However, my feeling is that not much help is provided, because wars of this kind are too diverse, and probably not well enough understood, for a modelling exercise, which is inevitably limited to the consideration of a very few variables if it is to be helpful.

The inductive study of war, pioneered by Lewis Richardson and Chauncey Wright a half century ago, seems to have languished in recent years. I think this is unfortunate, though I believe their methods need some adjustment. The comparative study of wars, taken in small groups so that researchers can become genuinely familiar with their histories, seems to me to offer considerable promise. Whether the level of characterization provided in this paper is the most appropriate level is unclear, but I believe the basic desideratum of small-scale comparative study is met: the study of each conflict generates a series of questions that may be asked of other conflicts, and the union of these questions, and the tendencies in the answers, provides an inductive theory of the course of some wars which can be extended in various ways.

Substantively, the most important suggestions deriving from study of the histories of the later stages of these regional conflicts are the following:

(1) When victory seems unattainable by either side, settlement may nonetheless be reached when a fighting stalemate is stabilized. A change in the correlation of forces may well be necessary for this to be achieved.

(2) A variety of social and economic conditions is compatible with this sort of conflict resolution: substantial ethnic or regional-based conflict, improving or deteriorating economic conditions, varying degrees of class conflict, and strong nationalist or anti-imperialist sentiments.

(3) A settlement based on compromise may well entail continued fighting, though at a reduced level. Since the disagreements that led to conflict have not been resolved, but only compromised, such settlements tend to be more fragile than those based on decisive victory by one side.

(4) The interests of regional powers in settling civil wars with external involvement have a varied structure. When spoiling is in the interests of some of them, regional solutions to problems will not be forthcoming, and this is a frequent though not ubiquitous situation.

(5) The four conflicts are historically atypical in that the Soviet Union supported the existing governments in the later stages of these civil wars while the United States supported the guerrillas. The "new thinking" in Soviet-American relations clearly was an aid to settlement, but may not have been decisive in any of the cases.

(6) Piecemeal negotiation was the major mode of discussion used to settle these conflicts. Regional powers played a central role in Nicaragua, and a significant role in Cambodia (not yet settled), but not elsewhere. An international conference involving all the interested parties did not occur and, had it occurred, seems unlikely to have had a positive impact on the process.

SOUTHEAST ASIA

SOVIET-AMERICAN CONFLICT AND COOPERATION IN INDOCHINA

Frederick Z. Brown

The conflict in Cambodia—still unresolved despite extravagant hopes—provides a rich example of a strategic world turned upside down in the post–Cold War era. The search for a compromise settlement in Cambodia suffers from all the complications arising out of this "new world order": conciliation among bitter rivals, the rebirth of politics based on nationalism and ethnicity more than ideology, a burgeoning multipolarity, unlikely alignments of convenience, and client states which refuse to take dictation from their patrons.

Speaking about the end of the Cold War in Europe, U.S. Deputy Secretary of State Lawrence Eagleburger has pointed out that the old era was in some ways easier. This was a statement of fact, not a complaint.[1] Washington and Moscow must now operate in a geopolitical environment that is more ambiguous and complex than the one they enjoyed after World War II. No longer must smaller states gauge their actions in fear of touching off a nuclear confrontation between the superpowers. At the same time, this allows uncommitted states greater latitude, and from Moscow and Washington's perspective makes them harder to deal with. This "inconvenience" duly noted, the world in the 1990s is indisputably better off thanks to the dwindling down of the Cold War environment the world has known since the 1940s.

For Cambodia, this is not necessarily so. The situation there remains murky, fluid, and as dangerous as ever. Sino-Soviet *rapprochement* and cooperation between the United States and the Soviet Union on a number of global issues have helped gain progress toward a compromise settlement during 1989 and 1990. We delude ourselves, however, if we believe that progress equates to a solution or even a temporary settlement. Peace is *not* at hand in Cambodia. The external powers have agreed to reduce the irritability quotient of Cambodia in order to ease their own political problems, but the situation on the ground in Cambodia and among the Cambodians themselves has not really changed for the better. It is possible, even probable, that despite the best of intentions on the part of the two superpowers—the Soviet Union and the United States—Cambodia will dissolve once again into chaos, and that the Khmer Rouge will ultimately return to a dominant position in that war-torn country.

Aside from the starting point of mutual U.S.-Soviet hostility, the Cambodia situation as it has developed since December 1978 has little in common with other superpower regional conflicts that have developed over the years in Southern Africa, Central America, or Afghanistan. Cambodia must be analyzed in terms of its peculiar ethnic, nationalist, and deeply rooted historical conditions, even going back a thousand years, when Cambodia (then the Khmer Empire) dominated Southeast Asia. From long before colonial times, Cambodia was trapped between powerful neighboring civilizations—the Siamese to the west and the Vietnamese to the east—as they pursued their "drive to the south" (*nam tien*) from the Red River delta, an Asian version of nineteenth-century American "manifest destiny." After World War II, Cambodia was a discardable geopolitical commodity in the great power struggle for Indochina. From 1975 onward the conflict in Cambodia was a function of Sino-Soviet rivalry and of noncommunist Southeast Asia's mistrust of Vietnam's regional intentions, a mistrust firmly shared by the United States. Moreover, for Americans, Cambodia is qualitatively different because of the trauma of the Vietnam War era, which is still alive in the United States politically and psychologically.

Second, Cambodia cannot be isolated from the rest of Southeast Asia or from the seminal source of the problem: Sino-Vietnamese hostility. The agony of the Cambodian people is tragically real and deplorable. The goals of current international negotiations are, correctly, to end the civil war, to remove all foreign forces, to help the Cambodian people choose their own government, and to create an independent, sovereign, nonaligned Cambodia. On the longer term, the issues of gut importance for the superpowers do not turn upon Cambodia itself but upon its neighbors. The issues that matter are: the future of the Association of Southeast Asian Nations (ASEAN)* and superpower relationships with that organization and its individual states (for the United States, most importantly Thailand), China's role and influence in the region, and Southeast Asia's relations with its sister regions of South and North Asia. Particularly crucial, though infrequently articu-

---

*ASEAN was formed in 1967. Its original members were Thailand, Malaysia, Singapore, Indonesia, and the Philippines. Brunei became a member in 1984.

lated, is the future direction of Vietnam—not so much Vietnamese *communism* as Vietnam *as a nation* which, irrespective of ideology, stands to become one of the most influential states in Southeast Asia early in the next century. While Cambodia has been the center of a regional drama, the stage on which the Cambodian tragedy is being played out is far broader. This sad reality explains in large measure why peace has been so elusive.

Third, China, more than the Soviet Union, is at the heart of the Cambodia conundrum. Let us admit that China is a superpower in Southeast Asia, if not all Asia. We err badly if we analyze events in Indochina primarily in terms of U.S.-Soviet rivalry. A settlement in Cambodia depends more on factors touching Sino-Vietnamese relations than on whatever Moscow and Washington may decide bilaterally. The direct concerns of the United States in Indochina's affairs are, by the United States' own choice, limited. They are a distant third to China's because of the latter's alliance with the Khmer Rouge, and to the Soviet Union's because of its own alliance with Vietnam, including support for Vietnam's invasion and occupation of Cambodia. While the United States has contributed political and economic backing for ASEAN's opposition to Vietnamese aggression, and has given material aid to the anti-Vietnamese resistance, only since early 1989 has Washington, through participation in the UN Security Council "Perm Five" negotiations, become an active, direct force in the Cambodia peace process. Surely this cannot be said about the U.S. involvement in Afghanistan and its massive support for the *mojahedin* forces. Nor can it be said of Central America, where its intimate association with the contras and activities in El Salvador, Honduras, Guatemala, and, most recently, Panama show the United States as the dominant external actor regardless of what the Soviets and Cubans may be doing there.

ORIGINS OF THE AMERICAN INVOLVEMENT

The Cambodia problem today is a direct consequence of the American defeat in Indochina in 1975. Its roots are traceable back to 1945 when the United States made the decision to support France's colonial claims in Indochina.[2] Although there were dissenting voices, the Eurocentric focus of U.S. foreign policy at that time, and the importance attached to France's political stability in the wake of the Soviet absorption of Eastern Europe and the perceived Soviet military threat to Western Europe, overrode the minor importance attached to independence for Vietnam. By 1950, the United States was firmly committed to the French struggle to maintain control over Vietnam one way or another; by 1954 it was bearing 80 percent of the financial cost of that effort.

When the first Indochina War ended with the French defeat at Dien Bien Phu and subsequent withdrawal, the United States in effect assumed responsibility for Indochina after the Geneva Conference. It backed Ngo Dinh Diem as the leader of South Vietnam and brought about the creation of the Republic of Vietnam as a bulwark against Ho Chi Minh's Democratic Republic of Vietnam. While Laos and Cambodia, the latter under Prince Norodom Sihanouk, achieved a degree of independence, both of these weak countries soon came under the shadow of the struggle for Vietnam. At issue was North Vietnam's determination to unite the entire country versus the American determination to prevent South Vietnam from being gobbled up by what was then seen as the red tide of communism, be it Chinese, Soviet, or Vietnamese, threatening all of Southeast Asia. In 1959–60, Washington drew the "line in the sand" (the Mekong River actually) in Laos to prevent presumed Pathet Lao and Vietnamese aggression against Thailand. Events in Vietnam itself, however, came to dominate U.S. strategy. The United States adopted Vo Nguyen Giap's concept of Indochina as a strategic unit, a single theater of operations. Because of its geographic proximity to the main arena as the southern terminus of the Ho Chi Minh trail and the use of its eastern provinces as North Vietnamese sanctuaries, by the end of the 1960s Cambodia was drawn more directly into the fighting.

In the 1940s and well into the 1950s, the United States defined its Indochina policy as part of the battle against a *Moscow-led* world communist movement. Under both Presidents Kennedy and Johnson, Vietnam was the quintessence of the Cold War struggle against international communism—an "Asian Berlin," a test of American resolve. In this concept of "monolithic communism," a contradiction soon became obvious. Mao's victory in China and then the Korean War demonstrated that the security threat in Asia was as much from Beijing as from Moscow. By the late 1950s the Sino-Soviet rift was an undeniable reality, and a few years later Hanoi's key material support was coming from the Soviet Union rather than China. American objectives in Vietnam soon became the prevention of the *Chinese* from taking over Southeast Asia. There were legitimate grounds for this fear. After 1949, China had been the essential supplier and safe haven for the Viet Minh during the first Indochina War. China supported (at least rhetorically) communist insurgencies in Thailand and Malaysia, and it gave comfort to the communist parties of Indonesia and other Asian nations. Beijing was explicit as to Mao's ultimate intentions.

Paradoxically, in the later stages of the Indochina conflict, it was the *Soviet Union* more than China that was positioning itself advantageously. The United States understood well enough how the Soviets benefitted in pure Cold War geopolitics from the bleeding of American power and manifold global repercussions of the Vietnam quagmire. Soviet policy, however, was not only to confront the United States in classic Cold War style, but also, in anticipation of a North Vietnamese victory, to begin the "encirclement" of China, which in Moscow's eyes had emerged as the greatest security concern for the Soviet Union in East Asia. At the same time, successive American administrations failed to comprehend the most elementary ethnic and cultural divisions between China and Vietnam—and the impact these would have on regional politics.

The American involvement in Indochina spanned the entire course of the Cold War, and it became by any calculation the most expensive and painful evidence of the nation's commitment. In March 1965, in the words of then Assistant Secretary of Defense John McNaughton, the United States was fighting "70 percent to avoid a humiliating U.S. defeat (to our reputation as a guarantor), 20 percent to keep South Vietnam (and the adjacent) territory from Chinese hands, 10 percent to permit the people of South Vietnam to enjoy a better, freer way of life."[3] The immense U.S. involvement in Indochina after 1954 thus became part of the larger American Cold War struggle against *both* China and the Soviet Union.

EVOLUTION OF U.S. CAMBODIA POLICY AFTER 1975

Cambodia a few years later became a geographical adjunct to the American commitment in Vietnam—a "throwaway" as much as a "sideshow." With all the American hand-wringing after 1975 over the fall of Saigon and its impact on U.S. credibility globally, little official concern was expressed over Cambodia's gruesome fate at the hands of the Khmer Rouge. In 1976–78, under President Carter, American policy focused upon normalization of relations with Vietnam. Beyond the admirable desire to "heal the wounds of war" and "put the past behind us," the central rationale for this policy was pure *realpolitik*: to preempt the Soviet

Union from moving permanently into the vacuum created by the American debacle. Diplomatic relations and commercial relations between the United States and Vietnam, it was hoped, might slow down or dilute growing Soviet-Vietnamese cooperation and provide Hanoi with a "Western option." Normalization with Vietnam was thus part of American Cold War diplomatic strategy.

Normalization under Carter failed for four reasons: Hanoi's insistence on reparations, the signing of the Vietnamese-Soviet mutual defense treaty in November 1978, the Vietnamese invasion of Cambodia a month later, and the primacy accorded U.S.-Chinese relations, formally established in January 1979. Washing its hands of Vietnam, the United States assumed a recessive role in Indochinese affairs which lasted until the summer of 1990.

After the Vietnamese invasion, U.S. policy was simple: "Let ASEAN take the lead" in reversing a situation that the Vietnamese claimed was irreversible—i.e., that any government in Phnom Penh must be Marxist-Leninist and responsive, if not subservient, to Vietnamese direction. In September 1979, the United States, together with ASEAN, the Europeans, Japanese, and much of the Third World, supported Democratic Kampuchea's (the Khmer Rouge's) claim to Cambodia's UN seat in order to demonstrate disapproval of Vietnamese aggression. In June 1982 the United States blessed ASEAN's creation of the Coalition Government of Democratic Kampuchea (CGDK), which joined the Khmer Rouge with the two noncommunist groups of Prince Sihanouk (Armée Nationale Sihanoukiste, or ANS) and Son Sann (Khmer People's National Liberation Front, or KPNLF). The three formed an armed resistance to the Vietnamese occupation, thus giving military teeth to the international political opposition to Vietnam and the surrogate People's Republic of Kampuchea (PRK, which changed its name to the State of Cambodia, or SOC, in 1989) installed by Vietnam in January 1979. The purpose of the alliance with the Khmer Rouge was not to defeat the Vietnamese army on the battlefield, but to drive Hanoi to the negotiating table. The United States began to supply covert assistance to the noncommunist resistance (NCR) groups sometime after 1980. In 1985 it instituted an overt assistance program of about $3.5 million annually, which was raised to $7 million in 1989. The scale of this aid was small, however, in comparison with that provided by China to the Khmer Rouge and by various ASEAN countries to all members of the CGDK.[4]

Perhaps it was hoped that the noncommunists would become strong enough to hold their own, but neither ASEAN nor the United

States did what was necessary to make the NCR genuine contenders either militarily or politically. Peace negotiations seemed far in the future, and the NCR by itself was not viewed as a political alternative in a future Phnom Penh government. Two Reagan administrations waffled, fearful of "another Vietnam" and reluctant to risk losing Hanoi's cooperation on the prisoner-of-war and missing-in-action (POW/MIA) issue through too energetic support for the NCR. The tough political questions concerning the NCR's organization, leadership, motivation, and *objectives* were never addressed seriously. Today, this failure by Washington is having extremely unfortunate consequences for its Khmer friends.

Another pillar of U.S. Cambodia policy was sustained high-profile political and diplomatic support for ASEAN at the UN and elsewhere, buttressed by the continuation of the embargo on trade and economic relations established in 1964 against North Vietnam and extended to the entire country in 1975. The embargo was a major coercive factor in getting Hanoi to withdraw the bulk of its military forces from Cambodia in September 1989.[5]

The Carter administration in its last two years and the Reagan administration throughout its two terms assigned a low priority to the Cambodia question and Indochina as a whole, as did the Bush administration in its initial year in office. On one level this policy reflected an inclination to shy away from any sort of involvement in a part of the world which caused American society such pain in the 1960s and 1970s—the "Vietnam syndrome." On another, it bespoke the conviction that ASEAN had matured politically, was doing well economically, and consequently should bear the primary responsibility for regulating affairs within its own region. Throughout there was an undercurrent of contempt for the Hanoi regime that had humiliated the United States in 1975 and a conviction that Indochina should remain near the bottom of the U.S. scale of global priorities.

The United States quickly answered Thailand's requests for additional military equipment—artillery, tanks, ammunition—when the Vietnamese staged brief incursions across the Cambodia-Thai border in the mid-1980s. But successive U.S. administrations refused to accept Cambodia as an American problem. Cambodia was an international responsibility, and in any event American resources were limited. U.S. activism, it was felt, could complicate the efforts of others to find a solution. When negotiations began to sprout up in various bilateral and multilateral forums, the Reagan administration reacted cautiously and repeatedly defined the American role as subsidiary to that of regional powers who had more direct interests in Cambodia and more influence in shaping events there.

In the absence of a complete withdrawal of Vietnamese military forces from Cambodia "in the context of a satisfactory settlement," the Reagan administrations showed little interest in normalization of relations with Vietnam. Washington demanded continued progress on humanitarian issues, such as resolving the fate of American servicemen still missing in Southeast Asia and the orderly departure program of former reeducation camp inmates and others with ties to the United States. Successive administrations maintained steadfastly that Vietnam knew clearly what it must do to advance the normalization process. Any dealings with the PRK were ruled out because it did not have "legitimacy," having been installed by force of arms. Washington argued that this regime was patently communist and in fact led by ex-Khmer Rouge cadres. In any event it was not strong enough to stand on its own without continued, pervasive Vietnamese support, a condition that was unacceptable. The Bush administration initially held to this policy line despite a growing uneasiness over the apparent contradiction of continued U.S. support for a resistance movement which was dominated by Pol Pot's Khmer Rouge, with the same senior leadership which had perpetrated the genocide of 1975–78.

Over the decade 1979–89, successive administrations judged the policy on Cambodia to be consistent with the apprehensive American public mood after the Vietnam War. The policy was compatible with ASEAN's goals by keeping pressure on Vietnam through the embargo and by providing a modicum of political and material support to the Cambodian resistance. This made sense in an anti-Soviet Cold War atmosphere. "Resistance to aggression" was the linchpin, and Vietnam had committed aggression against Cambodia, no matter how reprehensible its Khmer Rouge regime was. In domestic political terms, there was little to be gained through a more ambitious policy, and there was always the danger of criticism for getting the United States into "another Vietnam."

SOVIET POLICY IN SOUTHEAST ASIA AND COLD WAR IMPLICATIONS

Since 1989 fundamental changes have taken place within the Soviet Union and Eastern Europe, and a stunning improvement has occurred in U.S.-Soviet bilateral relations, demonstrated most dramatically at the Helsinki Summit and at the United Nations with regard to the crisis in the Persian Gulf. Is it time to abandon the Cold War precepts of four decades with regard to Southeast Asia and Indochina?

Three generalizations about the new look of Soviet East Asian policy since the advent of Mikhail Gorbachev seem warranted. First, Soviet policies in both domestic and foreign affairs (and this certainly applies to Indochina) changed because they were *forced* to change not only by internal contradictions but by external pressures as well. Second, what seemed important to the Soviet Union ten or twenty years ago is clearly less so today; priorities have changed. Gorbachev's current preoccupations are radical economic reform, disintegration of the Communist Party, restructuring the relationships with the Soviet republics, securing arms control agreements with the United States, and handling the Soviet military withdrawal from Eastern Europe. Third, and finally, in a positive sense the Soviets have redefined their objectives in Southeast Asia more rationally and have shaped policies in pursuit of these objectives with greater finesse, practicality, and subtlety.

Under General Secretary Brezhnev, the Soviet presence in Asia and the Pacific was manifested primarily in military—hence threatening—terms. The military alliance with Vietnam was the jewel in the crown of Soviet Southeast Asian strategy. With Gorbachev's landmark speeches at Vladivostok in July 1986 and Krasnoyarsk in September 1988, this image began to change. For Moscow, rapprochement with Beijing and a benign face toward ASEAN and the rest of noncommunist Asia became the central elements of a more nuanced Asian and Pacific policy initiative. Gorbachev's skillful use of Southeast Asian media (for example, in July 1987 the interview with the Indonesian paper *Merdeka* on arms control) underscored his intention to establish the Soviet Union as a peaceful Asia-Pacific power; it also signalled his intention to extend active Soviet interests well beyond Indochina. By assigning sophisticated Asian specialists to ASEAN and Pacific capitals to replace stereotypical Soviet Cold Warriors, and by stimulating an unprecedented exchange of high-level visits between Soviet and ASEAN leaders, Gorbachev sought to improve bilateral relations with the noncommunist countries of the region and with the association itself. Most Soviet aircraft stationed at Cam Ranh Bay were removed, and fleet activity in the western Pacific was reduced. Moscow seconded ASEAN's pet concept of a Southeast Asian Zone of Peace, Freedom and Neutrality (ZOPFAN). There was talk of increased two-way trade. All these gambits have helped establish the Soviet Union, really for the first time, as a nation whose influence in Southeast Asia is not based primarily on its military presence.

After years of expensive stalemate, both China and the Soviet Union decided in the mid-1980s to reduce the importance of Cambodia as an irritant in their bilateral relationship. A key element in this shift was the Soviet decision to put Cambodia in the perspective of larger Soviet foreign policy interests. From 1986 onward the Vietnamese occupation was one of three obstacles to a Gorbachev–Deng Xiao Peng summit meeting. The two other obstacles—Afghanistan and Sino-Soviet border problems—were moving toward satisfactory resolution. While both sides wanted a summit badly, China would not agree without a Soviet assurance of Vietnam's military withdrawal from Cambodia by a certain date. The Soviets were expected to deliver, and they did. With Vietnam's announcement in April 1989 that it would withdraw by 30 September, the way was open for the May 1989 Gorbachev-Deng summit.

In the view of many countries in and outside the region, Vietnam's invasion and occupation of Cambodia had been only the latest expression of Vietnam's historical drive for an Indochina federation or, at minimum, "hegemony." Inevitably, some of that taint rubbed off on Moscow. The obvious support for Vietnam's ambitions was an impediment to the other Soviet objectives regionally. Since late 1989 in meetings of the Perm Five and in bilateral dialogue with Washington, Moscow made clear that it favored a political settlement and was willing to put political capital on the line with Vietnam to promote a settlement. All this has helped U.S.-Soviet bilateral relations and also reinforced the image in Southeast Asia of the Soviet Union as a friend rather than a potential foe.

With the warming of relations with China and the dwindling of the Cold War, the strategic value of the alliance with Vietnam has diminished. While Moscow might have been content to see Vietnam dominate Cambodia indefinitely, the fact of ASEAN's sustained rejection of Vietnam's "irreversibility" doctrine and the continued American, European, and Japanese support for ASEAN's position obliged the Soviets to accept the impracticality of the Vietnamese hard line. The political and financial cost of Vietnam's occupation of Cambodia was a burden the Soviet Union could no longer bear. Beyond the direct costs (arms, ammunition, fuel), the absence of a satisfactory settlement ensured a continued U.S. economic and trade embargo and prevented multilateral international financial institution aid to Vietnam. Even before the changes in the Soviet Union and Eastern Europe were fully evident, the

Soviets had recognized the limits of their ability to help the Vietnamese develop under a "socialist model." And in any event Vietnam had in 1986 already embarked on its own version of *perestroika.* The Soviets began to reduce their economic and military assistance, which had been running up to $2 billion annually.

In 1990 it would be hard to imagine U.S.-Soviet hostility growing out of an incident in Southeast Asia escalating to the pitch of a shooting war. The region is not the raw nerve in the relationship it was at various times from the 1950s until 1975. Yet we need to differentiate between traditional Cold War antagonisms and a new multidimensional geopolitical and economic competition in which the Soviet Union (assuming it survives its grave economic and political travails) will have to be taken into account by American strategists. While the region and the world are better off without the Cold War's menace of military confrontation, the "post–Cold War" era presents other sorts of problems, in their own way equally challenging, for the United States as well as the Soviet Union. It would be naive to believe that *rivalry* between the United States and the Soviet Union in Southeast Asia—in all of Asia and the Pacific—has magically vanished because of the changes in the Soviet Union. Each country has its own interests; each will continue to pursue them. This point is especially important in view of the recent revival of conservative elements in the Soviet Communist Party and the army, which appear to be turning the clock back to the days of the old Cold War.

Certain underlying strategic considerations that shape the political and security policies of both superpowers are still active in Southeast Asia. Nuclear weapons–equipped submarines of the Soviet Union and the United States still patrol the waters of the western pacific and South China Sea. The Straits of Malacca, Lombok, and Sunda have lost none of their vital chokepoint importance: they remain the narrow passages through which the commerce and military ships of many nations must pass daily. Although the Cold War as we have known it has passed into history, several conditions will probably have to be met before this basic strategic character of Southeast Asia in "old Cold War" thinking is altered. There must be a comprehensive strategic arms control agreement between the Soviet Union and the United States which effectively removes the possibility of a nuclear exchange. Although there are hopeful signs, such an agreement and its full implementation could be many years distant. In addition, the profound political, economic, and social changes now underway in the Soviet Union must be accepted by the United States, Japan, and the West as immutable and not subject to destabilization, if not reversal, by Gorbachev's successors. An element of friction, even presumed hostility, will exist as long as the danger of nuclear war, however remote, exists.

With regard to the Soviet "withdrawal" from Cam Ranh Bay and the reduction of the Soviet military presence in Asia, we should distinguish between Soviet intentions and Soviet capabilities. The perception of a Soviet military threat in the minds of most Southeast Asians has certainly been reduced over the past two years. The modernity and effectiveness of these forces, however, have actually been enhanced under Gorbachev through modernization. Some U.S. military planners would argue that the Soviet military capability, both sea and air, in Asia and the Pacific is greater in 1990 than it was under Brezhnev. The Soviet Pacific Fleet and the U.S. Seventh Fleet remain juxtaposed. Even though their missions and potential adversaries extend well beyond traditional superpower conflict, their existence is a fact of geostrategic life and has implications for potential regional conflict in Southeast Asia. In fairness it should be noted that U.S. security alliances with the Philippines and Thailand (and of course Japan and Korea in North Asia) remain intact, and that these arrangements are a source of concern to Soviet planners, however they choose to define the threat to Soviet security interests. Moreover, Indonesia, Malaysia, and most obviously Singapore (which is negotiating a military basing arrangement with the United States) maintain security links to the United States through intelligence-sharing, military training, and purchase of U.S. armaments, notably aircraft. Thus, from the Soviet perspective as well, there would appear to be grounds for maintaining a degree of old Cold War thinking.[6]

The United States still smarts from the painful Indochina involvement; the Soviet Union's role as the major supplier of North Vietnam's advanced weaponry has not been forgotten.[7] It will be many decades before the concern over possible Vietnamese "hegemonistic designs" is dissipated. The 1978 Soviet-Vietnamese alliance and the Soviets' support for Vietnam's invasion and occupation of Cambodia sustain the contention by some Americans—even despite recent Soviet Perm Five cooperation—that the Cold War remains alive in Indochina, and that the United States must draw its security plans accordingly.

Finally, there are profound question marks in the Soviet-Vietnamese bilateral relationship, in part the result of the Cold War's demise. They will have a bearing upon the shape of the post–Cold War era. Change in the Soviet Union is moving faster than the Vietnamese would like. Even if hardliners in Moscow continue to gain strength and to reverse some of Gorbachev's initiatives, it seems doubtful that communist party-to-party links can remain as they have been over the past several decades. While the Soviets hope to maintain the political relationship, all three elements that have glued the countries together in recent decades—a common anxiety about China, the Cambodia question, and Soviet economic aid—have been eroded. The lure of relations with ASEAN and the United States is being dangled ever more tantalizingly before Vietnam's eyes, as exemplified by the September 1990 Baker-Thach meeting and other developments noted below.

One is tempted to ask, just what value do the ideological links of communism between Hanoi and Moscow have these days? The status of Vietnamese students and guest workers in Eastern Europe, particularly in what was East Germany, and the Soviet Union itself has become highly sensitive. Not only has the flow of remittances been sharply cut, Vietnam will soon be required to pay for its oil imports in hard currency.

In sum, the future of the Soviet-Vietnamese relationship and strategic opportunities for ASEAN and the United States must be counted as one of the most intriguing points of speculation among foreign analysts. It is conceivable that a more active U.S. involvement in the politics of Indochina will yield a different sort of friction with the Soviet Union, which for the past decade has had Vietnam pretty much to itself. This may not lead to a classic Cold War confrontation of the kind we saw in the region after World War II, but the potential for some intriguing geopolitical challenges—and opportunities—for the United States will be present.

WILL CAMBODIA GET A COLD WAR DIVIDEND?

Specifically, how do changes in recent superpower relations affect the Cambodia negotiations? We have already witnessed several significant consequences.

The first was the shift in policy toward Indochina announced by Secretary of State James Baker in Paris on 18 July 1990. Baker announced that the United States would no longer support the seating of the CGDK delegation at the forthcoming UN General Assembly, that it would open talks with Vietnam in order to expedite a Cambodia settlement, and that it would consider relaxing restrictions on the provision of humanitarian assistance to both Vietnam and the current Phnom Penh regime.[8] Shortly thereafter, Baker indicated in Jakarta, at the annual ASEAN ministerial consultations, that the United States was prepared to talk directly with the Hun Sen regime.[9] This was confirmed in Baker's testimony before the Senate Foreign Relations Committee on 4 September 1990. A line of communication to discuss POW/MIA matters was established between the U.S. and Cambodian embassies in Vientiane, and in early September the American ambassador to Indonesia, John Monjo, actually conferred with Hun Sen while the latter was in Jakarta attending the Indonesian-sponsored meeting of the four Cambodian factions—the first time an American diplomat has ever shaken hands with an official of the Phnom Penh regime.

During August and September, three meetings were held in New York between Vietnamese Permanent Representative to the United Nations Trinh Xuan Lang and State Department Assistant Secretary for East Asian and Pacific Affairs Richard Solomon, or his deputy for Southeast Asia, Kenneth Quinn.[10] On 29 September 1990, Secretary Baker met with Vietnamese Deputy Prime Minister and Foreign Minister Nguyen Co Thach in New York in what was described as "a step in the direction" of normalization of relations—but technically not "the commencement of normalization discussions." Thach reportedly stated Vietnam's intentions to remove all "advisors," as well as any regular troops that may remain in Cambodia, and to cooperate fully in the peace process. Baker announced that travel restrictions would be eased to permit Thach to travel to Washington in mid-October for discussions of the POW/MIA issue with General John Vessey, President Bush's special emissary to Hanoi for humanitarian matters. Thach also met with members of the Senate Foreign Relations Committee and House Foreign Affairs Committee while in Washington.[11] The Baker-Thach meeting was the highest level contact between Vietnam and the United States since 1973.[12] The meeting—indeed the thrust of bilateral events since July 1990—has modified the ground rules for American policy toward Indochina.

On 28 August 1990 the five permanent members of the UN Security Council announced agreement on five key elements of a comprehensive political settlement of the Cambodia conflict based upon an enhanced United Nations role. These elements were: (1) transitional arrangements regarding the administration of Cambodia during a pre-election period, (2) military arrangements during the transitional period, (3) elections under UN auspices, (4) human rights protection, and (5) international guarantees.[13]

Then there was the actual coming together of the four Cambodian factions in Jakarta, noted above, after which Hun Sen, Norodom

Ranariddth, Son Sann, and Khieu Samphan, after predictable squabbling, announced their acceptance of the Perm Five plan as a framework for a negotiated settlement.[14] Crucial to the next step was creation of a Supreme National Council, presumably twelve members—six drawn from the Phnom Penh regime and six from the resistance (two each from the Khmer Rouge, Sihanoukiste, and Son Sann factions). The first meeting of the SNC in Bangkok, 17 September 1990, yielded no agreement on the chairmanship of the SNC.[15] At the second meeting, 23 September 1990, the parties agreed to increase the SNC to fourteen members by adding Prince Sihanouk and a seventh member from the Phnom Penh government. Although this arrangement soon fell apart, Hun Sen and Sihanouk agreed in early June 1991 to a new SNC configuration keeping membership at twelve.*

The Cambodia peace process is still in an early stage, and it could be derailed momentarily by any of the parties. It is not yet certain that the Phnom Penh regime, regardless of its pledges at Jakarta, will agree to surrender its de facto control to the UN or agree to pre-electoral activity that would allow noncommunist Cambodians a fair chance. Many of the ranking leaders of the current Phnom Penh regime were themselves Khmer Rouge cadres (in some cases commanders) until they fled to Vietnam; the regime has been heavily dependent on Vietnam and remains tainted by this association.

Moreover, whatever its positive accomplishments since 1979, there is evidence that the Hun Sen regime has become deeply corrupted in recent years and has lost much of its claim to legitimacy in the eyes of the Cambodian people.[16] Western nongovernmental and voluntary agency representatives working in Cambodia, most of whom are favorably inclined to the current regime, are voicing increasing concern over corruption and nepotism reminiscent of the 1970–75 Lon Nol era. They report that the consequent decline of the government's authority, not only in Phnom Penh but also in the provinces, has become a major asset

---

*After an impasse of more than seven months, the Cambodian SNC finally met in Jakarta 2–4 June 1991 under UN and ASEAN sponsorship. Sihanouk and Hun Sen agreed on a formula in which Sihanouk would join the SNC simply as one of its twelve members, replacing one of the two Sihanoukistes, and Hun Sen would remain as one of six members from the Phnom Penh side. Thus, formally, the chairmanship question would be finessed, although clearly Sihanouk would be in position to lead the SNC's deliberations, and Hun Sen, with six votes, would be de facto vice-chairman. As of July 1991, however, it remained to be seen whether the SNC would be able to function effectively under this arrangement and whether the UN peace process would move forward.

to the Khmer Rouge. The drastic scaling down of assistance from Eastern European countries (and by necessity the Soviet Union) has further weakened the central government.

This development cannot please the Soviet Union. Beyond the direct benefits that would accrue to its ally Vietnam, the Soviet Union has an important interest in seeing an end to the present strife in Cambodia and to the instability that has plagued Indochina since 1975. The Soviets, of course, have their own investment in the Hun Sen regime, which they have supported with arms, fuel, and other essential supplies since 1979, either directly or through Vietnam. They also have limits to their capabilities. The best way to maximize the power of the ruling Khmer People's Revolutionary Party in a coalition government would be to dilute whatever is left of its Marxist economic character by establishing a working relationship, if not complete reconciliation, with the forces of Sihanouk and Son Sann. The settlement framework envisaged by the Perm Five provides for precisely such an arrangement. The big question mark, as noted previously, is whether Hun Sen and company would be willing to admit the noncommunists as an established political entity—that is, to embrace pluralism. As yet, however, there are no indications that the PRK's leaders are prepared to abandon their Leninist ways.

In a Cambodia settlement, the Soviets share Vietnam's objective of preventing any future threat to Vietnam's security stemming from Cambodia. In an era of growing regional interdependence, it is arguable that Vietnam's security can be most effectively protected by a Cambodia which is genuinely independent, pluralist, and economically strong through a free-market orientation and commercial ties to ASEAN and the West. This could also be the best means to prevent the Khmer Rouge from capturing exclusive power. Again, the Perm Five framework would seem to be supportive of the Soviets' long-term interests in this respect.

Also centrally important are Sino-Vietnamese relations. After years of diplomatic jockeying and small pacific gestures, Hanoi and Beijing have apparently agreed to move toward normalization. On 3–4 September 1990, Vietnamese Communist Party General Secretary Nguyen Van Linh, Prime Minister Do Muoi, and former Prime Minister Pham Van Dong, an old-line leader of great stature in the eyes of the Chinese, travelled to Chengdu, capital of China's Sichuan province, to meet with high-ranking Chinese officials. They reportedly met with Chinese party chief Jiang Zemin and Prime Minister Li Peng. Cambodia was obviously at the top of their agenda, and it is not coincidental that soon thereafter the warring Cambodian factions agreed, at least on paper, to accept the Perm Five formula. To what extent China is willing (or even able) to pressure the Khmer Rouge is not known, nor can we assess precisely the impact on the Hun Sen regime. But China and Vietnam appear to be seeking some sort of Cambodia arrangement both can live with; normalization of relations, after two decades of coolness and eleven years of outright hostility, is in the air. Underscoring this momentum was the presence of General Vo Nguyen Giap, Vietnam's most revered military man, as a "distinguished guest" at the Beijing Asian Games that began in late September 1990.[17]

WHO LOST CAMBODIA TO POL POT—AGAIN?

But by far the greatest threat to the Cambodia peace process comes from the Khmer Rouge. Their implacable long-term intention is to gain full power by whatever tactical means are necessary, and their current actions include the coerced movement of Cambodians from the displaced persons camps in Thailand (at Site 8 and Site K on the eastern Thai border, and O'Trao to the north) and continued intense political proselytizing in Cambodia's interior.[18] By early 1991 an estimated 100,000 people had been forced back into Khmer Rouge–controlled villages along the Thai-Cambodian border.

The Khmer Rouge have stockpiled arms and munitions caches in many areas. Even were China to cut off all material aid at once, the Khmer Rouge would be able to maintain themselves at a high level for years to come; observers who have travelled extensively with the Khmer Rouge believe they can obtain 90 percent of their essential supplies *inside Cambodia*, either through coercion or payment in gold, which they are said to have in ample quantity, thanks to a lively trade with Thailand in gems and timber.[19]

The dwindling down of the Cold War in Indochina may in the end have little favorable impact on Cambodia, and it *could* have adverse consequences. Even if agreement can be reached, UN peacekeepers may not be in place for many months. The United States and the Soviet Union are not prepared to send troops to keep the Khmer Rouge from returning to power. Would they ask Vietnam to do the job again? China has already done enough to assure the Khmer Rouge's survival regardless of what the international community does. Thanks to China's insistence on the inclusion of the Khmer Rouge in the Perm Five plan, and hence their legitimation, the Khmer Rouge have positioned themselves to move forward in open political competition while simultaneously reserving a military option from their Cardamom Mountain strongholds and employing their finely honed subtle coercion in the villages. Obviously a critical aspect of the Perm Five UN plan is effective disarmament of all Khmer factions, and this will be extraordinarily difficult to do with regard to the Khmer Rouge. By appointing former Democratic Kampuchea President Khieu Samphan and current Defense Minister Son Sen (the commandant of the notorious Khmer Rouge prison system in the 1975–78 period) as their delegates to the SNC, Pol Pot's men have served notice that they will not break with the past.[20] Corruption, inflation, declining military morale, and other signs of deterioration of the Hun Sen government all work in favor of the Khmer Rouge. In any event, there are immense problems in protecting human rights no matter what kind of regime is present in Cambodia.[21]

The change in U.S. policy vis-à-vis Vietnam and Hun Sen pursued since July 1990 is welcome and heads in the right direction. For Cambodia, unfortunately, it may be too little and too late. U.S. policy has been narrow and unimaginative; in a real sense it has been contrary to long-term U.S. strategic interests in Southeast Asia. Of particular concern has been the image—and the reality—of the United States acting in a manner which has tended to strengthen the Khmer Rouge, regardless of its declared intentions to the contrary. Moreover, the long-term geopolitical desirability of getting on with normalization of relations with Vietnam has been ignored by Republican administrations still mired in Cold War hatred for North Vietnam.

In 1991 the Khmer Rouge remains the dominant resistance faction, not only militarily but also politically. All too late the United States and others have confronted the baffling problem of how to get rid of Pol Pot. The price for "keeping the pressure on Vietnam"—preserving and strengthening the Khmer Rouge—is now being paid in the Cambodia end-game.

The United States has been deliberately vague as to what constitutes a "satisfactory settlement" in Cambodia: if the Cambodian factions can agree among themselves on the details of a political *modus vivendi*, including elections, will Vietnam be judged to have cooperated enough in the implementation of the agreement? Or must a functioning reconciliation government be in place? Will the Khmer Rouge rush into a vacuum if the Hun Sen regime crumbles? Can the noncommunist groups be sufficiently strengthened to play a meaningful role in a future coalition under UN protection? Although the Baker shift in policy has pulled the cork out of the bottle, and the way has been cleared for movement toward detailed discussions on normalization of relations with Vietnam, crucial judgments on the nature of a Cambodia settlement and on the precise timing of normalization must still be made by the administration. These decisions will be made in the new atmosphere of Soviet-American relations and evolving attitudes toward regional conflicts that should present opportunities for more creativity in foreign policy and, one would hope, improve the prospects for genuine peace in Cambodia.

NOTES

1. Testimony before the Senate Foreign Relations Committee, "The Challenge of the European Landscape in the 1990s," 22 June 1989, *Department of State Bulletin* 89: 37–38 (October 1989).

2. See Leslie H. Gelb and Richard K. Betts, *The Irony of Vietnam: The System Worked* (Washington: Brookings Institution, 1979)—the first extended examination of how the United States got involved in Vietnam, why it stayed, and why it had such trouble disengaging.

3. Memo: "Proposed Course of Action Re Vietnam" (first draft), McNaughton to McNamara, 3 March 1965; in *The Pentagon Papers* (Gravel Edition), vol. III, pp. 694–702 (Boston: Beacon Press, 1975).

4. For one interpretation of this program, see Kenton J. Clymer, "American Assistance to the Cambodian Resistance Forces," *Indochina Issues*, no. 90, April 1990; published by Indochina Project, 2001 S Street, N.W., Washington, D.C. 20036.

5. The definitive study of this subject is Nayan Chanda, *Brother Enemy: The War after the War* (New York: Harcourt Brace Jovanovich, 1986). See also Frederick Z. Brown, *Second Change: The United States and Indochina in the 1990s* (New York: Council on Foreign Relations, 1989).

6. For an analysis of Soviet capabilities in traditional Cold War terms, see Robert A. Manning, *Asian Policy: The New Soviet Challenge in the Pacific* (New York: Priority Press Publications, A Twentieth-Century Fund Paper, 1988).

7. See Douglas Pike, *Vietnam and the Soviet Union: Anatomy of an Alliance* (Boulder, CO: Westview Press, 1987).

8. *New York Times*, 19 July 1990.

9. *New York Times*, 28 July 1990.

10. The first meeting was reported in *New York Times*, 7 August 1990.

11. *New York Times*, 18 October 1990.

12. *New York Times*, 30 September 1990.

13. "Statement of the Five Permanent Members of the Security Council of the United Nations on Cambodia," issued in New York, 28 August 1990.

14. *New York Times*, 9 September 1990.

15. UPI, Bangkok, 18 September 1990.

16. The most detailed critique of the Hun Sen regime's human rights record and analysis of its composition is found in "Peace and Human Rights in Cambodia: Exploring From Within," by Kassie Neou with Al Santoli—an occasional paper published by Freedom House, 48 East 21st Street, New York, NY 10010.

17. *Washington Post*, 19 September 1990; *New York Times*, 20 September 1990.

18. *New York Times*, 3 September 1990.

19. Briefing by Nate Thayer, Associated Press correspondent resident in Thailand, before the Center for Strategic and International Studies, Washington, D.C., 31 July 1990.

20. For an extended discussion of Khmer Rouge tactics and criticism of the Perm Five "solution," see Nayan Chanda, "Pol Pot's Men Gain Legitimacy in Jakarta," *Asian Wall Street Journal*, 17 September 1990.

21. See "Human Rights Aspects of a Comprehensive Solution to the Conflict in Cambodia," by David Hawk and the Cambodian Documentation Commission, 251 West 87th Street, New York, NY 10024. The Perm Five deliberations over the past nine months reflect the thinking found in Hawk's paper.

A SOVIET VIEW OF THE CAMBODIAN CONFLICT

Gennady I. Chufrin

REVISION OF SOVIET ATTITUDES TOWARD REGIONAL CONFLICTS

After a very sharp debate at the 28th Congress, the highest political forum of the Soviet Communist Party, held in the first half of July 1990, its delegates gave their firm approval to the new foreign policy pursued by Mikhail Gorbachev since 1985. This policy, otherwise known as the "new political thinking," is said by the new Soviet leadership to be motivated exclusively by Soviet national interests and not by ideological dogmas, as it was so often in the past. The new Soviet leadership also emphasizes that under the "new political thinking" general humanistic values will take clear priority over class values in Soviet foreign policy and that its goal is to move from confrontation with the West to dialogue and cooperation on the basis of genuine respect of mutual interests and security concerns.

At the base of these dramatic changes in Soviet foreign policy lay several very important considerations, domestic as well as international. First, by the middle of the 1980s it became clear that the world was relentlessly moving toward open confrontation between the two major military powers and, unless some bold initiatives were taken to reverse this trend, a global nuclear catastrophe might become a grim reality.

Second, it was realized in the Soviet Union that the exhausting arms race with the West in which the Soviet Union had been involved for many decades not only had not increased Soviet security (although military parity with the United States was achieved), but it had also raised suspicions about the Soviet military buildup among a growing number of countries which, as a result, joined the ranks of Soviet critics and even became open opponents.

Third, growing economic and social domestic problems in the Soviet Union required that the new Soviet leadership divert some of the enormous human and material resources spent on defense to meet the pressing needs of the Soviet people. (Gorbachev later admitted that the share of defense expenditures in the Soviet GNP had at one time reached 18 percent.)

As a result, the new Soviet leadership started to reassess its domestic and international priorities and initiated the dialogue with the United States which later developed into a continuing process of frequent summit meetings accompanied by numerous meetings and conferences at other levels of Soviet and American officials and experts on political, economic, and military affairs. These meetings led to a number of very important agreements that radically improved the overall atmosphere of Soviet-American relations and, as a consequence, the state of global relations.

The same considerations that justified these changes in Soviet global policy can equally well be applied to the analysis of the Soviet foreign policy in the Third World. However, this policy has been characterized by a number of specific features.

For instance, the Soviet Union, driven by ideological zeal and competition with the West, has often taken part, directly or indirectly, in regional conflicts in the Third World without giving proper prior consideration to see if the risks involved were worth taking from the standpoint of genuine Soviet interests. This reckless involvement in Third World conflicts has not only been very costly economically, but it has also created many new political problems for the Soviet Union in its relations with other countries. The most recent example of such involvement was the direct Soviet intervention in Afghanistan, which not only brought to an end the policy of detente with the United States, but also seriously damaged the Soviet Union's relations with many other countries, including a number of Islamic states that until that time were generally quite sympathetic to the USSR.

The Soviet leadership rather belatedly recognized that it had only limited control over its allies in Third World regional conflicts, who pursued their own goals even to the point of putting the Soviet Union into extremely awkward positions. They could act in this way because they were certain that once the Soviet Union began to assist them in their conflicts, there was no way out for the Soviets because of ideological constraints. Thus the thesis of internationalist help that had previously been used by the Soviet leadership to justify some of its interventions became an ideological trap for the USSR.

As a result, the new Soviet leadership deemed it necessary to reassess Soviet behavior in the Third World and to set forth new guidelines for Soviet policy there. Those guidelines can be summarized as follows:

    a) The Soviet Union should stop using regional conflicts as a proxy war with the West;

b) Active steps should be taken to disengage the Soviet Union from regional conflicts, especially from those where it has been heavily involved;

c) A constructive dialogue should be established with the other countries concerned to resolve existing regional conflicts and prevent the emergence of new ones; and

d) The role of the United Nations and its machinery for resolving regional conflicts should be enhanced.

However, the new Soviet policy of disengagement from regional conflicts should not be interpreted as neo-isolationist or as meaning that the Soviet Union will remain passive in any future regional conflicts. Although such conflicts are caused, first and foremost, not by great power differences, but by various combinations of local political, economic, ideological, territorial, ethnic, religious, and other factors, they can have very definite geopolitical implications. Therefore, it will be only natural for the Soviet Union to take an active interest in those regional conflicts that may have a direct bearing on Soviet national interests. At the same time, in line with the governing mood in the Soviet parliament and Soviet society, it is very hard (in fact, impossible) to imagine any direct involvement by the USSR in any regional conflict. On the contrary, it is much more likely that the Soviet Union will exercise all its influence to resolve existing regional conflicts and to prevent new ones exclusively by political means, in close cooperation with the other countries concerned.*

THE SOVIET ATTITUDE TOWARD THE CAMBODIAN CONFLICT

These introductory remarks have been necessary, in my opinion, to explain the Soviet attitude toward one of the most prolonged regional conflicts of today—the conflict in Cambodia. It is one of those conflicts where the Soviet Union is involved only indirectly, although its outcome will be far from irrelevant to Soviet national interests.

First, the speedy resolution of the Cambodian conflict will remove one of the most serious irritants from current Sino-Soviet relations.

Second, the "Cambodia post-settlement era" in Southeast Asia is expected to be a period of rapid economic growth marked by the end of the Western economic embargo against Vietnam and Cambodia. This will

*This assertion, made prior to the Iraqi intervention in Kuwait, was vindicated by the Soviet government actions before, during, and after the war in the Gulf.

mean that these states will no longer have to rely largely on Soviet economic assistance, while this assistance itself will turn into mutually advantageous cooperation.

Third, the resolution of the Cambodian problem will have major implications extending beyond Southeast Asia and have a favorable impact on the overall international climate in Asia-Pacific through the removal of one of the "hot spots" in this area which has caused mutual suspicion and fear, a military buildup, and foreign interference in local affairs. The end of the Cambodian conflict could serve a good purpose by improving relations between Hanoi and Washington and by facilitating political and economic relations between the USSR and ASEAN countries.

However, these positive developments cannot materialize while the highly complicated Cambodian problem remains unresolved.

MILITARY ASPECTS OF THE CONFLICT

After the withdrawal of Vietnamese troops from Cambodia in September 1989, the tripartite Khmer opposition started a massive offensive against government troops. At first, taking advantage of the rainy season and the low combat-readiness of the government troops, the opposition forces managed to establish control over territory of approximately 1.5 thousand sq. km. in the western and northwestern areas of Cambodia. The peak of their military success was reached at the end of 1989 when the battle over Battambang, the second largest city in the country, started. However, after that, the government troops recovered the initiative in the battlefield and recaptured most of the previously lost territory. (The opposition accused them of using assistance from some Vietnamese troops, but that was neither admitted by Phnom Penh nor confirmed by an independent sources.)

It seems that the failure of their military adventure convinced Prince Norodom Sihanouk's FUNCINPEC and Son Sann's KPLNF (but not the Khmer Rouge!) that the only realistic way to resolve the conflict was by political methods. That conviction, it appears, lay behind Prince Sihanouk's position at the conference in Tokyo at the beginning of June 1990 where he—formally on behalf of the Coalition Government of Democratic Kampuchea (CGDK), but in fact on behalf of only two factions constituting the opposition—signed with Prime Minister Hun Sen a communiqué which called on both sides to voluntarily refrain from any further use of force.

However, the Khmer Rouge have not only refused to sign this communiqué, but they also continue to rely on military force in the conflict, thus presenting a very serious threat to any normal political process in Cambodia. According to some reports from inside the country, the Khmer Rouge appear to be making some headway on the battlefield in various parts of Cambodia, relying now on well-tested guerrilla methods of warfare. The military strength of the Khmer Rouge may even have increased because of continuing massive Chinese arms supplies.

POLITICAL ASPECTS OF THE CONFLICT

In spite of all the obvious difficulties, the political dialogue between the Phnom Penh government and the two opposition factions of the CGDK represented by Prince Sihanouk recently became more meaningful and helped to bridge at least some of their differences. This explains the much more sober approach of both sides to the Cambodian realities and the de facto recognition by the opposition that the Heng Samrin–Hun Sen regime is a genuine national political force sincerely interested in preserving the security and integrity of Cambodia. The political dialogue is clearly facilitated by the withdrawal of Vietnamese troops and advisers from the country, by the recent military victories of government troops, and by the shift of the Phnom Penh government from a leftist economic policy to liberal economic reforms aimed at the development of a free-market economy.

These positive trends are again counterbalanced by the stand taken by the Khmer Rouge, who refuse to participate in the negotiating process (as was the case in Tokyo). Their position does not change even if their representatives formally attend conferences in Paris or in Jakarta or even if they sign documents coordinated with other parties to the Cambodian conflict. The reason is obvious: the Khmer Rouge do not believe in normal, civilized political settlement, and they are afraid to test their popularity through a public vote.

PSYCHOLOGICAL ASPECTS OF THE CONFLICT

Inside Cambodia today one can see a definite improvement in the overall socioeconomic situation as well as in general living standards. Further prospects of economic improvement are connected with the transfer of land to peasants and with the rapid development of market forces, in particular of various forms of small private enterprise. After the withdrawal of the Vietnamese troops, there was also a definite decline in anti-Vietnamese feeling.

However, the Khmer people are very much afraid of the possible return to power of the Khmer Rouge. Those fears were especially high at the end of 1989 and the beginning of 1990—i.e., before the government troops managed to repulse the Khmer Rouge offensive—and they remain substantial. The population is war-weary and will favor any political solution that guarantees their basic human rights and lays down the foundations of a stable democratic society.

PEACE INITIATIVES

At present there are several peace proposals relating to Cambodia that are tabled for consideration at various international forums. The most comprehensive one is probably the proposal put forward by the Australian foreign minister, Gareth Evans, in February 1990. Its central idea is to give a prominent role to the United Nations in the peace process in Cambodia and especially in the transition period leading to free and fair elections. This plan received, in principle, the initial approval of all the opposing Khmer parties, who agreed that the purpose of the UN-organized elections should be to elect a constitutional assembly which would draft and adopt a constitution and then become the national assembly of the country.

Yet all these peace plans, including the Australian one, have failed so far to produce a final resolution of the Cambodian conflict, and the achievement of peace in Cambodia still looks a long way off. The basic reason for this, in my opinion, is that voluntary power-sharing between the two most important and influential parties to the Cambodian conflict—the Heng Samrin–Hun Sen regime and the Khmer Rouge—is impossible, at least for now. The present leadership of the Khmer Rouge will not accept the outcome of any proposed general election unless it clearly assures their return to power. On the other hand, the return of the Khmer Rouge to power is flatly rejected even as a possibility by the Phnom Penh government, although in April 1990 Hun Sen mentioned to a visiting delegation of the Europarliament that the Khmer Rouge would not be excluded on principle from future elections, but presumably could participate in them in their private capacities in the same way as any other citizens of Cambodia.

This attitude toward the Khmer Rouge may seem to be too rigid at first glance, but in fact it is similar to the stand taken on this issue by many other countries, including the United States. At least that would seem to be the import of a statement made by the U.S. Undersecretary of State for Political Affairs, Robert Kimmitt, who said in a speech given on 18 April 1990 to the Asia Society in Washington:

> I want to be clear on one crucial point about U.S. policy [on Cambodia]: the Bush administration is unalterably opposed to a return to power of the murderous Khmer Rouge. Our efforts to reach a comprehensive settlement are aimed at fashioning a structure of peace that contains effective measures to prevent the Khmer Rouge from returning to dominance. And under no circumstances can those Khmer Rouge leaders responsible for the policies of the past have any role in Cambodia's political future.

The question remains, however, what kind of participation by the Khmer Rouge in future general elections will be acceptable either to Phnom Penh (even taking into account the statement of Hun Sen) or to the United States, and what can be done with a political organization that has quite formidable military power, continues to receive regular supplies of arms from China, and exercises effective control over refugee camps being used by it as a rich source of fresh manpower, if this organization is given advance warning that it will not be allowed to come back to power under any conditions?

I am certainly not trying to build a case in favor of the abhorrent Khmer Rouge, but having come to this point in the analysis of the present stage of the Cambodian conflict, I think it would be worthwhile to consider a few suggestions that might be used to prepare the ground for any subsequent process of holding free and fair elections in Cambodia:

1. The international community should undertake concerted efforts to reduce the influence of the ultra-extremists among the already highly radical Khmer Rouge by reducing their ability to continue waging war. For this purpose, China should be approached with a proposal to stop the supply of arms to the Khmer Rouge on the firm condition that similar supplies to other opposing parties to the conflict, including the Phnom Penh government, will also be cut off immediately. To verify the stoppage of arms supply to Cambodia will not present an insurmountable problem because the number of air and sea ports in the country that can be used for the receipt, storage, and reloading of armaments is limited.

2. For the same purpose, independent observers could be sent to Cambodia to counter Chinese allegations about the continuing Vietnamese military presence there. Vietnam itself invited such observers to verify the Vietnamese troop withdrawal, but there was only a limited response to the invitation.

3. Greater prominence should be given to the peace efforts suggested or already undertaken by Thailand. The Thai government, in particular, should be actively supported in its efforts to relocate Khmer refugee camps away from the Thai-Cambodian border, deeper inside Thailand, and to establish effective international control over them.

4. The Khmer Rouge should again be offered participation in a Supreme National Council, but only as a part of the CGDK representation, which, as the UN Security Council Permanent Five already agreed, will have six seats in the "6 + 6" composition of the SNC.

5. Since the troop reductions in the transition period before the general elections are very difficult to verify, it would be advisable, after a cease-fire is announced, to keep the troops of the opposing Khmer parties in the places of their regular deployment and to establish observer posts to monitor any possible violations of the agreement.

6. During the transition period, the Phnom Penh government, as well as the CGDK, should carry out their routine administrative and economic duties in the areas they control, but without any interference in the election process, which will be the sole responsibility of the United Nations.

7. The United Nations should be given full authority to organize and supervise free and fair elections and to monitor the implementation of all international agreements on Cambodia.

The above suggestions are certainly not meant to replace the Australian peace proposal, which, being the most comprehensive so far of the peace initiatives on Cambodia, remains the basis for discussion at different levels and among the various parties concerned, including the Permanent Five. Rather, they are intended to supplement the basic provisions of that plan, are based largely on various proposals by the governments of the Soviet Union, Vietnam, Cambodia, and Thailand, and are meant to accommodate the interests of different parties to the Cambodian conflict, both inside and outside the country.

As for the practicability of the Australian peace proposal, there are two major points of criticism. The first one concerns its very large financial cost, and the second, its difficult logistical problems, including the number of UN personnel to be involved, availability of suitable UN personnel, availability of interpreters, etc. I would venture to introduce another note of caution in connection with the Australian proposals for the substitution of authority in Cambodia during the transition period. Although there are three possible options suggested, all of them, in my opinion, disregard or wrongly interpret Cambodian political traditions and customs. By this I mean that the Khmer population has traditionally shown respect for a central authority, a central government, which explains, on the one hand, the continuing influence of Prince Sihanouk (but not of his son) in the country, and, on the other, the notably increased authority of the Phnom Penh government (especially among the urban population) during the last two–three years. One of the latest evidences of the growing confidence in its popularity of the Phnom Penh government among the people is its willingness to distribute among them arms for the purpose of self-defense.

It would be wrong, therefore, either to try to apply an even-handed approach to the Phnom Penh administration and the CGDK structures, or to expect the Phnom Penh government to dissolve itself and completely hand over its prerogatives to UN personnel in the transition period. Rather, as has been suggested earlier, the Phnom Penh government and the CGDK should surrender to the United Nations only the right to organize and control the elections (as was the case in Namibia, where the South African authorities functioned until the results of the election were announced). Nor is it practical to expect the Phnom Penh government to accept a proposal, originally put forward by Prince Sihanouk, and supported since then by China, which is aimed at reducing the size of its troops to one-fourth of the total strength of a combined, four-part army.

During the twelve years that have elapsed since the outbreak of the Cambodian conflict, the Soviet Union has stood firmly by the side of Vietnam and the Heng Samrin–Hun Sen government of Cambodia, giving them all necessary political, materiel, and military assistance. Contrary to many speculations appearing from time to time in the international press, the Soviet Union has no intentions of abandoning its friends now in spite of its own economic and financial difficulties. Speaking at a press conference at the end of his visit to Singapore in February 1990, Soviet Prime Minister Nikolai Ryzhkov said that the USSR would stop supplying arms to the Hun Sen government only if other countries ceased supplying the Khmer opposition forces.

The Soviet Union, however, as is widely known, has urged, especially during the last few years, the conflicting parties—first of all, China and Vietnam—to begin a political dialogue that could lead to a comprehensive settlement of the Cambodian conflict.

The Soviet Union has not only used its influence with Vietnam to persuade it to make a complete military withdrawal from Cambodia, but also has welcomed the first official contacts between Hanoi and Peking and has actively participated diplomatically—at bilateral and multilateral levels—in preparing the grounds for the lasting political settlement of the Cambodian problem. By announcing its plans at the beginning of 1990 to drastically reduce its military presence in Cam Ranh Bay, the Soviet Union has effectively put an end to recent speculations about its alleged intentions to use the Cambodian conflict to project its military power to Southeast Asia.

The Soviet Union, as already stated, strongly supports a United Nations' role in peace efforts in Cambodia. Although it recognizes the Hun Sen government as the only legitimate government in Cambodia until elections are held to elect a new one, it is prepared to accept any results of future UN-sponsored elections—if they are indeed free and fair—just as it accepted the results of elections in Namibia and Nicaragua. And of course it is prepared to cooperate with a future government of Cambodia on the basis of mutual respect and economic benefit.

Moscow, 15 July 1990

POSTSCRIPT

By the end of 1990, the five permanent members of the UN Security Council managed to work out a five-point peace plan for Cambodia and presented it to the Khmer warring parties. The UN peace plan, accompanied by a radical change in U.S. policy toward Hanoi and Phnom Penh, as well as a coordinated decision of the USSR and China to freeze their arms supplies to the opposing Khmer parties, seemed at one time to be a workable arrangement for achieving a final resolution of the Cambodian problem. But not quite—for although the initial reaction of the Cambodian government and the opposition to the UN peace plan was rather favorable, very soon its inherent weaknesses (discussed earlier in this paper) became obvious.

March 1991

DEFERRING PEACE IN CAMBODIA: REGIONAL RAPPROCHEMENT, SUPERPOWER OBSTRUCTION

Ben Kiernan

The State of Cambodia—the Vietnamese-backed government of Hun Sen and Heng Samrin—has been in power for over twelve years. In 1989 Vietnam's troops withdrew from the country, preceded by all but a few Vietnamese military advisers. The State of Cambodia then offered its non-communist opponents, Norodom Sihanouk and Son Sann (but not their Khmer Rouge ally), a political role and free elections.[1] From 1988, neighboring Thailand's policy significantly shifted toward rapprochement with its Indochinese communist neighbors, best illustrated by the hosting of three visits by Cambodian Prime Minister Hun Sen to Bangkok in 1989. In the same period, regional—particularly Southeast Asian—diplomacy showed promise of an emerging consensus to exclude the Khmer Rouge as well as the Vietnamese.

But the great powers, particularly China and the United States, played a spoiling role, maximizing their influence with and support of their Cambodian protégés to outflank the regional diplomacy. Negotiations at great power level, in Paris and especially in the UN Security Council, displaced the regional ones, returning the Khmer Rouge to the diplomatic forefront. Such a UN settlement, a recipe for renewed civil war if not genocide, could now be imposed on Cambodia. Meanwhile the country remained diplomatically isolated, economically blockaded, and under military attack by Pol Pot's Chinese-backed Khmer Rouge and their U.S.-funded allies.

THE WAR IN CAMBODIA

During the Pol Pot period, from 1975 to 1979, Cambodia was subjected to probably the world's most radical political, social, and economic revolution. The country was cut off from the outside world, its cities were emptied, its economy was militarized, and its Buddhist religion and folk culture destroyed, and over a million of its eight million people were starved and massacred, while foreign and minority languages were banned and all neighboring countries were attacked.

Thus an international conflict was intertwined with genocide that provoked a civil war. On 10 May 1978, Phnom Penh radio broadcast a call not only to "exterminate the 50 million Vietnamese" but also to "purify the masses of the people" of Cambodia. When Cambodian communists rebelled in the Eastern Zone, Pol Pot was unable to crush them quickly. Over the next six months, 1.5 million easterners were branded as "Khmer bodies with Vietnamese minds," and at least 100,000 were exterminated by Pol Pot's forces. In 1979, surviving leaders of the Eastern Zone dissidents (like Hun Sen and Heng Samrin) succeeded Pol Pot, once Hanoi had driven his Khmer Rouge army into Thailand.

The Cambodia-Vietnam conflict had started in 1977, with Pol Pot's regime staging repeated savage raids into Vietnamese territory, massacring thousands of Vietnamese civilians and causing hundreds of thousands to flee from their homes.[2] Hanoi's complaints to this effect were corroborated at the time by both U.S. intelligence reports and the testimony of Vietnamese refugees fleeing abroad from the war zone, and they have since been extensively documented from both sides of the border.[3]

After Pol Pot's regime refused to negotiate peacefully or accept international supervision of the border,[4] Vietnamese forces intervened and overthrew it in early 1979. Western rhetoric aside, Hanoi's invasion of Cambodia was not "aggression" (unprovoked attack). Vietnam's immediate reason for intervention was self-defense. China joined Cambodia as an aggressor state when Pol Pot's ally Deng Xiaoping retaliated against Hanoi with his own invasion of Vietnam.

Vietnamese troops remained in Cambodia, offering to withdraw only in return for two concessions: the exclusion of Pol Pot's forces from the country, and the ending of the new Chinese threat to Vietnam itself. China, the Association of Southeast Asian Nations (ASEAN), and the West, on the other hand, demanded an unconditional Vietnamese withdrawal, recognized the ousted Pol Pot regime as the "legitimate" representative of the Cambodian people, and rearmed and supplied its forces. With this aid and in the sanctuary of Thailand, the Khmer Rouge rebuilt an army of about 25,000, and in 1982 were joined in a coalition government-in-exile by two small Western-backed groups nominally loyal to Norodom Sihanouk (the ANS) and Son Sann (the KPNLF).[5]

Nevertheless, from 1980 Hanoi began withdrawing its advisers, and in 1982 began official partial withdrawals of its troops, as the new Cambodian government consolidated its position. As we shall see, Vietnam successively dropped its two conditions for a withdrawal, which it completed *unilaterally* in September 1989. But then the opposition coalition intensified its attacks, although refusing to acknowledge the withdrawal or make reciprocal concessions, and possibly several thousand Vietnamese combat troops briefly returned to Cambodia in November 1989. They reportedly left again in January 1990. A few technical military advisers apparently remained.[6]

Vietnamese Troop Strength in Cambodia, 1979–89
(U.S. Sources)

Year	Troop Numbers
1979	224,000
1982	180,000
1983	150,000
1987	c. 120,000
1988	100,000
Early 1989	50,000
September 1989	0

The State of Cambodia forces have since held the country, belying Western predictions that a collapse would quickly follow any withdrawal. (A mid-1987 Australian intelligence assessment, for instance, had put the chances of a Vietnamese withdrawal by 1990 at "1 in 300," in which case the Phnom Penh regime would last only "seven months.")

In their ten-year occupation, the Vietnamese not only established a full-fledged Cambodian government led by Khmer nationalists,[7] but also trained a large Cambodian defense force. The three levels of the army—national, regional, and local—probably muster 100,000 regular troops and 200,000 militia. They have been hard pressed in the past year, but recent accounts suggest that the military situation has again stabilized.[8] The opposition has seized a swath of remote territory on the Thai frontier, but all cities and populous rural areas remain under Phnom Penh's administration. The Khmer Rouge remain a serious military threat, but one that unites most Cambodians against it. The economy has become the most pressing problem for Phnom Penh since the end of East European and much Soviet aid in 1990.[9]

The 1985 fifth congress of the ruling People's Revolutionary Party formally legalized and endorsed the private sector. More recent economic reforms in Cambodia have included the privatization of agricultural land, housing, and the industrial and commercial sectors. Political reforms have made Buddhism the state religion, legalized Christianity, officially declared neutrality in foreign policy, and changed (at Sihanouk's request) the official name of the country and the flag. Cambodia remains a one-party state, although Hun Sen favors a multiparty system for a postwar Cambodia.[10]

A settlement among the Cambodian parties that includes the Khmer Rouge, if achieved, could be a recipe for later breakdown and a new civil war far more destabilizing than the status quo. But there is potential for a settlement between the State of Cambodia and the noncommunist opposition groups should the latter break their dependence on the Khmer Rouge and take advantage of the rehabilitation of their country by the Cambodian government the Vietnamese established there. Whether Sihanouk and Son Sann would accept this is unclear. As head of the two smallest factions, they are most dependent on their great power backers, who require a Khmer Rouge role. But the Cambodian balance of forces is compatible with an emerging regional, Southeast Asian consensus to exclude the Khmer Rouge.

THE REGIONAL DIPLOMACY

In March 1980, Malaysian Prime Minister Datuk Hussein Onn and Indonesia's President Suharto met in the Malaysian coastal town of Kuantan. Their meeting produced a new term in international diplomatic parlance, the "Kuantan principle." The two Southeast Asian leaders released a statement noting their concern over the Soviet role in the Cambodia conflict, through Vietnam, but also over China's role in Indochina. As the *Far Eastern Economic Review* put it: "Hanoi's reaction was cool. But elsewhere, the principle was widely seen as a step in the right direction. Vietnam, it was generally thought, would withdraw only if there was no more Soviet aid to make the occupation viable, and if there was some guarantee that China would not leap into the breach after the withdrawal."[11] In other words, Hanoi had some legitimate concerns, which were shared in Southeast Asia. Indonesia, for instance, was not to establish diplomatic relations with China for another decade. These concerns had to be addressed in negotiations.

According to Nayan Chanda, Indonesian armed forces chief Benny Murdani made two secret trips to Hanoi in 1980 and 1982 to attempt to mediate the dispute.[12]

In 1983 Bill Hayden, Australia's new Foreign Minister, identified the two key issues dominating the Cambodian conflict. These were the problem of a threatened Khmer Rouge return to power, and the need for a Vietnamese withdrawal. Hayden launched an effort to "facilitate dialogue" on the Cambodian question.

Indonesia encouraged this effort, even expressing the vain hope that Australia would restore its aid program in Vietnam. In February 1984, Benny Murdani concluded a third visit to Vietnam with the statement that Hanoi posed no threat to Southeast Asia. He also recognized that Hanoi's invasion of Cambodia had been undertaken in self-defense, "to maintain Vietnam's own existence" against Pol Pot's attacks.[13] Soon after, Hanoi made a new diplomatic proposal, which Indonesia's Foreign Minister, Mochtar Kusumaatmadja, called "a significant step forward." The Thai Foreign Minister, Siddhi Savetsila, also welcomed unspecified "new elements" in Hanoi's position.[14]

These new elements became clear in 1985. Hanoi, after capturing all twenty of the Khmer Rouge and allied camps along the Thai-Cambodian border, dropped its demand that the Chinese threat would have to end before any full Vietnamese troop withdrawal from Cambodia.[15] In early March 1985, Hayden visited Hanoi, and heard further Vietnamese proposals from Foreign Minister Nguyen Co Thach which Hayden claimed were "a considerable advance." He asserted that his trip had "been quite successful and that will be proved."[16] Indonesia's Mochtar concurred that there had been another "advance in substance" in the Vietnamese position.[17]

While in Vietnam, Hayden had had a meeting with Hun Sen, becoming the first of many regional leaders to meet the Cambodian Premier. Hun Sen told him: "We are ready to make concessions to Prince Sihanouk and other people if they agree to join with us to eliminate Pol Pot." Hun Sen later announced that the Vietnamese troops would all leave Cambodia by 1990, or earlier if there was a settlement. (The previous date set by Hanoi had been 1995.)

Vietnam now insisted only that the Khmer Rouge be prevented from returning to power. This meant that the Cambodian problem could from that point be resolved within Southeast Asia, principally by Thailand, which could cut off sanctuary and supplies to the Khmer Rouge, and Vietnam, which could withdraw the rest of its own troops. China's cooperation in a settlement was no longer necessary. (As we shall see, however, China and the United States disagreed.)

Hayden then addressed the question of the Khmer Rouge. At the ASEAN Foreign Ministers' meeting in Manila in June 1986, Hayden proposed the establishment of a tribunal to try the Pol Pot leadership for its crimes. Although U.S. Secretary of State George Shultz declined to support the idea, it was immediately endorsed in principle by the Malaysian Foreign Minister,[18] and a few weeks later the Indonesian Foreign Minister added his own agreement.[19] (Along with Chinese and U.S. opposition to the idea, resistance also came from Australia's Prime Minister.)[20]

It was another year before Prince Sihanouk withdrew, even temporarily, from the Khmer Rouge coalition. He met Hun Sen for the first time in December 1987, and carried to Beijing Hun Sen's proposal to disarm the Khmer Rouge. As Kelvin Rowley points out, China rejected the idea, and Sihanouk cancelled his next round of talks with Hun Sen.

But in July 1988 the first round of the Jakarta Informal Meetings (JIMs) took place, attended by all ASEAN and Indochinese countries, and all Cambodian factions. This meeting leapt a major hurdle, the refusal of the Cambodian sides to meet face-to-face, each having long insisted it would negotiate only with the foreign backers of the other. In Jakarta the ice was broken by having the Cambodian parties meet first, with the Southeast Asian supporters of each then joining the conference.

The "consensus statement" from the meeting, released by the new Indonesian Foreign Minister Ali Alatas, stressed the two problems Hayden had identified: a Vietnamese withdrawal (promised for 1990) and prevention of "a recurrence of the genocidal policies and practices of the Pol Pot regime." In April 1989 the Vietnamese undertook to withdraw by September 1989. Sihanouk and Hun Sen met again in Jakarta the next month. They reached general agreement, and Sihanouk said he was prepared to go it alone without the Khmer Rouge should they prove recalcitrant.[21] However, he reneged on this undertaking immediately after leaving Jakarta.

The Prince had lost his nerve, becoming a genuine puppet of the Chinese and the Khmer Rouge. As the last Vietnamese troops were pulling out, Sihanouk called for a civil war in Cambodia to overthrow the Hun Sen government, threatening Cambodia's people with "danger to yourself" unless they rallied to his coalition to "avoid the charge of treason" after its victory.[22]

The third Jakarta Informal Meeting, in February 1990, broke down over the Khmer Rouge objection to use of the word *genocide* in the final communiqué. Although it had appeared in previous statements, the Khmer Rouge now opposed its inclusion, insisting instead on mention of "Vietnamese settlers," to which Hun Sen and Vietnamese Foreign Minister Thach objected. The Australian Foreign Minister, Gareth Evans, then proposed placing an asterisk next to each disputed phrase, with a note that these had not been agreed upon unanimously. Hun Sen and Thach agreed to this compromise. But the Khmer Rouge refused, and the talks broke up.[23] Again, Sihanouk and Son Sann had declined to break with the Khmer Rouge.

In Tokyo in June 1990, Sihanouk did go ahead in cease-fire talks with Hun Sen, despite a Khmer Rouge boycott. He signed an agreement on "voluntary self-restraint," and subsequently named six members of the non-communist forces to an agreed twelve-member Supreme National Council, with Hun Sen naming the other six. But again, Sihanouk tore up this agreement after the Khmer Rouge expressed opposition.[24] Hun Sen later commented: "It is regrettable that Prince Sihanouk rejects all our accords as often as I enter into agreement with him."[25] The Pol Pot-Sihanouk-Son Sann coalition has long held firm. It seems unwise to rely on any future commitment from Sihanouk, who revealed in September 1990 that he "would agree to anything the Khmer Rouge wanted."[26]

But meanwhile the policy of Thailand, the "front-line state" most threatened by Hanoi's 1979 removal of the Pol Pot regime, shifted. Thailand's first elected Prime Minister since 1976, Chatichai Choonhavon, held office from 1988 until he was ousted in a military coup in 1991. During this period, sensing advantage in the accelerating Vietnamese withdrawal, Bangkok moved closer to both Hanoi and Phnom Penh, hoping to turn Indochina from "a battleground into a trading ground." In Southeast Asia, the Cambodian issue is the major one dividing the region, and the momentum developed for a settlement.[27]

The Southeast Asian consensus, at the JIM meetings and elsewhere, usually favored a settlement that would exclude both Vietnamese troops and the Khmer Rouge—potential common ground with Hanoi. And the Tokyo meeting of Cambodian parties went ahead without the Khmer Rouge. Any likely regional settlement would exclude them as well.

These advances were possible because the great powers, particularly China and the United States, were not involved. But there was no settlement precisely because of Chinese and U.S. rejection of any such move to exclude the Khmer Rouge. The great powers have continued to offer the Khmer Rouge a veto, which has been regularly exercised.

A major role in this process has been played by Australia. In late 1989, Foreign Minister Gareth Evans came under intense domestic pressure from opponents of the Western/Chinese proposal, which Evans had publicly backed, to return the Khmer Rouge to positions of power as full partners in a new "quadripartite" Cambodian government. On 24 November 1989, the day after the John Pilger–David Munro film *Cambodia Year Ten* was shown on national television, Evans announced a new Australian plan to have the United Nations temporarily administer Cambodia and hold elections. He said its aim was to exclude the Khmer Rouge, with Cambodia's UN seat declared vacant. For eight months, international "support for the Australian plan" ignored the crucial latter point, which has not been implemented.

The proposal never involved any concrete action by Australia. It quickly degenerated into a refusal to take any action without Khmer Rouge "acceptance"—not at all a means to exclude them. Evans states: "The simple fact is that, in the absence of a comprehensive settlement supported by China and accepted by the Khmer Rouge, the Cambodian tragedy will continue."[28] Thus the Evans Plan to end the threat of the Khmer Rouge offered them veto power to paralyze the peace process and over a year's valuable time to advance their war aims.

THE REGION AND THE GREAT POWERS

"I do not understand why some people want to remove Pol Pot," Deng Xiaoping said in 1984.[29] "It is true that he made some mistakes in the past but now he is leading the fight against the Vietnamese aggressors." In May 1989, Prince Sihanouk revealed to foreign diplomats that Deng had threatened to "fight" him should he abandon his alliance with the Khmer Rouge.[30] Chinese support for the Khmer Rouge, including a large delivery of weapons in mid-1990[31] despite a previous undertaking to cut arms supplies in return for Vietnam's withdrawal,[32] has remained strong. China still provides the Khmer Rouge forces with U.S. $100 million per annum, according to American intelligence, and in late 1990 began supplying them with T-59 tanks, twenty-four of which had arrived by October. *Jane's Defence Weekly* described the Khmer Rouge tanks as "the most significant increase in firepower the resistance to the Vietnamese-installed government has ever received."[33] (Beijing possibly sees the Khmer Rouge and their two anti-Vietnamese allies replaying China's wartime anti-Japanese struggle, when the Chinese Communist Party's

United Front tactics also gave its bourgeois allies two of the "three-thirds" of coalition posts.)[34]

The USSR, while continuing to supply Vietnam and Cambodia at reduced levels (aid to Vietnam fell by 63 percent in 1990),[35] has rapidly lost interest in the region, owing to Vietnam's mismanagement of its aid and Soviet domestic problems. The Soviet Union, according to Steven Erlanger of the *New York Times*, "no longer has the money or, seemingly, the will to project an ideology onto developing countries anywhere."[36] The "virtual Soviet military withdrawal" from Cam Ranh Bay in Vietnam underscores that lack of interest.[37]

On the other hand, three major planks of American policy toward Cambodia have remained unchanged. The U.S. veto of aid, including UN, World Bank, and International Monetary Fund aid to Cambodia,[38] U.S. support for a Khmer Rouge role, and U.S. military support for the Khmer Rouge's allies ($17-32 million per annum),[39] all continued despite the Beijing massacre of June 1989, the Vietnamese withdrawal from Cambodia in September 1989, and Washington's policy "shift" of July 1990.[40]

Unlike the affected regional countries, great powers can afford to ignore for years the damage their policies inflict on small nations. A British diplomat expressed this distance when he remarked on Cambodia in 1986, "We're only talking about six million people."[41] France, too, like the United States, is unenthusiastic about any settlement arrived at independently in Southeast Asia.[42] And given the choice, China naturally blocks isolation of its Khmer Rouge client, as well as resisting moves toward regional concord, demonstrating its preference for a Balkanized Southeast Asia with "many roads to Beijing." Yet any agreement to isolate the Khmer Rouge between Vietnam and Thailand, if backed by ASEAN and the West, would be very hard for Beijing to subvert. China must live with Southeast Asia, and would accept a bipartisan Southeast Asian settlement.

The withdrawal of the Vietnamese army from Cambodia in 1989 belied the myth that Chinese and Western backing for Pol Pot's forces (and his allies) since 1978 was primarily aimed at forcing a Vietnamese withdrawal. As Deng Xiaoping had stated in December 1979: "It is wise for China *to force the Vietnamese to stay in Cambodia*, because that way they will suffer more and more."[43]

The real question, then, is who rules Cambodia. The Vietnamese presence was a pretext not just for China, but also for the United States, to oppose their Cambodian enemy candidate: the pro-Vietnamese, anti-Pol Pot, Hun Sen regime. Despite obvious difficulty in justifying it, the

West has maintained an embargo on Cambodia (renewed by Washington in September 1990 for its twelfth year), yet still supports Pol Pot's allies and opposes Pol Pot's Cambodian opponents, and continues to offer the Pol Pot forces a veto over any proposed settlement.

For over a decade, official Western support for Deng Xiaoping's China has spilled over into Western support for his protégé Pol Pot. Former U.S. National Security Advisor Zbigniew Brzezinski says that, in 1979, "I encouraged the Chinese to support Pol Pot. . . . Pol Pot was an abomination. We could never support him but China could."[44]

They both did. The United States, Brzezinski says, "winked, semi-publicly" at Chinese and Thai aid for the Khmer Rouge after their defeat by Hanoi. Washington also pressured UN agencies to supply the Khmer Rouge. In *Rice, Rivalry and Politics*, the major study of the relief effort for Cambodian refugees in Thailand, Linda Mason and Roger Brown, graduates of the Yale School of Management, revealed: "The U.S. Government, which funded the bulk of the relief operation on the border, insisted that the Khmer Rouge be fed." They add: "When World Relief started to push its proposal for aid to the Khmer Rouge, the U.S. was supportive, though behind the scenes . . . ; the U.S. preferred that the Khmer Rouge operation benefit from the credibility of an internationally known relief organisation." Congressional sources have also cited a figure of $85 million for U.S. aid to Pol Pot's Khmer Rouge since 1979.[45] This may explain why, under U.S. influence, the World Food Program alone handed over $12 million worth of food to the Thai army to pass on to the Khmer Rouge. "20–40,000 Pol Pot guerrillas benefitted," according to former Assistant Secretary of State Richard Holbrooke.[46] Mason and Brown note that the health of the Khmer Rouge army "rapidly improved" throughout 1980: "The Khmer Rouge had a history of unimaginable brutality, and having regained their strength, they had begun fighting the Vietnamese."[47]

In May 1980, the U.S. Central Intelligence Agency produced a "demographic report" on Cambodia which denied that there had been *any* executions in the last two years of the Pol Pot regime.[48] (The toll from executions in 1977–78 had in fact been around half a million people.) In November 1980, former Deputy Director of the CIA Ray Cline made a secret visit to a Khmer Rouge camp inside Cambodia.[49]

In the diplomatic arena, the United States led most of the Western world to line up behind China in support of the Khmer Rouge. Both the Carter and Reagan administrations voted for Pol Pot's representative to occupy Cambodia's seat in the United Nations. He did so until late 1990, and subsequently continued to run Cambodia's UN mission in New York. As of 1991, no Western country has voted against the Khmer Rouge in the eleven years that their tenure has been challenged.

In 1981, at an international conference on Cambodia, then U.S. Secretary of State Al Haig dismayed the Southeast Asian countries by backing China's firm support for the Khmer Rouge. Some of Haig's subordinates soon regretted this "shameful episode."[50] The next year, the United States and China cooperated to force the exiled Cambodian leader Prince Sihanouk to join a coalition with Pol Pot. The Reagan administration then justified the Khmer Rouge flag flying over New York by reference to its "continuity" with the Pol Pot regime.[51]

In 1983, U.S. Secretary of State Shultz described as "stupid" the efforts of Australian Foreign Minister Hayden to encourage dialogue over Cambodia.[52] In 1985, Shultz visited Thailand and again warned against peace talks with Vietnam. According to the *Bangkok Post* of 13 July 1985, "A senior U.S. official said Shultz cautioned ASEAN to be extremely careful in formulating peace proposals for Kampuchea because Vietnam might one day accept them."

Washington's fears were realized. Rapprochement in Southeast Asia, particularly between Thailand and Vietnam, facilitated the Vietnamese withdrawal and allowed the prospect of a settlement of the Cambodia question. The key remaining issue is the future of the Khmer Rouge, armed to the teeth by Deng's China, whom Washington gives "most favored nation" status.

By contrast, the Bush administration has threatened to punish Thailand for its defection from the aggressive U.S.-Chinese position. As the *Far Eastern Economic Review* put it on 2 March 1989: "Officials privately warned that if Thailand abandoned the Cambodian resistance and its leader Prince Norodom Sihanouk for the sake of doing business with Phnom Penh, it would have to pay a price. Thailand should consider whether the total value of any new Indochinese trade would even cover the U.S. trade access privileges it still gets under the Generalised Special Preferences, one administration official said." Soon afterwards, the U.S. ambassador in Thailand stated that the Khmer Rouge could not be excluded from the future government of Cambodia, while U.S. Secretary of State James A. Baker actually proposed their inclusion.[53]

The removal of the negotiations from the regional forum in Jakarta to the great power forum in Paris, with the introduction of a unanimity requirement, gave the Khmer Rouge both direct superpower backing and a veto over resolution of the conflict. At the International Conference on

Cambodia in Paris in August 1989, Baker restated his proposal to return the Khmer Rouge to positions of power. The conference failed to foster a Sihanouk-Hun Sen alliance against the Khmer Rouge. As the *Economist* put it on 30 September 1989: "The talk among the delegates is that the American State Department torpedoed the deal."[54]

Washington has sought not a mere independent Cambodian government, but an *anti-Vietnamese* one. According to the *Far Eastern Economic Review* of 7 September 1989, "Thai officials believe that, despite its publicly expressed revulsion toward the Khmer Rouge, the U.S. has been quietly aiding the Khmer Rouge war effort for several years." One senior Thai official said: "We would like to see a lead against the Khmer Rouge taken by the U.S."[55]

After ten years of U.S. opposition to its role in Cambodia, Vietnam withdrew. The Hun Sen government did not collapse. Then Washington moved the goal posts. "Hanoi has an obligation to do more than just walk away," Assistant Secretary of State Richard Solomon now said. Thus began the search for a "comprehensive settlement." The United States calls on Hanoi to force another change of government on the Cambodians, one that would appease Pol Pot's Khmer Rouge, if not return them to positions of power. Washington's policy demonstrates that it will not reduce its support for the genocidists, let alone take any action against them, before their only Cambodian opponents, the Hun Sen regime, are first displaced from power.

In November 1989, Australia's Foreign Minister Gareth Evans launched his proposal for a UN administration to run Cambodia and hold elections, with the UN seat being vacated by the Khmer Rouge and their allies. Although the Hun Sen government in principle accepted the idea,[56] the Khmer Rouge have on many occasions refused it, preferring to step up attacks on the country while keeping their enemies talking.

Roger Normand, fieldwork editor of the *Harvard Human Rights Journal*, obtained the contents of some of Pol Pot's confidential speeches, recorded in briefing notes taken by Khmer Rouge commanders who defected in 1989.[57] They show Pol Pot's conscious use of the veto the West has given him over the negotiation process through its push for a unanimous "comprehensive settlement." In 1988, Pol Pot secretly revealed plans to "delay the elections" until his forces "control all the country," when his officials "will lead the balloting work." In this secret briefing to Pol Pot's commanders, Khieu Samphan, his delegate to the negotiations, added: "The outside world keeps demanding a political end to the war in Kampuchea. I could end the war now if I wanted, because the outside world is waiting for me, but I am buying time to give you comrades the opportunity to carry out all the tasks. . . . If it doesn't end politically, and ends militarily, that's good for us." Here Pol Pot interrupted, saying that "to end the war politically" would make his movement "fade away": "We must prevent this from happening." Since then Pol Pot has been playing the international community on a break.

Yet the struggle for peace continues. After the breakdown of the Paris talks, *Asiaweek* reported on 13 October 1989: "The only sign of settlement is a conference of the four factions along with ASEAN and Vietnam, suggested by Thailand's fence-mending Prime Minister Chatichai Choonhavan. . . . Washington, whose say-so is important, has indicated that it disapproves. That has put a damper on the plan." The United States has since also opposed Thailand's proposals for a cease-fire and establishment of neutral camps to protect Cambodian refugees from the depredations of the Khmer Rouge and their allies.[58] According to diplomatic correspondent Nayan Chanda, writing in the *Christian Science Monitor* on 13 June 1990, Washington "politely dismissed" even Japan's peace plan, which called for "elections in Cambodia with a limited UN participation."

Before the 5 June 1990 cease-fire talks in Tokyo, Chanda reports, Richard Solomon made a secret trip to deliver a warning to the Thais.[59] The talks went ahead and did produce a shaky cease-fire agreement. But like the Khmer Rouge who boycotted them, Solomon publicized U.S. opposition, and the U.S.-backed KPNLF, ally of Pol Pot's forces, foreshadowed that it would not respect what it called "only a document . . . a play on words."[60]

On 14 June 1990, Thailand's Prime Minister Chatichai visited Washington and met with U.S. President George Bush. They disagreed on Cambodia. Chatichai called for U.S. pressure on China to reduce its support for Pol Pot's forces. Bush favored a "comprehensive solution" that includes them. As Richard Solomon remarked, "We're at a fork in the road."[61]

On 18 July 1990, Washington announced its readiness for talks with Hanoi over Cambodia, a modicum of humanitarian aid for children there, and a vote against the Khmer Rouge coalition for Cambodia's United Nations seat. Although Washington later began direct talks with Phnom Penh, U.S. leaders were aware that they could rely on the forthcoming UN "Perm-5" Plan (agreed on 17 July) to absolve them from casting the promised vote against the Khmer Rouge. U.S. goals had not changed: displacing the Hun Sen regime and returning the remnants of

Cambodia's pre-1975 regimes to power. These non-communist factions have not been able to translate ten years of covert and overt U.S. and allied military aid into significant military power. So in the absence of a settlement with Phnom Penh, their ambitions remained dependent on their Khmer Rouge partners inflicting critical damage to the State of Cambodia. This looked an easy road to follow, but it is blocked further ahead. Any Khmer Rouge defeat of Phnom Penh would likely turn Khmer Rouge aggression against their coalition allies, whom they privately regard as enemies.

Nevertheless, the American search for leverage over Cambodia's future demanded two things. First, increased power for its non-communist protégés. U.S. policy remained wedded to the hope of Sihanouk and Son Sann riding to power on the back of the Khmer Rouge. Washington has continued to aid them despite the explicit contrary undertaking of Under-Secretary of State for Political Affairs Robert Kimmitt, when he explained the policy "shift" on 18 July. When asked: "Are you telling the non-communist resistance to pull away from Pol Pot, or the United States will desert them ?," Kimmitt replied quite clearly: "Any time they are in any form of association with the Khmer Rouge, that makes U.S. support no longer possible."[62] Nevertheless, Washington extended overt and covert aid to Sihanouk and Son Sann's forces despite their unabated cooperation with the Khmer Rouge. Sihanoukist commander Kien Van boasted in early October 1990 that the Khmer Rouge would provide him with 2,000 troops for an attack on Siemreap, as well as twelve tanks plus jeeps, trucks, and heavy weapons provided by China to the Khmer Rouge in the previous two months. Sihanouk's son, Norodom Ranarridh, added, as if he had been warned to keep Washington's secret: "I have to say very frankly, and Washington will criticise me again—that against Siemreap the Khmer Rouge will be the major attacking forces."[63] U.S. policymakers have pursued a calculated risk of assisting an eventual Khmer Rouge takeover and prospects for another genocide.

Second, the United States naturally has more leverage over Cambodian discussions held in a great power forum than in the more finely balanced regional environment. If necessary to maintain U.S. leverage, Washington favors a great power forum, allowing the Chinese their say as well. That too entails a continuing Khmer Rouge role.

These two factors prompted the search for a "comprehensive solution," as designed by the United States with the other "Permanent Five" members of the United Nations Security Council. As American hopes for influence remained wedded to Khmer Rouge ambitions, Washington's policy refused any reduction in its continuing support for the Khmer Rouge until the only Cambodian opponents of these genocidists are first displaced from power.

PROSPECTS AND POSSIBLE SOLUTIONS

The Perm 5 proposal of August 1990 calls for the United Nations to introduce civilian personnel to "supervise or control" five key ministries of the State of Cambodia, and hold elections under the scrutiny of UN troops, who are supposed to disarm and cantonize all four Cambodian armies. Reflecting U.S. and Chinese interests, this proposal entails risks for Cambodia.

Gone is the Jakarta forum's earlier provision against "a recurrence of the genocidal policies and practices of the Pol Pot regime." The UN General Assembly first watered this down in November 1989 to "the universally condemned policies and practices of the recent past." Even that euphemism now reads blandly: "Necessary measures should be taken in order to observe human rights and ensure the non-return to the policies and practices of the past." In effect, the Perm-5 have condoned genocide.

Within days, the UN's Human Rights Subcommission decided to *drop from its agenda* a draft resolution on Cambodia. This resolution had referred to "the atrocities reaching the level of genocide committed in particular during the period of Khmer Rouge rule," and called on all states "to detect, arrest, extradite or bring to trial those who have been responsible for crimes against humanity committed in Cambodia," and "prevent the return to government positions of those who were responsible for genocidal actions during the period 1975 to 1978." "The sub-commission's chairman, Danilo Turk of Yugoslavia, decided to drop the text from the agenda after several speakers said it would render a disservice to the United Nations after the five permanent members of the UN Security Council issued a joint plan this week aimed at ending the fighting."[64]

The January 1991 version of the UN plan attempts to give Pol Pot's Khmer Rouge "the same rights, freedoms and opportunities to take part in the electoral process" as any other Cambodian, and specifically to "prohibit the retroactive application of criminal law.[65] The Perm 5 are signaling to future genocidists that the worst they can expect is to have their opponents disarmed and removed from office, and to face them in unarmed combat with immunity from prosecution.

Yet there seems no serious UN attempt to spell out how the Khmer Rouge forces are to be located, supervised, "disarmed," or "cantonized." This would be much more difficult to do to the Khmer Rouge, who are located in remote, jungled areas, than to the Hun Sen army, which defends fixed bases, cities, and populated areas. During the 1989 Paris Conference, the Khmer Rouge successfully kept the UN military investigation mission away from their secret military camps.[66] The likelihood now is that any effective disarming will be lopsided and will favor the Khmer Rouge. Even if all the Cambodian armies are in fact disarmed, the process would most disadvantage the Hun Sen army, easily the largest (over 200,000, compared to its opponents' combined 50,000). Thus genocidists, who threaten to repeat their crimes against humanity,[67] would undergo less UN control than those who have opposed them. This may be the reason China has agreed to the proposal.

The Khmer Rouge are not willing to hand over their arms, only to hide their troops if necessary.[68] A settlement that will not effectively disarm them is illusory. Popular support does not exist to offer the Khmer Rouge hope of power by peaceful means, and they could merely bide their time before attempting a coup, a return to insurgency, or "death squad" activity.

The concept of a UN government supported by an International Peacekeeping Force is misleading. The only army that can stop a Khmer Rouge offensive is the Cambodian one, and the only peaceful way to ward the Khmer Rouge off is to stop their supply of bullets before they are fired. This means cutting their supply lines in Thailand and denying them sanctuary and international recognition as a "legitimate" government. Normal diplomatic recognition should be accorded the long-established government of the country, the State of Cambodia; the world's denial of it is no act of neutrality. It has assisted the Khmer Rouge greatly, as any insurgency benefits from an embargo on its enemy. Normal international and bilateral aid must no longer be denied the long-suffering Cambodian people. With an end to this embargo, the threat of another Khmer Rouge genocide would recede.

As part of a new effort to break the Cambodian deadlock, Japan made three new proposals in early 1991: UN monitoring from the start of a cease-fire, expulsion from the settlement process of any group which violates the cease-fire, and establishment of a special commission to investigate the Khmer Rouge. In Bangkok on 18 March 1991, U.S. Assistant Secretary of State Richard Solomon criticized Tokyo's proposals as "likely to introduce confusion in international peace efforts." The next month, the new military strongman in Bangkok, Suchinda Krapayoon, told a visiting U.S. senator that he considered Pol Pot a "nice guy."[69]

In June 1991, the four Cambodian parties assembled in Jakarta once more. Sihanouk and Hun Sen agreed for the second time that the former would head the Supreme National Council, and the latter would be deputy chairman. The next day, once again, Sihanouk announced that his Khmer Rouge allies had rejected the agreement.[70] This scenario may recur.

The Cambodia conflict is played out on three levels: the national, regional, and great power levels. Within Cambodia, the balance of forces favors the incumbent State of Cambodia. In the UN Security Council, its opponents have hegemony. But at the intervening regional level, the forces are fairly evenly divided. Southeast Asia's ten nations are politically diverse, none has overall preponderance, and few can be ignored. Those who seek a solution to the conflict can be found on both sides of the ASEAN-Indochina divide, and unlike in the UN Security Council, none of the Southeast Asian countries readily identifies with the remaining obstacle, the Khmer Rouge. The only lasting solution to the Cambodia conflict is to be found in Southeast Asia.

NOTES

1. See Elizabeth Becker, "Vote the Communists out of Cambodia," *Washington Post*, 20 May 1990.

2. See, for instance, Bernard Edinger, "Cambodians Behead Vietnam Villagers," AAP-Reuters, *The Asian* (Melbourne), November 1977, p. 11. Edinger noted that "reliable sources said there was no doubt that the fighting was started by Cambodian central authorities." (Earlier, "during the summer . . . hundreds of people were killed when Cambodian troops stormed close to 40 villages set up within Vietnam's 'new economic areas' programme.")

3. According to *Asiaweek*, "Most intelligence analysts in Bangkok agree that Cambodian raids and land grabs escalated the ill-will . . . until peace was irretrievable" (22 September 1978). See also Ben Kiernan: "New Light on the Origins of the Vietnam-Kampuchea Conflict," *Bulletin of Concerned Asian Scholars* 12, 4 (1980): 61–65, esp. 64, and *How Pol Pot Came to Power* (London, 1985), pp. 413–21; Michael Vickery, *Cambodia 1975–82* (Boston, 1984), pp. 189–96; and Gary Klintworth, *Vietnam's Intervention in Cambodia in International Law* (Canberra: Australian Government Publishing Service Press, 1989).

4. Hanoi's proposal of 5 February 1978 offered a mutual pullback five kilometers each side of the border, negotiations, and consultation as to an appropriate form of international supervision. Phnom Penh rejected this.

5. See Ben Kiernan: "Kampuchea: Thai Neutrality a Farce," *Nation Review* (Melbourne), 24 May 1979, and "Kampuchea 1979–81: National Rehabilitation in the Eye of an International Storm," *Southeast Asian Affairs 1982*, Institute of Southeast Asian Studies, Singapore (Heinemann, 1982), pp. 167–95. Both Sihanouk and Son Sann reported being pressured by the United States to join the coalition with Pol Pot.

6. However, according to a *Bangkok Post* report by Richard Ehrlich from Phnom Penh on 8 July 1990, "several senior Western and Eastern diplomats in Cambodia and Vietnam agreed there is 'no evidence' to support reports that Vietnamese troops have been secretly fighting against the resistance in Cambodia."

7. For more recent information on this, see Steven Erlanger, "Political Rivals Jockey in Phnom Penh," *New York Times*, 11 August 1990.

8. The *Far Eastern Economic review* reported on 19 July 1990: "Government forces may be poorly paid and badly trained, but they have shown a marked willingness to fight in recent engagements." The *New York Times* on 22 July 1990 quoted Pol Pot's ally Prince Norodom Ranariddh as saying that "it seems we may have lost on the battlefield." After a visit to recently besieged Kompong Thom city on 18 July, former diplomat John Pedler concluded that the military situation is "fundamentally sound." (See also note 9.) Similar reports appeared a year later. See Jacques Bekaert, *Bangkok Post*, 20 May 1991.

9. Steven Erlanger reported from Phnom Penh in the *New York Times*, 6 August 1990: "No credible analyst or official here sees any imminent political or military collapse. The main concern, they say, is the economy, which the Khmer Rouge is trying to disrupt. Economic collapse could lead to the kind of panic that would quickly undermine an army that is *still holding its own*." [Emphasis added.]

10. In an interview with U.S. National Public Radio on 27 July 1990, Hun Sen said: "Once we reach a political solution, a multiparty system will be automatically adopted . . . to allow all political parties to participate in an election. I know we can be asked why we do not allow a multiparty system at this time. I'd like to argue that we do not want to fight simultaneously on two fronts, for the danger facing the Cambodian people is not the question of a multiparty system or a one-party system, but the return of the Pol Pot genocidal regime."

11. *Far Eastern Economic Review, Asia 1981 Yearbook* (Hong Kong, 1981), p. 191.

12. *Brother Enemy* (New York: Harcourt Brace Jovanovich, 1986), p. 393.

13. *Age* (Melbourne), 16 March 1984.

14. *Ibid.*, 16, 19, and 27 March 1984.

15. That the Hanoi position had been poised to change since the previous year is evident from a *Nhan Dan* article of November 1984, which began by proclaiming that Vietnamese forces would withdraw from Cambodia "when the Chinese threat and the danger of Pol Pot's return have been removed and when the

security of Kampuchea is fully ensured," but then revealed the coming offer of a new deal: "To discard the Pol Pot remnants, rather than calling for Vietnam to unilaterally withdraw troops from Kampuchea, is a crucial and imperative demand of peace in the region" (report by Michael Richardson in the *Age*, 29 December 1984).

16. Ben Kiernan, "Kampuchea: Hayden Is Vindicated," *Australian Society* 4, 8 (August 1985): 20–23.

17. *Age*, 21 March 1985.

18. *Sydney Morning Herald*, 27 June 1986.

19. This was at a press conference in Jakarta on 8 August 1986, reported in *Indonesia Times*, which claimed that his support was merely "tongue-in-cheek." However, a year later, Mochtar again publicly endorsed the proposal to try the Pol Pot regime before the World Court for genocide (*Christian Science Monitor*, 17 June 1987). Hayden's successor as Foreign Minister, Gareth Evans, ignored this record, merely stating that Hayden's proposal had not been greeted "with equal enthusiasm by ASEAN" (Evans, Beanland Lecture, Melbourne, 24 August 1989).

20. In the meantime, 2,000 Cambodians living abroad had signed a petition to Australian Prime Minister Bob Hawke (and leaders of other governments) asking for action against the Pol Pot regime in the World Court (see, for instance, *Far Eastern Economic Review*, 14 July 1988). Hawke refused. Opposition leader Andrew Peacock supported the idea, as did the Australian section of the International Commission of Jurists. The case is outlined in Ben Kiernan, "Cambodian Genocide," *Far Eastern Economic Review*, 1 March 1990, and "The Genocide in Cambodia, 1975–79," *Bulletin of Concerned Asian Scholars* 22, 2 (1990): 35–40.

21. "Sihanouk to Return as Cambodia's Head of State" and "Move to Dump Khmer Rouge," *Sydney Morning Herald*, 3 and 4 May 1989.

22. Kelvin Rowley quotes Sihanouk's speech on 24 September 1989, broadcast on the Voice of the National Army of Democratic Kampuchea: "You must get rid of the regime immediately. . . . Rally to the tripartite forces of our resistance movement before it is too late, so that the real patriots . . . can undoubtedly see that you are also patriotic. By so doing, you in Cambodia can avoid the imminent danger to yourself. . . . It is impossible this time for me to defend you." I am grateful to Rowley for this reference.

23. Roy Eccleston, "Evans Plan Stumbles over an Ugly Word," *The Australian*, 2 March 1990.

24. *Far Eastern Economic Review*, 19 July 1990, p. 14. Only a few weeks earlier, on 29 June, Congressman Stephen J. Solarz, a leading supporter of Pol Pot's allies and opponent of Pol Pot's opponents, had made the unfortunate claim that the Tokyo meeting proved Sihanouk was not a "front man for the Khmer Rouge." Solarz had said: "This is hogwash. The best evidence that it is hogwash is the fact that one month ago the Japanese convened a conference in Tokyo to move the peace process on Cambodia forward. . . . If Sihanouk is a front man to the Khmer Rouge, why would he be signing agreements opposed by the Khmer Rouge and which exclude the Khmer Rouge from

power?" After the House of Representatives had accepted Solarz's amendment to aid Sihanouk's forces, Sihanouk accepted the Khmer Rouge amendment of the Tokyo agreement.

25. Interview on U.S. National Public Radio, 27 July 1990. See also note 56 below.

26. *Indochina Digest*, no. 90-37, 15–21 September 1990.

27. For the background to this regional feeling in the common postwar anti-colonial struggles, see Ben Kiernan, "ASEAN and Indochina: Asian Drama Unfolds," *Inside Asia* 5 (September–October 1985): 17–19.

28. See Ben Kiernan, "Time Is Ripe for Evans to Dump Khmer Rouge," *Sydney Morning Herald*, 12 January 1990, and Nick Cumming-Bruce, "U.S. Tries to Allay Fears on Cambodia," London *Guardian*, 28 July 1990, quoting Evans.

29. Nayan Chanda, "Sihanouk Stonewalled," *Far Eastern Economic Review*, 1 November 1984, p. 30.

30. Gareth Porter, "Cambodia: The American Betrayal," unpublished paper, 1989.

31. *New York Times*, 1 May 1990.

32. This undertaking was given by Chinese Premier Li Peng on a visit to New Zealand in January 1989.

33. "Sihanouk: No Council without K. Rouge," *Bangkok Post*, 23 July 1990; *New York Times*, 19 July 1990; Nate Thayer, "Khmer Rouge Receive Chinese Tanks," AP, 7 October 1990; *Indochina Digest*, no. 90-40, 6–12 October 1990. On 4 February 1991, UPI reported from Phnom Penh that government forces said they were now facing these Khmer Rouge tanks in battle. See *Nation*, 23 March 1991, and *Bangkok Post*, 21 April 1991, for confirmation.

34. Kyoko Tanaka, "The Civil War and the Radicalization of Chinese Communist Agrarian Policy," *Papers on Far Eastern History*, vol. 8, September 1973, pp. 49–114, at p. 54, note 13.

35. *Far Eastern Economic Review*, 30 August 1990, p. 65, See also *New York Times*, 16 April 1990.

36. Steven Erlanger, "Cambodians Face Loss of Eastern Aid and Trade," *New York Times*, 12 August 1990.

37. Nayan Chanda, "For Reasons of State," *Far Eastern Economic Review*, 2 August 1990.

38. See Erlanger, "Cambodians Face Loss of Eastern Aid and Trade" (note 36). The similar U.S. blockade of international aid funds to Vietnam, including from the International Monetary Fund, was also said to be punishment for Hanoi's overthrow of Pol Pot's regime in 1979. But it actually began before that, when Vietnam had become the first communist country to join the IMF. And after the Vietnamese withdrawal from Cambodia, as the *Far Eastern Economic Review* (28 September 1989) reports: "To the profound disappointment of many officials at the IMF and the World Bank, the U.S. and Japan—countries with major voting rights in the two institutions—have blocked Vietnam's re-entry into the interna-

tional economic community, despite what is considered an exemplary Vietnamese effort at economic stabilisation and structural adjustment." British, West German, and French executive board members of the IMF, on the other hand, had "endorsed Vietnam's stabilisation programme and implied the county was ready for a formal IMF programme."

39. *Far Eastern Economic Review*, 12 July 1990, p. 14. $7 million of this is overt "non-lethal" military aid. Another $10 million is said to be provided by Singapore in "military hardware and other supplies" (*New York Times*, 19 July and 8 July 1990).

40. See Ben Kiernan: "Pol Pot Stomps in Deng's Footsteps, and with U.S. Support," *Sydney Morning Herald*, 13 July 1989, and "U.S. Policy Turn on Cambodia Is Incomplete," London *Guardian*, 23 July 1990.

41. Eva Mysliwiec, personal communication, 1987. See her book *Punishing the Poor: The International Isolation of Kampuchea* (Oxford: Oxfam, 1988).

42. See, for instance, "France in Bid to Gag Report on Cambodia," *The Australian*, 26 February 1990.

43. Nayan Chanda, *Far Eastern Economic Review*, 18 December 1979.

44. Elizabeth Becker, *When the War Was Over* (New York, 1986), p. 440.

45. Letter from Jonathan Winer, counsel to Senator John Kerry, member of the U.S. Senate Foreign Relations Committee, to Larry Chartienes of Vietnam Veterans of America, 22 October 1986, citing "information from the Congressional Research Service." The details cited included the following annual amounts of U.S. aid to the "Khmer Rouge" for "development assistance, food assistance, economic support, and in smaller amounts for the Peace Corps, narcotics enforcement and military assistance" (in FY 87 dollars): 1980—$54.55 million; 1981—$18.29 million; 1982—$4.57 million; 1983—$2.46 million; 1984—$3.70 million; 1985—$0.84 million; 1986—$0.06 million. This has since been denied by the U.S. State Department, while the Congressional Research Service has reportedly transferred its employee who provided the statistics. If their initial provision was a mistake, a convincing explanation for it does not appear to exist. In a subsequent letter to Noam Chomsky dated 16 June 1987, Jonathan Winer reported: "It is my understanding that U.S. funding to Cambodia has been restricted to non-Khmer Rouge recipients since 1985 (FY 86). An earlier such restriction on direct aid put into place in 1979 was repealed in part on December 16, 1980, when humanitarian assistance to the Cambodian people was permitted, and repealed entirely on December 29, 1981. . . . On August 8, 1985, aid to the Khmer Rouge was again banned, although small amounts have been since made available to non-Communist Cambodian resistance forces," who had allied themselves with the Khmer Rouge in 1982. Additional evidence of U.S. military support for the Khmer Rouge remains to be either corroborated or pursued. On 27 August 1981, syndicated columnist Jack Anderson reported that "through China, the CIA is even supporting the jungle forces of the murderous Pol Pot in Cambodia." On 10 October 1983, *Newsweek* reported that the American CIA "is working with the Chinese to supply arms to the forces of former Cambodian ruler Pol Pot." On 4 June 1987, the *Far Eastern Economic Review* published a letter

alleging that a U.S. consular official in Thailand had attempted to recruit a former British soldier "to a job smuggling guns to Pol Pot for payment in gold." "The American identified himself with a card issued by the U.S. Government," claimed the "witness." In the same year an Australian veteran told friends of his own claimed involvement in secret American supply operations on behalf of the Khmer Rouge. In late 1989, Sihanouk said he had "received intelligence informing me that there were U.S. advisers in the Khmer Rouge camps in Thailand, notably in Site B camp. . . . The CIA men are teaching the Khmer Rouge human rights!" (*Le Figaro* [Paris], 30 December 1989). (I am grateful to Jack Calhoun for this last reference.) On 14 August 1990, United Press International quoted a former U.S. Green Beret sergeant in Thailand, Bob Finley, as claiming that he had been ordered to destroy incriminating documents that "would have linked the U.S. Joint Military Assistance Group . . . with the security council and the Thai government" in the 1988 sale of U.S. ammunition and explosives on the Thai black market, where they may have fallen into the hands of the Khmer Rouge. The *San Francisco Examiner* on 12 August 1990 offered corroboration from the Pentagon Inspector General's Office. Another ex-Green Beret sergeant, Mike Bracy, who had been assigned as a part of an internal military investigation into the matter, stated, "U.S. Army Special Operations lost control of millions of dollars of American arms and ammunition over five years. . . . $1 million worth dropped off the books in a two-month period, including Russian ammunition anti-tank rounds, chemical agents, dynamite and C-4." According to *Indochina Digest*, "Sources in Bangkok say munitions sold on the black market make their way to the Cambodian resistance, including the Khmer Rouge." Another U.S. sergeant who reportedly "knew the details" of the illicit sales and "the most about the scandal" was killed in his office in Okinawa by a bomb (*Indochina Digest*, nos. 90-32 and 90-33, 11 and 17 August 1990).

46. William Shawcross, *The Quality of Mercy: Cambodia, Holocaust and Modern Conscience* (New York, 1984), pp. 289, 395, 345. Omang and Ottoway, writing in the *Washington Post* on 27 May 1985, also report that the U.S. government provided food-aid to the Khmer Rouge in 1979, but they say this was stopped by Congress in 1980. See note 45 above.

47. Linda Mason and Roger Brown, *Rice, Rivalry and Politics: Managing Cambodian Relief* (University of Notre Dame Press, 1983), pp. 136, 159, 135.

48. *Kampuchea: A Demographic Catastrophe*, National Foreign Assessment Center, Central Intelligence Agency, May 1980. For critiques of this document, see Michael Vickery, "Democratic Kampuchea: CIA to the Rescue," Bulletin of Concerned Asian Scholars (*BCAS*) 14, 4 (1982): 45–54, and Ben Kiernan, "The Genocide in Cambodia, 1975–1979," *BCAS* 22, 2 (1990): 35–40, and references cited.

49. "Thais Furious at Cambodians for Disclosing Visit by Reagan Aide," *Los Angeles Times*, 5 December 1980. I am grateful to Jack Calhoun for this reference.

50. Nayan Chanda, *Brother Enemy*, pp. 388–89, 457.

51. See Ben Kiernan, "Kampuchea 1979–81," *Southeast Asian Affairs 1982*, and John Holdridge (U.S. Department of State), Hearing before the Subcommittee on

Asian and Pacific Affairs of the Committee on Foreign Affairs, House of Representatives, 97th Cong., 2nd sess., 14 September 1982, p. 71.

52. "Peace Plan 'Stupid'—U.S. Rap," *Herald* (Melbourne), 28 June 1983. This report from Bangkok by Nikki Savva and Australian Associated Press added: "Mr. Shultz criticised and severely questioned Australia's motive and made it plain the U.S. was not expecting much success from Mr. Hayden's Hanoi visit. . . . Australian officials said Mr. Shultz had given Mr. Hayden 'an extremely tough time' . . . 'a hell of a hammering' . . . in the first closed session of the ASEAN five-minister summit. They claimed the U.S. had coordinated a strong anti-Australian stand before Mr. Hayden went into the closed meeting. . . . [But] by the afternoon session, when Mr. Hayden met the five ASEAN Foreign Ministers alone, the mood had changed. Mr. Hayden was able to gain strong support for the Australian initiatives. . . . Mr. Hayden was given ASEAN's approval for any progress Australia could make and will take a verbal message of goodwill to Hanoi tomorrow." However, through Australian Prime Minister Bob Hawke, Shultz managed to force Hayden to abandon the Labor Party's 1983 election pledge to restore bilateral aid to Vietnam, despite Indonesian support for such aid.

53. Mary Kay Magistad, "Khmer Rouge Are Closer to New Chance at Power," *Boston Globe*, 17 April 1989.

54. When the Paris Conference on Cambodia foundered in August 1989, Washington "reiterated its support for a Khmer Rouge role in a transitional government" (Associated Press, *Bangkok Post*, 1 September 1989). As a result of U.S. support, the Khmer Rouge emerged strengthened from the failed conference. As one diplomat put it, the Khmer Rouge "got the U.S. and Western countries to block a Vietnamese attempt to isolate and contain them" (Joseph de Rienzo of Reuters, Bangkok *Nation*, 31 August 1989).

55. See also the four "Cambodia" films by John Pilger and David Munro, and the 1990 American Broadcasting Company documentary, "From the Killing Fields," for further evidence on these lines, as well as the report by Raoul Jennar, for ten years a foreign affairs adviser to the Belgian Senate, "How the West Is Helping the Return of Pol Pot," Brussels, May 1990, in *Cambodia: And Still They Hope*, compiled by John Nichols (Australian Council for Overseas Aid [Box 1562, Canberra ACT 2601 Australia], July 1990), pp. 21–31.

56. See for instance, "New Hope for Cambodia Peace," *Australian Financial Review*, 14 December 1989: "According to news reports out of Cambodia, Mr. Hun Sen has agreed to the proposal, overcoming one of the first hurdles. However, Prince Sihanouk, who initially supported it, reversed his stand once Mr. Hun Sen came on board." See also "Evans Plan Finds Support in Hanoi," *Sydney Morning Herald*, 13 December 1989; "Cambodia Agrees to UN Role in Peace Process," *The Australian*, 2 February 1990; and Ruth Youngblood, "Cambodian Prime Minister Announces Support for Sweeping UN Role," United Press International, 28 February 1990. Nayan Chanda reports further that in May 1990 the Australian negotiator Michael Costello visited Phnom Penh and put to Hun Sen the version of the Australian plan known as Option II (b), which Hun Sen accepted. Subsequently, however, Costello was unable to get the agreement of the opposition coalition (Nayan Chanda, personal communication).

57. For some of the contents of these speeches, see Roger Normand, "The Teachings of Chairman Pot," U.S. *Nation*, 27 August 1990; also Roger Normand and Ben Kiernan, "Khmer Rouge Poised to Gain from U.S. Policy," letter to the *New York Times*, 6 August 1990; and Ben Kiernan: "U.S. Policy Turn on Cambodia Is Incomplete," and "Medieval Master of the Killing Fields," London *Guardian*, 23 and 30 July 1990. I am grateful to Normand for making this information available.

58. Paul Wedel, "U.S. Opposes Proposed Ceasefire in Cambodia," United Press International, 14 May 1990.

59. Nayan Chanda, "Japan's Quiet Entrance on the Diplomatic Stage," *Christian Science Monitor*, 13 June 1990.

60. *Indochina Digest*, no. 90-20, 25 May–1 June 1990, citing UPI, 31 May 1990.

61. *Indochina Digest*, no. 90-23, 18–22 June 1990.

62. MacNeil-Lehrer News Program, PBS-TV, 18 July 1990, interview with Jim Lehrer.

63. "We will have seized Angkor Wat and Siemreap by January at the latest," Kien Van predicted inaccurately. Nate Thayer, "Khmer Rouge Receive Chinese Tanks," Associated Press, 7 October 1990; *Indochina Digest*, no. 90-40, 6–12 October 1990.

64. *Agence France Presse* report from Geneva, 30 August 1990.

65. UN Security Council statement on Cambodia, released 11 January 1991, pp. 24, 27.

66. Michael Haas, "The Paris Conference on Cambodia," forthcoming in the *Bulletin of Concerned Asian Scholars* 23, 2 (1991).

67. In a secret 1988 briefing to his commanders, recounted by defectors to Roger Normand, Pol Pot blamed most of his regime's 1975–79 killings on "Vietnamese agents." But he defended having massacred the defeated Lon Nol regime's officers, soldiers, and officials. "This strata of the imperialists had to be totally destroyed," he insisted. In "abandoning communism" now, Pol Pot added, his movement discards its "peel," but not the fruit inside. "The politics has changed but the spirit remains the same." The Khmer Rouge predict their return with this slogan: "When the water rises, the fish eat the ants, but when the water recedes, the ants eat the fish."

68. Normand's Khmer Rouge defector informants quote Pol Pot as saying in 1988: "Our troops will remain in the jungle for self-defense," in the event of a settlement.

69. Senator Bob Kerrey, testimony before the U.S. Senate Foreign Relations Committee, 11 April 1991. The Thai general's compliment to Pol Pot is in line with that of Air Marshal Siddhi Savetsila, Thailand's foreign minister under the former military regime, who in 1985 described Pol Pot's deputy, Son Sen, as "a very good man" (Reuter, *Age* [Melbourne], 3 September 1985).

70. *Sydney Morning Herald*, 3 and 4 June 1991.

SOUTHERN AFRICA

THE SUPERPOWERS IN SOUTHERN AFRICA: FROM CONFRONTATION TO COOPERATION

Michael Clough

WINDHOEK, NAMIBIA, 21 MARCH 1990: U.S. Secretary of State James Baker sits with Soviet Foreign Minister Eduard Shevardnadze on a grandstand crammed beyond capacity with a host of international figures applauding F. W. de Klerk, the president of South Africa, as he hands over power to Sam Nujoma—leader of the South-West African People's Organization (SWAPO)—whom white South Africans had until recently regarded as a "Marxist terrorist." This act ended a conflict between the international community and South Africa over the political status of Southwest Africa/Namibia that began in the late 1940s. Coming after a year in which the Berlin Wall fell, Communist rule in Eastern Europe collapsed, and black leader Nelson Mandela walked out of prison to lead an unbanned African National Congress (ANC), this scene, marking the independence of Africa's last colony, seemed relatively unremarkable. Two years earlier it would have been unimaginable.

In late 1987 the worst fears of those who had predicted that a Reagan presidency would intensify U.S.-Soviet competition and exacerbate conflict in southern Africa seemed close to being realized. The civil war in Angola had grown more intense as the União Nacional para a Independência Total de Angola (UNITA), with increasingly open South African support, sought to broaden its range of operations and the Angolan government countered with larger and larger offensives aimed at UNITA's base in the country's southeast corner. Soviet military support for the government had increased dramatically, and the United States had resumed military assistance to UNITA rebels. Mozambique had been left in ruins by South African destabilization policies. Encouraged by their success in winning support for UNITA, American conservatives argued that antigovernment guerrillas in Mozambique should be added to the list of "freedom fighters" qualifying for support under the so-called "Reagan doctrine," which endorsed U.S. aid to insurgents fighting to overthrow Marxist governments in the Third World. And

South Africa seemed on the verge of a descent into racial violence and chaos that would create powerful pressures for superpower intervention. However, the cycle that had become so familiar in the Third World—local conflict, external intervention, escalating violence—was broken. As President Reagan prepared to leave office in late 1988, the world was witnessing the successful conclusion of negotiations linking Angola and Namibia—an unprecedented experiment in joint mediation by Moscow and Washington. At long last, peace seemed possible in southern Africa.

The diplomatic turnaround in southern Africa occurred well before the dramatic events of 1989 and 1990 made it appear so commonplace and inevitable. To appreciate its full significance requires going back to the beginning of the cycle in 1975, when the superpowers first began to view southern Africa as an important geopolitical arena.

THE BEGINNINGS OF SUPERPOWER COMPETITION IN SOUTHERN AFRICA

The United States and the Soviet Union came into conflict over Angola suddenly and unexpectedly in the spring of 1975. Before the collapse of Portuguese colonial rule following an April 1974 coup in Lisbon, neither superpower had shown much interest in southern Africa. When each decided to support rival nationalist parties in Angola, neither expected its actions to engulf it in a major international crisis. As each became aware of the other's involvement, however, the stakes changed. What had begun as low-cost efforts to provide limited support to regional allies became significant geopolitical gambits.

U.S. officials, with the exception of a handful of liberals and Africanists in the Kennedy administration, had long regarded southern Africa as a relatively secure and comparatively unimportant Western sphere of influence. This view was reinforced by a belief that the Brezhnev regime, in signing the May 1972 statement of "Basic Principles of Relations Between the United States and the Union of Soviet Socialist Republics," had committed itself to exercising restraint in the Third World. Based on this mistaken perception of Soviet policy and a belief that the white-dominated status quo in southern Africa was unlikely to be shaken, the Nixon administration adopted a policy of benign neglect in the region.[1]

The Soviet Union and—just as important—Cuba had never accepted the view of southern Africa as a Western sphere of influence. Both countries had provided political and military support to liberation movements in the region since the early 1960s.[2] Throughout the 1960s and early 1970s, however, the relative weakness of their local allies and their own military limitations afforded them few opportunities to seriously challenge Western claims. In the mid-1970s four developments fundamentally altered the situation: the collapse of Portuguese colonialism; the emergence of serious internal opposition to the apartheid state in South Africa; an increasingly anti-Western anticapitalist orientation of the leading nationalist groupings in the region; and the Soviet Union's development of an effective military capability.[3]

The Angolan civil war in 1974–75 presented Moscow with irresistible opportunities for influence in the region. The most immediate was the possibility of assisting the accession to power of a socialist-oriented party—the Movimento Popular de Libertação de Angola (MPLA)—in a potentially rich and strategically positioned African country. Of probably greater importance was the prospect that a favorable outcome in Angola would put the Soviet Union in a position to make gains elsewhere in the region, especially South Africa. Finally and most important, a successful demonstration of the newly developed reach of the Soviet military promised to validate the Brezhnev regime's claim to global superpower status and enhance its credibility as a reliable ally of socialist forces throughout the Third World. These attractions, combined with pressure from two Soviet allies with long historical ties to the MPLA—Cuba and the Portuguese Communist Party—as well as the probable assumption that the United States and other Western nations would not become significantly involved tilted arguments inside the Kremlin in favor of intervention.[4]

In January 1975 the Ford administration approved a small amount of covert financial assistance ($300,000) for the Frente Nacional de Libertação de Angola (FNLA). As the civil war in Angola escalated and Soviet-Cuban involvement became more apparent (while the United States was forced to stand aside as the U.S.-backed government in Saigon fell), Secretary of State Henry Kissinger decided to use the Angolan conflict to demonstrate to Moscow that the United States was still able to act as a great power.[5] But U.S. intervention was to no avail. With the held of Soviet arms, Cuban troops, and African diplomatic recognition, the MPLA triumphed, and the United States was forced to develop a new regional strategy.

In a historic speech on 27 April 1976 in Lusaka, Zambia, Kissinger committed the United States to working actively to achieve three objectives: a negotiated settlement in Rhodesia that would ensure majority rule while protecting minority rights, an internationally supervised transition to independence in Namibia, and a peaceful end to "institutionalized inequality" in South Africa. By intervening diplomatically to hasten political change, the Ford administration hoped to prevent escalating violence, reduce the appeal and influence of "radicals," and hence eliminate opportunities for more Soviet successes in the region.

When the Carter administration took office in 1977, it quickly declared its intention to remain actively engaged in southern Africa. U.S. objectives continued to be those identified by Kissinger, but new emphases emerged. Human rights were given higher priority. Geopolitics was downplayed. More effort was made to work with the United Nations and other multilateral actors. The concerns of African governments and nationalist movements were given greater attention. Relations with Pretoria chilled.

Results came slowly. Throughout 1977–78 the regional tides continued to flow in Moscow's favor. The new governments in Luanda and Maputo declared their countries socialist states and embraced the notion of a "natural alliance" between the Soviet Union and "progressive" parties in the Third World. Both signed treaties of friendship and cooperation with Moscow. Liberation movements hostile to Western capitalism gained ground politically and militarily in Zimbabwe and Namibia. In South Africa a race war, with the West entrapped by history on the side of the white minority, seemed increasingly likely.

By 1980, however, several factors changed the regional environment in ways that significantly reduced opportunities for Soviet gains. Efforts to negotiate settlements in Rhodesia and Namibia created a new basis of trust between regional leaders and Western officials. By brokering the settlement leading to the independence of Zimbabwe, accepting the election victory of Robert Mugabe—perceived as the most radical of the nationalist leaders—and providing substantial assistance to his new government, the United States and Great Britain demonstrated to regional leaders that conflict with the West was not inevitable. This lesson came just as the revolutionary euphoria of 1975–76 had begun to wear off. Despite incessant chants about natural alliances, the inability of the socialist bloc to provide the economic, political, and military support necessary to permit stable development in southern Africa was increasingly apparent to all but the most ideologically blindered. In short, both the perceived need for and the attraction of close ties with Moscow and its allies were diminishing in the region.[6]

CONSTRUCTIVE ENGAGEMENT AND REGIONAL CONFLICT

When the Reagan administration took office in 1981, it failed to appreciate that Soviet fortunes in southern Africa were already fading or to recognize the role its predecessors' policies had played in fostering and reinforcing this decline. Convinced that the Carter administration's policies had been naive and moralistic, Reagan's Africa policy team, under the direction of Assistant Secretary of State for African Affairs Chester Crocker, attempted to project what it considered a tougher, more "realistic" image. Geopolitical considerations once again became the driving force behind policy, the assumption that South Africa could be an important strategic ally resurfaced, and multilateralism fell into disfavor.

In his first televised interview, President Reagan referred to South Africa as "a country that has stood beside us in every war we've ever fought."[7] More subtly, in a May 1981 memo to Secretary of State Alexander Haig spelling out the basic assumptions of the strategy of "constructive engagement," Crocker argued as follows:

The political relationship between the United States and South Africa has now arrived at a crossroads of perhaps historic significance. After twenty years of generally increasing official U.S. Government coolness toward South Africa and concomitant South African intransigence, the possibility may exist for a more positive and reciprocal relationship between the two countries based upon shared strategic concerns in southern Africa, our recognition that the government of P. W. Botha represents a unique opportunity for domestic change, and a willingness of the Reagan Administration to deal realistically with South Africa. The problem of Namibia, however, which complicates our relations with our European allies and with black Africa, is a primary obstacle to the development of a new relationship with South Africa. It also represents an opportunity to counter the Soviet threat in Africa. We thus need Pretoria's cooperation in working toward an internationally acceptable solution to Namibia which would, however, safeguard U.S. and South African essential interests and concerns.[8]

The Namibian negotiations, which had been started by Kissinger in 1978, thus became central to the Reagan administration's regional strategy. However, a major new policy twist linked Namibian independence with the withdrawal of Cuban troops from Angola. Two main rationales for linkage were given. Crocker believed that linkage, by reducing the

Soviet-Cuban threat to South Africa, would provide a needed induce-
ment for Pretoria to go along with Resolution 435, the UN plan for
Namibian independence. More important, however, linkage offered
Crocker a means of winning support from senior administration officials
for continued U.S. diplomatic engagement in southern Africa. Without
the promise of removing the Cuban-Soviet presence from Angola,
Reagan and Haig would have had little interest in promoting Namibian
independence.[9]

If this strategy had succeeded relatively quickly (within two or
three years)—as Crocker evidently believed it would—U.S. credibility in
the region would have received a significant boost and the Soviets would
have been dealt a major political blow. But Crocker's strategy contained
two basic problems. First, it failed to take into account the changing
military situation in Angola. Second, it assumed that South Africa was
interested in a settlement for Namibia.

The major problem was the growing strength of the UNITA forces.
Although U.S. support for UNITA appeared to be waning, South African
assistance increased, and other countries—e.g., Morocco and Saudi Arabia—reportedly began to give aid. This assistance and repeated incursions by the South African Defense Force (SADF) into southern Angola
helped to improve UNITA's military position, making it increasingly
difficult for the Angolan government to accede to U.S. demands for a
Cuban withdrawal. At the same time, South Africa's destabilization
campaign began to engulf the region in a widening spiral of violence,
and officials in the Reagan administration were forced to rethink their
initial premise that the United States and South Africa had common
regional interests. These problems became more and more evident, and
by late 1982 the Namibian negotiations had stalemated.

As hopes for a settlement in Namibia began to dim, constructive
engagement entered a new phase. The first indication of a change in U.S.
administration thinking came in a little noticed speech by Frank Wisner,
Crocker's top deputy, in September 1982:

> [W]e need to understand that Namibia is not the alpha and omega of
> U.S. policy interests in the region; there is a long agenda to which we
> need lend our efforts, including working toward a more productive
> relationship with Mozambique and Angola, supporting the develop-
> ment of a strong, stable, and pro-Western Zambia and Zimbabwe, and
> assisting in the stable and democratic development of Botswana,
> Lesotho, and Swaziland.[10]

Nine months later, this reformulation of regional strategy found its way into a speech by Undersecretary of State Lawrence Eagleburger; it was billed as the most comprehensive and highest level statement on southern Africa since the administration had come into office. Eagleburger spelled out "a framework of regional security" based on respect for international boundaries, renunciation of violence, and political coexistence. Significantly he also observed, "A structure of regional stability is unlikely to take root in the absence of basic movement away from a system of legally entrenched rule by the white minority [in South Africa]."[11]

The clearest manifestation of a shift in U.S. strategy for the southern Africa region was the new importance attached to relations with Mozambique. Throughout 1983 Washington and Maputo engaged in discussions that led to the resumption of American food aid and the reestablishment of normal diplomatic relations. In 1984, when South Africa signed agreements with Mozambique and Angola which had been facilitated by the United States, the Crocker team credited constructive engagement and quickly predicted that peace in the region was at hand. Although these predictions proved premature, the U.S. rapprochement with Mozambique marked a watershed in superpower competition in southern Africa. Mozambique decided to turn to the West after it became clear that Moscow could not provide the economic and military assistance Maputo required. Once the material limits of the "natural alliance" with the Soviet Union became apparent, the concept's appeal faded quickly. Without Soviet assistance, the Mozambique government had few options.[12]

In choosing not to provide the requisite support for the survival of socialism in Mozambique, the Soviet Union abandoned any hopes of further strategic gains in the region. It made this choice for several reasons. Growing doubts about the prospects for socialist transformation in Third World regions such as southern Africa were reinforced by Moscow's increasing awareness of the limits of its ability to influence the behavior of states that it befriended. Moreover, a serious and sustained effort to assist Mozambique—much less other countries in the region—would have required far greater resources and commitment than the Soviet Union was able or willing to muster. In short, by the early 1980s Soviet officials had realized that they had overestimated the benefits and underestimated the costs of expansion into southern Africa. As a result, they began to spurn new commitments. Instead they concentrated on avoiding regional defeats that might have ramifications beyond southern Africa. Above all this meant preventing the military defeat of the MPLA regime in Angola.

According to the zero sum logic that shaped the Reagan administration's geopolitical calculations, Moscow's losses should have been Washington's gains, but something seemed to go wrong with the equation. Just as the Soviet threat in southern Africa receded, constructive engagement came under domestic attack.[13]

THE END OF CONSTRUCTIVE ENGAGEMENT

As originally conceived by Crocker, constructive engagement had two strands. Through quiet diplomacy, he hoped to persuade Pretoria to end apartheid. At the same time, he hoped to establish pragmatic relationships with the region's black leaders so as to produce a stable region resistant to Soviet advances. Because of his success in the region, by late 1984 Crocker was being hailed by some as a diplomatic superman. He quickly lost this status, however, because no visible progress was made toward ending apartheid. Between September 1984 and September 1986 political protest and violence in South Africa escalated, and apartheid became a major domestic political issue in the United States. These developments overshadowed the administration's regional successes and precipitated the collapse of constructive engagement. Responding to a growing public perception that the Reagan administration was "soft" on white rule, Congress passed the Comprehensive Anti-Apartheid Act of 1986. This accelerated the transformation of Washington and Pretoria into adversaries.

In this same period, constructive engagement came under serious attack from the right. In 1984–85 support for the Reagan doctrine began to swell. In one of his weekly radio broadcasts in early 1985, Reagan included UNITA on the administration's list of freedom fighters. Such rhetoric contrasted sharply with Crocker's carefully worded statements of prior years. For example, in early 1983 Crocker had told a congressional hearing that Angola's internal problems were not an issue to be dealt with by the United States. While reiterating the view that "UNITA was an important and legitimate nationalist movement," he added,

> Whether the Angolan government and others will conclude that in order for [the Cuban troop withdrawal issue] to be resolved there will need to be some kind of an agreement on the issue of UNITA, that is for them to say. We have no conditions on that issue.[14]

In mid-1984 conservatives in Congress began to push for a repeal of the Clark Amendment, which barred U.S. aid to UNITA, and Crocker was placed in a difficult bind. Given the President's personal preferences, Crocker could not openly oppose the repeal. Once the amendment was repealed, policy shifted quickly and Crocker's freedom to maneuver was greatly reduced.

Black unrest in South Africa and political developments in the United States precipitated the collapse of constructive engagement. More fundamentally, however, the strategy failed because it rested on a false set of assumptions about the underlying sources of regional conflict and the nature of South African regional interests and objectives. On 22 March 1982 Crocker had succinctly outlined the administration's early views on these issues:

> The Soviet Union alone has a vested interest in keeping the region in turmoil. It is to no one else's advantage, neither to that of the South Africans, the other southern Africans, nor certainly to the United States and the West.[15]

By 1985–86 it was clear that it was Pretoria, not Moscow, which believed that regional instability was in its interest. Slowly U.S. officials directly involved with southern African issues realized this.

Two factors had a particularly adverse effect on U.S. perceptions of South African regional policy. The first was Pretoria's failure to live up to the terms of the Nkomati Accord, a nonaggression treaty signed in 1984 by South Africa and Mozambique completely ending assistance to the Resistencia Nacional Moçambicana (RENAMO). As U.S. support for Maputo solidified, continued South African support for RENAMO increasingly placed the Reagan administration in direct conflict with South Africa. In June 1987 Crocker challenged Pretoria's repeated denials by testifying at a congressional hearing that South Africa was still supplying RENAMO.

The second cause for growing U.S. hostility toward South Africa's regional policy—less discussed but extremely important—was Pretoria's efforts to coerce Botswana into signing a nonaggression pact similar to the Nkomati Accord. Botswana has long enjoyed an extremely positive reputation in the United States as one of Africa's few multiparty democracies. It should have come as no surprise to Pretoria, therefore, when an SADF raid on an alleged ANC facility in Gaborone (Botswana) on 13 June 1985 provoked a strong reaction in Washington. Declaring that the raid "comes against a background that raises the most serious questions about [the South African] government's recent conduct and policy," the Reagan administration recalled its ambassador to South Africa for consultations.[16]

The growing tension in U.S.–South African relations and the development of a surprisingly positive U.S.-Mozambican relationship had a dual effect on U.S.-Soviet relations. It reduced the administration's tendency to view southern Africa through a geopolitical prism. U.S. officials continued to see the Soviet Union as a regional adversary—especially in Angola—but countering the Soviets became subsidiary to ending regional destabilization. At the same time, Soviet views were altered by evidence of a split between Washington and Pretoria and a rapprochement between Washington and Maputo. The new regional realities, which could no longer be represented in the simplistic ideological terms on which Soviet officials had for so long relied, forced Moscow to develop a new way of perceiving and portraying conflict in southern Africa. In a positive sense, it permitted Soviet analysts who had already begun to engage in "new thinking" on the region to raise the possibility of a convergence of U.S.-Soviet policy toward southern Africa, and thus begin to explore possible formulas for cooperation.

The conceptual basis for a common U.S.-Soviet posture toward southern Africa was developed through a series of policy-oriented binational discussions involving academics, government officials, and other opinion-shapers over the period 1983–87. Implicit agreement developed on the need for mutual acknowledgment on the following:

> Both the United States and the Soviet Union had important interests in southern Africa but neither had vital interests there;

> Neither superpower had the ability to shape the political and economic future of the region unilaterally;

> Regional conflicts must ultimately be resolved through political—and not military—means;

> Both nations had an interest in a more rapid, less violent negotiated transition to majority rule in South Africa.

These points of agreement had begun to take shape well before General Secretary Mikhail Gorbachev's rise to power. Regional realities would have forced changes in Soviet policy toward Africa no matter who emerged on top in Moscow. With Gorbachev in control, however, Soviet interest in a UN-supervised settlement in Namibia increased.

By 1987 the changes outlined above had created the potential for superpower cooperation in southern Africa. However, these changes were not sufficient to produce a diplomatic breakthrough in the negotiations on Angola-Namibia. That did not become possible until a dramatic series of military developments in southern Angola in late 1987 caused the main parties to the conflict—Luanda, Havana, and Pretoria—to reexamine their policies.

TOWARD COOPERATION

In early 1987 the Angolan government decided to launch a major conventional offensive against UNITA. After some initial successes, the Forças Armadas Populares de Libertação de Angola (FAPLA) suffered a major defeat attempting to cross the Lomba River in southeastern Angola. As FAPLA retreated to Cuito Cuanavale, a key government staging base, it was pursued by UNITA and SADF units. By November these forces were threatening to overrun Cuito Cuanavale. This threat prompted an emergency meeting between Angola's president, Jose Eduardo dos Santos, and Cuba's Fidel Castro.

Cuba had opposed the decision to launch a conventional offensive, believing that it would be costly and ineffective. However, with the survival of the MPLA government possibly hanging in the balance, Castro agreed to send more troops to Angola. The new units relieved Cuito Cuanavale and moved into position to directly threaten South African forces along the Namibian border. Had such a development occurred in the early years of the Reagan administration, alarm bells would have sounded in Washington. But in the winter of 1987–88 the United States remained calm as thousands of fresh Cuban troops arrived in Angola. Some U.S. officials, frustrated with Pretoria and convinced that Cuba and the Soviets were interested in a negotiated settlement, even hinted that Cuba's moves served U.S. interests.[17]

South Africa's crackdown on domestic opposition and its continued regional belligerence had embarrassed and frustrated Crocker, but the failure of constructive engagement and the administration's refusal to consider economic sanctions left Washington with little leverage over the Botha government. In these circumstances, Cuba's military moves provided a timely warning to Pretoria that it was reaching the limits of its capabilities.

The battle of Cuito Cuanavale was not a clear defeat for South Africa, as many have claimed, but the country experienced heavier casualties than ever before. If South Africa had not abandoned its effort to take Cuito Cuanavale, it would have risked a potentially devastating defeat. President Botha and his advisers reassessed their Angolan policy and became more interested in exploring diplomatic options.[18] The Cuban military threat thus ironically became Crocker's best source of leverage over Pretoria.

Equally important in explaining Washington's low-key response to the emerging military situation in southern Angola was the fact that the Cuban buildup was accompanied by signals from Havana and Luanda of a willingness to return to the bargaining table and resolve the stalemate over linkage and timetables for Cuban troop withdrawal. In August 1987 Luanda had offered a compromise on the timetable for Cuban withdrawal put forward in a "platform" presented to the United States in September 1984. Discussion of this offer was interrupted by the rapidly changing military situation. In January 1988, after the Cuban reinforcements had begun to arrive, the Angolan government informed Washington that it was ready to resume negotiations. These diplomatic gestures made it more difficult for conservatives to stir up fears that Cuba's moves indicated a commitment to a military resolution of regional conflicts.

A breakthrough occurred in late January 1988, when the United States accepted Cuban representatives to the discussions in exchange for Cuba's acceptance of the United States as official mediator. Cuba accepted this "deal" for three reasons. First, it gave Havana some much desired diplomatic recognition. Second, it offered Castro an honorable way out of the military quagmire in Angola. Finally, the Cubans hoped a settlement would clear the way for an improvement in U.S.-Cuban relations. The Reagan administration was willing to allow the Cubans into the negotiations because it had become convinced that Havana was willing to pressure the MPLA to compromise. For this deal to work, each side had to make a concession on Angolan issues. Angola and Cuba dropped their demand for an immediate end to U.S. support for UNITA, and Crocker agreed to keep demands for national reconciliation in Angola off the formal agenda. However, all parties recognized that these issues would have to be addressed eventually.

In early May 1988 Crocker convened a meeting in London of negotiators from Angola, Cuba, and South Africa. Also present as an observer was a senior official from the Soviet Foreign Ministry. The meeting established the basic terms for subsequent negotiations. Significantly all parties appeared to downplay differences on the UNITA issue in order to allow progress in the discussions of South African and Cuban withdrawal and implementation of UN Resolution 435.

After the London meeting, a period of intense maneuvering began. South Africa explored possibilities for a separate settlement with Angola that would not involve Namibian independence. When that gambit failed, its behavior, both diplomatic and military, indicated it was having second thoughts about the negotiations. For example, officials in Pretoria suggested that national reconciliation in Angola would have to precede rather than follow Namibian independence. At the same time, UNITA and the Angolan government sent high-level delegations to the United States to test and influence U.S. opinion. Nonetheless, all of the principals, prompted by fears about the potential costs of a breakdown in the talks, remained in the negotiations.

A critical threshold was crossed in talks in New York in mid-July 1988, when the parties agreed to a set of principles, including a formal acknowledgment of the mediating role of the United States. From then on Crocker's authority was not seriously challenged by any of the principals. Like the proverbial prophet, however, he remained without honor in his own country.

In the final months of the negotiations, the greatest threat to a settlement came from conservatives in the United States who sought to block any agreement that might weaken UNITA or lend legitimacy to Cuba. Their political clout in Congress and the White House made it impossible for Crocker to use U.S. aid to UNITA as a bargaining chip. The domestic constraints on Crocker's ability to maneuver were demonstrated clearly in mid-October, when the Senate voted to block the use of U.S. funds to support UN-supervised elections in Namibia until and unless the Angolan government agreed to national reconciliation with UNITA. Senate concerns were spelled out in a letter to President Reagan, signed by fifty-one senators, urging that UNITA be brought into the negotiations, that settlement of Namibian independence and Cuban troop withdrawal be linked to national reconciliation in Angola, and that U.S. aid to UNITA not be halted until all Cuban troops were withdrawn and the MPLA had agreed to a government of national reconciliation. An African-led initiative to bring the MPLA and UNITA together for preliminary talks finally provided all parties with the cover they needed to reach a settlement. An agreement was signed on 22 December 1988.

CONCLUSION

From 1974 through 1989 superpower involvement in southern Africa was driven by geopolitics. Moscow and Washington intervened in Angola in 1975 because they believed their actions (or inaction) would affect their credibility and influence throughout the Third World. They cooperated to settle the Angola-Namibia conflict in 1988–89 because they had come to believe that a settlement would reinforce the trend toward global accommodation. For neither superpower was the primary concern the likely effect their actions would have in southern Africa.

The ink on the 22 December agreement had not dried before both superpowers began to lose interest in Namibia. In the period leading up to independence, they joined forces at the United Nations to exact a reduction in the budget of the United Nations Transition Advisory Group (UNTAG), and both made it clear that they would not provide significant financial assistance to an independent Namibia. Even on independence day, Baker and Shevardnadze showed little interest in discussing southern Africa. For them the occasion provided a convenient opportunity for talks that just as easily could have been held elsewhere.

At the end of the 1980s both superpowers remained involved in Angola, but the nature and purpose of that involvement had changed significantly. Neither Washington nor Moscow seemed particularly concerned about the ultimate outcome of the internal conflict. Each remained involved for reasons that had little to do with Angola. For President Bush it was a matter of domestic politics: ending support for UNITA without achieving an acceptable settlement to Angola's civil war could anger conservatives at home. For Gorbachev it was a concern about further damaging his government's international credibility by appearing to desert an erstwhile ally.

U.S. and Soviet involvement in southern Africa had thus come full circle. By 1990 the positions were not all that dissimilar from those that had prevailed in the early 1970s, when neither superpower was greatly interested in the region. However, one big difference between 1974 and 1990 was apparent. With the cold war over and the struggle for independence and majority rule in southern Africa in its final phase, little prospect existed that unanticipated events would spark renewed geopolitical competition. For better or worse, the era of the superpowers seemed over in southern Africa

NOTES

1. Anthony Lake, *The "Tar Baby" Option: American Policy Toward Southern Rhodesia* (New York: Columbia University Press, 1976), and Roger Morris, *Uncertain Greatness: Henry Kissinger and American Foreign Policy* (New York: Harper and Row, 1977).

2. On Soviet policy toward southern Africa, see Seth Singleton, "The Natural Ally: Soviet Policy in Southern Africa," in *Changing Realities in Southern Africa,* ed. Michael Clough (Berkeley: Institute of International Studies, 1982). On Cuban policy, see William Durch, "The Cuban Military in Africa and the Middle East: From Algeria to Angola," *Studies in Comparative Communism,* Spring-Summer 1978.

3. On the changes in southern Africa, see John Marcum, *The Angolan Revolution* (Cambridge: MIT Press, 1978), vol. 2. On changes in Soviet military capabilities, see Bruce Porter, *The USSR in Third World Conflicts* (Cambridge: Cambridge University Press, 1984).

4. See Raymond Garthoff, *Detente and Confrontation: American-Soviet Relations from Nixon to Reagan* (Washington, D.C.: Brookings Institution, 1985), pp. 502–37.

5. On U.S. intervention in Angola, see Nathaniel Davis, "The Angola Decision of 1975," *Foreign Affairs,* Fall 1978, and William Hyland, *Mortal Rivals* (New York: Random House, 1987), pp. 130–47.

6. See Michael Clough, ed., *Reassessing the Soviet Challenge in Africa* (Berkeley: Institute of International Studies, 1986).

7. Office of the Historian, Bureau of Public Affairs, U.S. Department of State, *The United States and South Africa: U.S. Public Statements and Related Documents, 1977–1985* (Washington, D.C., September 1985), p. 58. Hereafter referred to as *The United States and South Africa.*

8. *Counterspy,* August–October 1981, p. 54.

9. See Michael Clough, "United States Policy in Southern Africa," *Current History,* March 1984.

10. *The United States and South Africa,* p. 122.

11. *Ibid.,* p. 192.

12. See Winrich Kühne, "What the Mozambique Case Tells Us about Soviet Ambivalence toward Africa," *CSIS Africa Notes,* August 1985, and Gillian Gunn, "Post-Nkomati Mozambique," *CSIS Africa Notes,* January 1986.

13. For a more detailed account, see Michael Clough, "Beyond Constructive Engagement," *Foreign Policy,* Winter 1985–86.

14. *The United States and South Africa,* p. 172.

15. *Ibid.*

16. *The United States and South Africa.*

17. The best accounts of these events and the subsequent negotiations are Gillian Gunn, "A Guide to the Intricacies of the Angola-Namibian Negotiations," and John Marcum, "Africa," both in *Foreign Affairs*, 1988–89.

18. See Michael Clough and Jeffrey Herbst, *South Africa's Changing Regional Strategy* (New York: Council on Foreign Relations, 1989).

SUPERPOWER CONFLICT AND COOPERATION IN SOUTHERN AFRICA: THE SOVIET UNION

S. Neil MacFarlane

INTRODUCTION

In 1975–76 Soviet-Cuban intervention in the war in Angola was one of the first major tests of the detente between the USSR and the United States. It ushered in a period of much more liberal unilateral use of force by the USSR and its friends in the Third World. Many Americans perceived the Angolan intervention—at a time when the Vietnam debacle had paralyzed the United States in much of the Third World—as a Soviet effort to take advantage of post-Vietnam American vulnerability and to use detente as a cover for Third World opportunism. As a result, in the leadup to the presidential elections of 1976, the advocacy of detente itself became a liability in American politics.

In December 1988 the United States brokered an agreement among the Angolans, Cubans, and South Africans which covered the withdrawal of South African and Cuban troops from Angola, independence for Namibia, and an end to the use of Angolan territory by the African National Congress (ANC) as a sanctuary and training base in its ongoing war of liberation in South Africa. The agreement contributed greatly to stabilizing the regional situation. The Soviets supported this U.S.-mediated negotiation and by offical American account contributed greatly to its success through constructive diplomàtic intervention at various critical phases of what were extremely sensitive and difficult talks. Soviet-American cooperation in this instance has been cited as a model for the enhancement of regional security elsewhere in the region and further afield.

The author's understanding of Soviet perspectives on southern Africa has been enhanced considerably by participation in a Soviet-American exchange on problems of international security sponsored by IREX and the Soviet Academy of Sciences.

Clearly there has been a substantial evolution in the superpower relationship in southern Africa. This evolution is characterized by a radical shift in the balance between cooperation and conflict in favor of the former. This shift has much to do with a substantial reformulation in Soviet policy in the region from zero-sum competitive objectives to mixed or positive-sum ends. Although it is a part of a broader shift in the Soviet approach to the superpower relationship and to policy in the Third World and reflects the deepening domestic crisis in the USSR, it has important regional roots and cannot be adequately explained without reference to them. This paper will analyze the evolution in Soviet theory and practice toward southern Africa, attempt to identify its sources, and assess its implications for regional security.

THE NATURE OF SOVIET INTERESTS IN SOUTHERN AFRICA

One can visualize superpower relations in any given region along a continuum between war on one end and condominium on the other. Where the superpowers fall along this continuum depends on the priority accorded various objectives and on how the objectives are perceived by the other. The latter in turn depends on both the regional and global context of their relations. The USSR has over the past two decades pursued an array of objectives in southern Africa—among them revolutionary transformation; exclusive relationships of influence; prestige and status as a player in the politics of the region; and the expansion of diplomatic and economic ties. The last may be objectives in their own right or vehicles to the first two. Some of these (e.g., influence, revolutionary transformation, military position) are clearly zero-sum in character. Others (e.g., the quest for a role in regional politics or the establishment of diplomatic and economic ties with regional actors) are not so intrinsically but may be perceived as such, particularly when the global relationship between the United States and the USSR is troubled, as it was in the late 1970s and early 1980s.

In addition to the positive objectives, there are avoidance goals in the calculus of Soviet interests in the Third World. Perhaps the foremost of these is a desire to prevent the escalation of competition in the Third World to direct superpower confrontation. The costs of such confrontation clearly exceed any potential benefit from activism in a region such as southern Africa. A second is the desire to avoid significant costs in the superpower relationship with regard to valued objectives in other theaters. How the Soviets place such goals in their hierarchy of objectives depends on how they appraise the leadership of the United States and the general trend of history at any given point.

The manner in which the USSR pursues its interests in the region is strongly colored by its capabilities and its history. The Soviet Union has suffered from an incapacity to compete economically with the West in this region as elsewhere. It is not a trading nation. It possesses few surplus resources. It has considerable difficulty integrating foreign economic activity into its system as a result of the structural characteristics of central planning. This deficiency has favored an emphasis on military instrumentalities. Since the late 1960s the USSR has enjoyed the capacity to deploy military instruments at distance in the Third World, particularly when the other superpower has been inclined to limit its involvement.

The historical heritage of the USSR handicaps its activities in the region, where it is a latecomer. Until the 1960s the colonial powers dominated Africa and controlled its politics, leaving little space for others. Southern Africa lagged behind other regions of the continent in decolonization, Portugal remaining in Angola and Mozambique until the mid-1970s and South Africa in Namibia until 1990. In South Africa itself, although formal decolonization occurred reasonably early, the extremely conservative and anti-Communist National Party (NP) has dominated politics since 1948. To the extent that the USSR could be involved in the politics of the region, this meant an emphasis on counter-elites—e.g., opposition to colonial rule in the Portuguese colonies and in Zimbabwe and support of the anti-apartheid movement in South Africa. The Soviets grasped this rather early in their history. The South African Communist Party (SACP) was established at the beginning of the 1920s and was an active participant in the affairs of the Comintern from 1921 forward. The USSR established contact with the ANC both indirectly (through the SACP) and directly in the 1920s. It established relations with the Movimento Popular de Libertação de Angola (MPLA) in Angola in the early 1960s. Relations with the Frente de Libertação de Moçambique (FRELIMO) in Mozambique—though less close than those with the MPLA—emerged at the same time, in the context of the emergence of low-level insurgencies against Portuguese rule in both countries.

THE INHERITANCE OF THE 1970s

In the mid- and late 1970s the Soviets interpreted their various objectives in clearly zero-sum terms. The stress was on competition and not collaboration. The Soviets viewed the world as divided between forces of progress and those of reaction. The basic paradigm explaining relations between the two camps was that of class struggle. The mid-1970s were seen as a period in which the "correlation of forces" between the two systems was clearly shifting in favor of the USSR. In Africa, and in particular southern Africa, the "positions of imperialism" were seen to be weakening. The Soviets perceived a substantial prospect that the most important citadel of imperialism in sub-Saharan Africa would fall in the immediate future. They were sanguine about armed struggle as an approach to revolution in South Africa and felt that the regime was showing considerable signs of weakening.

Prospects for the acquisition of state power by movements committed to some form of socialist orientation were judged to be good. The Soviet capacity in the prevailing historical conditions to render them assistance in doing so was high. The chances for such movements of making a reasonably rapid and easy transition to socialism were strong. Soviet belief in the achievement of such a transition through a reliance on the public sector, central planning, and dissociation from the international capitalist economy and integration into the international socialist division of labor was considerable.

The Soviet appraisal of the potential for substantial zero-sum gains at the expense of the West was, in other words, quite optimistic. Their assessment of the potential for cooperation with the West in the region was, by contrast, very pessimistic. Indeed the question simply did not arise. Imperialism, and specifically the United States, was the root cause of problems in the region rather than a potential participant in attempting their resolution. The United States was not and could not be a credible participant in efforts at conflict resolution. The stability that it purported to seek in the region was one of colonial and neocolonial oppression.

There was little stress placed on avoidance goals. The Soviet literature of the period displays little concern about the possibility of an escalation of conflict in the region to the level of superpower confrontation. In the Soviet view the growing power of the Soviet Union served to deter imperialism from involvement in local conflicts while denying it any advantage from escalating a conflict. Likewise, there was little consideration of linkage between Soviet behavior in the region (and elsewhere in the Third World), on the one hand, and the fate of critical issues in the superpower relationship, on the other. The United States had not chosen detente. Detente was a historically determined response to the growing relative power of the USSR. Since detente was not a matter of choice to begin with, it was unlikely that the United States would abandon it. Moreover, both sides had an interest in such basic issues as the control of the arms race, the expansion of trade between the blocs, and the stabilization of Europe, whatever might or might not be troubling their relationship in the Third World.

In short, the Soviet view of their (and American) policy in the region was highly competitive, and the Soviets apparently perceived the moment to be one which greatly favored them. Soviet practice reflected this very positive view of the potential for substantial gains at low cost. The military involvement in the Angolan conflict; enhanced military support of insurgencies by the South-West African People's Organization (SWAPO), the Zimbabwe African People's Union (ZAPU), and the ANC; support for rapid transformations to socialism in Angola and Mozambique; the signing of treaties of friendship with both these states—all suggest that Soviet optimism went well beyond encouraging rhetoric to an unprecedented degree of concrete involvement in the affairs of the region. The emphasis on revolutionary movements and on building exclusive ties of influence with the successor regimes in Portuguese southern Africa underscores the competitive essence of these policies.

This activism may be explained in terms of both external variables (in the region as well as in the global system) and domestic political and institutional variables. The region obviously presented an array of tempting opportunities as the Portuguese empire collapsed and as the insurgency in Zimbabwe intensified. The internal violence which beset South Africa in the aftermath of independence in Angola and Mozambique gave some reason (particularly to a policymaking elite utterly unfamiliar with the realities of power within South Africa) to assume that South Africa could not hold out much longer.

At the systemic level, the United States had just extricated itself from Vietnam. Its diffident reaction to the fall of Saigon in the spring of 1975 suggested that there was little reason to expect a significant hostile response to Soviet-sponsored military activities in southern Africa, a region of far less strategic importance. American unilateralism in the Middle East and Chile may have indicated to the Soviet leadership that analogous Soviet activity was consistent with detente. The Jackson-Vanik and Stevenson Amendments and the subsequent Soviet abrogation in January 1975 of the U.S.-Soviet trade agreement had in any case reduced the Soviet economic interest in detente with the United States. In the meantime, China had returned from its self-imposed isolation of the Cultural Revolution to contest the legitimacy of the USSR as a leading force in the world revolutionary process.

At the domestic level, Soviet policy toward the region was dominated by institutions (e.g., the International Department of the Central Committee) and personalities (e.g., Politburo proponents of Third World activism Mikhail Suslov and Boris Ponomarev) who were strongly committed ideologically to a global transition to socialism. The critical role that Suslov played in supporting Brezhnev in the Soviet leadership gave him considerable latitude in the pursuit of this agenda in peripheral theaters. The failure of the economic aspect of Soviet-American detente, moreover, may have strengthened the hand of those in the Politburo committed to foreign policy activism in the face of American weakness. The devolution of authority over the formulation and execution of Soviet policy in southern Africa away from the foreign ministry may have rendered that policy less sensitive to global consequences than it would have been had such functions been centralized in a single institution.

Thus one can account for the activism characteristic of the late 1970s in terms of a combination of systemic and domestic characteristics. Of these, it seems reasonably clear that external variables played the more important role.

REASSESSMENT UNDER GORBACHEV

The Gorbachev era displays a fundamental transformation in both Soviet theory and practice relating to the southern African region. The role of class struggle has diminished drastically. Soviet thinking about the region is substantially more attentive to concrete cost and benefit. Soviet analysts and policymakers are less enthusiastic about either the importance of the region in world politics or the course of the revolutionary process within the region. The region's significance to the USSR should be concrete and economic.

Just as the Soviets seem less committed to an autarkic approach to economic growth focusing on the international socialist division of labor, they are less sanguine about the capacity of the world socialist system to operate as a motor for development for the socialist-oriented states of southern Africa. As the Soviet Union itself seeks integration into the global economy, it is advising its friends in the region to do likewise. Its confidence in vanguard party regimes to bring about the transition to socialism has evaporated. Instead it recommends a moderate mixed economic model and pluralistic political structure, noting that the Soviet experience is not transferable.

The Soviets no longer cast the United States as the progenitor of regional instability and conflict, emphasizing instead the significance of local factors in stimulating conflict. They are unenthusiastic about force as a means for resolving the region's problems, and notably for bringing the process of liberation to fruition. Instead political settlement via national reconciliation is deemed to be the more promising approach to a stabilization of regional politics, which is now seen as a desired objective. The United States is considered a viable partner in the quest for regional security.

Much is made now of the relationship between regional events and the central Soviet-American relationship. Soviet writers stress the dangerous potential for escalation from regional conflict and the need for cooperative efforts to manage the problem. In a more general sense, they recognize that past disagreements over regional conflicts have significantly damaged the superpower relationship to the detriment of Soviet as well as American interests. It follows, therefore, that a cooperative search for political settlements of regional conflicts is an important means of stabilizing the superpower political and diplomatic relationship.

Significant change in practice has accompanied these conceptual reformulations. It is true that Soviet military assistance to Angola increased in the Gorbachev era, as did the direct involvement of Cuban troops in the struggle against South African forces occupying southern Angola. But events suggest that the point of this was to stimulate a regional agreement reducing pressure on the Angolan regime and increasing the costs of unilateral South African behavior. In this sense, the enhanced resort to force by the Angolans and Cubans, particularly in 1988 was an element of a strategy of political settlement rather than a unilateral quest for victory. At the same time, the Soviets, as noted, cooperated directly in the American-led quest for a settlement of the dispute between Angola and South Africa and the Namibia question. They pushed the Angolans and Cubans to accept the linkage of Cuban withdrawal from Angola to the self-determination of Namibia and an accelerated timetable for Cuban withdrawal. They dropped the demand for a cessation of U.S. assistance to the União Nacional para a Independência Total de Angola (UNITA) as a condition of settlement of the broader regional dispute. Soviet diplomats have quietly counseled the Angolan government to seek a compromise with UNITA based on power-sharing in order to resolve the internal war. They have supported a similar approach to the civil war in Mozambique, where the abandonment of Marxism as official ideology and transition away from the one-party system have not been resisted. They pushed SWAPO to accept a constitutional compromise in which the movement had to rely on the ballot box in a UN-supervised election and accept a transitional arrangement severely limiting its prospects for a monopoly of political power in Namibia. In South Africa they have clearly articulated their unhappiness with armed struggle as a means for attaining state power and have nudged the ANC toward negotiation with the South African regime. They have also moved to broaden their own base of contacts inside South Africa, opening discussions with the white moderate opposition, with liberation movements other than the ANC, and with the NP regime itself.

In the economic sphere the Soviets clearly support marketizing reform in Angola and Mozambique. They view with equanimity if not approval the efforts of these states to increase the levels of trade with the West and foreign private direct investment. There is much obvious interest in the expansion of economic ties with South Africa, as was evident (for example) in a recent formalization of an agreement with a subsidiary of the Anglo-American Corporation on the marketing of Soviet gem diamonds and South African investment in the Soviet diamond industry.

What we see in the region is a fundamental recasting of Soviet objectives away from a competitive and exclusive quest for influence and revolutionary transformation toward nonconfrontational if not cooperative objectives such as

1. The containment of damage to the superpower relationship emanating from continuing regional conflicts;

2. The resolution of these conflicts so as to further reduce the likelihood that they can operate as obstacles to the normalization of the superpower relationship and to legitimize and institutionalize the Soviet role in regional politics;

3. The stabilization of politics in Angola and Mozambique through the inclusion of opposition movements; and

4. The development of diplomatic and economic relationships with regional actors independently of questions of ideological orientation.

Two groups of questions suggest themselves at this stage. First, why did this fundamental change in Soviet perspectives and policy occur? To what extent was it a matter of leadership succession? To what degree does change in Soviet thinking represent "motivated bias" rather than learning? What are the comparative weights of domestic versus environmental factors in accounting for this evolution? Second, what will be the impact of this change for southern African regional politics? Let us look into these questions in some detail in the following two sections.

SOURCES OF CHANGE FOR SOVIET REGIONAL POLICY

There are three categories of explanation of change in Soviet theory and practice of foreign policy. Various observers stress the critical role of personality (notably that of Gorbachev), the domestic context, and the international environment. Regarding personality, it is worth mentioning at the outset that Gorbachev personally has little impact on the formulation of policy toward southern Africa. He has little knowledge of the region and little time to preoccupy himself with it. To the extent that there is a "Gorbachev factor," it has been the laying out of a more general design for Soviet international behavior and Soviet practice in the Third World. In general terms, Gorbachev's foreign policy preferences appear to be

1. The diminution of the role of class struggle as an organizing principle for Soviet foreign policy;
2. The integration of the USSR into the global community;
3. A focus in foreign policy on issues where concrete benefits to the USSR are at stake;
4. A reduction in what are perceived to be unprofitable activities and commitments; and
5. The fostering of an international environment conducive to the diversion of scarce resources into more productive domestic use.

With specific reference to the Third World, these preferences translate into

1. A reduction in commitment to anti-Western revolutionary movements and governments;

2. The cultivation of ties with economically significant Third World states;

3. Efforts to contain damage to the East-West relationship emanating from disagreements over Third World issues and, conversely, the exploration of the potential for cooperation between East and West in the Third World as a means of ameliorating the climate of the East-West relationship; and

4. A reduction in the degree of importance attached to the Third World in Soviet practice.

It is perhaps not so much the appearance of Gorbachev as personality which has conduced to change in Soviet policy in southern Africa but the disappearance of others who were—for various reasons—committed to class struggle in the Third World. To some extent, Gorbachev may have played a role (as with the retirement of Ponomarev). Suslov's death in 1982 was, as far as we know, a natural event. The demise of the principal high-level proponent of Third World activism greatly facilitated the turn in Soviet attitudes toward regional conflict. The same could be said, arguably, for the demise of Defense Minister Dmitrii Ustinov and his replacement by a political nonentity. Such changes created a vacuum, reducing greatly the potential for high-level resistance to the reorientation of Soviet foreign policy. Thus the process of populating the foreign affairs apparatus with figures sympathetic to Gorbachev's general approach to policy in the Third World was made much easier.

It seems rather artificial to consider personality as a category of explanation to be autonomous. Gorbachev is in many respects a creature of his times and of his prior experiences, both of which were defined largely by the Soviet domestic political and economic context. Hence many have argued that change in Soviet policy—particularly in regions peripheral to basic Soviet interests (e.g., southern Africa)—is driven by economic imperatives and domestic political implications. In this sense, change in official Soviet perspectives on foreign policy is a matter of rationalization for, or justification of, policies undertaken as a result of changing domestic conditions. This is a potentially disturbing conclusion since it implies that there is nothing permanent or necessarily enduring about these changes.

The argument here is well known and needs no substantial elaboration. The Soviet economy has been in a state of steady deterioration since the early 1970s owing to the exhaustion of cheap inputs and the incapacity of the central planning system to make the transition fron extensive to intensive growth. This has both direct and indirect implications. Most obviously, the growing crunch in resource allocation favors the reduction of nonessential costs and the concentration of resources on high-priority tasks of domestic economic restructuring.

In a related vein, Soviet policymakers have judged the normalization of relations with the West to be a necessary aspect of successful economic reform. This would facilitate the acquisition of technology and credit necessary to effect the transition from extensive to intensive growth, as well as foster an international climate conducive to the reallocation of limited resources from military to civilian use. This foreign policy implication of perestroika favored a winding up of conflicts in the Third World troubling Soviet-American relations. Angola specifically and southern Africa in general were prominent among these. This shift has been accompanied by a reduction in the role and authority of institutions such as the International Department of the Central Committee, intellectually ill-equipped to implement the more moderate, domestically generated foreign policy.

Moreover, the domestic economic crisis fostered changes in political structure, such as the empowerment of the legislature, and alterations in process, such as glasnost', which severely limited Soviet flexibility in pursuing traditional policies in southern Africa and elsewhere in the Third World. The Supreme Soviet has proven to be skeptical of the merits of devoting scarce resources to ideologically grounded commitments outside the country in the face of the privations of its own constituency. Openness has made it difficult to hide the extent and costs of these commitments from the public and the wider and more diverse political elite. One would expect the deepening decentralization of power—either to the republican or to still lower levels of government—to reinforce this effect by reducing the center's command over resources necessary to the pursuit of an activist foreign policy.

The deep transformation of the Soviet state, economy, and society that is occurring willy nilly at the moment could not have proceeded without a thorough ideological critique of the previous model—the vanguard party, its monopoly of political power and suppression of real political life within the country, the command economy and its suppression of individual initiative, and so on. The ideological precepts central to Soviet policy in southern Africa were derived from the interpretive, operational, and prescriptive dimensions of Soviet Marxism. Criticism of the source necessarily implied a recasting of the intellectual basis of the derivative. In this sense, the emergence of "new thinking" on the Third World from elliptical references in obscure journals and monographs into the realm of policy formulation followed from the rejection of dogmatism in the *domestic* political framework.

The salience of domestic factors as determinants of Soviet policy in southern Africa would be difficult to overestimate. The role that these factors play now in influencing policy is fundamentally different from the 1970s. They go a considerable distance toward explaining the deep shift that has taken place. To the extent that changing thinking on the Third World is purely a product of the dictates of the resource crunch and the need to focus on the internal situation, it may be characterized as motivated bias. New formulations on the regional situation justify a retrenchment of commitments and an unwillingness to pursue new opportunities. Given the seriousness and long-term nature of the domestic crisis, there seems little reason to expect the conditions underlying this tactical shift to change dramatically in the foreseeable future. Even if it is tactical, change in Soviet theory and practice regarding southern Africa is likely to endure. At the same time, it seems reasonably clear that we are seeing deep structural changes in Soviet politics and society. These reflect a rejection of Soviet Marxism as traditionally conceived. In this sense, change in thinking regarding the Third World goes well beyond tactical adjustment to changed domestic needs. It is a small part of a very broad intellectual and political revolution reaching to the core of the Soviet polity. As such, reversion to past practice is still less likely.

Just as it is difficult to extricate personality from its domestic political and social context, it is problematic to establish a clear boundary between the domestic and the international. Factors in the international environment considerably exacerbated the domestic economic crisis. Just as growth in GNP became negligible in the early 1980s, in part as a result of the excessive military burden, the United States was embarking on the largest military buildup in its peacetime history. The increase in U.S. and NATO efforts was not only quantitative, but also qualitative, focusing on the development of high-technology weapons systems. This increased the pressure on resources in the USSR. The level of Soviet defense spending slowly crippled the economy. Efforts to match the Americans at all technological levels (as apparently advocated by Marshal Nikolai Ogarkov) would have inflicted even more severe damage. A desire to avoid this may have occasioned efforts to limit the U.S. buildup through diplomacy.

Moreover, had policy under Brezhnev produced conspicuous and significant success at low cost, it would have been more difficult to effectuate rapid change in the domestic situation and the foreign policy which derived from the domestic evolution. But Soviet foreign policy was in many respects one of expensive failure. The bleak external record itself called for the revamping of international behavior. (In this sense, it significantly reinforced domestic forces compelling change.) That is to say, experience in the international environment suggested the need for a fundamental reformulation of Soviet foreign policy. The lessons from this experience provided the guidelines for the recasting of Soviet poli- cies under Gorbachev. As noted, the domestic political transformation permitted the new foreign policy framework to emerge into official discourse. The discrediting of previous approaches also cleared the way for the advancement of those who had questioned the policies of the past into positions of responsibility for the formulation and implementa- tion of a new foreign policy.

The southern African case displays the close connection between new thinking and prior experience in the region. Three examples suffice. First, Soviet experience in the region suggested that the attribution of the causes of local conflict to imperialism was not only inadequate, but also dangerous. The Angolan civil war is illustrative. It was not possible to explain the successes of UNITA in the early 1980s without reference to ethnic support for the insurgency. Attribution of the conflict to external causes—coupled with excessive optimism about the lack of staying power of the United States and South Africa—led to a costly underesti- mation of Angola's problems of internal security.

Second, the great difficulty that the MPLA and FRELIMO had in rooting the vanguard party system firmly in society and the catastrophic economic record of both Angola and Mozambique (which can be ex- plained only partially by the persistence of civil conflict) contributed to the empirical basis for rejecting the export of models based on Soviet ideology. A growing experience with the difficulty and costs of support- ing allies in the region underlined to the Soviets that material solidarity with the liberation movements after independence was a fundamentally more difficult (and expensive) proposition than was support for their struggle for power. Involvement with these and other Third World friends underlined the Soviet incapacity to sustain the economic costs of its wide-ranging commitments to impoverished client states.

Third, by the early Gorbachev years it was reasonably clear that the United States was not acting in close concert with South Africa, that the one was not the puppet of the other, and that the United States was capable of acting as a reasonably effective mediator in southern Africa. Reality was inconsistent with the purported identity of American and South African interest and action. Denying this reality carried substantial potential political costs, as elements of the Angolan and Mozambican leaderships displayed at various times a pragmatic willingness to ignore Soviet formulae in cooperating with American-mediated efforts at settlement. Holding out on this issue risked the Soviet Union's being closed out of the settlement process.

It would be difficult, therefore, to deny the role of learning from experience in accounting for the shift of the USSR from a unilateral, revolutionary, competitive agenda to a more moderate and collaborative one. Learning from experience supports the conclusion that such change may be durable, in that alterations in Soviet cognitive structures are likely to persist unless subsequent radically disconfirming experience emerges.

In summary, the transformation in Soviet regional policy is the product of interactive factors of personality, the domestic context, and the international environment. It is to some extent tactical (though probably durable nonetheless) but to some extent reflects deeper transformations in the Soviet domestic system and in Soviet understanding of regional and world politics.

REGIONAL IMPLICATIONS OF THE SOVIET POLICY TRANSFORMATION

The second body of questions (as noted) concerns the impact of the transformation in Soviet thinking and behavior for the evolution of regional politics. In particular, will the transition from competitive engagement to collaborative disengagement and diplomacy of conflict resolution have any significant impact on the region's security and the evolution of superpower relations? The competitive dimension of superpower relations in southern Africa fueled their propensity for involvement in regional conflict. This in turn played a role in intensifying the regional conflict. It increased the quantity and enhanced the quality of arms in the hands of local actors. External support reduced the propensity of local actors to compromise.

The universalistic pretensions of Soviet ideology and the close historical ties between the USSR and regional actors such as the MPLA,

ZAPU, SWAPO, and the ANC convinced many white South Africans that they faced an externally conceived conspiracy to impose a Communist regime controlled by the Soviet Union on South Africa as part of the global Soviet revolutionary struggle. The focus on this "total onslaught" obviated the necessity for internal reform. More cynically, for some the image of the total onslaught—all too easily conjured up in the context of global East-West struggle—served to justify the white defense of their privileges in South Africa—that is, it served in an instrumental capacity, legitimizing the regime's propensity to resist change.

As the competitive dimension of Soviet-American relations has diminished, so too has the degree of superpower involvement in regional conflict. Long-standing commitments, often in the form of treaties or other official agreements, no doubt inhibit this effect. But as cold-war-motivated arms transfer agreements come to term, they are unlikely to be renewed at the same level. One may expect as a result some diminution in the lethality of regional conflict and a weakening of the regional arms race.

The decline in the regional reflection of the cold war, and more particularly the growing incredibility of the Soviet image as a power wedded to violent global revolutionary transformation, has had at least three effects within the white community in South Africa:

1. It has clarified for Afrikaners the degree to which the USSR constitutes a threat;
2. It has devalued the total onslaught argument as a means of legitimizing domestic political repression; and
3. It has refocused political attention on the internal causes of instability in South Africa.

Arguably, moreover, a distancing of the USSR from the ANC has enhanced that organization's stature as a negotiating partner. It is now difficult to cast the ANC as the proxy of a foreign power. All of these conduce to settlement.

The concern of the superpowers about their central relationship also favors avoidance of confrontational behavior. More positively, it encourages the USSR and the United States to promote a settlement of conflicts in which they have been involved. Indeed the two powers' positions on South Africa—involving peaceful change through a negotiated settlement providing for the enfranchisement of the black majority and some reform of discriminatory economic and social practice—are close. For all of these reasons, the transition from a competitive to a relatively benign and more cooperative superpower relationship has improved prospects for a settlement of regional conflict.

However, the capacity of outsiders to influence a regional conflict depends substantially on the degree to which they possess leverage over parties to that conflict and on the degree to which regional parties possess reverse leverage. There is ample evidence that both superpowers have recently attempted to use their leverage in a parallel fashion to urge a peaceful settlement based on national reconciliation in South Africa and to some extent in Angola. There has been clear Soviet pressure on the ANC to enter negotiations with the NP and abandon the armed struggle. In Angola there is evidence that the Soviets have urged the MPLA to accept negotiations with UNITA and its leader, Jonas Savimbi. In both cases, however, Soviet diplomacy has been ambivalent, owing to the continuing Soviet vulnerability to reprisal by local clients. Although the ideological commitment of the USSR to revolution in southern Africa has waned, its desire to retain a diplomatic role in the region persists. The Soviets—cognizant of their comparative isolation—are attempting to diversify their diplomatic and economic ties, but their major links with the region depend on the ANC and the MPLA. These ties are threatened by reductions in Soviet arms transfers and in the perceived Soviet commitment to the objectives of their local allies.

Both the MPLA and ANC are themselves attempting to reduce their own isolation by diversifying contacts beyond what was the Soviet bloc. The Angolans have joined the IMF, giving them limited access to alternative sources of financial support. Domestic reforms in 1985–86 have considerably relaxed impediments to foreign private investment. Their relations with the United States are noticeably warmer, although U.S. diplomatic recognition has yet to come. The ANC's contacts with the West blossomed after the release of leader Nelson Mandela from prison. There was a concomitant rise in financial and other support from nontraditional sources. The unbanning of the organization and the gradual repatriation of its personnel reinforce these effects. In both Angola and South Africa, a further weakening of Soviet influence has resulted. It is not surprising that there is a reluctance in Soviet diplomacy to push local friends too far.

Just as the sources and dynamics of the conflicts are primarily indigenous, so too are the principal determinants of the process of conflict resolution. Even if the USSR were to take a more resolute approach to the process of reconciliation, the factors dominating MPLA decision-making on this subject have been and likely will continue to be

1. Deep distrust of and antipathy toward Savimbi;
2. The psychological impact of an extraordinarily bloody fifteen-year civil war; and
3. Concern about the MPLA's capacity to survive as the dominant party in a coalition including UNITA, given the ethnic structure of Angolan society.

In South Africa, change in the leadership of the NP, the unbanning of the ANC, the release of Mandela, and the opening of talks between the government and the ANC have shifted the locus of efforts at settlement into the country itself. The process appears to depend primarily on factors such as

1. The capacity of the ANC and the NP to dominate the process at the expense of other groups in both the white and black communities;
2. The capacity of the two to contain centrifugal ethnic forces in the black community; and
3. The capacity of the various parties to the negotiations to arrive at a formula which addresses white concerns about property rights and political domination by the majority while meeting the desires of the disenfranchised majority for self-determination and a bigger share of the nation's resources.

Although these issues are not completely isolated from external influences, the latter are likely to be no more than marginal. The shift in Soviet policy and the consequent transformation of the superpower relationship in southern Africa has facilitated the process of settlement by removing important material and subjective obstacles to it. In the process, however, the USSR and the United States have become more marginal to that process. The end of the cold war in Africa cannot in and of itself produce a settlement.

POSTSCRIPT

Since the writing of this chapter, there has been a followup agreement in Angola, which ostensibly ends that country's civil conflict between the MPLA and UNITA. The presence of Soviet Foreign Minister Aleksandr Bessmertnykh and American Secretary of State James Baker at the signing ceremony in Lisbon in May 1991 again raises the question of the causal role of superpower diplomacy in regional conflict resolution. Certainly the activities of the USSR and the United States in the period leading up to the agreement underline the continuing relevance of superpower policy to regional outcomes. Although the mediating role of the superpowers was perhaps less important than that of Portugal, the likelihood of change in Soviet and American arms transfer policy no doubt substantially affected the calculations of the major internal protagonists, predisposing them to negotiated settlement. However, ultimately it was the war-weariness of the Angolan population and the incapacity of either side to end stalemate with victory which brought the MPLA and UNITA to accept a compromise.

SOUTHERN AFRICA AND THE END OF THE EAST-WEST CONFLICT

Winrich Kühne

INTRODUCTION

Africa is experiencing a dramatic change in the international environment of its politics. The cold war in Europe—or as political scientists used to say, the "intersystemic, antagonistic confrontation" of East and West—has come to an end.[1] By 1989 orthodox Marxism-Leninism, which had dominated the Soviet Union since 1917 and Middle and Eastern Europe since World War II, had failed and lost its legitimacy for most people who had lived under its rule. Centralist Marxist-Leninist one-party systems disintegrated almost overnight. In Hungary and Poland, and later in Czechoslovakia and the GDR, the Marxist-Leninist parties renounced their claims to exclusive popular representation in favor of multiparty systems. A conversion to market economies was also initiated. On 7 January 1990 the Central Committee of the Communist Party of the Soviet Union (CPSU) abdicated the party's monopoly of power. In late 1990 a much debated plan to introduce the market economy in the Soviet Union was adopted.

In fall 1990 the euphoria following the collapse of the oppressive and unproductive regimes in the former "socialist camp" came to an end. Disenchantment arose. In economic and ecological respects the situation in Middle and Eastern Europe as well as in the Soviet Union is much worse than was assumed before the iron curtain disappeared. The economic decline has just begun, and it will not stop for years. While the old systems no longer function, the new market-oriented systems do not work yet. In the Soviet Union, Bulgaria, Romania, and Poland even famines cannot be excluded (and serious energy shortages in the wintertime). Only the former German Democratic Republic (GDR), united with its economically booming neighbor, the Federal

Republic of Germany (FRG), will probably escape such a fate. Economic and political restructuring will most probably be accompanied by explosive political and social problems. Ethnic and nationalist conflicts may escalate into violent confrontations (consider Yugoslavia and Romania) and present a serious test to the European capability of conflict management and peacekeeping. Europeans will have to stop referring exclusively to Africa when speaking of "tribal conflicts." One expert on Eastern Europe recently counted more than forty potentially violent minority conflicts in Europe.[2]

Given these events, it is evident that in the 1990s not only the attention, but also the material resources of Western Europe, the United States, and Japan will be concentrated on Eastern Europe and the Soviet Union. Hundreds of billions of deutsche marks (DM) and dollars must be invested to get the economies of these countries going again. The costs of German unification are skyrocketing. Twelve billion DM will have to be paid for the support of Soviet troops on German soil in the next four years. The infrastructure is run down and outmoded in all the East European countries, and even more so in the Soviet Union. Its modernization is a precondition to foreign investment and economic growth. Billions of dollars will also have to be invested for ecological aid. More Chernobyl-like catastrophes or explosions of gas and oil pipelines are feared in Europe. Africa will be in direct competition with Middle and Eastern Europe and the Soviet Union not only for economic resources and cooperation but humanitarian aid as well.

In Africa and the Third World in general, the East-West rivalry of past decades has dissolved. Namibia's independence was the first outcome of this change. With respect to the conflicts in South Africa, Angola, Mozambique, and Ethiopia, there are no significant differences left between Washington and Moscow. They even agree in not wanting to get vigorously involved in solving these conflicts. Other issues are much more important to them. The same is true for the West and East European states, and it will be even more so if the internal disintegration of the Soviet empire continues. Not only the Baltic republics, but also by far the largest republics of the Soviet Union, the Russian SSR and the Ukraine, have declared their sovereignty and the priority of their legislation over all-Union legislation. Others—indeed the overwhelming majority of the fifteen Soviet republics—have followed suit. Given these changes, we may be witnessing the end of Soviet Third World policy. Even if General Secretary Mikhail Gorbachev manages to stop the disintegration of the Soviet empire and renegotiate a confederative scheme for the Soviet republics, foreign policy decisionmaking in such a confederation will be of a completely different character compared to what it was under centralized decisionmaking. Deliberations on the possible end of a centralized Soviet foreign policy therefore are not just wild speculations. In Africa there is already a remarkable case in which such a possibility has proved to be more than speculation. In late summer 1990 South Africa's De Beers Centenary signed an official contract with the Soviet central government to market the USSR's uncut diamonds. Gosbank admitted the USSR had a pressing need for $2 billion to cover arrears on import bills. De Beers paid $1 billion cash as a five-year advance, thus helping to resolve this problem.[3] In August 1990 the parliament of the Russian republic proclaimed the contract with De Beers "null and void" because it violated the republic's sovereignty over its natural resources (which had been declared by the parliament in summer 1989).[4] Later it agreed de facto to accept the treaty for the time being.

This sketchy overview for the changed environment of African politics raises a number·of difficult questions, only a few of which will be dealt with in this paper. Part 1 will address issues relevant to Africa as a whole: What are the lessons to be learned from the collapse of Marxism-Leninism in Middle and Eastern Europe? Has socialism failed and capitalism succeeded? What conclusions have to be drawn for the debate about socioeconomic and sociopolitical development in Africa? There are strong indications that in Africa, like in Eastern Europe, the era of one-party rule is coming to an end. A wave of unrest and popular demands for multiparty systems are sweeping through Africa. In the 1980s, democratization and redemocratization were topical in Latin and Central America. Now it seems to be Africa's (and Eastern Europe's) turn. In southern Africa the debate about multiparty rule has gained momentum in a very specific way: free and fair elections for a multiparty democracy have become the generally accepted formula for ending violent regional conflicts. Regional conflict resolution in the post–cold-war era and the enormous difficulties it still encounters are therefore the topic of part 2.

THE COLLAPSE OF MARXISM-LENINISM: LESSONS FOR AFRICA

> "History vigorously poses the question
> of whether socialist ideas can survive."
> —Mikhail Gorbachev[5]

IS SOCIALISM COMING TO AN END?

In the West the collapse of the regimes in Middle and Eastern Europe and the crisis in the Soviet Union are generally celebrated as a "victory of capitalism." Many claim that socialism is finished. Such a conclusion may turn out to be premature. At least it is much too simple. For one thing, there is not just one socialism, as there is not just one capitalism. For example, democratic socialism and its multiple social-democratic variations in Western Europe are successful and still viable, whatever their particular significance may be. The argument that these models are not really a type of socialism is compelling only for orthodox Marxists; by the same token, dogmatic capitalists claim that there is only one type of capitalism. Both lines of argument are founded on abstract and rigidly ideological thinking.[6] The idea of socialism in Europe pre-dates Marx. After Marx, the socialist debate in Europe as well as in developing countries was not restricted to orthodox Marxism and Marxism-Leninism.[7]

There is no doubt, however, that Marxism-Leninism, or socialism as it really exists, has completely failed to produce a model superior to capitalism in terms of economic productivity and an efficient, humane organization of labor. The shocking economic and ecological state of Eastern bloc countries is ample proof of this fact. The economic failure undermines the legitimacy of Marxism-Leninism as a whole and the legitimacy of one-party domination based on the principle of a dictatorship of the proletariat in particular. Both derive their justification from Marx's teaching of historical materialism, through which he claimed to have scientifically proven the inevitable superiority of socialism. This superiority has not materialized; as Fred Halliday recently wrote, "At the theoretical level, communist parties operated with two assumptions that were shown to be fatally flawed: one was the inevitable crisis and secular decline of capitalism; the other was of the ability of the communist countries to constitute an alternative, rival and self-contained bloc."[8] (German conservatives have used this theoretical insight for an ironic punch in their campaigns: "Proletarians of the world, forgive: Errare humanum est! Karl Marx.") The objection by some dogmatic Marxists that this conclusion is premature—because all these countries did not practice the "right" Marxism and other, more successful models are conceivable—is an exercise in escapism considering the great number of countries in which Marxist models have been tried.

In South Africa the quest for a post-apartheid South Africa has triggered a vigorous and fascinating debate about socialism's past failures and future prospects. Although the South African Communist Party (SACP) is the oldest Communist party in Africa and is considered extremely orthodox (if not Stalinist), it and its leader, Joe Slovo, drew some radical conclusions from the developments in Eastern Europe. The party now concedes that "over-centralized and commandist economies of the socialist world helped to entrench a form of socialist alienation." It claims, furthermore, that socialism is going through its greatest crisis since 1917.[9] In a discussion paper, Slovo makes a remarkably blunt statement: "These were popular revolts against unpopular regimes [in Eastern Europe]; if socialists are unable to come to terms with this reality, the future of socialism is indeed bleak."[10]

If the conclusions of the SACP are correct, the left in South Africa, in Africa, and in the world in general has to make a far-reaching reassessment of what role is left for the teaching of Marxism in the future. It will not be enough to stop half way, as Slovo and others have done, and merely state that "the major weaknesses which have emerged in the practice of socialism are the results of distortions and misapplications" and that these weaknesses "cannot be traced to the essential tenets of Marxist revolutionary science."[11] Pallo Jordan, a member of the National Executive Committee of the African National Congress (ANC) in a critical review of Slovo's analysis has correctly noted that such a statement "is just identifying the symptoms of the illness, but not its basic causes," a stance inappropriate for a Marxist as "Marxism prides itself in its ability to uncover the reality that lies behind appearances."[12]

The question which has to be answered, therefore, is why Marxist regimes failed so dismally in the area of economics and did not become superior to capitalist ones in terms of economic productivity—as should have been the case according to Marxist theory.[13] Furthermore, the left has to explain why socialist regimes, claiming to be based on the most revolutionary and progressive ideology, in practice turned into utterly static and conservative systems, hostile to any innovative social forces. It is surprising, even dismaying, to what extent old-fashioned "petty bourgeois nationalist thinking" has been preserved in the former socialist countries of Eastern Europe instead of having created the "new man" in the process of the revolutionary struggle. If honest and convincing answers to these and other questions are not forthcoming, Marxism and the left will become irrelevant for the future debate on social problems. Slovo's unshaken confidence in the "inherent moral superiority" of socialism is somewhat hollow.[14] It may even be that the conservative German historian Ernst Nolte is correct in coming to a somewhat paradoxical conclusion: "Today it should be clear that de facto there is only one socialism, i.e., the western 'social state' with more or less 'capitalist modifications,' in which in the near future the Soviet Union will also have to be counted."[15]

THE VICTORY OF CAPITALISM?

While socialism in Africa has not succeeded, there is not much reason for capitalism to triumph either. The developments under capitalist banners in such countries as Kenya, Zaire, and the Ivory Coast are not impressive. The differences from Benin or the Congo, for instance, are marginal. Indeed the last is one of the few African countries with a continuous economic growth rate, though moderate.* Differences from Mozambique, Angola, and Ethiopia would not be as blatant if these countries had not been in a state of war for decades, followed a misguided economic policy, and suffered natural disasters. Soviet economist Gleb V. Smirnov correctly pointed out that the disappointing economic results in Africa are not confined to countries with a socialist orientation but are a general phenomenon.[16]

The controversy between capitalism and socialism is less relevant to African development than many assume, although it fills numerous books and articles. The overwhelming dominance of the state—more precisely the more or less centralist, authoritarian-bureaucratic state and party structures which are a common feature of most African states—is much more important than this ideological controversy. On the one hand, the authoritarian-bureaucratic structures, which have their origins in

*Botswana is an even more remarkable exception to the general failure of development in Africa. Because of the sound management of its mineral resources and dependence on South Africa, it has managed to have an average annual growth rate of about 8 percent over the years. In contrast, the Ivory Coast, long praised as a miracle of economic development along Western lines, is in a deep economic and social crisis.

colonialism, and on the other the authoritarian style of government of the new urban elites, partly based on African traditions, have joined in a repressive symbiosis unanticipated at independence. The lack of indigenous African capital reinforced this tendency because for Africans the state became the main—if not the only—access route for the accumulation of capital.

It would be hypocritical to unilaterally castigate African elites for taking this direction. It coincided with mainstream thinking in development theory in the 1960s and early 1970s all over the world that the state would have to act as the main "agent of development" and accumulator of capital to compensate for the lack of internal private capital. In practice, a more or less corrupt, more or less repressive, and more or less socialist- or capitalist-oriented "state class" evolved and became a widely discussed phenomenon in the development literature of the 1970s and 1980s. The results, however, were almost always the same: mismanagement, patronism, severe human rights violations, and ultimately the paralysis of private initiative and human creativity in the economic area, especially in the rural sector.

It is too easy to blame the failure of economic development, the abuses of power, and corruption (among other things) on the personal faults of elites or individual leaders. The incredible difficulties some of the new governments had to face at independence must be taken into consideration: economic and bureaucratic deformation through colonialism; arbitrary borders; the lack of education of officials, technicians, doctors, and professors, etc. In some countries, such as the Portuguese-speaking nations, the illiteracy rate was up to 90 percent at independence. Reasonable politicians would have refused to enter office under these circumstances. Unfavorable global economic conditions (a deterioration in the terms of trade, for example) further hindered economic development. One study points out that in just three years, from 1986 to 1988, Africa lost $50 billion (one quarter of its export income) because of a fall in commodity prices.[17] To what extent internal or external factors are responsible for the failure of African development is not yet clear. However, "colonial or post-colonial dependence" or external factors alone are not a sufficient explanation, as Hartmut Elsenhans, for instance, has shown.[18]

THE INDISPENSABLE MARKET

A thorough examination of the reasons for the economic failure of the centrally planned economies all over the world leads to the conclusion that the failure is mainly due to the dogmatic negation of the market and private initiative. Most orthodox Marxists (and similar schools of thought) made the mistake of perceiving the market and private initiative merely as forms of exploitation. Although this is one aspect of the market and private initiative, they also have vital functions for economic growth: information (through prices) on the low-cost allocation of resources, creativity, flexibility, and the ability to innovate (among others). These functions were strangled by the centrally planned command economies. In fact, attempts to enact an all-encompassing system of planning did not lead to more, but often to less rationality, freedom, and humanity, in addition to economic failure. In other words, Marxist socialism does not have a workable, refined theory and program for the construction of a socialist political and economic order and has not been able to develop one since the October Revolution. This is not surprising, as Marx's writing is mostly about capitalism and its contradictions. His few remarks on what a socialist society should be like are not very enlightening or definite. The same holds true for Engels. "Naive organizational formulas like the withering away of the state [are used]," as Dieter Senghaas has noted.[19] Recently a Marxist from the GDR labeled the systems in the Soviet Union and Eastern Europe as "feudal absolutist socialism."[20]

In Africa the negation of the market and private initiative had negative effects particularly on the rural sector, where the majority of Africans live and work. Rural communities and peasants lost interest in producing for the private market or were not even allowed to do so. Consequently they remained in or withdrew to a subsistence economy. The production of food in Africa has shown an increase of only 1.5 percent since the 1960s. In relation to the population growth of 3.0 percent, this is a de facto decrease. Exacerbated by protracted wars, natural disasters (in the mid-1980s about thirty African countries suffered severe droughts), and other problems, poverty and famine are now endemic in several parts of Africa. In the Horn of Africa, about 10 million people are near starvation; in Angola, about 1 million; in Mozambique, several hundred thousand. Africa today harbors twenty-eight of the world's forty-two least developed countries.

The nationalization of trade, implemented particularly in countries with a socialist orientation, was disastrous. The interchange between city and countryside, which in colonial times had been maintained by small tradesmen despite great difficulties, broke down. Farmers could not get rid of their products or did not see any sense in selling them in national buyouts at fixed prices. In the cities, markets and shops grew empty.

The urban elites for a long time had a facile explanation: because of the social and economic backwardness of African small farmers and peasants, they could not be expected to achieve quick and extensive production growth and supply the cities sufficiently. Because of their attachment to traditional cultural values, African farmers were unable to modernize. Therefore the state had to promote development, either through nationalized farms, collectivization, and nationally operated collectives—in countries with a socialist orientation—or through "agrobusiness," jointly managed by the state and multinational companies—in countries with a so-called capitalist orientation. Neither model benefited the African economies. Nationalized farms turned into unproductive capital mongers, and agrobusiness did not care in the least about the needs of the indigenous population.* Urban elites in Africa were not the only ones to articulate prejudices about African peasants, however. Western agro-technocrats and Soviet experts on developing countries, as well as many orthodox Marxists, were equally convinced of the peasants' inability to modernize.[21] The negative attitude of the Soviets toward the peasants is not surprising considering Stalin's liquidation of millions of Soviet farmers in the 1930s and Marxism's primary orientation toward urban industrial societies.[22]

This one-sided perception of the African peasants' inability to modernize has proven to be a crude prejudice. Agricultural production rose several percent in countries which did not force peasants into the tutelage of bureaucratic structures and rigid pricing systems or which stopped doing so. Zimbabwe, Tanzania, Mali, and Ghana are telling examples since they have enacted reforms. Thus traditional values do not keep African peasants from increasing their production and from modernization if prices are adequate and the political framework supportive. In Ethiopia a land reform benefiting the peasants immediately after Haile Selassie's downfall resulted in continuous production growth

---

*As Michael Lofchie and others have emphasized, state farms ironically increased the dependence on foreign capital which they were supposed to decrease. More financial and material assistance from Western donors became necessary. In Sweden, for instance, 80 percent of all foreign currency is used for investments in Mozambican farms. In Ethiopia, President Mengistu Haile Mariam put 90 percent of the investments into state farms, which produced only 6 percent of the country's grain revenues (Michael Lofchie and Stephen Commins, "Food Deficits and Agricultural Policies in Tropical Africa," *Journal of Modern African Studies* 20, 1 [March 1982]: 7–25).

until Mengistu stopped it with his policies of forced collectivization and nationalization. After a decade of failure Mengistu is capitulating. In March 1990 he announced reforms in favor of private peasant farming.

The significance of shadow economies and black markets in several countries—especially those with a socialist orientation—highlights the creative entrepreneurial potential of the African population. In Luanda, for instance, black markets called "cadongas" are more important than official markets. Acknowledging this fact, the government has labeled black markets "parallel markets" (however, they are still only hesitantly shown to foreigners). A study on Zaire found that "unofficial sectors" were maintaining the economy of the country. Actual economic activities are three times as high as stated in official statistics, especially in the wide field of "informal foreign trade" or smuggling.[23] Similar observations can be made in many other African countries.

WHAT KIND OF MARKET ECONOMY: THE DEBATE ABOUT ECONOMIC AND SOCIAL JUSTICE

The revival of the market and private initiative is not the remedy for all problems, as free marketeers maintain (encouraged by events in Eastern Europe). As German economist Meinhard Niegel has written, "The market economy is not a plant which prospers always and everywhere. It is rather, especially its social variant (the social market economy), a cultivated (cultural?) plant, which needs . . . intensive nursing."[24] The fact that all economically prosperous states have a market economy should not mislead one to the conclusion that the introduction of a market economy is a guarantee for economic growth and prosperity. In fact, the majority of market economies are failures. Possibly Zaiki Laidi is correct that the rapid conversion of Africa to the neoliberal model seems as illusory today as was its widespread Sovietization ten years ago.[25]

As noted, the market is a multifunctional and multidimensional phenomenon. Exploitation—the focus of Marxist class analysis—is just one dimension. However, to ignore or underestimate the relevance of this dimension and its potentially inhumane and dangerous sociopolitical effects would be a mistake. Exploitation and social antagonism are possible in market economies; they may be called class struggle, social stratification, or whatever. The extremely uneven distribution of wealth in developing countries is one strong case in point. The horrendous and widening gap between rich and poor on the North-South axis, which is in danger of becoming irreversible, is another aspect of this problem. On the one side are the three industrial powerhouses—North America (and potentially Mexico), Europe, and Japan (and the four small tigers—Hong Kong, Singapore, South Korea, and Taiwan)—whose economic productivity continues to rise with amazing speed, and, on the other side, the rest of the world, which faces unchecked population growth but is falling behind economically. One telling figure may suffice to underline this gap: from 1980 to 1987 the share of the developing countries in global GNP decreased to 16.8 percent, although two-thirds of mankind lived in these countries.

This difference in productivity growth (because of accelerated technological innovation and social modernization) may render ineffective all structural adjustment policies to lead Africa out of its economic decay. There are few, possibly too few pockets left for Africans to successfully compete on the world market or—even worse—in Africa itself.* In most business sectors, cheap labor is no longer a very relevant cost factor. Good infrastructure, administration, and technical education are much more relevant. The marginalization of raw materials and cheap labor will prove to be a more decisive reason for the marginalization of Africa than the end of the cold war and the competition with Eastern Europe. Past debates and theories about imperialism and imperialist exploitation seem to be of little value for explaining this partition or for supplying practical advice to overcome it.

How can the process of deindustrialization in Africa, which has gone on for about a decade, be stopped? It may be that South Africa is the only country in Africa which still has a chance to close the gap and catch up—if there is a speedy and peaceful solution to its race conflict. On the other hand, a further decline cannot be ruled out, considering that a post-apartheid South Africa will go through a difficult, unstable phase of internal social, political, and economic adjustments and (as a prime exporter of minerals) will be specifically affected by the marginalization of raw materials. For the time being, even the South African economy is deindustrializing.

A sociopolitical discussion of the limits and risks of the market and private initiative will therefore be as important in the future as it was in the past. The fact that the controversy between socialism and capitalism is outdated does not mean that the problems which brought about the

---

*The negative social and political effects of the structural adjustment policies of the World Bank and the International Monetary Fund (IMF) have been discussed extensively and need no further elaboration here.

controversy have been resolved. The debate on social and economic justice will go on and has to go on. Unlike the past debate, which was little concerned with the real mechanism of economic productivity and focused in the abstract and almost religiously on the "the masses," the new debate will have to based on the realities of market economies and the forces functioning therein. As Richard L. Sklar wrote, "Plainly stated, there is no substitute for capital; it is the driving force of economic development."[26]

THE NEW CONSENSUS ON THE "MIXED ECONOMY"

The "mixed economy," a combination of state intervention and the private sector, has already become the new catchword for the debate on economic and social justice. In South Africa the ANC and most other liberation forces, including the SACP, have postulated this model as the basis for a post-apartheid economy. Similarly, in Mozambique, Angola, Zimbabwe, Benin, the Congo, and Ethiopia, this notion has become the centerpiece of new economic policies.

In South Africa leading social and political forces like the ANC and the Congress of South African Trade Unions (COSATU) are looking for a new balance between state intervention and private initiative. They also have a much more differentiated view now on the merits and dangers of nationalization. Sweeping, old-style socialist nationalization is no longer their policy. A consultative workshop organized by the ANC and COSATU in Harare in April–May 1990 produced some interesting suggestions concerning the future organization of the South African economy. Although the necessity for overall macroeconomic planning was reaffirmed, both organizations are aware of the need to avoid an overcentralized state-command approach to economy policy.[27]

The role of independent trade unions is also an issue not yet sufficiently discussed in Africa, with the exception of South Africa. Mixed economies have no built-in guarantee for social justice and redistribution. Therefore they need trade unions and other social groups to struggle for social change. Such organizations are just appendages to the ruling parties and heads of state in most African countries and are of no help in this respect. Indeed "trade union autonomy is a prime marker for the great divide between democratic and Leninist socialism."[28]

In January 1990 President Joaquim Chissano of Mozambique criticized the traditional dominance of the party and its so-called mass organizations. He demanded that trade unions be independent and that

they be guaranteed the right to strike. In other countries similar suggestions have been made. In South Africa the ANC and COSATU agreed
that independent trade union rights should be enshrined in the constitution.[29] South Africa's strong, independent trade union movement, experienced in both fighting and negotiating, could become a guide for
Africa for the sound organization of labor relations in a mixed economy.
This could have a healthy impact on the role of trade unions in the
southern African region in general. If South Africa eventually joins the
Southern African Development Coordination Conference (SADCC),
trade unions in the region would be well advised to take a more regional
approach in order to counter the regional maneuverings of business in
labor relations.

GUIDELINES FOR THE DEBATE ABOUT THE TRANSFORMATION OF THE STATE

The mixed economy concept derives much of its popularity from
the fact that it leaves most questions open. Both politicians and experts
in and outside of Africa will be challenged to define its practical implications more precisely. Which mixture of private and state elements
will be optimal for Africa considering its various material, social, and
cultural conditions? Which mixture will be optimal in the respective
sectors? Have there been experiences either inside or outside Africa
which could be generalized?

There is a danger in Africa (as well as in Eastern Europe) that after
a phase of too much state intervention, the debate will concentrate
exclusively on how to cut back on it, in the belief that the rest can be
left to free market forces. However, as noted, to flourish, market economies (especially social ones) need a state to provide an efficient and
predictable legal and administrative framework and an infrastructure.
This is the secret of almost all successful market economies, not only in
Europe, but also in Asia.

Africa therefore needs a much more explicit debate about the
transformation of the state (and its bureaucracy). A neglected part of this
debate (in Eastern Europe as well as in Africa) is what sequence of
reforms and timing would be economically and socially the least harm-
ful. Furthermore, the market and planning are not dichotomies, as standard Marxist thinking insinuates. Planning by business and local,
regional, and national state actors is a vital part of successful market
economies, although the planning geared to market forces is of course

very different from the central planning of command systems. Current developments in Poland (for example) show how difficult it is for the old bureaucracy to switch from one type to the other. It is more than just an institutional and legal problem; it is a difficult and painful process of mental adjustment. This is also true for the shattered state bureaucracies in Mozambique and Angola which have to get rid of a double evil: Portuguese colonial and Marxist-Leninist bureaucratic hypertrophy and inertia.

The technocratic role of the state to provide an adequate legal and administrative framework and infrastructure for market forces is very much related to questions about democracy and political organization (one or multiparty rule, type of government structure, separation of forces, etc.) which are currently being discussed in Africa. Much has been said recently about the lack of accountability, or—to use a broader and more fashionable term—bad governance in most African states.[30] Accountability in fact is a link between these issues.

There is little doubt that in Africa the era of one-party rule is coming to an end. Encouraged by the events in Eastern Europe, a wave of popular revolts is sweeping the continent. The first spectacular case, in late fall 1989, was Benin, one of the first African states to adopt Marxism-Leninism as its official ideology (in 1974). Particularly discouraged by the downfall of Erich Honecker and Nikolai Ceaucescu, African rulers did not dare suppress these uprisings, as some of them would have done a few years ago. Rather most of them have tried to accommodate popular discontent by taking up the issue of multiparty rule.

Africans are disappointed not only by the lack of economic development during the first decades of independence, but also by persistent and gross human rights violations, abuses of power, and political patronism. With a few exceptions hopes for democracy have not materialized. The postcolonial state has lost the confidence of the populace.[31] African leaders and regimes will have to learn that their struggles against colonialism (and the national and international legitimacy resulting therefrom) do not guarantee lifelong power and legitimacy. This lesson may be easier for the new generation of leaders to accept because internal and external forces will press for more accountability, economically as well as politically. As noted, the authoritarian style of the first generation of leaders was tied closely to the bureaucratic structures of colonialism. As a British Africanist correctly pointed out, "If the colonial state provided a model for its inheritors it was that government rested not on consent but on force."[32] In Marxist-Leninist–oriented countries the concepts of class struggle, the dictatorship of the proletariat, and the vanguard party were a powerful argument in favor of one-party rule.

African ruling elites were not alone in considering one-party systems as the most authentic expression of traditional African values. The majority of the African populace shared this view. In a survey in Namibia shortly before the election of a constituent assembly in November 1989, two-thirds of black Namibians, given the choice of a one-party system, a multiparty system, or an all-party government, voted for the first.[33] In contrast, Western multiparty systems were mostly considered incompatible with the African identity. "There is only one bull in the kraal" is a well-known African saying, or, as Zimbabwe's President Robert Mugabe said in 1984, "You never have two chiefs in a given area."[34]

Here we do not propose to discuss either the viability of multiparty rule or whether democracy is a precondition for successful economic development.[35] Concerns of African politicians about the polarizing force of multiparty systems cannot be easily dismissed in view of the ethnic diversity and the strength of ethnic loyalties in Africa. However, the record of one-party rule in this respect has not been impressive. No doubt it has helped to contain ethnic conflicts in some cases, but with respect to a lasting integration of ethnic diversity, the results are meager. In some cases, one-party rule has even served to entrench the domination of one ethnic group over another. Suffice it to say that the one-party versus multiparty controversy is but one element of the complex debate about the transformation of the African state. Moreover, as empirical evidence has shown, more democracy tends to bring another potential role of the state to the fore. It can become society's agent to fight the exploitative and destructive tendencies of market forces (e.g., through social welfare, redistribution by taxation, and participatory labor laws).[36]

Let us stress, however, that all efforts to transform and improve the African state will fail if a far more basic malaise is not corrected: the division—even antagonism—between the modern territorial state and ethnicity. The defamation of ethnic structures and loyalties as hostile to modernization has driven a dangerous wedge between the urban-dominated state and the majority of its people, who live in the rural areas. All endeavors in postcolonial nation-building to suppress ethnicity as an illegitimate and backward force have failed. In most parts of Africa a revival of traditional ethno-hierarchical structures can be observed. One may even say ethnicity is very much alive, whereas the African state is not.

A reconciliation of ethnicity with the African state as a vital force for socioeconomic development is of the utmost urgency, however difficult it may be. (It may not be to the liking of the urban elites, as it will mean shifting the political focus to the rural areas.) If it does not take place, African states will be plunged into violence and bloodshed—like Liberia recently—be they governed by one-party or multiparty rule. For post-apartheid South Africa such a demand seems almost unfair because of the abuse of ethnic diversity by apartheid divide-and-rule strategies which has culminated in the creation of the so-called home-lands or bantustans, homes of poverty and misery. Judging from the current violence in South African townships (which is not simply black on black), South Africa will have little choice but to reintroduce ethnicity in a positive sense into the post-apartheid debate.

CONFLICT RESOLUTION IN SOUTHERN AFRICA

EFFECTS OF THE COLD WAR

In a short period Gorbachev's perestroika has led to a fundamental reevaluation of the significance of regional conflicts in the relations between Washington and Moscow. Whereas in the past national libera-tion wars and armed conflicts in the Third World were perceived as opportunities to shift the ideological and military balance of power between East and West, they have now become burdens. A greater realism regarding the role of military power in the resolution of regional conflicts—stemming from superpower experiences in Vietnam, Afghan-istan, Ethiopia, and Angola—has reinforced the trend for a new approach to conflict resolution.[37]

During the summit meeting with President Ronald Reagan in Reykjavik in 1985, Gorbachev indicated an interest in cooperating with Washington to resolve Third World conflicts, starting with Afghanistan. The Reagan administration responded positively. In 1988 Soviet troops started pulling out of Afghanistan. At the same time, American-Soviet cooperation to end the conflict in Namibia intensified. In May 1988 U.S. Under-Secretary of State Chester A. Crocker and his Soviet counterpart, Deputy Foreign Minister Anatoly Adamishin, agreed on a framework for implementing UN Security Council Resolution 435 of September 1978. For a decade its implementation (among other things) had been stalled by the global confrontation. On 22 December 1988 treaties for the im-plementation of Resolution 435 and for the retreat of Cuban forces from Angola were signed.

Further steps have marked the Soviet commitment to change its Africa policy. In 1989 Soviet and Mozambican officials announced the departure of about 800 Soviet military advisers from Mozambique by 1990–91. Most of them have left the country. The ice was broken for meetings of Soviets and white South Africans in October 1989, when a group of more than 20 predominantly Afrikaans speakers met with a delegation from Moscow and leading members of the ANC and the SACP in Leverkusen (FRG).[38] The Soviet government had already increasingly stressed its preference for a negotiated solution to the apartheid dilemma. Dialogue is the new bottom line. Neil van Heerden, Director General of Foreign Affairs in Pretoria, visited Moscow recently—the first contact on such a high diplomatic level in Moscow since the termination of consular relations in 1956.

In Ethiopia, the most important Soviet ally in Africa since the 1970s, Moscow is putting greater pressure on Mengistu to end the war in Eritrea, Tigre, and other parts of the country, as well as to terminate his mistaken "barracks communism." Arms supplies to the Ethiopian army have decreased, and Gorbachev is supposed to have threatened stopping deliveries altogether. Soviet military advisers have been withdrawn from the battle lines. The retreat of Soviet troops from Ethiopia is turning out to be more difficult, although public pressure is increasing to get rid of these costly failures.*

In late May 1990 Soviet diplomats met with representatives of the União Nacional para a Independência Total de Angola (UNITA) in Miami.[39] They have also supported American efforts to establish peace corridors to save Angolans from a hunger crisis brought about by the long war and a drought. In Ethiopia the two superpowers have exerted pressure on the fighting factions to accept shipments of food and humanitarian aid from the harbor of Massawa. However, apart from these and other rather low-level diplomatic activities, Washington and Moscow show little interest in conflict resolution in southern Africa. (Ironi-

---

*In late 1989 the GDR suspended its deliveries of military materials and ceased all activities in Ethiopia. By and large, the same holds true for Czechoslovakia. Cuba withdrew its remaining troops from the Ogaden in fall 1989. Its units in Angola are on schedule concerning withdrawal by July 1991. It seems that with Namibia's independence, Havana is concluding its internationalist phase in Africa. The engagement in Ethiopia has been very expensive for Moscow. The value of arms supplies has been estimated at more than $7 billion. Moscow cannot seriously hope for repayments. Ethiopia is one of the poorest countries in the world. These debts have apparently been written off to 1.5 billion rubles in Soviet books.

cally U.S. diplomacy vis-à-vis Angola now seems to be mostly the responsibility of Deputy Assistant Secretary of State Jeffrey Davidow, who is of Russian origin.) Superpower disinterest rather than superpower condominium (as many Africans had feared) turns out to be the main feature of the post–cold-war era in southern Africa.

By and large, the same holds true for the Europeans. The difficult task of harmonizing German unification with the advancement of European integration and the need to transform the old confrontational and bloc-based system of security and cooperation into a cooperative one will absorb European public attention and politicians for many years. In France the high costs of keeping its *chasse gardée* have become a political issue since its allies in Western Africa have run into deep economic and social trouble. French investments are getting out of Africa at an amazing speed (20 percent disinvestment during the last two years). British business and political interest is declining too. The Germans are busy managing the accumulating economic, political, and social problems of unification. Portugal may be an exception to this European trend because of its considerable involvement regarding the Angolan peace process. However, it is too small an actor to make a difference in the overall assessment. In Eastern Europe very little enthusiasm, if any, is left for engagement in southern Africa. For national economic interests Hungary has entered into an official relationship with South Africa. GDR ambassadors have been called home and have left the keys to their embassies in West German embassy offices.

All major actors now agree on a new (and old) demand: African solutions to African problems, reached by Africans. For the superpowers this is in stark contrast to their substantial and sometimes heavy-handed cold war involvement in the region, particularly in Angola. However, while the cold war is over, its effects are not—i.e., huge human losses, millions of displaced persons, the destruction of the economies and infrastructures as well as the fragmentation of the societies in Angola and Mozambique. One may well argue that it is not enough for the Soviets, Americans, and Europeans to declare the end of global rivalry and just walk away without helping to clear up the mess they have left behind.

AFRICAN CONFLICT RESOLUTION ON THE RISE?

In June 1989 African politicians tried their luck at regional conflict resolution by endorsing a cease-fire agreement for Angola proposed by

Zaire's president, Mobutu Sese Seko. A few days later it broke down because of vagueness and a lack of agreement concerning its implementation. Other, more astute mediators such as Cape Verde, South Africa, and Portugal took over and tried to put the peace process back on track; they were supported by Washington and Moscow. Finally, Lisbon arranged for direct talks between UNITA and the Angolan government of the Movimento Popular de Libertação de Angola (MPLA). De facto this put Lisbon into the position of chief mediator. The first meeting took place in Portugal at the end of April 1990 and a second in mid-June. In early July the Central Committee of the MPLA voted in favor of a new, multiparty-based constitution to be worked out once a cease-fire was negotiated.[40] The UNITA Central Committee had already recognized José Eduardo dos Santos as the head of state. However, it refuses to recognize the government because it did not take office through free elections. A third round of direct talks in Lisbon, scheduled for 8 August, had to be postponed because of renewed UNITA attacks against government forces in southern Africa. The talks took place at the end of the month, and a breakthrough was reported. In fact, the mediator, Portuguese Minister of Foreign Affairs Duaro Barroso, felt compelled to call for the United States and Soviet Union to join in the peace process.[41]

In Mozambique the involvement of Presidents Daniel arap Moi of Kenya and Robert Mugabe of Zimbabwe has turned out to be more enduring than Mobutu's in Angola. On 31 July 1990 President Chissano announced that the Political Bureau of the Frente de Libertação de Moçambique (FRELIMO) government had decided unanimously that the conditions for the creation of a multiparty system had now been met. Elections are scheduled for 1991. Chissano did not envisage that the Resistencia Nacional Moçambicana (RENAMO) would have trouble meeting the criteria for political parties.[42] In January he had presented a liberal draft constitution which (inter alia) outlawed the death penalty and stipulated basic individual freedoms, including the right to strike and to own property. Yet the first official direct talks between RENAMO and the FRELIMO government, which took place in Rome in August, got bogged down for reasons which are only partly clear. No cease-fire agreement was announced. RENAMO would not yield to requests to recognize the government. Apparently it wants a share in government power before free elections, as it is not sure of its popularity. Rumors about RENAMO's insistence that Kenya continue as a leading mediator support this suspicion. According to the government in Maputo, however, both parties had agreed that mediation should end once direct talks had begun.[43] In late August it was reported that the Kenyan government had allowed RENAMO to establish at least one training camp in Kenya, thus increasing the already existing doubts about Kenya's impartiality.[44]

MULTIPARTY RULE AND FREE AND FAIR ELECTIONS AS A NEW FORMULA FOR PEACE

Although peace has yet to come to Mozambique and Angola, it now appears that conflict resolution in southern Africa has made a quantum leap in recent months. Free and fair elections in a multiparty system have become the accepted formula for peace. The successful termination of conflict in Namibia by free and fair elections and the breakdown of one-party systems in South Africa (as well as Eastern Europe) have had their effect. The ANC's clear commitment to a multiparty democracy in its constitutional guidelines (published in spring 1988) was a crucial intermediate step for a rapprochement with the white government. Surprisingly this commitment is now vigorously shared by all relevant liberation forces, not least because it guarantees them a political niche in a future South Africa ruled by an ANC/National Party (NP) coalition. Endorsing the concept of a multiparty democracy, Slovo stated, "We have had sufficient experience of one-party rule in various parts of the world to perhaps conclude that the 'mission' to promote real democracy under a one-party system is not just difficult but, in the long run, impossible."[45]

Zimbabwe is a notable exception to this trend toward multiparty systems. The government in Harare can even (and does) claim that its December 1987 Unity Agreement ended the bloody conflict between the Shona-based government of the Zimbabwe African National Union (ZANU) and the Ndebele-based opposition party, the Zimbabwe African People's Union (ZAPU). The old alliance from the liberation war, ZANU-PF (Patriotic Front), was recreated. However, since the Unity Agreement was more or less forced upon ZAPU, its longer-term peaceful effects remain to be seen. In the agreement ethnic conflict is contained by institutionalizing the hegemony of the stronger party. Following up on Mugabe's quest for one-party rule, on 22 December ZANU-PF concluded its congress with the solution of transforming Zimbabwe into a de jure one-party system on the basis of Marxism-Leninism. Critics in Zimbabwe point out that the date of the party's decision coincides with the day when despotic one-party rule was overthrown in Romania. Furthermore, it has started a heated debate on the merits of one- and multiparty rule

among the Zimbabwean elite. (Unfortunately there are no new arguments.) The majority of the urban elite is clearly against de jure one-party
rule, whereas Mugabe claims that the rural population—i.e., the majority
of the population—backs his plan for implementing one-party rule as
the authentic African form of democracy. Even Mugabe's critics agree
that his assessment is probably correct. However, in a recent vote in the
Politbureau of the party only five of the twenty-five members voted to
change the constitution to stipulate a de jure one-party system. The
majority of the Politbureau seems content with the de facto one-party
rule and fears international repercussions of a move toward de jure
one-party rule, particularly with respect to the benefits of the economic
liberalization program announced on 5 July 1990. There is a general
mood in Zimbabwe that the era of sloganeering is over.

CONCLUSIONS: THE UNRESOLVED PROBLEM OF IMPLEMENTING CONFLICT RESOLUTIONS IN SOUTHERN AFRICA

The acceptance of free and fair elections as a formula for ending
violent conflicts in southern Africa is an important breakthrough, but it
raises difficult questions about the implementation of cease-fire agreements and political solutions based on this principal. In Namibia the
international community made a decisive contribution by bringing in
the United Nations Transition Assistance Group (UNTAG). Its presence
was a sine qua non for the (relatively) peaceful transition of power.

In Mozambique and Angola the obstacles for implementing a cease-
fire and free and fair elections seem to be almost insurmountable. One
can no longer refer to functioning state structures. Both countries will
have to be rebuilt almost from scratch. In Mozambique and in most parts
of Angola violence has become a way of life as well as economic survival.
How far local and regional warlordism has spread will become evident
only after cease-fires have been agreed upon. Obviously in both countries
peacekeeping and monitoring forces much larger than those in Namibia
would have to be brought in to give free and fair elections a chance.
Angola has one and a half times the territory of Namibia and about eight
times the population, and Mozambique has approximately the same area
but about thirteen times the population. In Angola, where a mine war
worse than in Afghanistan has been fought, experienced mine-sweeping
forces would be needed to make the war-torn parts of the country safe
for elections (and for observers). In both countries peacekeeping forces
would be in danger of being drawn into fighting with local warlords.

In South Africa the ANC, the government, and other actors may agree on an implementation formula which could dispense with comparable international effort. State structures in South Africa are intact and could take care of implementation. It remains to be seen whether the contending parties will find a formula to handle state power in the interim phase. Whatever they agree upon, the actors will be well advised to integrate an international element into their internal solution. An impartial international presence would diffuse mistrust (not least with respect to violence by black and white groups) and create confidence regarding the fairness of elections. The legitimizing effect of an international presence is a well-established fact.

NOTES

1. See Fred Halliday, "The Ends of Cold War," pp. 5–24, and Mary Kaldor, "After the Cold War," pp. 25–40, both in *New Left Review* 180 (March/April 1990).

2. See *Die Zeit*, 24 August 1990.

3. *Financial Mail* (Johannesburg), 3 August 1990.

4. *BBC-SWB, Middle East*/WO142, 21 August 1990.

5. Cited in "Die sozialistische Idee und die revolutionäre Umgestaltung," *Der Spiegel*, January 1990, p. 2.

6. It is questionable whether the so-called New Left of the 1960s, with its simultaneous rejection of Stalinist communism and social democracy in Western Europe, can be considered as a school of thought clearly distinguishable from either orthodox Marxism or social-democratic thinking; see *New Left Review* 180 (March/April 1990): 2.

7. See R. W. Davies, "Gorbachev's Socialism in Historical Perspective," *New Left Review* 179 (1990): 5–27.

8. Halliday, p. 17.

9. Internal discussion paper of the SACP, partly reprinted in *Weekly Mail*, 19–25 January 1990.

10. Joe Slovo, "Has Socialism Failed?," *South African Communist* 121 (Second Quarter 1990): 25–51.

11. *Ibid.*, pp. 32 and 34.

12. Pallo Jordan, "Crisis of Conscience in the SACP," *SAPEM*, June 1990, pp. 28–34.

13. Slovo hints at this problem: "At the purely economic level this form of alienation often turned out to be the worst of both worlds" (Slovo, p. 43).

14. *Ibid.*, p. 15.

15. Cited in *Frankfurter Allgemeine Zeitung*, 17 February 1990.

16. Gleb. V. Smirnov, "Economic Development of Socialist Oriented African Countries," *Front File: IAIS Conference Special* 3, 17 (December 1989): 6.

17. *Africa Research Bulletin* (Economic Series), 28 February 1990, p. 9823.

18. Hartmut Elsenhans, *Abhängiger Kapitalimus oder bürokratische Entwicklungsgesellschaft, Versuch über den Staat in der Dritten Welt* (Frankfurt and New York, 1981).

19. Dieter Senghaas, *Europa 2000: Ein Friedensplan* (Frankfurt, 1990), p. 71.

20. Martin Robbe, "Jahrhundertwende in Sicht: Versuch einer Standortbestimmung"; unpublished conference paper.

21. See, for instance, I. Andreyev, *The Non-Capitalist Way: Socialism and the Developing Countries* (Progress Publishers, 1977). Some independent Marxists opposed this opinion. As early as the 1960s S. Amin presented the thesis that progressive regimes with a socialist orientation had to "break up" the traditional agrarian sector with capitalist development (S. Amin, "The Class Struggle in Africa," *Revolution* 1, 9 [1964]: 43).

22. Even before perestroika several authors upheld the thesis that Marxism-Leninism would fail in Africa, not least because of its proletarian urban bias against development. See (inter alia) Peter Aaby, *The State of Guinea-Bissau: African Socialism or Socialism in Africa?* (Uppsala: Scandinavian Institute of African Studies, 1978; research report no. 45), p. 18; Winrich Kühne, *Die Politik der Sowjetunion in Afrika: Bedingungen und Dynamik ihres ideologischen, ökonomischen und militärischen Engagements* (Baden-Baden, 1983).

23. Janet MacGaffey, *Perestroika without Glasnost: The Need for a New Approach to the Real Economics of African Countries* (Atlanta, Georgia: Carter Center of Emory University, 1989), p. 132; *Beyond Autocracy in Africa: Working Papers for the Inaugural Seminar of the Governance in Africa Program*, 17–18 February.

24. Meinhard Niegel, *Die Zeit*, 4 May 1990, p. 41.

25. Zaiki Laidi, "Le déclassement international de l'Afrique," *Politique étrangère* 53, 3 (1988): 667–75.

26. Richard L. Sklar. "Beyond Capitalism and Socialism in Africa," *Journal of Modern African Studies* 26, 1 (1988): 15.

27. The product of this workshop was a document called "The Economy beyond Apartheid," reprinted in *New Nation*, 15–21 June 1990, pp. 8–11.

28. Sklar, p. 9.

29. "The Economy beyond Apartheid."

30. For instance, see Carter Center of Emory University, *Beyond Autocracy in Africa.*

31. See *ibid.*, p. 21.

32. Michael Crowder, "Whose Dream Was It Anyway? Twenty-Five Years of African Independence," *African Affairs* 86, 342 (1987): 13.

33. See Heribert Weiland, "Namibia auf dem Weg zur Unabhängigkeit," *Europa-Archiv* 23 1989): 711–18.

34. Interview in *Moto* 28 (October 1984).

35. On these issues, see Peter Anyang' Nyong'o, "Political Instability and the Prospects for Democracy in Africa," *Africa Development* 13, 1 (1988), and Thandika Mkandawire, "Comments on Democracy and Political Instability," *Africa Development* 13, 3 (1988): 77–82. See also "Debates: Questions about Democracy," *Review of African Political Economy* 45/46 (1989): 83–97.

36. See A. W. Stadler, "A Contribution to the 'Conditions of Democracy Debate': A Working Paper," *International Affairs Bulletin* 12, 3 (1988): 25–34.

37. See *Front File: Southern Africa Brief* 12, 2 (August 1988): 1.

38. On changes in the Soviet–South African relationship, see Winrich Kühne, "A 1988 Update on Soviet Relations with Pretoria, the ANC, and the SACP," *CSIS Africa Notes* 89 (1 September 1988): 1–8. An extensive discussion can be found in Kurt M. Campbell, *Soviet Policy Towards South Africa* (New York: St. Martin's Press, 1986).

39. *Monitor-Dienst (Afrika)*, 7 June 1990.

40. *Ibid.*, 5 July 1990.

41. BBC-SWB, Middle East/0859 ii, 30 September 1990.

42. BBC-SWB Service - Middle East, ME/0832 ii, 2 August 1990.

43. *Monitor-Dienst (Afrika)*, 21 August 1990.

44. *The Herald* (Harare), 29 August 1990.

45. Slovo, p. 41.

AFGHANISTAN

SOVIET POLICY IN AFGHANISTAN

Robert S. Litwak

For over a decade, Soviet policy in Afghanistan has been a key factor defining and shaping the superpower relationship. The Soviet invasion of December 1979 culminated a period of radical activism in the Third World by the USSR and dealt a final body blow to détente. Jimmy Carter asserted that the Soviet move constituted "the greatest threat to peace since World War II" and enunciated the doctrine now bearing his name designating the Persian Gulf a zone of vital American interest. He stated that the invasion had done more to shape his perception of Soviet intentions than any other event during his presidency. In its wake came the election of Ronald Reagan, the most vocal anti-communist American president in memory, and his administration's subsequent return to a more militarized form of containment.[1]

The unique conjunction of superpower interests and regional instability in Southwest Asia under the political circumstances of the late 1970s led to heightened fears that the United States and the Soviet Union might be drawn, inadvertently or otherwise, into direct conflict. Many observers pointed to ominous analogies with 1914 and warned of the danger of a new Sarajevo—that is, a regional flashpoint that might escalate and spread geographically, thereby leading to general war. This danger of a "catalytic conflict" in which a war might start in the Persian Gulf and feed back into Central Europe was one of the principal scenarios that dominated NATO thinking about the strategic environment during this period.

If the Soviet invasion of 1979 was instrumental in shaping American perceptions of an expansionist USSR in the early 1980s, Soviet General Secretary Mikhail Gorbachev's decision to withdraw the Red Army from Afghanistan, a process completed in February 1989, was equally important in persuading the public at large that the Cold War was indeed drawing to a close, if not over. Up to that time, skeptics of Soviet domestic reform within the Bush administration, notably Secretary of Defense Richard Cheney and Deputy National Security Adviser Robert

Gates, had spoken of Afghanistan as a key "litmus test" of Gorbachev's "new thinking" in foreign policy. Although the April 1988 Geneva accords on Afghanistan paved the way for the Soviet withdrawal, they have not ended the conflict. The Afghan conflict has reverted to the civil war which existed prior to, and indeed precipitated, the December 1979 invasion. The Najibullah regime in Kabul has demonstrated surprising political resilience in the face of a continuing challenge from the Afghan *mujaheddin* based in Pakistan. For its part, the resistance, without the unifying force of the Soviet presence in Afghanistan, has had difficulties maintaining political cohesion. Superpower efforts to end the Afghan civil war have foundered on unbridgeable differences between the combatants over the composition of a new regime in Kabul—specifically, the personal role of President Najibullah in a postwar Afghan government.

This essay will address three key issues that relate to the three phases of Soviet involvement in Afghanistan. The first is why the Soviet leadership decided that direct military intervention was ultimately necessary in December 1979—and that it would lead to the attainment of the Kremlin's desired political objective. The second key issue is that of Gorbachev's decision to withdraw Soviet forces from Afghanistan. As in the discussion of the initial phase of Soviet involvement, this section will focus on the respective roles of domestic and external factors in Soviet decision-making. The third issue relates to the post-withdrawal period: how will "the end of the Cold War," as well as the USSR's evolving internal situation, affect the future of Soviet policy in Afghanistan?[2]

At the outset, one must, of course, acknowledge the perennial difficulty in the Soviet studies field of obtaining adequate and reliable sources to permit rigorous foreign policy analysis. As a consequence of *glasnost'*, the Soviet Union is no longer the "black box" that it once was. Scholars and journalists have risen to Gorbachev's challenge to fill in the "blank spots" of the USSR's history. Following Gorbachev's announcement in February 1988 that all Soviet forces would be withdrawn from Afghanistan within a year, there appeared a number of articles in the Soviet press purporting to explain the inner workings of the Brezhnev regime when it decided to invade in December 1979.[3] These writings featured interviews with civilian and military leaders, both current and former, as well as academic specialists from the relevant USSR Academy of Science institutes who had served in various advisory capacities. Some articles (for example, a detailed account of Soviet decision-making during 1978–79 that appeared in the Soviet military newspaper *Krasnaya zvezda*) were reportedly based, in part, on archival research.[4] These new sources provide fresh insights into the roles played by the major institutions and key policymakers in the months leading up to the invasion. In some instances, these products of glasnost' challenge conventional wisdoms about how and why decisions were taken. One striking example of this phenomenon is a March 1989 interview in the weekly *Ogonek* in which General Valentin Varrenikov, Deputy Minister of Defense and commander of USSR ground forces, disputes the widely held view that the KGB had repeatedly cautioned against direct intervention, while the military as an institution had been a major proponent.[5]

Notwithstanding the publication of these new source materials, many gaps in our understanding of Soviet decision-making remain. A special commission of the Supreme Soviet was created to provide a fuller accounting of Soviet policy in Afghanistan and to address outstanding questions. The problem in attempting to fill in this particular "blank spot" in Soviet history goes beyond the need for fuller archival access. As the principal officials on the Politburo who were reportedly involved in the decision to invade in December 1979 are now deceased, our ability to sort through the selective and often contradictory accounts that glasnost' has produced remains limited. There is the very real possibility that the new source materials are, at least in part, self-serving exercises in post-hoc rationalization by the interested parties. A similar problem of sources exists with respect to Gorbachev's decision to withdraw Soviet forces from Afghanistan. Although the more open political environment within the USSR of the late 1980s gives us a better picture of the interplay of forces influencing Soviet decision-making, there have, as yet, been only hints of how the withdrawal process unfolded. Despite glasnost', there exist no authoritative insider accounts of how and why the decision was taken.

In the analysis that follows, it will be evident that Soviet policy toward Afghanistan from Brezhnev to Gorbachev has been shaped by an amalgam of domestic, regional, and international factors. Clearly no single factor in isolation can adequately explain Soviet policymaking at key decision points. The resort to direct military intervention in December 1979 was not solely the product of the peculiarities of the Brezhnev regime, nor can it be attributed exclusively to anxieties about the danger of an Islamic resurgence in Soviet Central Asia in the wake of the Iranian revolution. Likewise, in analyzing Gorbachev's decision to withdraw, it would be misleading to place too much emphasis on the military impact of Stinger missiles at the expense of other salient factors. In assessing Soviet policy, the challenge is to prudently use the available source material to make judgments, however preliminary and couched, about the relative importance of the various domestic and external factors affecting Soviet decision-making.

1. THE DECISION TO INTERVENE

Viewed in historical terms, the Brezhnev Politburo's decision in December 1979 to invade Afghanistan was the culmination of Moscow's efforts since the early nineteenth century to assert influence, and ultimately, control over that strategically situated state on its southern border. During the pre-revolutionary period, Afghanistan served as a buffer between the Russian and British empires. The two imperial powers vied for influence in what was then called the "Great Game."[6] In the wake of the Bolshevik Revolution, Lenin feared that the British might attempt to use Afghanistan as a base for intervention in Central Asia. For this reason, he moved quickly to establish diplomatic relations with Kabul in May 1919 and then went on to conclude a Treaty of Friendship in February 1921. During the period between the Revolution and the end of World War II, the Kremlin continued to define its interests in Afghanistan primarily in military-strategic terms. The overriding objective of its policy was to prevent any hostile power from using Afghanistan as a base of operation against the USSR.[7] With the advent of the Cold War, the Soviet Union viewed the Kabul regime's avowed policy of nonalignment as a useful means for circumscribing Western influence in that country. The USSR's assiduous efforts during the 1950s and 1960s to expand economic and military ties with Afghanistan yielded considerable political results. Afghan reliance on Soviet economic and technical aid fostered a foreign policy that was generally more accommodating to Soviet preferences and interests.[8]

A pivotal event on the road to intervention was the creation in January 1965 of an underground communist party—the People's Democratic Party of Afghanistan (PDPA)—under the leadership of Nur Mohammed Taraki. The founding of this pro-Soviet party was followed little more than two years later by its split into two main factions: Khalq ("the masses"), led by Taraki, and Parcham ("the banner"), headed by Babrak Karmal, the man who would later lead the PDPA regime in Kabul after the December 1979 invasion.[9] The schism reportedly resulted both from personal and policy differences within the PDPA's Central Committee. In June 1973 King Zahir Shah was overthrown by former Prime Minister

Mohammed Daoud, and Afghanistan was declared a republic. Most informed observers believe that Daoud acted in his own right, although some of the participants in the 1973 coup reportedly had PDPA links. Following his seizure of power, Daoud sought to reduce Afghan reliance on Soviet aid and began to pursue a more independent foreign policy line. The consequent cooling of Soviet-Afghan relations was reflected in the communiques issued during the visit of Soviet President Nikolai Podgorny to Kabul in December 1975 and Daoud's return visit to Moscow in April 1977. The attempt by Daoud to diversify his diplomatic options came amidst a deepening economic and political crisis within Afghanistan.

The chain of events that precipitated the PDPA/military coup against Daoud in April 1978 began with the murder of a prominent Parcham labor leader. The issue of Soviet participation in the Saur ("April") revolution remains one of contention. For a decade, Moscow had sought to bring about a reunification of the Khalq and Parcham factions; this was achieved in mid-1977 and was an important prerequisite for the success of the subsequent coup.[10] The coup unfolded when the Daoud regime made a bungled attempt to arrest the PDPA leadership following the murder of the Parcham labor leader. During the course of these events, Soviet military advisers (then numbering some 350) were observed with Afghan armored units and at the Bagram airbase outside Kabul, where they reportedly assisted in the servicing of MiG-21s and SU-7s.[11] Given the close links that then existed between the Soviet embassy and PDPA, as well as the extent of the USSR's close ties to the Afghan army, it is likely that Moscow had some foreknowledge of the coup. That said, the ad hoc nature of Soviet actions once the coup began would indicate that they were not part of an orchestrated plan, but rather were responses to unfolding events.

Once the coup occurred, the Kremlin moved quickly to consolidate relations with the PDPA regime headed by Taraki and vigorously denied Western charges of complicity in the overthrow of the Daoud government. Moscow's efforts to consolidate relations with the Taraki regime were reflected in the conclusion of more than twenty bilateral agreements and the doubling of Soviet military advisers by mid-1978. As part of a political strategy emphasizing the creation of Leninist institutions, Soviet personnel were assigned to key governmental bodies.[12] This emphasis on institution-building along Marxist-Leninist lines was a product of a learning process dating to the late 1960s and early 1970s during which Moscow grappled with the problem of maintaining pro-Soviet regimes in the Third World. Political turnabouts in Ghana, Egypt, and Chile, among others, had convinced the Soviet leadership that this type of political engineering offered the best means for maintaining "socialist-oriented" regimes in power and thereby ensuring a long-term influence relationship. Although such an institutionalization strategy was pursued in Afghanistan, it ultimately proved insufficient. By late 1979, only direct Soviet military intervention could save the PDPA regime from the growing insurgent threat that challenged its very existence.

Domestic opposition to PDPA rule stemmed, in large part, from the draconian domestic measures adopted by Taraki following the April revolution. Taraki's program included radical land reform and the banning of certain religious practices. These moves engendered deep resentment of the PDPA regime in both urban and rural areas, such that in mid-1978 incidents of armed resistance to the regime were reported. By late 1978 the first training camps and supply routes had been established by the Afghan resistance, the mujaheddin, across the Durand line in Pakistan. Taraki's adoption of this radical, ideologically motivated domestic program coincided with the revival of intense factionalism within the PDPA. Since his rise to power, Taraki had moved aggressively to consolidate both his personal position and that of his faction, the Khalq. In practice, this consolidation translated into the removal of Parcham members from positions in the government, schools, and military. Diplomatic postings abroad was a method used by Taraki to exile key Parcham leaders; Babrak Karmal, who would later return to Kabul alongside Soviet tanks, was named ambassador to Czechoslovakia in early July 1978.

A key figure in this factional infighting between the Khalq and Parcham was Hafizullah Amin, a politburo member and PDPA party secretary. In addition to assisting in efforts to consolidate Khalqi control within the PDPA regime, Amin played a leading role in the implementation of Taraki's radical domestic program. Motivated by ideological fervor, Taraki called for nothing less than the wholesale transformation of Afghan society. Although aware that Taraki's program was generating heated opposition within Afghanistan, Moscow, for its part, took no discernible steps during 1978 to moderate the Khalq leader's actions.

When Taraki visited Moscow in early 1978, the conclusion of a twenty-year Treaty of Friendship, Neighborliness, and Cooperation signified a further solidifying of bilateral relations. This agreement included Afghan acceptance of the Brezhnev 1969 Asian collective security plan, as well as a provision (Article 4) pledging both parties to take "appropriate measures" to ensure their mutual security. In Soviet press commentaries and leadership statements, Afghanistan under PDPA rule was lauded along with other states of a "socialist orientation," such as Angola, Mozambique and Ethiopia. Assured of strong Soviet political and materiel support, Taraki continued his efforts at home to radically transform Afghan society. The level of popular opposition, spearheaded by mujaheddin resistance groups operating both within the country and from base camps in Pakistan, rose accordingly.

With PDPA rule under threat, the Soviet leadership dispatched Soviet General Alexei Epishev, then in charge of the ideological and political supervision of the Soviet armed forces, to Kabul in early April 1979.[13] This visit would be the first of several missions by senior Soviet military delegations to Afghanistan during the course of 1979 to assess the internal security situation and advise the PDPA regime. Amidst these deteriorating conditions, Vassily Safronchuk was posted to Kabul in June 1979 to be Soviet ambassador Aleksandr Puzanov's deputy. Serving in this capacity as chief liaison official between the embassy and the PDPA regime, Safronchuk coordinated Moscow's efforts to stabilize conditions within the country.

One of Safronchuk's chief objectives was to end the incessant factionalism that was devouring the PDPA from within and preventing it from mounting an effective response to the insurgent threat posed by the mujaheddin. The Taraki-Amin leadership was urged to rescind or modify some of its more extreme social measures in order to broaden the regime's popular base.[14] Informed observers differ over whether the Soviets were open to a coalition government (i.e., incorporating non-communist elements into the ruling of the PDPA regime). This possibility, although perhaps entertained by Safronchuk, is doubtful on two grounds. First, serious non-communist officials (such as those who served in King Zahir Shah's government) would probably have viewed it as merely a cosmetic attempt to legitimize PDPA rule. Second, and perhaps more importantly, there would probably have been opposition to this possibility within the Soviet leadership. Although there have been periods when Moscow has pursued a "popular front" strategy (i.e., seeking working coalitions between non-communist and communist parties), it should be recalled that the late 1970s was a period in which Soviet Third World policies were strongly influenced by Politburo hardliners such as Mikhail Suslov and Boris Ponomarev, head of the Central Committee's International Department.[15] As noted above, these defenders of the ideological faith viewed the creation of Marxist-Leninist institutions as the best means for ensuring that pro-Soviet regimes in the Third World would remain in power.

As a follow-up to the Epishev military mission, Soviet Deputy Defense Minister General Ivan Pavlovskii was dispatched to Kabul in August 1979 to provide a fresh assessment of the deteriorating internal political situation. At that juncture, Soviet decision-makers confronted two stark options: Moscow could either up the ante and intensify efforts to maintain the PDPA in power, or curtail its commitment and permit events to run their course within the country. On 14 September, Taraki, reportedly acting with Soviet approval, moved to oust Amin from the PDPA leadership; this abortive effort resulted instead in Taraki's own murder and replacement by Amin. One persistent theory about this bizarre episode is that Moscow hoped that Amin's departure would permit Taraki to reconstitute the PDPA, perhaps through a rapprochement with Karmal's Parcham faction.

The murder of Taraki, who was reportedly well regarded by Brezhnev, set in motion the events that culminated in the December 1979 invasion. While ostensibly offering to work with Amin during the autumn of 1979, the Soviet leadership initiated steps to oust him from power. The groundwork for the coup against Amin was laid by Lieutenant General Viktor Paputin, a First Deputy Minister of Interior, who arrived in Kabul in late November.[16] At the time of the Paputin mission, the size of the Soviet military contingent had increased to some 4,000 troops who controlled such key installations as the Bagram airbase outside Kabul. This airbase presence was bolstered three days prior to the invasion by the deployment of an additional 10,000 airborne troops. It was these forces that moved into Kabul on 27 December and overthrew the Amin regime. Meanwhile, seven Soviet mechanized divisions (estimated at a strength of 80,000 men) crossed the frontier and fanned out across the country, occupying the major urban centers. Babrak Karmal, broadcasting from the Soviet Union, announced that Soviet forces had been invited into the country under the terms of the 1978 Treaty of Friendship. The first detailed Soviet commentary on the Afghan crisis appeared in *Pravda* on 31 December under the pseudonym A. Petrov. The article charged that Amin had been a "helpmate" of reactionary forces that had overthrown the "legitimate" government headed by Taraki.[17] The Soviet commentary further asserted that the United States, still recovering from its disastrous political setback in Iran, was seeking to "subjugate the Afghan people" in order to create a new strategic outpost on the USSR's southern border.

In his initial public statement following the invasion, Brezhnev asserted that "it was not a simple decision for us to send military contingents to Afghanistan."[18] Despite the recent publication of new source materials, many questions remain about how and why the decision to invade was taken in December 1979. A variety of sources indicate that the specific decision to overthrow Amin and deploy a large-scale contingent of Soviet forces into Afghanistan was made by a special Politburo commission that included President and CPSU General Secretary Leonid Brezhnev, Soviet Premier Alexei Kosygin, KGB Chief Yuri Andropov, Defense Minister Dmitrii Ustinov, chief ideologue Mikhail Suslov, and Foreign Minister Andrei Gromyko.[19] Former Soviet Foreign Minister Edouard Shevardnadze, who was a candidate member of the Politburo at the time of the invasion, reported to an October 1989 session of the Supreme Soviet that he and Mikhail Gorbachev "happened to be together at the time, and we learned about it from the radio and newspaper reports. A decision which had grave consequences for our country was made behind the party's and people's back. They were presented with a fait accompli."[20]

The absence of serious consultation by Brezhnev's inner circle within the Politburo was not confined to other party and governmental officials. Academic specialists from the USSR Academy of Sciences, as well as those officials, such as Safronchuk, who had spent extended periods inside Afghanistan were evidently frozen out of the decision-making process. In early 1989, the role of academic specialists during this episode became the focus of a lively exchange between novelist Alexandr Prokhanov and academician Oleg Bogomolov in *Literaturnaya gazeta*. Prokhanov, known for his hard line pro-military views, charged that the academic specialists had provided incorrect assessments of the Afghanistan situation; Bogomolov's response was that expert advice had been systematically ignored.[21] In the case of Safronchuk, the Soviet official with probably the best feel for conditions on the ground in Afghanistan, his assessment was recorded in a strikingly candid and prescient conversation with the U.S. Chargé d'Affaires J. Bruce Amstutz; Safronchuk approvingly cited the Leninist dictum that "every revolution must defend itself" and predicted that the deployment of Soviet forces into the country would have adverse internal and international repercussions.[22]

With respect to the military, glasnost' era publications have challenged the conventional wisdom in the West prior to 1989 that the military had supported the Politburo decision to intervene. This view had taken root following the publication of an interview in 1982 with a KGB defector, Major Vladimir Kuzichkin, who reportedly stated that the KGB high command had opposed further Soviet entanglement in Afghan affairs, while the military complained about allowing events to "get out of hand."[23] According to General Varrenikov, who was interviewed in a March 1989 issue of *Ogonek*, both Chief of the General Staff Nikolai Ogarkov and Marshal Sergei Akhromeev had argued against the decision to intervene. These entreaties, however, were ignored by the civilian Minister of Defense Ustinov, who reportedly directed the General Staff to prepare for military operations in Afghanistan on 10 December.[24] No information is available whether the leadership requested estimates from the military or civilian experts on the length of time that would be required to defeat the mujaheddin insurgency and stabilize political conditions within the country. Although no rigorous assessment was made prior to the intervention, the evident belief within the leadership was that the mujaheddin could not stand up to the power of the Red Army and would be quickly routed. The issue of Soviet expectations going into the conflict was addressed by Shevardnadze in his revealing speech of October 1989 before the Supreme Soviet. The then Soviet Foreign Minister observed that "the people who made the decision . . . did not plan to stay in Afghanistan for any length of time, nor to create the sixteenth or seventeenth Soviet republic."[25]

In assessing the Soviet decision to intervene in Afghanistan, it is important to bear in mind the broader regional and international context within which Soviet decisions were taken. On the strategic level, the period 1978–79 witnessed a further deterioration in Moscow's relations with its principal great power rivals—the United States and China. The possibility of a nascent Sino-American alliance against the USSR was suggested by the January 1979 visit of Chinese Vice-Premier Deng Xiaoping to Washington, during which plans for closer strategic cooperation were discussed. Given this development, the importance of Afghanistan as a strategic buffer on the USSR's border took on a new light. Andrei Kokoshin, Deputy Director of the Institute of the USA and Canada, recently stated that Soviet policy toward Afghanistan during 1978–79 was motivated in part by the desire to open up "a new line of communication and collaboration between the Soviet Union and India" in order to offset the Sino-American challenge.[26]

In addition to the China factor, three other developments were important in shaping the political context of Soviet decision-making on Afghanistan: first, NATO's decision in early December 1979 to proceed with the modernization of new medium-range nuclear systems in Central Europe; second, the declining political fortunes of the SALT II Treaty in the U.S. Senate; and third, the American naval buildup in the Persian Gulf and Arabian Sea over the course of 1979 in response to events in Iran (i.e., the February revolution and the seizure of the American embassy in November). The deployment of American military power in Southwest Asia further reinforced the perception of Afghanistan as an important strategic barrier. In the wake of the invasion, Soviet commentaries maintained that the American military presence in the region posed a direct threat both to Iran and Afghanistan. Although there is no evidence that the Carter administration entertained direct military intervention in Iran, let alone Afghanistan, this theme continues to be struck by some Soviet officials and analysts even in the era of glasnost'.[27]

Another factor affecting the regional milieu was the resurgence of Islamic fundamentalism that accompanied the Iranian revolution and its uncertain domestic political impact in the Soviet Union. The importance of the Islamic factor in Soviet decision-making remains an issue of contention. Given the closed nature of the Brezhnev system, there were, of course, no public indicators (e.g., leadership statements) that the fear of an Islamic contagion into Soviet Central Asia was a major factor bearing on Moscow's policy in Afghanistan in 1978–79. That said, Soviet decision-makers could not have been oblivious to the fact that dynamic demographic growth rates in Central Asia were then projected to produce a Turko-Muslim population of approximately 80 million by the year 2000. Given this demographic trend, as well as the deteriorating internal security situation within Afghanistan and the Islamic orientation of the mujaheddin resistance, the Soviet leadership could not have dismissed the possibility that the Iranian experience might be replicated in Afghanistan. Within this context, the preservation of PDPA rule in Kabul would have appeared the best means of preventing the rise of an Islamic republic in Afghanistan, with its attendant danger of political and religious spillover into Soviet Central Asia. In this sense, the requirements of Soviet border security, discussed above, may well have been seen as serving an important domestic objective—the maintenance of Soviet power in Central Asia.

In the short space available, this discussion has highlighted a range of domestic, regional, and international factors affecting Soviet decision-making: the closed nature of the Brezhnev system that prevented the adequate integration of expert advice into the process, a commitment by some within the Soviet leadership to an ideologically motivated foreign policy (e.g., the support of Marxist-Leninist vanguard parties, such as the PDPA, in the Third World), possible concern about the spread of Islamic fundamentalism in Central Asia in the wake of the Iranian revolution, and the challenge to the USSR's strategic position posed by the creation of a tacit Sino-American alliance in Asia. This confluence of factors shaped the milieu of Soviet decision-making. They were necessary, but not sufficient, conditions for intervention. The key determinant triggering the December 1979 decision was the deteriorating political situation within Afghanistan itself. Faced with an erratic PDPA regime under Amin and a growing insurgency threat, the Soviet leadership evidently concluded that only direct large-scale military intervention could forestall the collapse of a Marxist-Leninist regime in this strategically situated state on the USSR's southern border. The Brezhnev Politburo's decision to act upon this perceived imperative was buttressed by three key political calculations: first, the prevailing belief that the war would be short in duration; second, the recognition that the likely alternative to a PDPA government in Kabul would be an Islamic one—an outcome with uncertain implications for domestic stability in Soviet Central Asia; and third, the view that superpower relations had already deteriorated to such a point by late 1979 that there was indeed little left to forfeit in the bilateral relationship.

2. THE DECISION TO WITHDRAW

The Soviet decision to withdraw from Afghanistan reflects the complex and subtle interrelationship between domestic and foreign policy factors in Gorbachev's calculations. During the period between Brezhnev's death in November 1982 and Gorbachev's ascent to power in March 1985, there were no public indications of any reevaluation or serious debate over Soviet Afghan policy within the ruling oligarchy. At the Brezhnev funeral, Andropov did hint at some flexibility in the Soviet position when he told Pakistani President Zia ul-Haq that the Soviet Union would leave Afghanistan "quickly" if Pakistan ended its support for the mujaheddin. By and large, however, Soviet leadership statements and press commentaries merely echoed earlier pronouncements that the march toward socialism in Afghanistan was "irreversible." Despite these public affirmations, some criticism was directed at the Taraki-Amin regime that preceded Babrak Karmal in power; this included an acknowledgment that the harsh domestic measures adopted by Taraki and Amin had done much to generate the widespread popular opposition to PDPA rule that had necessitated direct Soviet military intervention.

The antecedents of the withdrawal decision date to the brief Andropov interregnum from 1982 to 1984—the period which Gorbachev later acknowledged had laid much of the groundwork for his strategy of domestic *perestroika* and "new thinking" in foreign policy. By the time Andropov assumed power, in November 1982, initial hopes that the Afghan war would be a short one had been dashed; the period of "military romanticism," as Alexandr Prokhanov has it, had ended.[28] The USSR's twin military and political strategies, far from producing their desired objectives, had led to stalemate. In its conduct of the ground war, the Soviet military had proved surprisingly slow in adapting to the challenge of counter-insurgency warfare within Afghanistan. Although it does have well-developed doctrines of mountain and desert warfare, the Red Army pursued the war as though it were operating on the European central front. Unlike the United States in Vietnam, the Soviet military did not attempt to exert control over the countryside; rather, emphasis was placed on the security of the major urban centers and the road network connecting them. The size of the USSR's "limited contingent" rose to 115,000 troops by early 1980 and remained constant at that level throughout the years of Soviet military involvement in Afghanistan. This force was large enough to forestall a mujaheddin victory over the PDPA, but proved insufficient (both in terms of size and choice of strategy) to quell the rebellion.

Moscow's political strategy was hamstrung by the ineffectual nature of the Karmal regime. The Afghan leader sought to legitimize his regime at home by repealing the extreme social measures that his Khalq predecessors had adopted and which had led to the large-scale disaffection of the Afghan populace. Given Karmal's identification with the Soviet occupation force, this "hearts and minds" campaign yielded no concrete political results. Likewise, no progress was made in revitalizing the two key institutional underpinnings of PDPA rule: the armed forces and the party. The DRA (Democratic Republic of Afghanistan) Army was militarily ineffective and politically unreliable; the constant problem of desertions and defections over to the guerrillas increased the Kabul regime's reliance on Soviet troops. Amidst this further deterioration of the DRA Army, the problem of fratricidal factionalism within the PDPA continued. Karmal's ruling Parcham faction dominated the major party and governmental organs (notably the KHAD, the Afghan intelligence service).

From 1980 to 1985, Soviet policy in Afghanistan was in a state of inertia. As noted above, there was very little effort to innovate on either the political or military levels. This can be explained, in large part, by the fact that throughout this period the Soviet leadership was preoccupied by a long, drawn-out succession struggle. The war in Afghanistan did not figure as a major factor in this process. Despite evidence that the stalemated conflict was becoming increasingly unpopular at home, Moscow's steady state policy kept its political and economic costs within tolerable limits. In his address to the CPSU Central Committee Plenum in June 1983, Andropov did express irritation with client regimes whose commitment to socialism appeared more rhetorical than real: "It is one thing to proclaim socialism, but another to build it."[29] Although this may have been a veiled reference to the PDPA regime, there was no explicit questioning of the political bases of Soviet policy in Afghanistan. One can only speculate whether Andropov would have initiated a fundamental change in Soviet Afghan policy had he lived. As it was, this radical reassessment awaited Gorbachev's ascension to power in March 1985.

In his February 1988 speech announcing the USSR's intention to withdraw from Afghanistan, Gorbachev stated that "[f]ollowing the CPSU Central Committee April [1985] Plenum, the Politburo conducted a hard and impartial analysis of the position and started even at that time to seek a way out of the situation."[30] This private reassessment was belied by Gorbachev's initial public statements on Afghanistan in which he indicated an intention to stay the course. For example, in a meeting with Pakistani President Zia following the funeral of Konstantin Chernenko, he warned against the dangers of continued Pakistani assistance to the mujaheddin and again affirmed that Afghanistan's transition to socialism was "irreversible." While maintaining this public posture, Gorbachev, as later acknowledged by the Soviet leader, sought to make major changes in the twin political and military strategies in Afghanistan that he had inherited. His effort to revitalize Soviet military strategy was symbolized by the appointment of General Mikhail Zaitsev, the young and energetic former commander of Soviet forces in East Germany, to command the USSR's "limited contingent."[31]

Under Zaitsev's direction, Soviet military tactics changed and military performance improved significantly. One particularly important change was the innovative use of helicopter gunships (e.g., the HIND Mi-24 and Mi-25) and special forces units (*spetznaz*). These capabilities permitted the Soviet military to operate deep behind mujaheddin lines. By mid-1986, the innovations implemented by Zaitsev were beginning to erode the military effectiveness of the resistance movement. Ironically, just as Soviet military performance was beginning to improve, the Reagan administration, after a prolonged period of deliberation, decided in April 1986 to provide the mujaheddin with Stinger anti-aircraft missiles. The provision of these new American weapons marked a turning point in the war.[32] The increased air losses that the Stingers produced forced the Soviet military command to drop the use both of helicopter gunships for deep penetration raids and of tactical aircraft for close ground support. In response to the Stinger threat, the Soviet military fell back onto old tactics that had failed to produce significant results during the earlier years of the war (i.e., increased reliance on artillery and high-level aerial bombardment). In short, the arrival of the Stingers brought an end to Zaitsev's activist strategy based on the mobile use of Soviet forces.

General Zaitsev's attempt to overhaul Soviet military strategy during 1985–86 was complemented by Moscow's adoption of a new political strategy to revitalize the PDPA regime. In early May 1986, the Soviets dropped the ineffectual Babrak Karmal in favor of Dr. Najibullah, a former top official in the KHAD. The "hearts and minds" campaign was intensified to try to increase public support for the new leadership in Kabul. Soviet press commentaries approvingly reported that "the social base" of the Afghan revolution was being expanded and drew sharp contrast with the "adventurist" strategy pursued by Taraki and Amin prior to the Soviet intervention.

Amidst these efforts to politically reconstitute Afghanistan, Gorbachev gave his first public hint that the withdrawal of Soviet military forces was perhaps being contemplated. In his political report to the CPSU's Twenty-Seventh Party Congress in February 1986, he dramatically described the Afghan as a "bleeding wound." At the time, the use of this phrase was taken as a sign of increasing Soviet frustration and fatigue with the war, but not as one indicating that a fundamental decision to cut losses and withdraw from the country had been taken. It should be noted that when Gorbachev made this statement, General Zaitsev was working assiduously through the implementation of a new military strategy to turn the ground war around. In addition, at the UN-sponsored negotiations on Afghanistan in Geneva, the Soviets maintained their long-standing insistence that any settlement must include guarantees for the continued survival of the PDPA regime. In retrospect, Gorbachev's candid characterization of the Afghan war in his Twenty-Seventh Party Congress address may have been a signal to the Soviet populace (which until then had heard only upbeat assessments from the Soviet leadership) and the PDPA regime itself that a change in Soviet policy was being contemplated. From the outside, however, it was at best a mixed signal because of what the Soviets were doing on the ground militarily in Afghanistan, their efforts to revitalize the PDPA regime politically, and their continued hard-line stance in the UN negotiations.

In January 1987, Foreign Minister Shevardnadze and Central Committee International Department Chief Anatoly Dobrynin visited Kabul in an attempt to break the political logjam. As noted above, the mission occurred against the backdrop of a deteriorating military situation within the country following the American transfer of Stinger missiles to the resistance. Following his meetings with Shevardnadze and Dobrynin, Najibullah issued proposals for an immediate cease fire and the formation of a "national reconciliation government" that would include elements of the mujaheddin. This overture was rejected out of hand by the resistance leadership from their base camps in the Pakistani border town of Peshawar. Six months after the Shevardnadze-Dobrynin visit, Najibullah went to Moscow for a comprehensive review with Gorbachev of the political and military situation within Afghanistan. It was reportedly at this July 1987 meeting that Gorbachev informed Najibullah that the Soviet leadership had decided upon a definite timetable for the withdrawal of Soviet forces from Afghanistan.[33] Shevardnadze hinted at this possibility in September 1987 when he publicly stated that the Kremlin hoped that Soviet troops would be out of the country before the end of the Reagan administration.

The real turning point in the UN-sponsored negotiations on Afghanistan came in November 1987 during a meeting between Soviet Deputy Foreign Minister Yuli Vorontsov and U.S. Undersecretary of State Michael Armacost in Geneva. It was in the course of those discussions that Vorontsov unveiled a decisive shift in the Soviet negotiating position. As noted above, until that time the Soviet delegation had steadfastly maintained the position that an Afghan settlement must include concrete guarantees for the continued survival of the PDPA regime in Kabul. For years, this issue—the composition of the post-settlement government in Kabul—had been the primary stumbling block precluding a settlement; differences over the timetable for a Soviet withdrawal had always been a secondary issue. When Vorontsov finally yielded on this point, the primary obstacle to the attainment of a settlement had been removed. Rapid progress in the Geneva negotiations permitted Gorbachev to publicly announce on 8 February 1988 that the USSR intended to withdraw all of its troops from Afghanistan over a twelve-month period with the initial pullback beginning as early as 15 May 1988.[34]

The final arrangements for the withdrawal of Soviet forces from Afghanistan were agreed upon by Gorbachev and Najibullah when they met in Tashkent on 7 April. One week later, on 14 April 1988, the foreign ministers of the United States, the Soviet Union, Afghanistan, and Pakistan met in Geneva to sign the UN-brokered agreement. The extent of Gorbachev's desire to conclude an Afghan accord was manifested in his willingness to accept a last minute American demand that the cutoff of military supplies to the Kabul regime and the resistance should be "symmetrical." This shift reflected a toughening of American terms for a settlement; the prior American position, articulated by Secretary of State George Shultz, had been that U.S. military assistance to the mujaheddin would be ended in tandem with a Soviet withdrawal from Afghanistan. By the end of July 1988, some 30 percent of the USSR's total 115,000-man force had reportedly been withdrawn.

One striking feature of the Soviet withdrawal decision was that it did not provoke an intense domestic debate over credibility and superpower responsibility of the kind that the United States experienced during the Vietnam War. While Gorbachev's program of radical domestic reform has come under intense criticism, the Afghan decision did not become a source of contention within the Soviet leadership. The decision to withdraw from Afghanistan was evidently a consensual one that was supported (or at least acquiesced to) by such noted hardliners as Yegor Ligachev. In addition to the civilian leadership, the military as an institution also appears to have been supportive of the withdrawal decision. In his address to the Nineteenth All-Union CPSU Conference in July 1988, General B.V. Gromov, the final commander of Soviet forces in Afghanistan, stated simply that Soviet forces were returning from the country after fulfilling their internationalist duty.[35]

Prior to the February 1988 withdrawal announcement, many Western analysts believed that a major factor militating against Soviet acceptance of a settlement was the impact that a foreign policy setback in Afghanistan might have on the stability of Gorbachev's position within the ruling oligarchy. In fact, over time, the impact of Soviet domestic politics on the Kremlin's Afghan policy cut precisely the other way. By the late 1980s, the adverse consequences of the conflict on Soviet society were more evident and were being discussed more openly, thanks to glasnost'. These problems included increased drug use and the return of thousands of disaffected veterans (*"Afgantsy"*) from the war. For the first time, public opinion, which by then had decisively swung against the war, became a major factor that the Soviet leadership had to take into consideration.[36] Within this context, Gorbachev must have increasingly viewed the war as a liability. The continued, demoralizing presence of Soviet forces in Afghanistan was undermining the support of key constituencies for his ambitious program of domestic reform—most notably, the youth and intellectuals. The success of perestroika relied upon the harnessing of a new voluntaristic spirit within the country, and continued warfare in Afghanistan threatened to undermine that political strategy.

External factors clearly shaped the political context within which the Soviet decision to withdraw from Afghanistan was taken. As discussed above, the situation within Afghanistan was at a military and political impasse. The PDPA, which remained divided by internecine party factionalism, proved unsuccessful in its efforts to woo non-communist coalition partners into the regime and thereby increase its public popularity. Militarily, the Reagan administration's decision to provide Stinger anti-aircraft missiles frustrated General Zaitsev's new tactics, and the Soviet military reverted to essentially a garrison strategy. While these developments were unfolding within Afghanistan, the Soviet Union continued to come under significant international pressure to withdraw its "limited contingent" from Afghanistan. These external factors were necessary prerequisites for a withdrawal decision. Had Soviet strategy proved successful in Afghanistan and had the international community acquiesced to the Soviet presence there, the pressure to reach this decision would have been eased considerably. Thus external (i.e., extra-Soviet) factors were necessary, but not in themselves sufficient, to bring about this decisive shift in Soviet policy.

The key determinant was the Gorbachev revolution that transformed the relationship between Soviet foreign and domestic policies through the adoption of a wholly new perspective on national security issues. Gorbachev has repeatedly stated that a primary objective of Soviet foreign policy is to serve the ends of domestic perestroika. Toward this end, the Soviet leader has assiduously attempted to foster a tranquil international environment within which his program of radical reform could be implemented at home. While Gorbachev's pivotal personal role in the decision to withdraw Soviet forces from Afghanistan should, of course, be fully acknowledged, it is important to bear in mind that he was part of a generational turnover in the leadership that brought with it a new perspective on security requirements.

During 1986–87, as the political and military stalemate in Afghanistan continued, Gorbachev had three options. The first option was to do something that his three predecessors had resisted—namely, escalate the fighting (perhaps including attacks on mujaheddin base camps in Pakistan) and increase the size of the USSR's "limited contingent" above the 115,000-man level. Such a move to up the ante of the conflict would have produced an immediate crisis with Washington in which the likely outcome would have been the Reagan administration's abandonment of détente and a renewed American arms buildup. Not only would military escalation have generated a superpower crisis, but it offered no assurance that the mujaheddin insurgency would be defeated. Under such conditions of renewed Cold War, it is inconceivable that Gorbachev could have pursued a program of domestic reform with any vigor.

The second option was to "stay the course" at the existing level of commitment. This alternative was equally untenable as a long-term strategy because of the debilitating social consequences of the Afghan war that threatened to undermine his ability to implement perestroika. As noted above, the war had already demoralized key constituencies that Gorbachev was depending upon to help spearhead domestic reform. In addition, with the more candid depictions of the war in the Soviet media following the advent of glasnost', public opinion began to turn against it. Many questioned whether the USSR could any longer continue to devote scarce economic resources, desperately needed at home, to the putative defense of socialism abroad. Because of glasnost', it had become impossible to conduct the war any longer in secret and hide the human and economic costs from public scrutiny.

If neither escalation nor staying the course were viable alternatives, the third and remaining course, ultimately adopted by Gorbachev, was the extrication of Soviet forces from Afghanistan—despite the admitted uncertainties and dangers. In taking this action, Soviet decision-makers had to accept the very real possibility that the PDPA regime would collapse (as American government specialists forecast) and that the likely successor regime would be dominated by the mujaheddin with their Islamic orientation. Soviet experts, however, in contrast to their American counterparts, believed that the Najibullah regime would stand a reasonable chance for survival after the withdrawal of the Red Army. This assessment was based on several key assumptions: first, that Najibullah's popularity within the country would rise with the departure of the Soviet occupation force, especially among those who wished to perpetuate a secular society and rejected the creation of an Islamic republic on the Iranian model; second, that the mujaheddin, without the political glue created by the Soviet presence, would fragment into an assortment of competing tribes and ethnic groups; and third, that the Soviet Union, even after the withdrawal of the Red Army, retained enormous military and economic resources to influence events within Afghanistan such that any regime in Kabul, of whatever political composition, would have to work out a pragmatic accommodation with Moscow.

The withdrawal option also offered tangible benefits in the foreign policy realm. The decision defused the regional conflict that had revitalized the Cold War in the early 1980s, and served to convince many skeptics in the West who had spoken of "litmus tests" that there was indeed real substance in Gorbachev's "new thinking" in foreign policy. The Soviet leader emerged from the conflict with enhanced international prestige. Moreover, while the decision reflected the final recognition of a failed policy, the withdrawal was carried out in an orderly fashion with no humiliation; Deputy Foreign Minister Vorontsov noted that there were no scenes of helicopters evacuating personnel from the roof of the Soviet embassy in Kabul. When General Gromov walked across the Friendship Bridge into Uzbekistan on 15 February 1989, he completed the withdrawal process. The human and economic costs of the eight-year war to the Soviet Union have been placed at 15,000 dead and $100 billion.[37] With the withdrawal of the USSR's "limited contingent," the Afghan conflict reverted back to the civil war that had precipitated the Soviet intervention.

3. THE POST-WITHDRAWAL PERIOD

Since the withdrawal of Soviet forces from Afghanistan, Western observers have been impressed by the staying power of the PDPA regime. In February 1989, most specialists, both in the governmental and academic communities, had predicted a rapid mujaheddin victory. This assessment had been based on the inability of Najibullah to broaden his government's popular base and the poor performance of the DRA Army. Given the dominant role played by the Red Army in the counter-insurgency campaign against the mujaheddin, few believed that the Kabul regime could survive in the absence of a large-scale Soviet presence. Certainly when Gorbachev decided to withdraw from Afghanistan, the collapse of the Najibullah regime had to be considered a strong possibility by Soviet planners.[38] That this has not happened can be attributed to a combination of factors.[39]

First, without the unifying presence of a Soviet occupation force, the guerrilla movement began to fragment. A particularly important rift developed between the mujaheddin commanders operating within Afghanistan and the Peshawar-based parties backed by Pakistan's Inter-Service Intelligence (ISI). Second, in addition to this primary political problem, the guerrillas have found it difficult to manage the military adjustment from guerrilla to conventional warfare. This inability was manifested, for example, during the siege of Jalalabad in March 1989. Third, the PDPA, now freed of the political liability of Soviet occupation forces, has improved its popular standing—particularly with those secularly oriented Afghans who fear the specter of a mujaheddin-run Islamic republic. Indeed, Najibullah has gone over to the political offensive, portraying himself as the standard bearer of Afghan nationalism and charging that the guerrillas are the pawns of a foreign power—Pakistan.

A fourth critical factor explaining the unanticipated success of the PDPA during the post-withdrawal period is the pattern of outside military assistance to the combatants. As will be recalled, the Reagan administration at the time of the April 1988 Geneva accords had pushed for Kremlin acceptance of "positive symmetry," under which both Moscow and Washington could continue to supply their respective allies. Since February 1989, the Soviets have maintained an air bridge of supplies to the PDPA regime estimated at some $300 million per month. At the same time, Washington, having advocated "positive symmetry," is now practicing "negative symmetry" by reducing its military assistance to the mujaheddin. With this development, the military balance has shifted in favor of the Kabul regime. To the surprise of many, including evidently the Bush administration, the Soviets have not simply cut their losses and permitted events to run their course.[40] Gorbachev has sought more than just a "decent interval" between the withdrawal of Soviet forces and whatever political fate might await Najibullah. Through tangible military and political support, he has endeavored to give this ally every means available to survive short of a direct Soviet ground presence.

Within this altered political and military context, a search for a diplomatic solution to the civil war in Afghanistan continues—and Moscow is strongly committed to that process. The Soviets, in seeking to preserve a role for the PDPA, have repeatedly emphasized that the United States has a joint interest with the Soviet Union in preventing the proliferation of Islamic republics on the Iranian model in the Middle East. Hopes that a political settlement might be near were buoyed in November 1990 with the report that Najibullah had met in Geneva with representatives of the Peshawar-based coalition. In his press conference announcing the meeting, the PDPA leader made no mention of resigning, as demanded by the resistance, but did indicate his support for the creation of a multi-party joint commission to oversee UN-sponsored elections. The mujaheddin subsequently denied that any of their representatives had met with the "puppet Najib."[41] The Afghan war was reportedly discussed during the several meetings between U.S. Secretary of State James Baker and Soviet Foreign Minister Shevardnadze that took place during the latter half of 1990. The American administration was, of course, preoccupied by the Gulf crisis throughout this period, but did hope that some progress could be made when Shevardnadze visited Houston on 10–11 December 1990. The primary impediment to a settlement is not the lack of superpower will, but rather the inability of the local parties to work out the terms of a political transition among themselves. Outside powers cannot impose a settlement on the regional actors. The mujaheddin remain intransigent that Najibullah must go, while the Soviet leadership sees no reason to accept this maximalist demand so long as the PDPA regime continues to hold its own both politically and militarily.

Given the end of the Cold War and the ideological framework that sustained it, what is the likely course of Soviet policy in Afghanistan? At a time of extreme economic and political crisis, when the very future of the Soviet Union itself is in question, foreign policy has been eclipsed by domestic concerns. To the extent that the Third World is an issue in Soviet policy, it is viewed as a problem—namely, how to reduce the economic burden. The one major exception to this general pattern of disengagement from the Third World is the southern border areas of the USSR, which will remain a zone of primary interest. Indeed, during a period when the status of the southern republics within a new confederation is in question, one could well argue that relations with Turkey, Iran, Afghanistan, and China will remain as important as ever. The status of these relationships could significantly affect Moscow's ability to deal with potential instability in its southern border republics. Here there is a clear linkage between Soviet foreign and domestic policies, particularly with respect to the USSR's nationalities problem. In the Soviet Central Asian republic of Uzbekistan, for example, the future status of the local leadership will in no small part be shaped by political outcomes in adjacent Afghanistan (i.e., whether Najibullah survives or is replaced by an Islamic-oriented regime).[42]

Given the current structure of American and Soviet interests, there is no objective impediment to broadly cooperative superpower policies in the Third World, including the southern border areas of the USSR. In the post–Cold War era, the danger of superpower conflict developing out of a regional dispute has diminished greatly. In the Western policy community, this was what gave such disputes their salience during the 1980s. One can only shudder to think what would have happened if the Iraqi invasion of Kuwait had happened in the political climate of the early 1980s. During the Gulf crisis, the legacy of the Soviet involvement in Afghanistan was in evidence. Some officials in Moscow, for example, claimed that an impediment to the USSR's participation in the multi-national coalition was public resistance to the deployment of Soviet forces abroad. At the same time, Moscow's multi-faceted diplomacy prior to the onset of the ground war in late February 1991 reflects the Soviet Union's continuing commitment to an activist policy in this key geographical zone along its southern border.

NOTES

1. This new approach was manifested in the Reagan Doctrine under which the United States funnelled military assistance to anti-Soviet insurgencies in the Third World, including the Afghan mujaheddin.

2. I have earlier examined many of these issues in a paper presented at the June 1990 conference on "Political-Military Intervention: From Commitment to Disengagement," co-sponsored by Tel Aviv University and the University of California at Davis.

3. See Cynthia Roberts, "*Glasnost'* in Soviet Foreign Policy: Setting the Record Straight?," *Report on the USSR* 1, no. 50 (15 December 1989), pp. 4–8.

4. A. Oliinik, "Vvod voisk v Afganistane: kak prinimalos' reshenie" (The introduction of troops in Afghanistan: how the decision was taken), *Krasnaya zvezda*, 18 November 1989, pp. 3–4.

5. *Ogonek*, no. 12, March 1989; reported in Michael Dobbs, "Soviet Dissent on Afghan War," *Washington Post*, 20 March 1989; see also Roberts (note 3), pp. 5–6.

6. For a detailed historical treatment of the Soviet-Afghan relationship, see Ludwig W. Adamec, *Afghanistan's Foreign Affairs to the Mid-Twentieth Century* (Tucson: University of Arizona Press, 1974).

7. Alvin Z. Rubinstein, *Soviet Policy Toward Turkey, Iran and Afghanistan: The Dynamic of Influence* (New York: Praeger, 1982), pp. 134–35.

8. This assistance included infrastructural developments (highways, etc.) that further solidified Soviet-Afghan relations and indeed later facilitated the December 1979 invasion. See Mahnaz Z. Ispahani, *Roads and Rivals: The Political Uses of Access in the Borderlands of Asia* (Ithaca, NY: Cornell University Press, 1989), pp. 126–41.

9. The development of the PDPA is discussed in Anthony Hyman, *Afghanistan Under Soviet Domination, 1964–83* (London: MacMillan Press, 1984), ch. 4.

10. *Ibid.*, pp. 80–81.

11. Henry S. Bradsher, *Afghanistan and the Soviet Union* (Durham, NC: Duke Press Policy Studies, 1984), p. 83.

12. See Rubinstein (note 7), pp. 159–68.

13. See Jiri Valenta, "Soviet Decisionmaking on Afghanistan, 1979," in *Soviet Decisionmaking for National Security*, eds. Jiri Valenta and William Potter (London: George Allen & Unwin, 1984), pp. 218–36.

14. Raymond L. Garthoff, *Détente and Confrontation: American-Soviet Relations from Nixon to Reagan* (Washington: Brookings Institution, 1985), pp. 902–5; Bradsher (note 11), pp. 103–4.

15. The evolution of Soviet Third World policy during this period is discussed in Francis Fukuyama, "The Rise and Fall of the Marxist-Leninist Vanguard Party," *Survey*, no. 2 (Summer 1985), pp. 122–27.

16. Thomas T. Hammond, *Red Flag Over Afghanistan: The Communist Coup, the Soviet Invasion, and the Consequences* (Boulder, CO: Westview Press, 1984), p. 98.

17. A. Petrov, "On Events in Afghanistan," *Pravda*, 31 December 1979; reprinted in *Current Digest of the Soviet Press* 31, 52 (23 January 1980), pp. 5–7. The Soviets accused Amin of developing "secret contacts" with Washington and Beijing. See, for example, P. Demchenko, "Afghanistan: Na strazhe zavoevaniy naroda" (Afghanistan: standing guard over the people's gains), *Kommunist*, no. 5 (March 1980), pp. 71–78.

18. *Pravda, 13 January 1980;* reprinted in *FBIS/Soviet Union*, 14 January 1980, pp. A1–A6.

19. According to Anatolii Gromyko, son of the late Foreign Minister, in an interview with correspondent Igor' Belyaev in *Literaturnaya gazeta*, 20 September 1989.

20. Speech entitled "Foreign Policy and Perestroika" by Foreign Minister Edouard Shevardnadze before the Supreme Soviet on 23 October 1989 in *FBIS/Soviet Union*, 24 October 1989, p. 45.

21. See Prokhanov's charge in *Literaturnaya gazeta*, 17 February 1988, and Bogomolov's response in *Literaturnaya gazeta*, 16 March 1988.

22. Garthoff (note 14), p. 917, cites confidential documents reconstructed by Iranian militants after the seizure of the U.S. embassy in Tehran.

23. See "Coups and Killings in Kabul: A KGB Defector Tells How Afghanistan Became Brezhnev's Vietnam," *Time*, 22 November 1982; discussed in Roberts (note 3), pp. 5–6; Garthoff (note 14), pp. 926–27.

24. *Krasnaya zvezda*, 18 November 1989; see note 3 above.

25. Cited in Roberts (note 3), p. 935.

26. Quoted in Eric Miller (rapporteur), "Beyond Afghanistan: Changing Soviet Perspectives on Regional Conflicts," p. 4—a 1990 conference report published by the Center for Naval Analyses, Alexandria, VA.

27. See, for example, G.A. Trofimenko, "Rukoi neposvyashchennoi" (By the uninitiated hand), *SShA*, no. 6 (1989), pp. 70–77.

28. Miller (note 26), p. 7.

29. *Pravda*, 16 June 1983; reprinted in *Current Digest of the Soviet Press* 35, 25, p. 8.

30. Gorbachev speech at the CPSU Central Committee Plenum on 18 February 1988 in *FBIS/Soviet Union*, 19 February 1988, p. 56.

31. For an analysis of Soviet military performance in the Gorbachev era, see Alexander Alexiev, *Inside the Soviet Army in Afghanistan*, no. R-3627-A (Santa Monica, CA: Rand Corporation, May 1988).

32. David B. Ottaway, "Stingers Were Key Weapon in Afghan War, Army Finds," *Washington Post*, 5 July 1989.

33. See Don Oberdorfer, "The Soviet Decision to Pull Out," *Washington Post*, 17 April 1988.

34. *Ibid.*

35. Gromov's speech appeared in *Krasnaya zvezda*, 2 July 1988.

36. See Sallie Wise, "The Soviet Public and the War in Afghanistan: Discontent Reaches Critical Levels," report no. AR 4-88, Radio Free Europe/Radio Liberty, May 1988.

37. Western casualty estimates were confirmed by Nodari Simoniya, a leading Soviet academic specialist on the Third World, in *FBIS-Soviet Union*, 19 May 1988, p. 22. The estimate of the economic costs was made by Foreign Minister Edouard Shevardnadze; see *Washington Post*, 27 May 1990. These figures may not be exact, but most observers believe they are of the right order of magnitude.

38. In a July 1988 issue of *Ogonek*, Major-General Kim M. Tsagolov offered a pessimistic assessment of the PDPA's prospects, predicting that the Kabul regime might collapse; reported in Bill Keller, "Soviet General Declares Kabul Could Collapse," *New York Times*, 24 July 1988. In contrast, Yuri Gankovsky, a top Afghan specialist at the Institute of Oriental Studies in Moscow, predicted that the Najibullah regime stood a reasonable chance of survival after the February 1989 withdrawal of Soviet forces.

39. For an assessment of the post-withdrawal period, see *Strategic Survey 1989–1990* (London: Brassey's for the International Institute for Strategic Studies, 1990), pp. 159–64.

40. David B. Ottaway, "U.S. Misread Gorbachev, Offical Says," *Washington Post*, 9 October 1989.

41. Reported in *Keesing's 1990*, 36, no. 11, p. 37855.

42. At this and other points in this section, I am indebted to Dr. Barnett Rubin of Columbia University.

SUPERPOWERS, REGIONAL POWERS, AND THE BALKANIZATION OF AFGHANISTAN

Selig S. Harrison

Despite the withdrawal of the last Soviet combat forces from Afghanistan in February 1988, Moscow and Washington are still embroiled in the intractable Afghan civil war that set the stage for the Soviet occupation. This continuing superpower involvement has in turn stimulated and facilitated intervention by increasingly assertive regional powers pursuing their own conflicting purposes. Initially polarized between narrowly based Communist and Islamic fundamentalist factions, the Afghan conflict has now become a broader and more complex process of social upheaval and territorial Balkanization. Gone is the loose but well-ordered unity of a traditional power structure based on the unchallenged control of tribal and ethnic patriarchs in their respective domains. Tribal and ethnic warlords must now compete for local power with some two hundred heavily armed resistance commanders, who are themselves competing for access to burgeoning economic and military assistance pipelines.

In this jungle of overlapping and frequently shifting jurisdictions, two major power groupings have emerged: the Soviet-supported Communist city-state in Kabul, with its dispersed outposts in Jalalabad, Herat, and Mazar-i-Sharif, and an American-subsidized network of local commanders in the eastern districts near Pakistan, linked primarily to Pakistani and Saudi Arabian intelligence agencies. Iran-backed factions are dominant in north-central Hazarajat and certain other Shia-majority areas, and orthodox Saudi Wahabi groups have been seeking with limited success to establish control of Kunar and surrounding eastern districts. However, most of the Afghan countryside, though awash with aid, is not firmly linked to either Kabul or any of its rivals.

While the disengagement of the superpowers would greatly reduce its intensity, the Afghan struggle could well continue indefinitely in any case, given the entrenched strength of the Kabul regime in its enclaves and the clashing goals of the regional powers involved. The Pakistani role in particular is driven by a sense of compelling geopolitical purpose.

In a conversation with me six weeks before his death, President Mohammed Zia Ul-Haq argued that Pakistan had earned the right as a "front-
line state" to pursue a sweeping postwar "strategic realignment" in
South Asia.[1]

Zia made no secret of his desire to install a Pakistani satellite state
in Kabul, reversing what he perceived as a pro-Indian, pro-Soviet tilt on
the part of prewar regimes. Zia's strategic objectives, still pursued by his
successors, explicitly included a pan-Islamic confederation linking Pakistan and Afghanistan that would influence and possibly annex the
adjacent Tajik and Uzbek areas of Soviet Central Asia. For the Soviet
Union, with its restive Central Asian republics, the possibility of a
fundamentalist-dominated Afghanistan has been a focus of serious concern. For India it has been even more alarming, since fundamentalist
leaders in Pakistan have made the liberation of Indian-held areas of
Kashmir a companion objective. Together with its activities in Afghanistan, the Pakistani Directorate of Interservices Intelligence (ISI) in Islamabad has since 1988 supported a Kashmir insurgency in which
American-equipped Afghan fundamentalist groups have been involved.

The Afghan conflict is inseparably linked with the overarching
struggle between India and Pakistan over the terms of the balance of
power in South Asia. Pakistan sees a secure rear in Afghanistan as a
key element in its defense posture against its giant neighbor. India, for
its part, views Pakistani policy in Afghanistan in the context of the
larger regional challenge posed by the rise of fundamentalist influence
in Islamabad following the ouster of Prime Minister Benazir Bhutto in
1990 and by the growth of the Pakistani armed forces resulting from
the flow of American military assistance to Islamabad during the
Afghan war years. To be sure, the United States froze its military aid
to Pakistan in 1990 following a rupture over the issue of Pakistan's
nuclear weapons program, and the Islamabad-Washington alliance was
further strained by the American role in the Persian Gulf war in early
1991. Although Pakistan sent token forces to Saudi Arabia after the
Iraqi occupation of Kuwait, the Army Chief of Staff, General Aslam
Baig, later condemned American military intervention against an Islamic
state, reflecting a widespread popular upsurge of anti-Americanism.
Nevertheless, New Delhi remained suspicious that the net effect of the
Gulf war would be to reinforce the alliance and thus American support
for the Pakistani role in Afghanistan. In Indian eyes, the wartime
establishment of American military bases in Saudi Arabia and other
Gulf states with military links to Islamabad makes it more important

than ever to support the Kabul Communist regime as a buffer against fundamentalist influence.

The prospects for a mutual termination of Soviet and American aid to Afghanistan—often described as "negative symmetry," a concept originally proposed by the United States in March 1988—depend upon the readiness of Pakistan, Saudi Arabia, Iran, and other regional powers to discontinue their own aid in conjunction with that of the superpowers. Barring such a comprehensive regional agreement, the Soviet Union, while continuing to promote the transition to a more broad-based Kabul regime, is not likely to end its military aid role. In order to understand the Soviet posture and project the future course of the conflict, it is first necessary to take a fresh look at the UN-mediated Geneva Accords, under which the Soviet Union agreed to withdraw in 1988 and, above all, at the reasons for the Soviet withdrawal.

From the outset of the UN negotiations Moscow emphasized its special geopolitical interest in Afghanistan as a country with which it shares a common border of more than 1,000 miles. The Geneva Accords were acceptable as a framework for the withdrawal precisely because they gave Moscow complete freedom of action in seeking to maximize future Soviet influence in Kabul. The accords were shaped within parameters solidly defined by *realpolitik*. By design, UN mediators focused on the goal of a complete withdrawal within a specified time, linked to a termination of foreign aid to the resistance. The replacement of the Kabul Communist regime with a more representative government was viewed from the outset of the Geneva negotiations as a companion goal but was relegated to a separate "second track."

This approach reflected a pragmatic judgment that the removal of foreign involvement in the Afghan civil war was a more realistic goal than the resolution of the conflict itself. But the United Nations also confronted a basic legal reality: the status of the Kabul regime as an accredited member of the General Assembly. As a party to the negotiations, the Communist regime could not be expected to participate in its own liquidation. More important, Moscow made clear that it would not join in an agreement requiring it to abandon the regime that it had intervened to defend or to cut off military assistance to Kabul.

In Soviet eyes, the projected withdrawal itself was viewed as a momentous concession that would inevitably be perceived as a retreat. Thus the essential tradeoff in the accords—i.e., a complete pullout within an agreed period in exchange for a U.S. cessation of aid to the resistance—

was perceived as an equitable bargain. Apart from the legal distinction between a UN member-state and an insurgent movement, realpolitik made it necessary for the United Nations to ignore the issue of Soviet military aid to a client regime in a neighboring state.

Despite their asymmetrical character, the emerging accords were provisionally accepted by the United States in December 1985, subject to agreement on a satisfactory withdrawal timetable. Moreover, the projected aid cutoff, coincident with the start of the withdrawal, was explicitly defended by Secretary of State George Shultz in Senate Armed Services Committee testimony. Badgered by Republican Senator Gordon Humphrey of New Hampshire, a leading critic of the accords, Shultz argued that the cutoff would be acceptable if the withdrawal schedule was "front-loaded and fast." He added that the resistance groups would have sufficient stockpiles inside Afghanistan before the agreement entered into force "and would be able to give an account of themselves without being further supplied."[2]

It was not until the end game in March 1988 that the Reagan administration upped the ante by demanding a termination of Soviet military aid to the Kabul regime. Significantly, however, while the United States unilaterally asserted its right to provide further aid to the resistance if the Soviet Union continued to aid Kabul, the concept of "positive symmetry" was not incorporated into the Geneva Accords. The U.S. position was presented to the Soviet Union in a letter on 9 April. Moscow, replying on 10 April, implicitly acknowledged the U.S. stand but did not accept it, notwithstanding administration efforts to make it appear that Moscow had done so. Indeed Senator Humphrey, stating that the unpublished exchange of letters had been shown to Congressional committees, alleged on 6 October 1988 that the Soviet reply "rejected the State Department's claim to a unilateral right to continue aid."[3]

In retrospect, just as the asymmetrical character of the accords was necessitated by the facts of life in Moscow, so the administration's use of "positive symmetry" to placate Congressional critics may well have been unavoidable in the face of political realities in Washington. The critical fact is that the Reagan administration did sign the accords in the face of opposition from critics who wanted to keep the Soviet Union pinned down or, at the very least, to condition an agreement on prior replacement of the Communist regime.

The withdrawal is often attributed exclusively to the bravery of the Afghan resistance and the firepower provided by American weaponry. But a balanced assessment shows that it resulted from a combination of military pressure and effective diplomacy.[4] Militarily the Soviet Union was stalemated, not defeated. Soviet forces did not retreat in the wake of a Waterloo or a Dien Bien Phu. To be sure, the deployment of Stinger missiles and other sophisticated American weaponry had a major impact on Soviet military strategy. Soviet forces were compelled to downgrade aggressive offensive operations that required close air support, especially the use of helicopters to transport troops. The Red Army was forced to return to its initial holding strategy of protecting urban centers and transportation networks. However, to equate the resulting stalemate with a defeat would be a gross distortion. Soviet forces were securely entrenched throughout the country when the Geneva Accords were signed.

The withdrawal decision was clearly governed in part by the economic and military costs of the war, as well as by strong domestic anti-war pressures. But in his cost-benefit calculus, the decisive consideration for General Secretary Mikhail Gorbachev appears to have been his new diplomatic priorities. Soviet pronouncements have emphasized that the Afghan withdrawal reflected a broad reappraisal of the global economic and political environment confronting the Soviet Union. In Gorbachev's "new thinking," Soviet interests required a relaxation of international tensions that would open the way for a reduction of defense spending and an influx of critically needed technology and credits, especially from Western Europe, the United States, and Japan. The Afghan withdrawal was perceived as essential for the achievement of these objectives as well as for new relationships with two critically important neighbors, China and Iran.

Gorbachev, unlike his predecessors, was prepared to risk the collapse of the Kabul regime. This explains why he went ahead with the withdrawal even when the United States reneged on its initial acceptance of the asymmetrical military aid formula in the accords. In the light of events since 1988, however, it is still more significant that he was not prepared for a "negative symmetry" agreement when the United States proposed one on the eve of the accords. Moscow was gambling that the Kabul regime, with continued support, might show greater staying power than generally expected.

In explaining why the regime has in fact survived, many observers have focused solely on military factors: massive Soviet military aid, effective Soviet training of the Communist-armed forces, Kabul's monopoly of air power, and the inability of resistance groups trained for hit-and-run guerrilla warfare to carry on conventional warfare against

Communist-led regular forces entrenched in fortified cities. All of these factors are important, but another, increasingly critical reason for Kabul's strength is that it has capitalized on nationalist antipathy toward resistance groups tarred by identification with Pakistan.

In my contacts with Afghan Communists over several decades, including visits to Kabul in 1978 and 1984 after they took power, I have been impressed with their dedication and patriotic self-image.[5] They see themselves as nationalists and modernizers carrying forward the abortive modernization effort launched by the reformist King Amanullah from 1919 to 1929. During the Soviet occupation, they rationalized their collaboration with the USSR as the only way available to consolidate their revolution in the face of foreign "interference." Most other Afghans will not easily forget and will certainly not forgive their collaboration. Since the Soviet force withdrawal, however, the Communists have successfully used nationalist appeals to temper the bitterness left over from the war years.

The turning point for Kabul in its psychological warfare with the resistance came when the Pakistani ISI and its fundamentalist allies in the resistance created the Afghan Interim Government (AIG) in their own image at a *shura*, or council, near Islamabad in February 1989. The fact that the gathering was held in Pakistani territory was itself damaging. But the world press also emphasized the heavy hand of ISI agents in rigging the proceedings and buying votes.[6] Three months later, when the resistance launched its abortive offensive against Jalalabad, angry Afghan commanders openly accused the ISI of pushing them into premature action that had needlessly sacrificed Afghan lives.

The fact that identification with Pakistan is a kiss of death among many Afghans was underlined when one of President Najibullah's key generals led an unsuccessful coup attempt against him in early 1990. At first, it looked as if the coup leader, Shahnawaz Tanai, might rally significant support. But Najibullah was able to discredit the coup easily by pointing to credible evidence of Pakistani complicity.[7]

The impotence of the AIG since early 1989 has reflected a basic division within the resistance between Pakistan-supported and Pakistan-based fundamentalist factions, on the one hand, and a wide range of Afghan nationalist forces on the other, including local commanders inside the country; leaders of the Pushtun tribes, Afghanistan's dominant ethnic group; respected figures associated with earlier regimes, notably former King Zahir Shah; and Shia resistance leaders who do not want to see a Sunni fundamentalist regime. This division reflects a basic social cleavage between the fundamentalists and the traditional Muslim leadership in Afghanistan. It is reinforced by deeply rooted historical animosities between Pakistan and Afghanistan that have led Islamabad to view the Pushtuns with suspicion and to build up anti-Pushtun minorities as Pakistani surrogates.

The established clergy in Afghanistan is identified with the Hanafi school of Islamic law and various Sufi sects. The power of the local mullah is reinforced by a symbiotic relationship with Pushtun tribal chieftains. By contrast, the fundamentalist groups, preaching more purist Islamic doctrines, are seeking to destroy the tribal system as incompatible with their concept of a centralized Islamic state linked to a pan-Islamic revival. Rejecting Afghan nationalism, they argue that Islam knows no national borders. They oppose most of the modernization measures initiated by previous regimes, especially those liberalizing the status of women.

There are three nonfundamentalist resistance groups, which work closely with the Pushtun tribes. By contrast, the Jamiat Islami is rooted primarily in the Tajiks, an ethnic minority. The ISI-supported Hezbe Islami embraces both Tajiks and detribalized Pushtuns from migrant families in northern Afghanistan no longer attached to the tribal structure. Given their lack of a strong social base inside the country and the rejection of fundamentalist doctrine by the traditional Afghan Islamic leadership, the fundamentalists do not have large territorial strongholds in Afghanistan except in the Tajik-dominated Pansjer Valley, where a local Jamiat Islami leader had built a potent local political machine on an ethnic basis before the war. As the conduit for U.S. and other foreign aid, the ISI has given some help to all of the resistance groups but has downgraded Pushtun elements and favored the fundamentalists, especially the Hezbe Islami.

Numbering at most 1,100 in the early 1970s, the Afghan fundamentalists faced severe repression under King Zahir Shah and during the republic which followed under Mohammed Daud. In 1975 most of them fled to Pakistan. There they linked up with the ISI, staging raids against the Daud regime, then at odds with Pakistan. Their ISI connections were already well established when the Afghan Communists staged their 1978 coup. As Islamabad's favored Afghan proteges, they have grown both financially and militarily, but their political influence inside Afghanistan remains negligible, especially in Pushtun areas.

The roots of Pakistan's animus toward the Pushtuns dates back to the early nineteenth century, when the original Afghan state created in

1747 by the Pushtun tribes under Ahmad Shah Durrani embraced the Pushtun areas of what is now northwest Pakistan. Later, as part of the "Great Game," the British Raj annexed 40,000 square miles of Afghan territory between the Indus River and the Khyber Pass. It was adding insult to injury when the British imposed the Durand Line in 1893, formalizing their conquest, and then proceeded to hand over their ill-gotten territorial gains and half the Pushtun population to the new Pakistani government in 1947. By dividing the Pushtuns, the British bequeathed an issue that has preoccupied Pushtun-dominated Afghan regimes ever since and has poisoned the relations between Afghanistan and Pakistan.

At various times, Zahir Shah's monarchy, Mohammed Daud's republic, and post-1978 Communist governments in Kabul have all challenged Pakistan's right to rule over its Pushtun areas. Against this background, Pakistan's approach to the Afghan war has been dominated by its desire to prevent the emergence of a unified, armed Pushtun force on its territory. It is the historic Afghan-Pakistani conflict over the Pushtun areas that explains why the ISI has consistently downgraded resistance groups linked to the Pushtun tribal structure, channeling most American aid to fundamentalist groups that share its opposition to the restoration of Pushtun dominance.[8]*

In my conversation with Zia, he emphasized that he regarded the Geneva Accords as a setback for Pakistan.[9] The United States, he declared, should have heeded his advice by insisting on the removal of the Communist regime in Kabul as a condition for conclusion of the accords. Even if this had meant the breakdown of the settlement process in April, the Soviets "would have come back sooner or later. Gorbachev pulled a fast one by agreeing to the withdrawal with the regime in place, and the bait was swallowed." Zia frankly defined his goal in Afghanistan as "a very friendly regime":

> By helping you we have earned the right to have a regime to our liking. We took risks as a front-line state, and we won't permit it to be like it was before, with Indian and Soviet influence there and claims

---

*One Pushtun group that has received ISI aid is that of Yunus Khalis, who has links with the Khogianis, a subtribe affiliated with the Ghilzai wing of the Pushtuns. Some observers have noted that fundamentalist leader Gulbuddin Hekmatyar is also a Ghilzai. However, Hekmatyar and those of his followers who are Ghilzais are detribalized Pushtuns from migrant families in the north no longer affiliated with the Pushtun tribal power structure.

on our territory. It will be a real Islamic state, part of a pan-Islamic revival that will one day win over the Muslims in the Soviet Union.

In the confederation that Zia envisaged, Pakistanis and Afghans could travel back and forth freely without passports, and "who knows, perhaps one day Turkey and Iran may join, even Tajikistan and Uzbekistan."

Zia's ghost has continued to dominate Pakistani—and American— policy in Afghanistan since his death. The elaborate ISI structure that he built up with American help still exercises largely unrestrained control over weapons aid and technical support for the resistance, successfully resisting civilian pressures for a new Afghan policy.

In March 1989 Air Marshal Zulfiqar Ali Khan, former head of the air force who later became ambassador to Washington, met with ISI Director Hamid Gul. The air marshal had just been appointed to review the structure of Pakistani intelligence agencies by newly elected Prime Minister Benazir Bhutto. In an interview, he recalled having argued that Pakistan should require Afghan resistance groups receiving its aid to recognize the Durand Line, the disputed Afghan-Pakistani border demarcated by Britain. "We don't need to," replied Gul. "Our border will be the Oxus."

Before her election, Bhutto had repeatedly criticized Zia's Afghan ambitions, calling for negotiations to create a broad-based compromise regime in Kabul dominated neither by the Communists nor the fundamentalists. Pakistan's interests require such a government, she told me in late June 1988, since "continued civil war means the continued presence of three million refugees." Bhutto said flatly that the Afghan fundamentalists "do not have enough popular support to establish a stable regime." In a subsequent July interview with *The Nation* (Lahore), she warned more explicitly that efforts to establish a Pakistani satellite state in Kabul might stir up a Pushtun backlash:

> It is dangerous to go in for a Greater Pakistan because that can invite counter-moves for a Greater Afghanistan [from Pushtuns on both sides of the border]. Continued civil war would mean that some Afghan nationalist can get up and say, well, this side of the border there are Afghans and that side of the border there are Afghans, and hence we are for Greater Afghanistan.

Markedly diluting her position, Bhutto moved cautiously after her election to avoid a showdown with ISI that she feared would trigger an army attempt to unseat her. Under Zia, ISI had become a Pakistani-style blend of the CIA, the FBI, and the powerful Savak developed by the late

Shah Mohammed Reza Pahlevi in Iran. In addition to expanding its foreign intelligence machinery, Zia had systematically built up a vast, ubiquitous apparatus of agents inside the country that he often used against his political opponents. Despite Bhutto's replacement of Gul as director with Shamsur Kallu, the ISI leadership bequeathed by Zia remained largely intact during her tenure, and she made no serious attempt to gain control over Afghanistan policy.

For Pakistani generals who dream of a satellite state in Kabul, nationalism and the geopolitical goal of balancing Indian power have been the driving motives. For their allies among Pakistani fundamentalist leaders, however, Afghanistan is merely one important theater in a grander pan-Islamic struggle. The combined impact of the Islamic movements in Afghanistan, Kashmir, and Soviet Central Asia, writes a leading Pakistani journalist, Ahmed Rashid, "have led to a resurgence amongst Pakistani Islamic fundamentalist parties, who are hoping to turn Pakistan into the base area of an Islamic upsurge in the entire region."[10] Agha Murtaza Pooya, Information Secretary of the Combined Opposition Party and publisher of *The Muslim*, a leading Islamabad daily, declared that "as the foremost Muslim country in the region, the onus is on us to help coordinate such movements, especially in Central Asia."[11]

With its four million Tajiks, northern Afghanistan is an especially tempting "base area" for the subversion of Soviet Tajikistan. The Soviet ambassador in Kabul formally accused the CIA and the ISI in early 1990 of sending weapons, money, and propaganda materials into Soviet Tajik areas, utilizing the ISI-sponsored Union of Northern Afghan Peoples. A defector from the Soviet armed forces was sentenced to an eight-year jail term for allegedly working as an ISI agent to create an Islamic underground in Tajikistan.[12] Pakistani interest in Central Asia was underlined when an Australian Defense Academy specialist reported after a visit to the Pakistani-Afghan border that "some generals would like to extend their strategic borders into Soviet territory through Afghanistan."[13]

When Ahmed Rashid visited Uzbekistan in July 1990, he heard reports that the Hezbe Islami was stockpiling arms in the Fergana Valley to support the new "Islamic Party," which calls for a federation of Central Asian republics independent of Moscow. Uzbek students expressed fears to Rashid of a possible power struggle in the new group between elements favoring a pan-Turkic grouping, oriented to Ankara, and Sunni fundamentalist forces linked to Pakistan and Saudi Arabia.[14]

The linkage between Afghanistan and Kashmir in Pakistani fundamentalist rhetoric has been paralleled by a long-standing organizational integration of ISI Afghan and Kashmiri operations. After a visit to Muzaffarabad, the capital of Pakistan-occupied Kashmir, the correspondent of *The Guardian* of Manchester reported that

> the links between the Afghan and Kashmiri jihad are well-established. Between 1,000 and 2,000 Kashmiris are said to have fought in the Afghan war since 1986, thus providing the struggle with an experienced corps of veterans. Foreign volunteers inside Afghanistan, bored with a rundown jihad there, are looking for a fresh field of action. Arabs have been sighted loitering on Muzaffarabad street corners outside the new offices of the Kashmiri guerrillas.[15]

The degree of ISI integration between the Afghan and Kashmiri fronts remains unclear. Indian officials have frequently emphasized this linkage to show that American weaponry intended for Afghanistan has been diverted to Kashmir. However, a secret Indian intelligence report circulated among key members of the U.S. Congress cited only one specific case in point, that of a Kashmiri who told interrogators of procuring arms and receiving a month of military training in late 1988 at an Afghan Hezbe Islami camp on the Afghan border, in addition to other training in Pakistan-occupied areas of Kashmir.[16] The report asserted that the "identity cards of Afghan *mujahideen* belonging to Hezbe Islami were intercepted while they were crossing over into Indian territory from Pakistan."[17] Since Hezbe Islami has a tight working relationship with ISI and totally depends on its support, this allegation points directly to ISI integration of its Afghan and Kashmir operations. However, it is not substantiated. The president of Pakistani-occupied Kashmir, Abdul Qayyum Khan, told the *New York Times* in January 1990 that "a big number of youngsters from both parts of Kashmir have been fighting with the Afghan mujahideen for many months, and most of them have now gone back with weapons."[18] Without citing its sources, a U.S. Congressional staff study reported that since Zia's death in 1988,

> ISI has increasingly used its Afghans for diversified operations ranging from "settling scores" to training Sikhs and Kashmiris to conduct "deniable" special operations inside India's Kashmir. With the escalation of the ISI-supported, if not ISI-incited, insurgency in Kashmir, this Afghan force has been further expanded.[19]

In a climate of growing Indo-Pakistani tension, fanned by the Kashmir insurgency, Indian concern over the fate of Afghanistan will grow, especially in the context of continuing U.S. military aid to Islamabad. In Indian eyes, Pakistan has cynically exploited the Afghan issue for the past decade to improve its balance of power with New Delhi through U.S. aid. This has posed a more immediate security threat than the hypothetical danger of a direct Soviet move into the subcontinent. Behind the Indian perception lay an assessment of the events leading up to the occupation in which Afghan-specific factors were emphasized and the concept of a Soviet push to the "warm waters" was discounted.

As the quality and quantity of U.S. military aid to Islamabad was upgraded, India coupled its criticisms of the Soviet presence with equally sharp or sharper objections to the American role in aiding the resistance. Indian perceptions of the Afghan struggle have also been strongly influenced by the fact that so much of the U.S. aid to the resistance has gone to fundamentalist cadres linked to the Rabitat al-Alam al-Islami and other well-financed orthodox Wahabi groups in Saudi Arabia, as well as to the Moslem Brotherhood and the Khomeini regime in Iran. As pan-Islamic forces in the Middle East and Persian Gulf have consolidated their influence in the resistance, in concert with their long-standing hold over Pakistani fundamentalist groups, India has increasingly identified its interests with the Kabul regime. In the Indian calculus, Kabul is a barrier to an emerging Afghan-Pakistani fundamentalist combination that could link up, in time, with Saudi-financed fundamentalist groups operating among the Indian Muslims.

The financial impact of Saudi Arabia has been powerful in helping the United States to sustain its massive military aid pipeline through Pakistan. In addition to some $2 billion in Congressionally appropriated U.S. weapons aid, Riyadh has contributed at least another $1 billion. For example, leaks from Congressional intelligence committees have suggested that Saudi aid totaled $525 million in 1985 and 1986 and $435 million in 1989.[20] Politically, however, Saudi efforts to use aid leverage to establish independent political beachheads in Afghanistan have produced dubious results. Despite lavish spending, the Wahabi-backed Salafi party has faced continuing local opposition in Kunar district.[21] Representatives of the Rabitat and other Wahabi groups have encountered stiff doctrinal opposition not only from Afghans, but also from rival Arab fundamentalist groups, notably the Muslim Brotherhood. Afghan antagonism toward Rabitat increased when it was blamed for the 1989 assassination of a well-known Brotherhood operative, Abdullah Ezzam, who had a loyal following among Wahabi fundamentalist leaders.

In contrast to Saudi activities in Afghanistan, carried out from afar through Pakistan, Iran has direct physical access along a 950-mile border. Iranian efforts to project power in Afghanistan have long been primarily targeted on the sprawling north-central Hazara region, with a population variously estimated from 2 to 4 million and possibly more.[22] Thousands of Hazaras and other Shias from areas closer to the border have been going back and forth to Iran as migratory workers since the 1960s, and a majority of the Hazara Muslim clergy have traditionally studied in Shia institutions in Iran and Iraq.

Following the Communist takeover in 1978, Hazara leaders immediately rebelled against centralizing measures that challenged their long-established autonomy, forming a United Islamic Council under Sayed Behesti to counter Kabul's incursions. Dominated by the traditional landowning elite, the council was rapidly pushed aside in the aftermath of the Soviet occupation and the Iranian Revolution. Teheran initially supported an existing orthodox Shia Hazara party, Sazman-i-Nasr, that professed loyalty to the Ayatollah Khomeini. But by 1982 Iran had decided to form its own group, Sepah-i-Pasdaran, manned largely by returning Hazara migrants and theologians trained in Iran.

As Arthur Bonner observes, despite Nasr's Shia orthodoxy, Teheran "wanted to counter its nationalistic tendencies and assure complete domination by Iran."[23] With Iranian backing, Nasr and Sepah rapidly dominated the Hazara scene, devoting more attention to liquidating their rivals than to countering Soviet forces.[24] By 1984 most Hazara areas were under effective Iranian control, a pattern that still continues. Remittances from Hazara workers in Iran reinforce ties with Teheran. Behesti and some non-Hazara Shia leaders such as Asaf Mohseni are making desultory efforts to oppose Iranian influence, advocating a federated Afghanistan in which Shia areas would enjoy wide autonomy. But they appear to be losing ground. "Nasr and Sepah don't want the unity of Afghanistan," one of Behesti's lieutenants told Bonner. "They don't even think of the motherland. They want to collect all of the Shias into an international empire of the Shias."[25]

Pakistani and Saudi efforts to promote a Sunni fundamentalist regime in Kabul have aroused predictable Iranian resistance. Teheran has consistently pushed Shia groups to take a hard line in bargaining over the terms of Shia representation in the AIG. This has led to the repeated failure of efforts to bring Shia resistance groups into the AIG framework. Significantly, by helping to deny the AIG legitimacy, Teheran has reinforced its broader diplomatic effort since 1988 to moderate tensions with the Soviet Union. While continuing to reaffirm the goal of an Islamic Afghanistan, Iran is not actively assisting military operations against the Kabul regime, and Kabul has reciprocated by treating the Hazara areas, for all practical purposes, as an Iranian sphere of influence.

For nearly a decade the war in Afghanistan attracted world attention primarily as a dangerous flashpoint of the superpower rivalry and secondarily as a human tragedy of enormous magnitude for the Afghan people. But there has been relatively little recognition of the profound impact of the war on the South Asian region. This impact has not been limited to the immediate social and political problems created for Pakistan by the refugee influx and its accompanying growth of smuggling, narcotics trafficking, and black marketing in weaponry. Zia was able to use the Afghan specter to justify and prolong his military rule. The war also provided a rationale for the renewal of American military assistance to Islamabad, which in turn prompted India to increase its own military spending in order to maintain what it considers an acceptable margin of military superiority. Against the background of an accelerated Indo-Pakistani conventional arms race, the pressures for a nuclear military capability in both countries have greatly intensified. Moreover, by poisoning the atmosphere of Indo-Pakistani relations, the Afghan conflict has impeded the hopeful effort led by Bangladesh to create a larger regional unity in the form of the South Asian Association for Regional Cooperation (SAARC).

Progress toward arms control in the Indian Ocean was directly undermined by the Soviet occupation. Other factors also contributed to the escalation in the superpower military rivalry in the Indian Ocean and the Persian Gulf after 1977. But it was the Soviet occupation that finally led the Carter administration to break off the hopeful Soviet-American negotiations on Indian Ocean arms control initiated during 1977 and 1978.[26]

As efforts to promote a political settlement proceed, the basic dilemma confronting Moscow and Washington alike is that neither the Kabul regime nor the AIG, the government-in-exile established by Pakistan and the United States, represents the majority of Afghans. Neither can serve as the nucleus of a broad-based regime because both bear the stigma of foreign parentage.

The challenge confronting the international community is to create new, independent processes of intra-Afghan political dialogue and accommodation that will give equitable representation to the unorganized, voiceless majority in shaping a political settlement. Such processes would swamp both the Communists and the fundamentalists, who now enjoy a degree of importance out of all proportion to their following. The secretary general of the United Nations is uniquely positioned to set in motion what would necessarily be a protracted search for a political solution. His efforts would not be likely to succeed, however, unless the United States and the Soviet Union are able to negotiate a mutually acceptable agreement to terminate military aid.

The Soviet Union is likely to accept negative symmetry, but, as noted above, only if it is part of an overall regional agreement in which Pakistan, Saudi Arabia, and Iran cooperate.[27] Such an agreement could be achieved if the superpowers made it a compelling priority and used their maximum leverage. Whether it would be observed, given the interests of the regional powers involved, is another matter. Nevertheless, the attempt should be made, together with a sustained UN effort to promote the establishment of a broad-based central government. Success in the UN effort would presuppose not only the complete military disengagement of the superpowers, but also their economic support for a multilateral effort to carry out the awesome tasks of reconstruction.[28] Just as the process of Balkanization has been accelerated by the influx of aid into the hands of local warlords, so it can be reversed most effectively by channeling future aid resources to the Afghan people through an internationally recognized central authority.

NOTES

1. Selig S. Harrison, "Avoiding Afghan Civil War," *New York Times*, 14 November 1988, p. A23. The conversation with Zia was on 29 June 1988.

2. *National Security Strategy*; Hearings before the Committee on Armed Services, United States Senate, One Hundredth Congress, First Session, 3 February 1987 (Washington, D.C.: U.S. Government Printing Office), p. 822.

3. Gordon Humphrey, "'Afghan Model' A Disaster?," *Washington Times*, 6 October 1988, p. F4.

4. This assessment is elaborated in Selig S. Harrison, "Inside the Afghan Talks," *Foreign Policy* 72 (Fall 1988): 31–60.

5. See Selig S. Harrison, "Afghanistan: Soviet Intervention, Afghan Resistance and the American Role," in *Low Intensity Warfare: Counterinsurgency, Proinsurgency*

and Anti-Terrorism in the Eighties, ed. Michael T. Klare and Peter Kornbluh (New York: Pantheon, 1988), pp. 183–206.

6. For example, see Christina Lamb, "Shura Decision Exposes Deep and Bitter Divisions," *Financial Times,* 24 February 1989, p. 10, and James Rupert, "Key Afghan Rebel Attack Delayed by Quarrel Over Strategy," *Washington Post,* 25 February 1989, p. A15.

7. In "Afghanistan: A Propitious Time for a Superpower Pact," *International Herald Tribune,* 6 April 1990, I discuss this evidence. See also Richard Mackenzie, "Pitfalls on the Path to Kabul," *Insight,* 9 April 1990, esp. p. 14.

8. See my discussion of the origins of Pakistani conflict with Afghanistan over the Pushtun areas in "Ethnicity and the Political Stalemate in Pakistan," in *The State, Religion and Ethnic Politics: Afghanistan, Iran and Pakistan,* ed. Ali Banuazizi and Myron Weiner (Syracuse: Syracuse University Press, 1986), esp. pp. 285–96.

9. Pakistani opposition to the accords is discussed in Harrison, "Inside the Afghan Talks," pp. 56–57.

10. Ahmed Rashid, "Fundamentalism in Pakistan," *The Friday Times* (Lahore), 8–14 March 1990, p. 8.

11. *Ibid.*

12. *Ibid.*

13. William Maley, as paraphrased by Barbara Crossette, "Central Asia Rediscovers Its Identity," *New York Times,* 24 June 1990, p. E3.

14. Ahmed Rashid, "Central Asia: A New Awakening," *The Herald* (Karachi), July 1990, pp. 106–7. See also Graham Fuller, "The Emergence of Central Asia," *Foreign Policy,* Winter 1989–90, esp. pp. 51, 61, and 64, for a discussion of the interaction of Afghanistan and Central Asia.

15. Kathy Evans, "New Jihad Follows the Pattern Set by the Afghan Rebels, Though It Lacks American Money," *The Guardian,* 1 May 1990, p. 3.

16. The unpublished secret report, "Involvement of Pakistan as Revealed in the Interrogation of Important Extremists of Jammu and Kashmir," pp. 4–5, cites the case of Abdul Rashid Jatal, code name Manzoor, arrested on 29 August 1989.

17. *Ibid.,* p. 14.

18. Barbara Crossette, "Protesters in Pakistan Vow to Free Kashmiris in India," *New York Times,* 27 January 1990, p. 5. Qayyum Khan made similar statements in an interview with the Karachi weekly *Newsline,* 24 September 1990, p. 6.

19. "Pakistan's Afghan Army"; Task Force on Terrorism and Unconventional Warfare, House Republican Research Committee, U.S. House of Representatives, 17 April 1990, p. 3.

20. Walter Pincus, "Iran Arms Cash Is Tied to C.I.A.-Run Account Aiding Afghan Rebels," and Bob Woodward, "Saudis Gave $500 Million in Afghan Aid," both in *"Washington Post,* 3 December 1986.

21. "Election in Kunar," *Monthly Bulletin*, no. 108 (March 1990), Afghan Information Center, Peshawar, Pakistan, pp. 11–14.

22. Jan Heeren Grevemeyer, "The Dual War: The Afghan Hazaras Between Resistance and Civil War," *Arbeitsheft* (Berlin: Berliner Institut für Vergleichende Sozialforschung, 6 October 1985), p. 4.

23. Arthur Bonner, *Among the Afghans* (Durham and London: Duke University Press, 1987), p. 325.

24. Jean-Jose Puig, "Voyage en Hazaradjat et au Pandjshir avec Jean-Jose Puig," in *Les Nouvelles d'Afghanistan* 17 (1984): 15–16. See also Olivier Roy: "Retour d'Afghanistan: Le cinquieme voyage," *Defis afghans* 1 (1984): 8–9, and "La Situation au Hazaradjat: La Choura," *Les Nouvelles d'Afghanistan* 16 (1984): 10–12.

25. Bonner, p. 328.

26. See my extended discussion of Indian Ocean arms control in relation to Afghanistan in *Superpower Rivalry in the Indian Ocean: Indian and American Perspectives*, ed. Selig S. Harrison and K. Subrahmanyam (New York: Oxford University Press, 1989), esp. pp. 278–83.

27. See my account of conversations with Soviet officials in "Fighting to the Last Afghan," *Peace and Security* (Ottawa), Autumn 1989, and in my testimony before the Subcommittee on Asian and Pacific Affairs, Committee on Foreign Affairs, U.S. House of Representatives, 21 February 1989 (*Developments in Afghanistan and Their Implications for U.S. Policy* [Washington D.C.: U.S. Government Printing Office, 1990], pp. 88–89).

28. The problems of Afghan reconstruction and their interplay with political factors are discussed in my essay in *After the Wars* (Washington, D.C.: Overseas Development Council, 1990).

CENTRAL AMERICA

THE UNITED STATES AND CENTRAL AMERICA AFTER THE COLD WAR: SEAL, PEEL, OR REPEAL THE SPHERE OF INFLUENCE?

Robert A. Pastor

On the twenty-fifth of November 1989, barely one week before a scheduled superpower summit on Malta, an unmarked plane flying from Nicaragua crashed in El Salvador with twenty-four surface-to-air missiles. The shipment was destined for the Salvadoran guerrillas, the Frente Farabundo Martí de Liberación Nacional (FMLN), and was a clear violation of pledges given by the Soviet Union and Nicaragua to the United States and the rest of Central America. Although the summit was supposed to focus on a nuclear arms agreement, the timing of the shipment escalated the issue of Soviet-Nicaraguan subversion in Central America to the top of the agenda. Secretary of State James A. Baker publicly warned the Soviet leaders: "Soviet behavior in Central America remains the biggest obstacle to an across-the-board improvement in United States-Soviet relations." When the summit ended, Baker stated, "All I can gather is that either the Nicaraguans are lying to the Soviet Union or the Soviet Union is lying to us. We [Baker and President George Bush] would prefer to believe it's the former."[1]

In the middle of the Mediterranean, the leaders of the two superpowers met and revised the contours of world politics. Their agenda was so laden and Central America was so remote that neither seemed aware that they had jettisoned the basic tenets that had defined U.S. foreign policy toward Central America during the past forty years. Baker's comment was an unwitting acknowledgment of the change. It seems straightforward unless one places it in historical context. The most vital U.S. interests in Central America have stemmed from the fear that foreign rivals of the United States could gain a foothold from which they could attack or subvert the United States or its friends.

Pleading with Congress for aid to the contras on 27 April 1983, President Ronald Reagan pointed out that the Nazis during World War II and the Soviets later recognized the Caribbean and Central America as vital to U.S. interests, so we should also. The point, sometimes lost amid the apocalyptic rhetoric, was that Central America could *not* endanger U.S. national security; a Central American regime could only affect U.S. security if it invited the Soviet Union—or to a lesser extent Cuba—to use its territory as a base for offensive weapons, a platform for subversion, or an opportunity to expand Communist influence at the expense of that of the United States.

This national security rationale, which had been at the core of U.S. foreign policy toward Central America, was impugned by the emergence of a new partnership in Malta. General Secretary Mikhail Gorbachev apparently informed Bush that even if the Central Americans invited the Soviet Union into the region for a political or military reason, Gorbachev would decline. More important, Baker's comment confirmed that he and Bush believed the Soviets, not the Nicaraguans. It meant that a little nation in Central America had replaced the Soviet Union as America's biggest problem in its neighborhood. The changing relationship, like the dawn of nuclear weapons, was so profound that not even the principals absorbed its implications at that time.

During the 1980s, the divisive U.S. debate on Central America turned on the question of the imminence of the threat in the region to the United States; the cardinal assumption of U.S. policy—that the most serious threat was that posed by the Soviet Union — was never seriously questioned. After President Reagan's address to a Joint Session of Congress in April 1983, where he warned that U.S. national security was at stake, Senator Christopher Dodd, a liberal critic of Reagan's policy, gave the Democrats' response:

> First of all, let me state clearly that on some very important things, all Americans stand in agreement. We will oppose the establishment of Marxist states in Central America. We will not accept . . . the creation of Soviet military bases in Central America. And, we will not tolerate the placement of Soviet offensive missiles in Central America—or anywhere in this hemisphere. Finally, we are fully prepared to defend our security and the security of the Americas, if necessary, by military means. All patriotic Americans share these goals.[2]

The debate in Congress was over the means, not over the ends.

In the light of the new relationship between the superpowers begun at Malta and deepened by subsequent cooperation in the Persian Gulf, the question is whether anti-Soviet goals are still valid and anti-communism is still relevant. What are the implications of the end of the Cold

War for Central America? Is this the time to construct a different relationship between the major powers and their "spheres of influence"? What would that relationship look like, and specifically what should the United States seek in Central America?

COLD WAR IN THE TROPICS

To understand the implications of the decline of the Cold War for Central America, one needs first to explain the nature of the conflict in the region and, second, the role of the United States. Because the nations of the region are so small and poor, it is natural to view the conflicts in the region from the outside looking in; indeed the two dominant perspectives for viewing the region—conservative and radical—tend to view outsiders as primarily responsible for the region's problems.[3]

Ronald Reagan and all of the Soviet general secretaries before Gorbachev had clear, undiluted, and essentially the same view of the global struggle. According to the "Cold Warrior" perspective that these rivals shared, the world was divided between two incompatible camps. Except for a disagreement as to which side wore the white hats, each believed that it was the source of goodness and light and the other of evil and darkness. To Reagan in 1980, the Soviet Union was the cause of all the world's instability, particularly in Central America: "The trouble that is going on down there comes from outside the area; [it] is revolution exported from the Soviet Union and from Cuba and from others of their allies."[4]

The radical perspective agrees that outsiders shape the region, but it views the United States as the principal problem. Some, like Mexican analyst Jorge Castañeda, consider the region a victim of both the United States and the Soviet Union—i.e., of "superpower confrontation." Castañeda argues that Latin America and the Third World "bore the brunt of the Cold War's destructive nature."[5]

Reagan, of course, changed with the times, and by the end of his term, he had negotiated with Gorbachev the kind of nuclear arms control agreement that he had disparaged at the beginning of his administration. If Reagan had been consistent and his vision accurate, the change in the Soviet Union would have brought peace and prosperity in Central America. Similarly, if Castañeda's basic argument were correct, then the destructive wars in the region would have ended as U.S.-Soviet detente began.

Today the prospects for Central America are better than they have been for a decade, but the region cannot be described as stable or prosperous, and many of the old conflicts are still being fought. There can be no doubt that detente between the United States and the Soviet Union has contributed to a more favorable climate for negotiations and democracy and that it has affected the calculations of local actors, though often with a lag and with some distortion.[6] Nonetheless, the direct causal link between superpower detente and local elections or negotiations is overstated. It was not responsible for the free elections in Nicaragua or the toppling of General Manuel Antonio Noriega of Panama, and it has had a marginal effect on the negotiations between the governments of El Salvador and Guatemala and their guerrillas. *The converse is probably more accurate: Superpower competition exacerbates divisions within a country, prolongs conflict, and transforms local disputes into geopolitical struggles, but making peace is far more difficult.* P. J. O'Rourke made the same point more graphically: "It's one thing to burn down the shit house and another thing entirely to install plumbing."[7]

The answer to the riddle of regional conflict can be located in the region itself, not in the motives or actions of the superpowers. The nations of Central America have lacked a tradition of moderate democratic change. "Peaceful changes between different factions of the ruling classes, which have been rather frequent in other Latin American countries, have not taken place in Nicaragua," wrote Carlos Fonseca Amador, the founding father of the Sandinistas. "This traditional experience predisposed the Nicaraguan people against electoral farces and in favor of armed struggle."[8] Fonseca was talking about his own country, but his statement applies to all of Central America except Costa Rica.

Central American governments traditionally viewed their oppositions as weak, fragmented, and ineffectual and did everything they could to keep them that way. The opposition viewed the governments as coercive and corrupt. When elections were called, some opposition groups would participate; others would ask the people not to vote, lest they provide a veneer of legitimacy to a dictatorial regime. To displace an incumbent, the opposition has always sought outside help, first from its neighbors, and then from either the United States or its rival. In that way, internal division was indissolubly connected to international intervention. Those who condemned the United States or other outside powers for Central America's fate identified only one half of the problem. An illegitimate structure for perpetuating dictatorship inevitably generates instability and entreaties for outside help.

The first flagrant case illustrates the pattern. In 1855, frustrated over their inability to remove the Conservatives from power in Nicaragua, the Liberals invited an American adventurer, William Walker. The popular mythology has not only omitted that the request came from the Nicaraguans, but it also neglects to note that U.S. President Franklin Pierce tried to discourage Walker by issuing an executive order to prohibit Americans from joining him. Walker had his own interests and was determined to remain in Nicaragua and govern after his victory. In the end, he made too many enemies and was killed.

In 1927, after U.S. intervention on one side and then another in Nicaragua's tragic civil war over an eighteen-year period, President Calvin Coolidge finally sent Colonel Henry Stimson to try to mediate an end to the war. Stimson persuaded both sides to agree to a cease-fire and a free election that would be supervised by the United States. Only Liberal General Augusto Sandino refused to abide by the agreement. He took his troops to the mountains of Nicaragua to harass American soldiers until they withdrew from his country. Sandino sought and received outside support from Mexico, which at that moment was perceived in the United States as Bolshevism incarnate. The United States condemned Mexico for interference and radicalism and increased its support for the incumbent government.[9]

This was not the first time that the United States deepened its involvement in Central America due to concern that a foreign rival, even one as weak as Mexico in the 1920s, would expand its influence in the region at the expense of that of the United States. And it certainly was not the last time.

U.S. motives in the region have remained reasonably consistent since Alfred T. Mahan, an influential naval strategist at the turn of the century, urged American leaders to assert U.S. naval power and make the region "America's Mediterranean." Because of the increasing importance of the Caribbean Basin as a transit between the Atlantic and Pacific coasts of the United States, Mahan wrote that Central and Caribbean America would be brought in turn into greater prominence. And this is as it has remained.

Primary U.S. interests in the region have not stemmed from a desire to extract resources or to implant a political philosophy, although history is replete with examples of both. From Mahan's guiding vision, the United States has been motivated not so much to control the region but to keep things from veering out of control, where they could be exploited by others viewed as hostile. The distinction is important: controlling a nation means imposing a total political system; not letting events take their course means that the United States intervenes only when it perceives a direct threat, generally the prospect of a rival gaining a foothold in the area. One could argue that U.S. tolerance for uncertainty was so low that it sought a high degree of control, but the number of interventions were few as compared to the lengthy period of instability in many of the countries. And many countries have pursued quite independent paths without provoking the United States to counter their policies. Has the United States controlled Mexico since 1916 or Venezuela since 1958? In fact, during the twentieth century the United States could be accused more legitimately of disinterest than of imperialism.

A related security motive is that the United States, like all other nations, does not want hostile neighbors. The fear that nearby hostile regimes would invite a powerful adversary is one that moves the United States to action. But even if there is no immediate prospect of such an invitation, the United States would not be passive or indifferent to the establishment of such a regime. The specific U.S. problem in Central America stems from the facts of proximity, vulnerability, and chronic instability.

The mellowing of the Cold War provides a *partial* test of which of these diverse motives are most important. It is partial because other variables are involved, and these are not constant. For example, each president will define a security threat differently, and his judgment of the extent to which a change in regime constitutes a threat will also differ. The definition of a threat will affect the policy response. If a president views a threat as immediate and dangerous, he is likely to suggest a strong military response. If he views a threat as distant and indirect, he might suggest no response or just a diplomatic demarche. Even if two presidents agree on the seriousness of a problem, they might very well adopt totally different responses. For example, faced with a leftist Sandinista regime in Nicaragua, Jimmy Carter used aid to try to influence it, and Reagan tried to organize a guerrilla group (the contras) to overthrow it. Faced with a Marxist offensive in El Salvador, the Carter administration conditioned its support to the government on internal changes, and the Reagan administration offered unconditional support. *In brief, there is nothing predetermined in the way in which U.S. interests are defined, threats are perceived, or responses are formulated.*

The U.S. response during the Bush administration has probably been influenced more by the legacy of eight years of Reagan's ideological crusades than by the declining interest and capacity of the Soviet Union.

The United States was fatigued by the constant executive-congressional brawls over the contras, and the region was in a state of unparalleled deterioration. Both of these factors led the Bush administration to back away from confrontation. Instead Baker negotiated a bipartisan accord with House Speaker Jim Wright to deny the contras military aid but provide them with humanitarian aid through the Nicaraguan elections in February 1990. It was a quintessential Bush compromise: he would not abandon the contras, nor would he support them. In practice, the United States withdrew from Nicaragua, and the timing proved fortuitous. The Nicaraguan government invited former president Carter, as the chairman of the Council of Freely-Elected Heads of Government, to observe the elections together with the United Nations and the Organization of American States (OAS). These three groups actually mediated the terms of the election; because of them, the opposition had the confidence to participate, and the government was compelled to accept and respect the results.

In a gesture to the changing strategic relationship, the Bush administration's Assistant Secretary of State for Inter-American Affairs Bernard Aronson made his first foreign trip to Moscow, not to Latin America. Nicaragua was at the top of his agenda. The Bush administration would later claim that a secret U.S. partnership with the Soviets was "behind the Sandinistas' stunning election loss."[10] The Soviet Union passed an explicit message that it favored free elections and two implicit signals. The message was sent by the Soviets' own free election for a parliament, but more influential was the obvious economic breakdown in the Soviet Union and the likely reduction of Soviet support for the Sandinistas. President Daniel Ortega would have to seek support elsewhere.

Still one should not overdraw the importance of a U.S.-Soviet understanding on Nicaragua. If a prior agreement had been reached, it is hard to explain the constant U.S. criticism during the electoral period of both the Sandinistas and the Soviets for supplying arms to the FMLN and denying a fair and equal playing field for the opposition. Frustration, not satisfaction, with the Soviets on these two key issues characterized the Bush administration's view before the election; to suggest after the election that there was a secret arrangement seems intended mainly to secure some credit for the outcome, which surprised most officials. Whether or not the superpowers had much influence on their clients or on the outcome, there is no question that their efforts were helpful. To bridge the gulf separating the region's adversaries, however, direct mediation was necessary. Bush's greatest contribution was not to block mediation.

Panama had more of an impact on U.S.-Soviet relations than U.S.-Soviet relations had on Panama. The U.S. invasion of the country in December 1989 raised concerns among hard-liners in the Kremlin as to whether the United States intended to take advantage of the more tolerant Soviet foreign policy. In an extraordinary encounter with the Soviet parliament, Baker heard the following comment from a Latvian deputy:

> I don't want to speak about the norms that the United States violated in Panama, but . . . you must have weighed the positive and the negative in taking these decisions. I would like to inform you of one negative aspect that you did not take into account.
> In this country, we also have our hawks and doves, and the actions of the United States in Panama provided additional arguments to our hawks, especially after the summit meeting in Malta left the impression that our relations have undergone a qualitative change, and then all of a sudden your intervention in Panama happened. There is no question that this will complicate our Parliament's consideration of our proposal to proceed along the road of disarmament.[11]

The deputy's point was driven home at a meeting of the Central Committee in February 1990. One conservative member, Vladimir Brovikov, criticized Gorbachev's perestroika for destroying the nation and its international relationships: "The point is well understood by Western leaders," he said. He argued that the invasion of Panama demonstrated that the United States would never permit itself to lose control of its allies.[12] Soviet hard-liners were looking for opportunities to persuade Gorbachev to seal, not repeal, the Soviet "sphere of influence" in Eastern Europe.

These arguments neatly paralleled those heard in the United States during the Carter administration. In the late 1970s National Security Advisor Zbigniew Brzezinski argued that if the United States did not respond strongly to the Soviet-Cuban intervention in Ethiopia, the Soviets would expand into other areas and jeopardize U.S. interests. The argument seemed validated by the Soviet invasion of Afghanistan in December 1979. The debate was parallel and connected. The harder-line approach of the Soviet Union elicited a harder-line approach by the United States, first by Carter and then in a much sharper variation by

Reagan. Now the argument is joined; it is clear to both sides that hawkish policies by one strengthen hawkish policies by the other, and as long as Gorbachev remains, the converse also works: cooperation can lead to cooperation. That equation has never been as precise as it became in 1990.

The United States and the Soviet Union have worked together to encourage both sides in the Salvadoran and Guatemalan conflicts to negotiate within the terms of an agreement known as Esquipulas II. No doubt this has helped in bringing both sides to the bargaining table, but it is questionable whether it will be sufficient to broker a deal.

The case of El Salvador might very well define the parameters of U.S. policy toward Central America in the post–Cold War period. The coalition of Salvadoran guerrilla groups—the FMLN—include a Communist Party and other Marxist-Leninist offshoots. Many of the leaders had been moved by the repression and social injustice of their country and inspired by Castro's revolution in Cuba. In 1980, energized by the Sandinistas' success, they formed the FMLN. These groups have ideological branches that connect them to Castro and the Soviet Union, but they have firmly planted indigenous roots. As the Soviet Union has changed, they have stressed their roots more. As communism has become discredited, Marxist groups have searched for new gods. The Sandinistas were the swiftest to revise their ideology in favor of free elections and genuine pluralism. In El Salvador, Joquin Villalobos, military commander of the guerrillas, underwent an ideological conversion in 1991, criticizing communism as "extreme" and Marxism as "just one more political theory, like any other." He announced his opposition to one-party rule and said that his goal was political participation in a pluralistic "competitive" democracy.[13]

Of course, all guerrillas insist that they rely solely on their domestic supporters, but with the rare exception of the Sendero Luminoso in Peru, guerrilla groups have needed foreign support to become credible threats to the government. The FMLN has built a powerful military organization and stockpiled large amounts of weapons, and it might not need as many arms from abroad as it once did. Cuba has the resources to supply the FMLN's needs even if the Soviets oppose such actions.

What should U.S. policy be? The Bush administration requested an $85 million military aid program to El Salvador in 1990, but Congress balked and pressed the administration to reduce its aid by at least half until the Salvadoran military brings to justice the killers of six Jesuit priests in 1989. The administration has been sensitive to such concerns but is unwilling to push Salvador as hard or as far as Congress is.

Clifford Krauss of the *New York Times* drew a connection between the changes in the Soviet Union and the U.S. debate on aid:

> The argument for cutting back the United States commitment to El Salvador has been strengthened by the realization that with the cold war over, the threat of Soviet expansion in Central America has diminished, no matter who wins the Salvadoran civil war.[14]

Krauss is correct that those who want to reduce aid have been strengthened, but the argument on the other side remains. No one in Congress wants to see the FMLN win the war, but the legislators are not as frightened about that possibility as some had been in the 1980s. What this means is that the United States will try to resist an FMLN victory, but it will not use "all means necessary," as Reagan administration officials once put it.

The United States can and should push the Salvadoran military further to reorganize itself, to accept the rule of law, and to bring its criminals to justice. This would increase the prospects for peace, as the military is a major cause of the problem in that country. The other part of the problem is the FMLN, which originated as a consequence of the repression but soon was used to justify its continuance. The FMLN has changed its doctrine fundamentally; it now accepts elections as the basis of legitimacy, but an important element in the FMLN is skeptical that the military will ever permit it to participate in elections. This element believes that armed struggle is the only feasible way to accomplish its ends, and of course this strategy provokes the government to a military response.

This circular dilemma did not start with foreign intervention, nor will it end with foreign support for negotiations. Indeed Salvadoran President Alfredo Cristiani argues that the FMLN launches offensives when U.S. support declines. This, in turn, provokes more repression, forcing the country into another downward spiral. The continued war and the stalemate in negotiations require that the United States use its leverage to persuade its client to negotiate seriously.

This brings us back to the central point: the connection between civil war and foreign intervention. As the Esquipulas II Agreement prescribed, and as subsequent events in Nicaragua have demonstrated, the best way to sever the connection is to focus on the divided country, not the foreign intervention, and develop a democratic and conciliatory process that the opposition trusts. If the opposition believes that it has a fair opportunity to attain power, it has no need or justification to pursue an armed struggle. Even Che Guevara acknowledged that violent revolution cannot succeed against a government "which has come into power through some form of popular vote, fraudulent or not, and maintains at least an appearance of constitutional legality."[15] As noted, foreign intervention in Central America has always been invited by at least one local party. If all parties trust the democratic process, they will have no grounds for inviting foreigners, and foreigners will not have a path to intervene.

Democracy, in brief, is the single best vehicle not only for securing freedom and peaceful change in each country, but also for excluding foreign intervention. As the mode of political change shifts from armed struggle to the ballot box, the mode of foreign involvement changes from intervention to influence. In small countries, relatively small amounts of money can influence an election outcome, thus giving some groups a feeling that they do not have a fair and equal chance and that the United States can have more influence on the outcome than they do. This raises an important question for U.S. policy: should the United States be neutral with respect to the candidates, and should it respect the process even if the winners are hostile to it? This brings us back to the central question of this essay: Should the United States seal, peel, or repeal its sphere of influence in Central America?

SPHERES OF INFLUENCE

Where colonialism or imperialism were not options, major powers have asserted "spheres of influence"—areas of vital interest where sovereignty was grudgingly recognized, deviant behavior was proscribed, and other powers were unwelcome. When respected, such spheres diminished the opportunities for confrontations between major powers; conflict was not necessarily diminished, but it was contained within and among small nations.

Geography and an instinct for overachievement impelled the United States to extend its sphere over an entire hemisphere. At least that was the way President James Monroe's 1823 message to Congress was interpreted in what came to be known as the Monroe Doctrine. In reality, the United States asserted its influence in the Caribbean Basin only in the twentieth century. For the first three decades of the century, the United States used marines to keep Cuba, Nicaragua, Haiti, and the Dominican Republic stable enough so as to deny an opportunity to a European rival. By 1928 the United States concluded that the costs of intervention exceeded the benefits, and it gradually withdrew U.S. troops.

The complete withdrawal of U.S. troops from the region occurred under Franklin D. Roosevelt. His "good neighbor policy" promised and delivered on trade reciprocity and nonintervention. Roosevelt was committed to sealing the hemisphere from European intervention, but he understood that the best way to achieve that was by collective, not solely U.S., defense and by building new cooperative relationships. As World War II ended, Roosevelt tried to construct a world order without spheres of influence, but his two principal interlocutors, Winston Churchill and Joseph Stalin, saw Roosevelt's vision as unrealistic, and they decided to allocate quotas of relative influence in the major strategic area that was contested—Eastern Europe. As Stalin secured his sphere in Eastern Europe, the United States secured its sphere in Latin America, first by negotiating the Rio Pact in 1947 and the establishment of the OAS the next year, and subsequently by a series of covert actions—successfully in Guatemala in 1954 and Chile in 1970–73, and unsuccessfully in Cuba in the 1960s.

Since the late 1940s, both the United States and the Soviet Union have rejected the other's right to a sphere, even while asserting their own rights. Critics in the United States had long noted the contradiction, but it took Gorbachev's reforms before a Soviet citizen would write, "We rejected the concept of a division of spheres of influence in 'theory' yet pursued it in practice."[16] The Brezhnev Doctrine, which asserted the right of the Soviet Union to keep its neighbors in the Communist camp even if they should prefer an alternative, made the Monroe Doctrine seem modest in comparison.

The Soviets were sensitive to the slightest diminution of their control in Eastern Europe; the United States allowed much more space for change but drew a line to preclude Marxist governments in Central America. The hotter the Cold War, the more sensitive each side became and the more determined to avoid any encroachments. While both spheres shared these similarities, there were still important differences that stemmed from the distinct ways that each nation organized itself internally and projected its influence internationally.

In the United States, freedom *from* government control is a central value, and it is maintained by dividing power and by guaranteeing that public and private institutions check and balance any attempt by a single institution to consolidate power. The United States projects this pluralistic premise abroad. In contrast, the Soviets have centralized power and authority internally and projected it internationally. Therefore, Soviet foreign policy has reinforced the power of friendly ruling elites, while U.S. policy, however unintentionally, has sometimes weakened friendly governments by insisting on pluralism and due process. This explains why Soviet control has seemed total and why U.S. policy has seemed reactive, managing crises rather than anticipating future problems.

Gorbachev changed this. By making it clear that he would let Eastern Europe go its own way—"the Sinatra doctrine"—he opened the door to the most profound series of peaceful transformations in the postwar period. Within one year, free elections brought democratic, non-Communist governments to power in Poland, Czechoslovakia, Hungary, and—most incredibly—East Germany. Though the people in each of these countries had deep-seated anti-Soviet fears, which had been one of the reasons why Gorbachev's predecessors had been so loath to let go—the new governments were less anti-Soviet than his predecessors had expected. The fact that the Soviets permitted the Warsaw Pact to end also took the wind out of the sails of anti-Soviet feeling.

A similar dynamic has been at work in Central America. After a decade of U.S.-supported war against the Nicaraguan government, many expected that the Nicaraguan people would vote against the United States and in favor of the Sandinistas that had fought the U.S.-backed contras. The Sandinistas themselves thought that the war and their nationalism were their most formidable political assets. But the Nicaraguan people voted overwhelmingly for Violeta Barrios de Chamorro. They did so for many reasons, but one of the most important was that they expected Mrs. Chamorro to be able to forge a better relationship with the United States. Democracy in Central America and a less belligerent policy by the Bush administration has evoked popular support for independent governments that are friendly to the United States.

The first concern of a democratic regime is development, and in Central America development is simply not sustainable in the context of a hostile relationship with the United States. Even if the United States adopts a patient and tolerant stance, as the Carter administration did initially with the Sandinistas in 1979–80, the regime's anti-American rhetoric will unsettle its businessmen, dampen foreign and domestic investment, and thereby harm development prospects. That is why the United States has little to fear from free elections in the region, and because of the centrality of human rights, the United States has much to gain by promoting elections.

When the United States confronted a freely elected regime—such as in Guatemala in 1954 or Chile in 1973—it committed a grave, short-sighted mistake because it projected to the Latin American left that U.S. support for democracy was not genuine. Believing that the United States would not permit them to take power peacefully, many on the left pursued revolution. In other words, the United States unintentionally contributed to a strategy of violence by not accepting unfriendly democratic regimes. There were signs that the Reagan administration learned that lesson—for example, in Alan Garcia's Peru—and that the Bush administration understands it as well.

The United States would have no problems with a democratic, non-conflict-ridden Central America. However, it would also have little interest. To its credit, the Bush administration did not withdraw from Panama and Nicaragua after friendly regimes took power; it sought large packages of aid and pressed Congress until they were approved. The question is how much longer the United States will help the region in the absence of a security threat. The answer most probably is not long.

The key to the region's development and future stability is at the national and regional level. The nations will receive international support for a period, but their success will depend, first, on their national capacity to save and invest and, second, on their ability to forge a newly invigorated Central American Common Market. The United States should provide incentives for the nations of the region to accomplish these goals. It should strengthen democracy and regional integration in Central America. This is the best guarantee against a repetition of the crisis that has harmed the region during the last decade and impoverished it since independence.

The United States should explore ways to increase the incentives for the five nations of Central America to develop a system to guarantee democracy by collective security. All of the nations should systematically reduce their armed forces and pledge to take collective action if the military in one country tries to take power.

Beyond this regional approach, the United States has two options for dealing with its "sphere" in Central America. First, it can deny it has a choice by proclaiming its adherence to nonintervention, self-determination, and peaceful resolution of disputes. This is the language of international law; it is the right thing to do, and it is unrealistic. The United States will adhere to the language until there is another crisis in the region; then it will treat problems in the region as it has always done.

Second, the United States can negotiate with the Soviet Union, Cuba, and the countries of Central America a framework agreement that could prevent the next internal crisis from becoming internationalized. This option is based on the historical fact that the United States remains sensitive to shifts in the region toward its rivals. These shifts are unlikely to occur during the Gorbachev era, but they could occur under his successor. Moreover, the United States will always be wary of a shift toward any of its rivals, even relatively minor irritants like Libya or Cuba. An excluded group or a hostile government will always seek help from other countries if it judges the electoral process to be rigged. If the incumbent is close to the United States, the opposition will turn to the enemy of the United States.

The second is the more complicated option, and given the current detente, it is less likely to be chosen. Everyone is lulled into thinking that as the problems diminish, they will never return. History suggests otherwise, but politicians rarely look at the larger picture. Yet this is the best moment to negotiate a superpower framework agreement—precisely when the United States and the Soviet Union are working so closely together and when the nations of Central America have their greatest sense of security and independence. The best time to fix a roof is when it is not raining.

The principal aim should be to construct a relationship that permits freedom of action for the nations of the region. A second but related objective is to prevent any changes in the region from becoming a cause for tension or involvement by the superpowers or U.S. adversaries. To accomplish both objectives, all parties should observe the entire negotiations, though not all would be parties to each agreement. The negotiations should be aimed at reaching agreements on the following points:

1. The Central American nations would agree not to invite any outside power to install missiles or establish military bases or naval facilities in their countries. The United States, Cuba, and the Soviet Union would agree that they would not undermine such an agreement.

2. In the course of negotiations to reduce their own military, the Central Americans would agree never to invite more than fifty foreign military advisors at any one time and to set limits on arms purchases, and the United States, Cuba, and the Soviet Union would agree to respect that agreement.

Both agreements would help extract the strategic issues from intra-Central American relations. While this approach appears to acknowledge a spheres of influence perspective, in practice it aims to repeal the concept. Such a proposal was unacceptable during the Reagan administration, which was unapologetic about maintaining the U.S. sphere of influence. But the Soviet Union justified Reagan's approach by maintaining a tighter grip on Eastern Europe than the United States ever had on Central America. When the Contadora countries (Mexico, Venezuela, Colombia, and Panama) suggested that both the United States and the Soviet Union remove all of their forces from Central America, Reagan responded that the region was too close to the United States, which was a force for good; it was unacceptable to him to equate the roles of the two superpowers in the region.

With the liberalization and liberation of Eastern Europe, however, the Soviets have gone beyond what Franklin D. Roosevelt had originally envisaged and have become a model for the United States to consider replicating. Not only have they let Eastern Europe go, but they have also let it associate with NATO. The proposal outlined above is a way to reduce external involvement that could exacerbate regional conflict.

From a U.S. perspective, the spheres of influence concept is simply the wrong answer to the wrong question. Instead of asking how we can keep the Soviets out of "our sphere," and instead of answering the national security question in terms of military aid and advice, we ought to be finding ways to reinforce democracy, increase development, and improve the prospects for justice. Rather than dividing the world geographically or ideologically according to a single formula, we would be better served by mapping the sociopolitical divisions in each country and pursuing strategies developed by the Inter-American Foundation and international development organizations. They avoid sterile debates about "exporting" democracy or development; instead they identify and support the individuals, groups, and projects in each country that offer the greatest promise for democracy and development. Similarly, the United States should identify and offer moral and in some cases material support to groups that share our values and principles, which, after all, are universal—human rights, social justice, economic development, and self-determination.

The United States should refrain from supporting candidates or political parties in electoral contests. It is true that the global Christian Democratic and Social Democratic movements support their affiliated parties in Central America just as the Communist parties have long received aid from the Communist Party of the Soviet Union. It would be best for all such aid to end as Central America's democracies seek to shape their own future. But regardless of what the Europeans choose to do, the United States should not subsidize political leaders or parties in the region because the weight of the United States is simply too heavy to permit democratic politics in each country to find its own natural equilibrium. If the United States supports a single candidate or party, it will unbalance the politics and could unintentionally disrupt the democratic process.

One could argue as to whether U.S. support for the Unión Nacional de Oposición in the 1990 Nicaraguan elections was justified, given the far greater resources available to the Sandinista governing party. Incumbency has traditionally been one of the main reasons for undemocratic politics in Latin America. The Mexican initiative in the 1930s to prohibit reelection has proven to be one of its greatest contributions to peaceful political change in Latin America. There are many in the Nicaraguan National Assembly who would like to amend the constitution to prohibit reelection of the president, as Nicaragua is the only Central American country that does not have such a prohibition. If they succeed, then the democratic playing field in all of Central America will become more level, and the United States will have an even stronger reason *not* to help any side.

REPEAL THE SPHERE: A SUMMARY

The history of U.S. relations with Central America can be viewed as a grudging acceptance by the United States of the region's autonomy and a gradual recognition by Central Americans that they were responsible for their own division and often for inviting foreign intervention. The Esquipulas II Agreement and the Nicaraguan elections were the answers to recurring problem of civil war and foreign intervention.

The Cold War was just the most recent variation of a problem that extends back to Central America's independence. The problem stemmed from the absence of a mutually agreeable framework for peaceful political change. The currency of political change was violence, not elections, and every ambitious leader sought help from abroad, from a neighbor, from the United States, or from an adversary of the United States. Thus internal division was linked irrevocably to international intervention. As the United States became the preeminent power in the Caribbean Basin with a significant stake in the region's stability because of the Panama Canal, it found itself on one side of every civil conflict, while its adversary was on the other side. The question, often debated, as to which side provoked the other—who pushed first?—was a futile and meaningless exercise. The fact is that involvement by one almost always led to the other's involvement.

This secondary layer of conflict—i.e., international intervention—exacerbated the struggle on the primary layer—i.e., internal political change. The end of the Cold War provides an opportunity to remove the second layer. U.S.-Soviet cooperation, combined with the collapse of world communism, has stopped exacerbating the region's conflicts. But these conflicts can be resolved only by the parties to the disputes.

The long-standing connection between civil war and foreign intervention has not been broken forever. Because such a connection is always possible in a region of small, open, vulnerable nations so close to the world's most powerful ones, definitive steps need to be taken to reduce the possibility that crises like those of the 1980s could occur again. Because the United States and the Soviet Union have proven that they can reach understandings on difficult regional issues, the leaders of the two countries should negotiate to remove any possible military cause of tension in Central America.

As noted, the best way to insulate local problems is to guarantee a democratic system. The nations of Central America should seek to deepen and secure their embryonic democracies by new collective security arrangements. They need to negotiate dramatic reductions in their military forces. They need to work with the superpowers and with Cuba to develop a mechanism that will constrain the use of violence to settle local, regional, or international conflicts.

In September 1989 Eduard Shevardnadze, then Soviet foreign minister, outlined a world without spheres in a speech to the UN General Assembly:

> It is no secret that we were not enthusiastic about the election setback of the Polish Communists. . . . Nevertheless, we see nothing threatening in the fact that in accordance with the will of the Polish people a coalition government has been formed. . . . Tolerance is the norm of civilized behavior.
>
> But if it is obligatory for us in our attitude toward the Government of Poland, why are others so intolerant toward, for example, Cuba? And if a non-Communist Prime Minister is possible in a socialist country, why should the appearance of a Communist as head of a

Western government be perceived as heresy? The days of traditional demarcation lines are numbered.[17]

One month later Gorbachev declared that his country had no moral or political right to interfere in the affairs of its East European neighbors. His spokesman made Gorbachev's point more succinctly: "The Brezhnev Doctrine is dead."[18] The Soviet Union long trailed behind the United States in its respect for self-determination on its periphery. Now it is far out in front in repealing its sphere of influence.

Before Gorbachev's daring dismantlement of the Soviets' East European sphere, President Bush had stated that he hoped to help "the Soviets understand that we have very special interests in this hemisphere, particularly in Central America, and . . . I don't think they really have substantive interests in this part of the world, certainly none that rival ours."[19] Now that the divisive problems of Nicaragua and Panama are behind us, it is incumbent on the United States to accept Gorbachev's challenge and repeal, not seal, its sphere of influence. The United States should engage the Soviets and Cuba in seeking new, nonmilitary, cooperative relationships in Central America. The superpowers cannot solve the region's problems, but they can help, and—more important— they can keep them from getting worse.

NOTES

For incisive comments that helped me to strengthen this essay, I am indebted to Thomas Remington, Albert Fishlow, Abraham F. Lowenthal, Svetlana Savaranskaya, and Marcin Meller.

1. Cited in Andrew Rosenthal, "Bush Hoping to Use Malta Talks to Speed Strategic Arms Pact," *New York Times*, 30 November 1989, pp. 1, 11.

2. Transcript of Dodd's address, *New York Times*, 28 April 1983, p. A12.

3. For an elaboration of these two perspectives and a third, interactive one, see Robert Pastor, "Explaining U.S. Policy Toward the Caribbean Basin: Fixed and Emerging Images," *World Politics* 38, 3 (April 1986): 483–515.

4. Transcript of Reagan's press conference, *New York Times*, 27 July 1983, p. A10.

5. Jorge Castañeda, "Latin America and the End of the Cold War," *World Policy Journal*, Summer 1990, p. 469.

6. I am indebted to Thomas Remington for encouraging me to sharpen this point.

7. P. J. O'Rourke, *Holidays in Hell* (New York: Random House, 1989), pp. 213–14.

8. Cited in Robert A. Pastor, *Condemned to Repetition: The United States and Nicaragua* (Princeton: Princeton University Press, 1988), p. 17.

9. For the history, see Pastor, *Condemned to Repetition*, ch. 2.

10. See Michael Kramer, "Anger, Bluff—and Cooperation: Behind the Sandinistas' Stunning Election Loss in Nicaragua Is the Secret Story of U.S.-Soviet Partnership in Central America," *Time*, 4 June 1990, pp. 38–45.

11. Cited in Thomas Friedman, "Baker Braves the Gauntlet in the Moscow Parliament," *New York Times*, 11 February 1990, p. 20.

12. "Excerpts from Remarks by Soviet Ambassador Brovikov to the Soviet Communist Party Central Committee," *New York Times*, 8 February 1990, p. A10.

13. Mark A. Uhlig, "Top Salvadoran Rebel Alters His Goals," *New York Times*, 7 March 1991, p. A3.

14. Clifford Krauss, "El Salvador Leader Lobbies U.S. in Effort to Block Aid Reduction," *New York Times*, 24 September 1990, p. A9.

15. Cited in Samuel P. Huntington, "The Modest Meaning of Democracy," in *Democracy in the Americas: Stopping the Pendulum*, ed. Robert Pastor (New York: Holmes and Meier, 1989), p. 24.

16. Andrey V. Kozyrev, "What Soviet Foreign Policy Went Sour," *New York Times*, 7 January 1989, p. 17.

17. Excerpts in *New York Times*, 27 September 1989.

18. Cited in Bill Keller, "Gorbachev, in Finland, Disavows Any Right of Regional Intervention," *New York Times*, 26 October 1989, p. 1.

19. "President's News Conference," reprinted in *New York Times*, 7 February 1989, p. 34.

THE USSR AND THE CONFLICT IN CENTRAL AMERICA

Nikolai G. Zaitsev

As the cold war era seems to have come close to its inglorious end, it is a good time to draw the necessary lessons from the past so as to avoid repetition of the costly errors committed by the two superpowers in their long-standing confrontation, *inter alia*, through involvement in the regional conflicts of the Third World.

Central America, despite the insignificant economic and military potential of the countries directly involved, at certain periods of the past decade came to play a major role in the superpowers' relations, in particular as far as the foreign policy of the United States is concerned. Moreover, the tension around the situation in Nicaragua in the mid-1980s was so high that direct large-scale military confrontation might have been possible. Luckily the growing degree of political responsibility of the Central American countries themselves within the framework of the Esquipulas process, inspired to a large extent by the preceding Contadora and Rio Group activities, as well as the progressive *rapprochement* between the two superpowers, have substantially diminished the danger of an overall military conflict, while the peace process in the region has been gaining momentum. Although this process, both in Nicaragua and El Salvador, does not appear to be irreversible, the chances for the nonviolent evolution of the two countries, as well as of the region as a whole, are now much higher than in the first half of the 1980s.

The Soviet involvement in the conflict in Central America has been the subject of both excessive political speculation and serious study in the United States. Surprisingly, the official political rhetoric on the issue has not changed much until very recently—ranging from strong criticism of the "intervention of the totalitarian coalition"[1] (in Central America) at the beginning of the decade to the blunt rejection of "the Soviet Union's . . . legitimate interest in Central America"[2] at the very end of it.

American scholarly research on this subject, comprising dozens of bibliographical listings, has also been generally critical of the Soviet policy in the region and has not as a rule provided a comprehensive picture. Soviet scholars (this author included)[3] have not gone beyond mere interpretation of official policy and have not managed to provide much rethinking of the dangerous situation created in Central America and of the superpowers' relationship there.

It is necessary, therefore, to undertake a sincere, objective, concise appraisal of Soviet policy vis-à-vis Central America during the last decade to identify its origins, evolution, and prospects for the future.

The Central American conflict was primarily viewed by the Reagan administration as having its roots in "the Soviet-Cuban penetration into the area," thus becoming part of the East-West confrontation. It is true that at a certain stage, in particular from the mid-1980s on, this conflict became an important component in the American-Soviet relationship, and as such an East-West issue. However, we would strongly argue that the Soviet Union was in no way responsible for the emergence of the guerrilla movement in Nicaragua, nor did it contribute to the Sandinistas' victory in July 1979. Moreover, the early period of Soviet-Nicaragua relations was slow and uneventful compared with the first years of links with Cuba, and they have never reached a comparable political, ideological, military, or economic dimension.

Thus the roots of the conflict can be identified not within the East-West (i.e., American-Soviet) context but rather within the perspective of North-South relations, in the sense that economic underdevelopment and social tensions along with the lack of democratic traditions have been the most important factors conducing to the political crisis in Central America.[4]

It is true that the new situation in Nicaragua after the Sandinistas took power, as well as the growing tensions in El Salvador resulting in a virtual civil war there after 1980, were a cause for legitimate concern in the United States. However, in my view, the Reagan administration overreacted to the potential threat emanating from this new situation in the region, and made its reversal the top priority issue on its foreign policy agenda. The substantial increase in economic and especially military assistance to the government of El Salvador and the provision of military and logistical support to the "contra" forces in Nicaragua led progressively to the direct involvement of the United States in the regional conflict. The U.S. invasion of Grenada in October 1983 should also be seen as part of the overall American strategy to counteract "communist penetration" into the Caribbean basin. After Grenada, the threat of U.S. direct intervention in Nicaragua was taken quite seriously not only by the leaders of Nicaragua but also in many quarters of the world political community. It was the danger and unpredictability of the situation in the region that gave impetus to the efforts of the Contadora group, later supported by other key countries in Latin America.

Under the circumstances, the Sandinista government in Nicaragua could legitimately look for extra-regional support in economic and defense matters, relying mainly on the Soviet Union and Cuba. As Robert Leiken puts it: "Paradoxically, Soviet 'penetration' of Nicaragua has been promoted more eagerly by the Sandinista National Directorate than by the Kremlin."[5]

Although it is my strong conviction that the American belligerent position on Central America was not commensurate with the dimensions of the threat to the United States emanating from the new realities in Central America, as well as with the degree of Soviet "penetration" there, the analysis of Soviet motivations is of paramount importance for the purposes of this paper.

Let us take as the point of departure the notion expressed by Zbigniew Brzezinski that "for the Soviet Union the Central American issue is at best a secondary front."[6] Notwithstanding the above, the degree of Soviet involvement in Central American affairs (directly bilateral with Nicaragua but indirectly through its having a strong regional and global component) has become quite significant during the last decade in both economic and political terms. My personal view of the underlying factors cannot be substantiated by official statements or by solid analytical work by Soviet researchers because the first are well-known for their general character, and do not go beyond routine "solidarity" and "anti-imperialist" rhetoric, and the second is virtually nonexistent. My views, based mostly on independent analysis, with its own strengths and limitations, can be summarized as follows:

First, the Sandinista revolution in Nicaragua, which came as quite a surprise to Moscow, fit into the framework of the "glorious revolutionary anti-imperialist" movements in Africa (the Portuguese colonies, Ethiopia) and Asia (Vietnam and Afghanistan)—to cite only the most prominent examples of the late 1970s. It was easy to be tempted by the prospect of having a new progressive regime in close proximity to the United States, providing additional evidence of the changing "global correlation of forces in favor of socialism."

I see the 1970s and early 1980s as a period of serious miscalculations in Soviet foreign policy vis-à-vis the developing countries, giving priority to ideological factors which turned out to be extremely costly in economic and military terms and counterproductive from the standpoint of obtaining tangible global benefits following the deterioration of relations with the Western countries after Afghanistan.

However, in the case of Nicaragua, the notion of "solidarity" was justified to a certain extent by the high degree of pressure on the country from the United States. Thus, the unusual combination of a sincere desire to support the weak against the powerful, on the one hand, and the inertia in global foreign policy, seemingly taking advantage of the "post-Vietnam syndrome" in the United States, appears to have been a major factor in the initial period of Soviet involvement in the Central American conflict.

Second, although never explicitly expressed, the unexpectedly high degree of international opposition to Soviet conduct in Afghanistan might have provoked the leaders of the USSR to endeavor to put increased pressure on the United States "in their corner of the world," and thereby reduce the pressure on them in Afghanistan.

Third, while Cuba was the first country to give material support to the Sandinistas, this support could not have decisively strengthened the Sandinista regime if not supplemented by strong Soviet aid. The prospect of forming an enlarged "triangular" alliance, in addition to the long-standing bilateral relationship with Cuba, might also have had some value in the eyes of Soviet foreign policy planners.

Fourth, geostrategic considerations—the opportunity for an enlarged presence in the Caribbean basin, a strategically important area for the United States—could also have played a role in making decisions to expand cooperative links with Nicaragua.

There were certainly strong factors running against these "pro" considerations for greater Soviet involvement in Central America. Among these were the overstrained state of the Soviet economy, the danger of further damaging relations with the United States as a result of the U.S. preoccupation with Soviet activities in this strategically sensitive area, the absence of any apparent economic benefits in promoting relations with Nicaragua, the unforeseeable reaction of other Central and Latin American countries to the enlarged presence of the Soviet Union in the Western Hemisphere, etc.

However, on the threshold of the 1980s, the arguments in favor of expanding the Soviet Union's presence in the region could not help but dominate the counter-arguments, given the prevailing thinking of the leadership in the USSR.

What were the results of Soviet policy in Central America in the pre-Gorbachev years? In my view, they can be seen as somewhat contradictory.

In the first half of the 1980s, trade and economic relations between Nicaragua and the Soviet Union were substantially expanded from a negligible level of 10 million rubles* in 1981 to over 212 million rubles in 1985—almost totally represented by Soviet exports on credit terms. According to Western estimates, military deliveries also substantially increased, with the Sandinista army progressively enlarging the Soviet-made armaments component in its materiel base.

One can argue whether Soviet assistance to Nicaragua was commensurate with its defense and economic needs or "excessive" (the view generally held by American politicians and scholars), but the fact is that Soviet aid to Nicaragua was the decisive factor in assuring the economic survival of the country and a defense level sufficient to counteract successfully the "contra" forces' attacks and provide a serious deterrent to a U.S. invasion. As such, Soviet assistance to Nicaragua can be seen not as a destabilizing factor (as generally believed by the American public), but rather as a peace component securing a balance of forces in the region. Thus, for the Sandinista government, Soviet assistance has been crucial in helping it achieve its policy objectives.

As far as the cost-benefit ratio of the Central American component in global Soviet foreign policy is concerned, it tended to be negative rather than positive, with the aforementioned counterproductive factors adversely affecting the nation's foreign policy and security interests. Because the American behavior in Central America was excessively belligerent and inflexible, the Soviet Union further damaged its relations with the United States without getting any substantial benefit from its involvement in the region's affairs. The economic and financial aid to Nicaragua diverted resources badly needed for internal development, etc.

The situation was even more tragic from the Central American point of view. The region was virtually transformed into a military camp, and the cost of war became intolerable. Over 160 thousand people perished as a result of military activities or internal terror, and the total number of emigrés and displaced persons exceeded 2 million. The direct economic losses of Nicaragua alone reached 12 billion dollars during the decade. The military actions in the region further aggravated its social

*Until 1985 the official rate of exchange was approximately 0.75 ruble = 1 dollar; from 1986 on it was approximately 0.6 ruble = 1 dollar.

problems: 60 percent of the population live under conditions of dire poverty, and 30 percent are illiterate.[7]

There are reasons to believe that the superpowers' involvement in the regional conflict, by giving it a strong international dimension, aggravated the situation and reduced the prospects for peaceful settlement. With the Contadora and later Rio Group activities virtually blocked by 1986, a peaceful outcome of the conflict appeared anything but likely. The nearly miraculous start of the Esquipulas process in 1987, on the basis of the Arias peace plan, clearly demonstrated the willingness of the regional parties to the conflict to overcome existing obstacles to peace. On the other hand, the implementation of the Arias peace plan only became feasible within the evolving global framework resulting from the thaw in the American-Soviet relations. The latter was the product of the mutual efforts of the two superpowers, which were given a decisive initial impetus by the policy of "new political thinking" pursued by Mikhail Gorbachev from his first year in office. With many difficulties and strains accumulated and/or aggravated in the years of *perestroika*, this resulted in remarkable initiatives in the foreign policy sphere. The new Soviet approach, announced at the beginning of 1986 and aimed at "reactivating collective efforts . . . to unblock the conflict situations in . . . Central America,"[8] signaled the genuine desire of the new Soviet leadership to disengage from its excessive involvement in regional conflicts, the Central American one being, in my view, the least necessary from the standpoint of the global interests of the USSR.

In the second half of the 1980s, the Soviet position vis-à-vis the Central American crisis has substantially evolved and become more comprehensive. The strong anti-American component has been gradually replaced by a genuine desire to find the most practical ways to a solution to the crisis. This approach, along with the changing (very slowly at first) American position both toward the peaceful settlement of the regional conflict (seeing such a solution as acceptable) and toward the overall relationship with the Soviet Union, made it possible for the two countries to engage in meaningful discussions of Central American issues within the framework of periodic consultations of the high-ranking foreign policy officials of the two countries.

What are the main building blocks of the current Soviet position with regard to the peaceful settlement of the conflict in Central America? Drawing upon various statements on the subject by President Gorbachev and Foreign Minister Eduard Shevardnadze, as well as declarations by the Soviet government and by the Ministry for Foreign Affairs, it would comprise the following major elements:

The Soviet Union stands for a just political settlement in Central America under strict observance of the fundamental principles of international law: respect for sovereignty, noninterference in internal affairs, the right of the people to the free determination of their development paths. It highly approves the results of the peaceful efforts of Central American and Latin American countries within the Esquipulas and, prior to that, the Contadora processes.

Within this global approach, the USSR gives preference to the Latin American solution of the conflict on the basis of the balance of interests of all the parties involved and supports the efforts of the United Nations and the Organization of American States to settle the regional crisis.

In promoting cooperation with Central American and other Latin American countries, the Soviet Union does not look for any political, military, or strategic dividends in the Western Hemisphere or seek to undermine the interests of other countries in that part of the world, which by no means should be an area of East-West confrontation.

The Soviet Union does not have now or intend to have in the future any military bases in the region. It strives for the establishment of a zone of peace and cooperation in Central America and the Caribbean basin.

Within this context, the Soviet Union considers that one of the major preconditions for peace and security in the region is the need to stop military supplies to Central America. Guided by this belief, it stopped military deliveries to Nicaragua at the end of 1988.

Of paramount importance is the fact that some of the principal elements of the positions of the Soviet Union, including some of those mentioned above, and of the United States on the Central American issues have now become part of the joint approach of the two countries. Thus in a joint statement by Secretary of State James Baker and Foreign Minister Shevardnadze, as a result of their discussions in Moscow in February 1990, the parties, in expressing their full support for the Esquipulas process, specifically stressed their opposition to the use of the territories of any Central American state for providing support to paramilitary groupings, as well as to the similar support by extra-regional states. They also strongly supported a negotiated peaceful settlement in El Salvador and gave full backing to the efforts of the UN Secretary-General to secure this settlement, as well as the use of UN machinery to monitor current and future agreements in Central America.[9]

The Soviet Union recognizes in broad terms the need for an increase in the UN efforts in peace settlement in Central America and closer cooperation between the UN, the United States, and the USSR. It also supports substantive combined efforts by the international community to assist in reviving the Central American economies badly damaged by the combined effects of war and severe economic crisis. The Soviet Union gave its backing to the Special Economic Cooperation Program for Central America adopted by the United Nations.

In this respect, it is important to note that the USSR throughout the 1980s has been one of the biggest donors to Central America by providing economic assistance to Nicaragua, the country most badly hit by war and economic malaise. Thus the total amount of Soviet economic and financial assistance to Nicaragua, including grants, during 1981–1988 exceeded 2 billion rubles. Soviet deliveries to Nicaragua in 1988, amounting to nearly 250 million rubles, were carried out exclusively on credit terms, with the repayment period extended to 1991. The total volume of Soviet commitments to economic assistance projects in such fields as energy, mining and textile industries, agriculture, fishing, geological prospecting, and others amounted to about 115 million rubles.[10]

What are the prospects for the Soviet position vis-à-vis the Central American conflict? It appears that they would be largely determined by the future evolution of the political situation in individual Central American countries and the region as a whole as well as by the state of U.S.-Soviet relations on a global scale.

As far as the regional situation is concerned, the key issues remain: the future evolution of the internal political situation in Nicaragua, including demobilization of the "contra" forces, and the outcome of negotiations between the government and armed opposition in El Salvador. The Soviet Union recognized the results of elections in Nicaragua and is willing to continue to further cooperate with the country on the basis of mutual benefit. However, one can hardly expect the maintenance of the same high level of Soviet exports to Nicaragua on credit terms—both because of the internal economic constraints in the Soviet Union and the drastic change in public opinion in the USSR against assistance to Third World countries and because of the low level of efficiency in Nicaragua's utilization of Soviet aid in the 1980s. Shipments of armaments to Nicaragua can hardly be expected either, although a reasonable level of cooperation with the army could be desirable for both parties to secure proper maintenance of military equipment.

The most critical factor in the future evolution of the situation in Nicaragua is the continuing economic crisis there and the unpredictability of the political situation. The "contra" movement does not seem to be totally neutralized, while the tensions between the Sandinista opposition and the government coalition, as well as within the coalition itself, remain high.

Still more complicated is the situation in El Salvador. The military activities cannot secure victory for any of the parties, and thus the political and military impasse continues. Additional conciliatory efforts are required by both the government and the opposition to end the war so as to allow the country to come to a peaceful resolution of the conflict.

Additional opportunities could open up for a more constructive role for the Soviet Union in Central American affairs if it would widen its diplomatic ties within the region. Until recently normal diplomatic relations were maintained only with Costa Rica and Nicaragua and *de jure* with Guatemala since 1944. There is reason to believe that the readiness of the Soviet Union to establish diplomatic relations with all the countries of the region interested in such ties has met with a positive response. Thus recently diplomatic relations were established with Honduras and will be reestablished soon with Guatemala. If the political situation in El Salvador stabilizes, progress toward diplomatic relations can be expected with that country as well.

Generally good, though modest, opportunities also exist for the promotion of trade and economic links between the USSR and Central American countries—in particular through agricultural purchases in those countries and deliveries of Soviet goods, especially machinery and equipment, as well as cooperation in various economic projects, including the establishment of joint ventures.

The expected further U.S.-Soviet rapprochement cannot but generally be beneficial for peaceful settlement in Central America. However, the United States, by its proximity to and special interests in the region, will bear special responsibility for the events in that part of the world, which requires a substantial degree of responsibility in its political and military behavior. In the second half of the 1980s, U.S. policy toward Central America became more cooperative and less belligerent, but there is room for further constructive steps. It appears that the U.S. administration is in a position to exercise greater pressure on the military in El Salvador, which still blocks productive dialogue between the government and the opposition forces. More economic assistance could be provided to Nicaragua—the country which has suffered most from American policy in the region.

One cannot expect durable peace in the region if the United States is able to use force and commit acts of aggression, as happened in Panama, no matter what justifications may be offered.

As far as the Soviet Union is concerned, the attempts to establish "linkage" between American-Soviet economic relations, Soviet assistance to Cuba, and Soviet policy vis-à-vis Central America appear to be fruitless and counterproductive.

This does not exclude the need for all extra-regional countries to adhere to the internationally agreed commitments to abstain from interference in the internal affairs of the Central American countries.

In concluding, let me emphasize that while the Central American countries on the threshold of the 1990s have much less turbulent situations than a decade ago, they are still at a very dangerous crossroads. The region can evolve toward a peaceful and prosperous future, or it can become involved in a new cycle of military activities, as happened at the beginning of the 1980s. The superpowers should do everything possible to avoid the repetition of the tragic events of the last decade.

NOTES

1. Joseph Cirincione, ed., *Central America and the Western Alliance* (New York, 1985), p. 108.

2. U.S. Department of State, *Selected Documents*, no. 36, 1989, p. 2.

3. See N. Zaitsev, "Política exterior de la URSS y relaciones con los países de America Central," *Relaciones Internacionales* (San José), no. 18 (First trimester, 1987).

4. This view is widely shared by many politicians and scholars in the United States, Latin America, and Europe. See, for instance, *Report of the International Commission for Central American Recovery and Development*, February 1989, ch. I; Andrew V. Pierre, ed., *Third World Instability: Central America as a European-American Issue* (New York, 1985), pp. 106–36; Howard J. Wiarda, ed., *Rift and Revolution: The Central American Imbroglio* (Washington, 1984), pp. 3–23, and many others.

5. See his article in *Central America and the Western Alliance*, ed. J. Cirincione, p. 164.

6. Article by Brzezinski in *ibid.*, p. 106.

7. See *Estudios Internacionales* (Guatemala), no. 1, 1990, p. 44.

8. "Materials of the XXVII Congress of the CPSU," Moscow, 1986, p. 70 (in Russian).

9. See *Pravda*, 11 February 1990.

10. For details, see *Estudios Internacionales* (Guatemala), no. 1, 1990, p. 48.

CENTRAL AMERICA AT THE END OF THE COLD WAR

Terry Lynn Karl

For Central America the effect of the winding down of the Cold War is mixed. To oversimplify, two contradictory scenarios are likely to emerge. On the one hand, the elimination of the perception of a Soviet threat to U.S. security in this hemisphere offers the hope that the United States will alter its traditional opposition to radical or reformist movements to its south, therefore creating new space for political change in the region. In the past such movements were inextricably linked by U.S. policymakers to the existence of a Soviet threat in "our own backyard" and met with hostility, especially in the Caribbean Basin.* With the basic anti-Soviet geopolitical underpinning to U.S. policy in the region removed, Washington's ostensible rationale for intervening militarily in Central America is no longer credible. This alone makes intervention less feasible in the future—at least on the sustained scale that has characterized U.S. relations with Nicaragua or El Salvador over the past decade.

In this scenario the potential effect on Central America is striking. The de-linking of the strategic concerns of the United States from the political consequences of changes in governments to its south could create more room for local governments to arrive at the type of fundamental pacts with their oppositions which are the basis for long-run social peace. The removal of the sword of Damocles of U.S. military intervention could increase the incentives for both sides to bargain directly with each other. For the right, though no longer able to rely on its traditional guarantee of U.S. military assistance and support for authoritarian rule, the end of Cold War rivalry has given a significant

*Indeed anti-Sovietism provided an indispensable justification for the overthrow of the government of Jacobo Arbenz in Guatemala in 1954, the Bay of Pigs invasion in 1961, the landing of marines in the Dominican Republic in 1964, U.S. support for military dictatorships in South America in the 1960s and 1970s, the overthrow of Chile's democracy in 1973, the invasion of Grenada in 1983, and the wars against the Sandinistas in Nicaragua and the Frente Farabundo Marti de Liberación Nacional (FMLN) in El Salvador in the 1980s.

boost to neoliberal economics and eliminated, at least temporarily, the threat of alternative socialist models. Thus it may see increased incentives to devise programs, consistent with its interests, that can win support in a democratic context.

The left, though weakened by the lack of a socialist model, is liberated from the past burdens of having to demonstrate that it is not pro-Soviet or pro-Cuban, that its accession to power would not lead to the creation of a new Soviet satellite, and that it is not a mortal enemy of the United States. To the extent that it can make the ideological adjustments required by the collapse of the Eastern bloc and the fading of the socialist paradigm, it may now be free to conceive of coherent and innovative alternatives to a "free-market" consensus.* It will do so in a context defined by the twin trends of economic crisis and democratization, precisely the context that historically has been most favorable to leftist activity. Thus there is reason to believe that the future could afford more political space for negotiated bargains to be struck between the right and the left and for disputes to be resolved through diplomacy rather than military confrontation.

On the other hand, the conclusion of the Cold War may encourage the United States to reassert its hegemonic vision of the region based on the defense of capitalist property relations and its own economic interests. This traditional vision predates the Cold War and is rooted in the early days of the republic. It is most succinctly captured in the Monroe Doctrine, whose direct association between the security of Latin American nations and the United States created the notion that the United States has both the right and the responsibility to monitor the character of Latin American regimes. This has been raised to a first principle of policy in the hemisphere, especially in Central America, where the United States has intervened repeatedly and where in 1927 Under-Secretary of State Robert Olds wrote:

> We do control [their] destinies . . . and we do so for the simple reason that the national interest absolutely dictates such a course. . . . Until

*Making such ideological adjustments is no easy task. The collapse of the socialist bloc calls into question basic beliefs about the Marxist notion of linear progress, the role of the state in the economy, and the desirability of revolution. As Jorge G. Castañeda notes, the traditional orthodox left, already weak, in Latin America has been devastated by events in Eastern Europe. Castroist political-military organizations, new social democratic movements, and even the traditional, more conservative social democratic parties have been affected. (See "Latin America and the End of the Cold War," *World Policy Journal* 7, 3 [Summer 1990]: 477–78.)

now Central America has always understood that governments which we recognize and support stay in power, while those we do not recognize and support fall.[1]

A continuation of this vision undoubtedly would mean "business as usual" in Central America—that is, firm U.S. support for status quo armies and oligarchies in the region regardless of the end of the Cold War. There are several strong motivations for a new U.S. reassertion in the region. First, the end of the superpower rivalry presupposes the removal of foreign counterweights to the United States, and it has greatly enhanced the legitimacy of capitalist and liberal democratic institutions. Although Central American nations never succeeded in playing one major power against another, the Soviet bloc and Western Europe, especially through Social Democratic and Christian Democratic parties, were sometimes seen as potential alternative models to the United States, and their actions placed some effective constraints on U.S. behavior. This countervailing potential has been removed due to the preoccupation of all of these powers with events in Eastern Europe.*

Second and more significant, as regional trading blocs in Europe and Asia emerge, and as the United States continues to lose its relative strength in the world economy, there will be a strong temptation for the United States to fall back on its sphere of influence in the Americas to establish free trade areas and enhanced economic interdependence.† The current preoccupation with Eastern Europe temporarily obscures the fact that U.S. exports to that region are less than 2 percent of those to Latin America and that the hemisphere could become a major export market in the 1990s. Such strictly economic motives are augmented by a concern

---

*"It is one more tragic Latin American paradox," Castañeda comments, "that at the same time that the Soviet Union and the 'socialist bloc' disappear as effective counterweights, Western Europe consummates a gradual withdrawal from its scant Latin American involvement, precisely because of events in Eastern Europe." Even Japan, Castañeda notes, has recently reduced its promised support for Latin America from $10 billion to $4 billion over the next five years, targeting the $6 billion difference to Eastern Europe ("Latin America and the End of the Cold War," p. 474).

†In Deputy Secretary of State Lawrence S. Eagleburger's words, "For all of our stake in peace and stability in Europe, we know that our West European friends will have primary responsibility for integrating the newly democratic regimes in the East, whereas our energies will be increasingly and inevitably drawn towards our own hemisphere—an area which is a natural place for U.S. economic cooperation" (address to the Washington Conference of the Council of the Americas, 21 May 1990).

with drug enforcement, especially since Latin American countries now produce or tranship more than 80 percent of the cocaine and 90 percent of the marijuana that enters the United States. To a lesser extent, immigration deterrence is also a factor, as well over 10 percent of Central America's total population has already fled that war-torn region.[2]

Regardless of which scenario is most likely to occur, there is little question that the alteration in superpower relations has already influenced the perceptions, actions, and relative power of regional forces and may transform them more fundamentally in the future. But it would be a mistake to overemphasize the impact of these changes on the resolution of the two "hot" conflicts in Central America: Nicaragua and El Salvador. As the following pages will show, these conflicts did not originate from Cold War dynamics, although they were intensified and prolonged by the rivalry between the superpowers; thus the end of the Cold War will not automatically resolve them. Furthermore, the broad outlines of a possible settlement of the Nicaraguan conflict and to a lesser extent the Salvadoran civil war were already spelled out *prior* to the termination of superpower rivalry, largely by regional actors themselves who were anxious to limit the hegemonic pretensions of the United States and were far less concerned about the Soviet Union. The end of the Cold War should facilitate reaching agreements along the lines established by these regional actors, but it cannot guarantee the viability of these accords.

THE LOCAL ROOTS OF REGIONAL CONFLICTS

When the Sandinistas marched into Managua in August 1979 and the civil war in El Salvador broke out in full force one year later, policymakers in Washington saw the roots of these events through Cold War lenses. Influenced by the writings of neoconservatives, they argued that the Soviet Union had financed and trained a Cuban military establishment which subsequently had become a major instrument of Soviet expansion in Central America and the Caribbean. "The first fruits of these efforts," Jeane Kirkpatrick wrote, "are the new governments of Grenada and Nicaragua. . . . El Salvador . . . is threatened by progressively well-armed guerrillas."[3] These were the latest indications of a domino move to encircle the United States.[4]

Given this vision, the stakes in Central America were great. U.S. policymakers argued that the Soviet Union, by establishing bases in the region, sought to lend logistical support to local insurgencies and to disrupt part of NATO's contingency plans in the area.* The United States could ill afford such footholds. To prevent them, policymakers developed the "Reagan Doctrine," which meant rolling Soviet influence back inside the borders of the Soviet Union through the combined pressures of a massive U.S. military buildup and the defeat of insurgencies, especially those in the U.S. sphere of influence. From the Reagan Doctrine the roots of the conflicts in Central America were understood to be largely Soviet-inspired, and therefore their resolution depended on lending military and other support to "freedom fighters" or governments bent on shaking off Marxist rule.[5] Thus the United States adopted the dual policies of the contra war against the Nicaraguan government and low-intensity warfare against the FMLN in El Salvador.

In Latin America, and especially throughout Central America, however, the revolution in Nicaragua and the outbreak of civil war in El Salvador were largely seen through the region's own domestic lenses. Few local forces shared the intensity of Washington's anti-Sovietism, and since the Cuba crisis of the 1960s, governments on the continent have been consistently reluctant to sanction their counterparts for developing relations with the Soviet Union.† For knowledgeable observers across the political spectrum, the origins of these conflicts lay in the intertwining of inequitable land use and repressive political regimes bolstered by the United States, not in the superpower rivalry. The primary feature of Central America's development model since colonial times has been

---

*According to the Reagan administration, these bases could disrupt U.S. trade routes, especially in the Caribbean, where more than 50 percent of U.S. oil imports pass. With the triumph of the Nicaraguan revolution, a new menace was envisioned. Nicaragua (and later the rest of Central America) could become a solid base for neighboring pro-Soviet insurgencies by lending logistical support systems and elaborate supply networks. (See R. Bruce McColm, "Central America: The Larger Regional Scenario," *Strategic Review*, Summer 1983.)

†Latin American governments did not support U.S. sanctions against Chile in the early 1970s or U.S. pressure on Peru in the 1960s, both aimed at breaking ties with the USSR. But anti-Communist rhetoric has been much in evidence on the continent, especially when governments are seeking to extract significant levels of aid from the United States. In El Salvador, for example, where I have carried out interviews for almost a decade, a number of government officials and rightist spokespeople did not speak of Soviet- or Cuban-inspired insurgencies until the aid battles raging in the U.S. Congress began to affect their rhetoric. They gradually changed their descriptions of (and even insistence upon) the domestic origins of the crisis as they realized that the Cold War meant the possibility of extracting higher levels of aid from Washington.

overdependence on the export of a few agricultural crops.* While this strengthened local oligarchies by partially transforming them into a modern capitalist class and produced regional rates of growth that were among the highest in the world from 1950 to 1978, it also brought about an extremely unequal distribution of land, widespread misery, and a slow decline in economic opportunities for the peasant majority.† The expansion of cash crop production on extensive landholdings pushed tens of thousands of small farmers off the land, a process which not only freed land for the planting of more export crops by landlords, but simultaneously "freed" the peasants to be seasonal wage laborers for the expanding farms—if they could find work. The consequences for the rural poor were disastrous. In El Salvador, for example, a UN study found that the proportion of the rural population that was landless increased from 12 percent in 1960 to 41 percent in 1975, while a 1977 study found that 83.5 percent of the rural population earned less than the AID-estimated poverty line of $225 per capita per year.[6]

Central America's development model relied on "reactionary despotism," a distinctive form of authoritarian domination which protected the interests of traditional oligarchies at the expense of the peasant majority, in order to maintain economic privilege and some of the highest concentrations of income in the world.[7] To secure the property and labor relations which benefited them, oligarchies built national militaries and local security forces, and they constructed a legal system to suit their interests. In Nicaragua, where the landlord class was especially weak, this task was accomplished by the United States, which put the Somoza dynasty in power. As early as the 1930s, in the wake of massive peasant protests throughout the region, these oligarchies were forced to cede control to the very military forces they had created in order to protect the status quo; subsequently they had to remain content with ruling

*In 1979 coffee, bananas, sugar, cotton, and cattle contributed over 60 percent of the exports of every country. In Guatemala these crops contributed 56 percent. (See John Weeks, *The Economies of Central America* [New York: Holmes and Meier, 1985], pp. 76–77.)

†This was true in every country but Costa Rica, where land has been distributed far more equitably since the time of the Spanish. Because of its remoteness from the center of the colonial empire and the absence of a large indigenous population, capitalism in Costa Rica developed on the basis of small landholdings based on family labor. This was qualitatively different from the plantation model developed in the rest of Central America. (See Mitchell Seligson, *Peasants of Costa Rica and the Development of Agrarian Capitalism* [Madison: University of Wisconsin Press, 1980].)

indirectly in a partnership with the region's armed forces. As officer corps were strengthened, largely through U.S. aid,* they acquired substantial power and autonomy from civilian elites and grew wealthy on the fruits of corruption. The repeated violations of human rights and democratic rules by these militaries belied their supposed role as modernizers who would serve as reformists rather than as guardians of the status quo.

Had the ruling alliance of oligarchies and the military not closed the avenue for peaceful reform in Nicaragua, Guatemala, and El Salvador, it is unlikely that armed guerrilla movements would have gained a strong foothold in those countries. In each case, the burgeoning of protest and the growth of armed movements can be traced to key historical junctures in which the national oligarchies responded to pressures for reform with increased repression. In Nicaragua the assassination of nationalist leader Sandino in 1934 was a turning point leading to the entrenchment of security forces dedicated to the interests of the Somoza dynasty. In Guatemala the 1954 U.S.-sponsored coup against the Arbenz government deposed a democratic regime that had attempted to redress the stark inequalities defining that country's social and political landscape and paved the way for a forty-year cycle of repression and resistance. In El Salvador the military slammed the door on peaceful reform by denying José Napoleón Duarte his electoral victory in the 1972 elections.[†] When economic crisis struck at the end of the 1970s, provoked by

*Through the Alliance for Progress and other mechanisms, the United States developed an economic program to encourage nontraditional exports, such as cotton and cattle, and a military security program which included military training, arms, antiriot equipment, and communications and transportation technology and which was designed to defeat any revolutionary challenge. Between 1950 and 1976 Central Americans trained under the Military Assistance Program and International Military Education and Training Program included 5,167 Nicaraguans, 3,213 Guatemalans, 2,888 Hondurans, 1,925 Salvadorans, and 696 Costa Ricans; 4,389 Panamanians were trained as well. (See U.S. Defense Security Assistance Agency, *Foreign Military Sales and Military Assistance Facts* [Washington, D.C., 1977], pp. 30–31.)

[†]In Honduras and Costa Rica, where ruling groups were more flexible in their ability to respond to pressures for change, armed guerrilla movements never appeared in force. In this respect the cases of Honduras and Costa Rica stand in sharp contrast to the historical pattern of reliance upon repression, death squads, and even genocide in the cases of Guatemala, El Salvador, and Nicaragua. In Honduras and Costa Rica economic and political reform undermined the narrow reliance on political repression to sustain the agro-export model—with the result that they were the only two countries in which the oligarchies were not threat-

falling prices for Central America's principal exports and high interest rates on the debt accumulated to pay for increased oil costs after the 1973 boom, the region descended into war.[8]

What is striking in this discussion of the roots of the conflicts in Central America, at least at the time of their outbreak, is the absence of any strong evidence that Cold War dynamics were a causal factor in the region's problems.* Indeed for most political actors, the Soviet Union was never considered a primary force, while the role of the United States and the consequences of a particular economic and political model, to the contrary, were evident. Although U.S. policymakers during the Reagan administration viewed the rise of oppositional movements as Soviet-inspired terrorism, the movements now known as the Frente Sandinista de Liberación Nacional (FSLN) in Nicaragua and the FMLN in El Salvador in fact rested on a peasant base, augmented by new urban middle and working class movements of students, professionals, trade unions, and the church. To the extent that local Soviet-allied Communist parties participated in these movements, they were never dominant and were joined by socialists, liberation theologians, Christian Democrats, and Social Democrats.

In Nicaragua, for example, the precursors to the FSLN had early links with the Moscow-aligned Communist party of Nicaragua (the Partido Socialista de Nicaragua—PSN), but these were definitively severed by FSLN founder Carlos Fonseca Amador in 1960, and thereafter relations were never good. The PSN remained so distant from the Sandinistas that it played virtually no role in the Nicaraguan revolution, and Moscow, which undoubtedly got most of its information from its

---

ened by insurgent movements in the 1970s. In Honduras the historical absence of a strong coffee oligarchy made possible a pattern of protest that culminated in a land reform sponsored by the military in the early 1970s. In Costa Rica the coffee oligarchy lost control of political institutions in the civil war of 1948; in its aftermath, a model of social democratic reform was institutionalized.

*The absence of obvious links between the origins of Central American conflicts and the Soviet Union led the Reagan administration to produce an infamous State Department 1981 White Paper on "Communist Interference in El Salvador" (*State Department Bulletin*, no. 2048). Its shoddy research and determination to advocate a Cold War–based policy, whether or not the evidence sustained it, became a source of acute embarrassment to the administration. Some of the supporting documents turned out to be forgeries, others were extremely vague, and none linked the USSR to the supply of guerrilla forces in El Salvador. (See *Wall Street Journal*, 8 June 1981.)

allied party, was taken totally by surprise by the event.* Nicaraguan relations with Cuba, however, were very close, and many of the Sandinistas saw the Cuban revolution as a possible model for the future.† But essentially the FSLN's ideological identification with the socialist camp arose more from the intimate identification of the United States with the Somoza tyranny, which created a deeply rooted animosity toward the United States and predisposed it to view the enemy of its enemy as a friend.

In El Salvador, to the contrary, the Soviet-allied Communist Party had always been in the thick of the struggle against authoritarian rule. But its intellectual hegemony was repeatedly challenged by radicalized religious activists and "political-military fronts" that split off from it, and the Salvadoran left was generally unreceptive to the socialist models stemming from Eastern Europe.** This is perhaps because the U.S. presence was more diffuse than in Nicaragua, and revolutionaries concentrated their attention on the "fourteen families" rather than external actors. For these reasons the left has fundamentally questioned an alliance with the Soviet Union and Cuba from the beginning, and the Communist Party guerrilla organization, the Fuerzas Armadas de

---

*In fact, the Nicaraguan revolution forced Soviet analysts to reassess the prospects for revolution in the rest of Central America, leading them to eventually endorse "broad political-military fronts" as the model for other Central American countries and support groups which they had previously castigated as ultra-leftist or adventurist. (See Cole Blasier, "The Soviet Union," in *Confronting Revolution: Security Through Diplomacy in Central America*, ed. Morris Blachman, William LeoGrande, and Kenneth Sharpe [New York: Pantheon Press, 1986], pp. 261–62, and C. G. Jacobsen, "Soviet Attitudes towards Aid to and Contacts with Central American Revolutionaries," report prepared for the Department of State, June 1984, p. 6.)

†Nicaraguan-Cuban links date from the early 1960s, when Cuba lent support to the FSLN after its founding. It subsequently refrained from providing material aid in the 1970s until the massive uprisings in Nicaraguan cities in September 1978 persuaded it to lend material assistance not just to the Sandinistas but to the guerrilla movement in El Salvador as well. The Soviet Union, however, did not follow suit until well after the victory of the Sandinista revolution. (See U.S. Congress, House of Representatives, Subcommittee on Inter-American Affairs, *Impact of Cuban-Soviet Ties in the Western Hemisphere: Hearings*, statement of Martin J. Scheira, Defense Intelligence Agency, 96th Congress [Washington, D.C.: Government Printing Office, 1980].)

**Indeed the most acrimonious internal debates throughout the 1970s revolved around the controversy over whether the Soviet Union was an ally or an imperialist enemy to the left (interviews with leaders of the FMLN, Mexico City, 1983).

Liberación (FAL), is the smallest of all five armed groups comprising the FMLN.[9]

This is not to argue that the Cold War has been unimportant. To the contrary, as Cold War competition heated up after the victory of the Sandinista revolution, an escalating cycle of U.S. hostility and Eastern bloc involvement set off the greatest and most rapid military buildup in the history of Central America.* In a mere five years the region's military forces increased a whopping 211.2 percent and its military purchases from the United States 1396.5 percent (see Table 1). For Central America

Table 1

Military Buildup in Central America

Country	Year	Purchases (*Millions of dollars*)	Security Forces
Costa Rica	1981	None	5,000
	1986	$6	9,500
El Salvador	1981	10	16,850
	1986	122	57,640
Guatemala	1981	Negligible	18,050
	1986	5.1	43,600
Honduras	1981	4.2	14,200
	1986	79.4	24,200
Nicaragua	1981	None	14,700
	1986	None	80,000
Total	1981	14.2	68,800
	1986	212.5	214,140
Increase, 1986/1981		1396.5%	211.2%

Source: Defense Department and International Institute of Strategic Studies, cited in *New York Times,* 19 April 1987.

*A full description of the actions of the superpowers is beyond the scope of this paper and will be offered by other contributors to this volume. Briefly, in 1981 the United States launched the contra war. This was followed by the quadrupling of aid to El Salvador, the construction of nine military bases in Honduras, the invasion of Grenada, the mining of Nicaragua's harbors, the introduction of the first sophisticated weaponry in the region, and the invasion of Panama. The Soviets and Cubans, for their part, provided small arms, heavy equipment, military technicians, and training to Nicaragua, and the Soviet Union gave credits, loans, and crude oil (see Jacobsen, p. 22).

the single greatest impact of this buildup has been the strengthening of military over civilian forces and the systematic increase in civilian murders and other violations of human rights, especially by the armed forces of Guatemala and El Salvador. The armed forces dominate every government in Central America. Indeed superpower largess has permitted them to become more sophisticated, more resistant to civilian authority, more violent, and wealthier than ever before.

A second major consequence has been the economic devastation of the region. Although wars and civil strife were not the precipitating factors for the economic crisis that hit the region at the end of the 1970s, the intensification of conflict provoked by the Cold War added immeasurably to the profound crisis of Central American economies. The official indicators of regional economic decline are formidable: drastic declines in growth and gross domestic product per capita, high inflation, drops in urban wages to less than their pre-conflict (1979) levels, soaring international indebtedness, and plunging export volumes, prices, and earnings (see Table 2). By 1987 Central America had suffered approximately $30 billion in economic losses since the outbreak of regional conflicts.*

Table 2

Economic Indicators for Central America, 1980–89

Region or Country	GDP Growth, 1980–87 (Percent)	GDP/Capita Growth, 1989 (Percent)	Export Earnings Index (1980 = 100)
Latin America	10.7%	-5.5%	124
Costa Rica	8.7	-9.5	132
El Salvador	-6.8	-14.5	46
Guatemala	-3.1	-20.5	77
Honduras	9.6	-14.5	114
Nicaragua	4.5	-17.2	58

Source: ECLAC, *Preliminary Overview, 1987, 1989*; cited in Michael Conroy, "Political Economy of the 1990 Elections," unpublished draft, 17 February 1990, pp. 7–8.

*This figure was provided by Guatemalan economist Jorge Gonzalez del Valle, director of the Center for Latin American Monetary Studies. He estimated that $15 billion has been lost as a direct consequence of the war and that the rest could not be accounted for. This is despite $15 billion in U.S. aid and credits to the countries of the region for both development and military aid. (See *Excelsior*, 15 December 1987.)

REGIONAL ATTEMPTS AT CONFLICT RESOLUTION

In the present climate, there is a presumption that the end of the Cold War has been the main development in resolving local conflicts. In fact, more than any other single factor, it was the threat that the combination of militarization and economic devastation posed to the survival of other regional actors in Latin America which prompted these actors, rather than the superpowers, to assume the task of conflict resolution in the region. Always believing that the rivalry between the United States and Soviet Union did not figure prominently in the roots of the turmoil in Central America, these actors nonetheless understood that the Cold War dimensions of the conflict would have to be neutralized if peace and economic recovery were ever to result. Expressions of their new level of political engagement were visible as early as 1979 through the actions of countries like Mexico and Venezuela. By 1983 individual expressions took a collective form with the formation of the Contadora Group, which included Mexico, Venezuela, Colombia, and Panama. Four years later, Contadora ceded its attempts at regional negotiations to the Central American countries themselves, who subsequently signed a peace treaty known as Esquipulas II, or the Arias Plan, in August 1987. Most recently, Esquipulas II has given way to UN-sponsored and mediated negotiations between the government and the FMLN in El Salvador.

Together these various efforts have determined the outlines of possible settlements and the forums through which such negotiations should take place. They demonstrate a surprising degree of political initiative and a striking break from past foreign policy behavior on the part of regional actors, both provoked by and aimed at containing the actions of the United States above all else. Indeed the militarization of Central America, sponsored largely by the United States, was the chief catalyst pushing neighboring countries to involve themselves in these conflicts.

Solutions to the Central American crisis were first proposed unilaterally by Mexico. Believing that the security of its own borders and the stability of the Partido Revolucionario Institucional (PRI) were threatened by massive U.S. involvement to its south, never sharing the Cold War preoccupation with the Soviet Union that colored U.S. perceptions of Central America, and confident from its newly discovered oil wealth, the Mexican government took a number of actions to limit U.S. military intervention.* Having led Latin American countries to rebuff the Carter

*As one high official of the PRI succinctly explained, "We already share one border with the United States. We do not want to share two" (interview with

administration's proposal to the Organization of American States (OAS) for a "peacekeeping force" in Nicaragua that might block the Sandinista victory—the first diplomatic rebuff from the OAS to a U.S. request for the use of force on the continent—it proposed to act as a bridge between the United States and Central America. Specifically it initiated high-level talks in 1981 between Secretary of State Alexander Haig and Foreign Minister Jorge Castañeda to seek ways of mitigating conflict and developed a formula for political negotiations involving a three-part dialogue between the United States and Cuba, the contending parties in El Salvador, and Nicaragua and its neighbors. This so-called Declaration of Managua led to new momentum for broadly linked negotiations throughout the region until it was blocked by the Reagan administration, which was suspicious of Mexico's sympathy for the Sandinista revolution.* It openly pressured the government of José Lopez Portillo and made no secret of its desire to eliminate Mexico as an intermediary in the region.[10]

Venezuela also attempted to undertake unilateral policy initiatives from 1979 to 1982 in order to protect its national sovereignty and regime stability from potential threats posed by the Central America conflict, although it never put forward a potential peace plan.† By 1982 both

---

official of the Foreign Ministry, Mexico City, September 1983). The Mexican government was also concerned about the number of Central American refugees fleeing across the border into the oil-rich south.

*The Mexican government lent significant economic and diplomatic support to the Sandinistas and the FMLN. Mexico guaranteed Nicaragua's external debt after the revolution, became an important aid donor, and was its major source of much needed petroleum. With France, it jointly recognized the Frente Democrático Revolucionario (FDR)—FMLN as "representative political forces" and called upon the international community to help reestablish peace in El Salvador. This joint declaration was important because it elevated power-sharing to an important position in regional diplomacy and was contrary to the U.S. position favoring the holding of elections as a replacement for negotiations. (See Terry Karl, "Mexico, Venezuela and the Contadora Initiative," in Blachman et al., eds., pp. 274–76.)

†Motivated by its Social Democratic and Christian Democratic parties and those of Central America and an oil-propelled desire to project itself as a continental leader, Venezuela's long-term commitment to promote democracy in the hemisphere, known as the Betancourt Doctrine, often fit nicely with U.S. objectives. Unlike Mexico, with its overriding fear of a U.S. military presence, the Venezuelan regime was haunted by the memory of its defeated guerrilla movement, which had been supported by Cuba in the 1960s. This promoted a strong anti-communism, a decision to "export" democracy, and a firm commitment to prevent "more Cubas." While this meant that the Christian Democratic government of Luis

Mexico and Venezuela had learned that it was too costly and ineffective to "go it alone." While individual countries could propose negotiating strategies as paths to the resolution of the region's conflicts, such initiatives were easily abrogated or simply ignored by the United States, leaving countries vulnerable to the displeasure of the Reagan administration. Yet while rapidly increasing militarization made political initiatives even more urgent in the perception of regional actors, no adequate forum for cooperation existed. The OAS was viewed with suspicion because it had traditionally served as a vehicle for the United States, a member and a key protagonist in militarization. The United Nations, itself ridden by Cold War tensions, was seen as generally ineffective and insufficiently representative of Latin America.

In this context, the Contadora Group was formed in January 1983 with the sole aim of finding a diplomatic settlement to the problems of Central America. Initiated by Venezuela and Mexico and instantly expanded to include Panama and Colombia, by 1985 it had a "support group" of Latin American democracies: Brazil, Argentina, Uruguay, and Peru.* Aimed at offering their collective good offices to help bring peace to Central America, the Contadora Group identified its primary task to be the intensification of dialogue on the Latin American level in order to "reduce tensions and establish the bases for a lasting climate of peaceful coexistence and mutual respect between countries."[11]

The Contadora initiative challenged U.S. policy because it explicitly contradicted the dual goals of overthrowing the Sandinista regime in Nicaragua and militarily defeating the FMLN in El Salvador. Thus it is

---

Herrera Campins was willing to pressure the Sandinista regime for early elections, condition aid on the Sandinistas' political behavior, support conservative private-sector organizations, and give full backing to fellow Christian Democrat Duarte in El Salvador, there was a divergence between Venezuelan and U.S. policy, especially after the Falklands-Malvinas War in 1982. Furthermore, the strong identification with U.S. policy and the equation of Christian Democratic Party interests with national interests had a domestic price tag, as Social Democratic critics from Accion Democrática vehemently criticized Venezuelan involvement in covert activities in support of Duarte. These pressures led Venezuela to back off from an alignment with the United States and eventually lean toward Mexico. (See Karl, "Mexico, Venezuela, and the Contadora Initiative.")

*Some observers trace the origins of Contadora to General Omar Torrijos's 1976 effort to elicit the support of Mexico, Venezuela, Colombia, and Costa Rica in his negotiations with the United States over the Panama Canal Treaty. These same nations later attempted to isolate Somoza in the region, and after his overthrow sought to extract promises of political pluralism, a mixed economy, and nonalignment from the Sandinistas.

not surprising that the Reagan administration met Contadora's formation with counteractions of its own and quiet hostility.* It insisted that
all discussion regarding Central America take place in the OAS, where
it could influence outcomes directly. But in a striking example of declining U.S. authority on the continent, both the United Nations and the
OAS declared that the latter was not an appropriate forum for the
problems of Central America.[12] After the OAS Council rejected an April
1983 attempt by Costa Rica to bring accusations against Nicaragua to
the organization, Contadora successfully insisted that any discussions
about Central America in the OAS or the United Nations "be based on
the documents and resolutions of Contadora and not on the request of
one of the parties in conflict." It subsequently established a commission
to investigate border tensions between Nicaragua and Costa Rica, temporarily diminishing tensions between the two countries.

For a time, it looked as though the Contadora process might help
to settle the conflicts in Central America. Adopting the Cold War framework that so preoccupied the United States, the Contadora Group proposed an agreement which would defend the sovereignty of Central
American nations in exchange for keeping the Soviet Union out of the
isthmus and stopping armed subversion against existing governments.
By 1984 all Central American countries agreed in principle to the following program: the creation of demilitarized zones, the elimination of
foreign advisers, arms control, a proscription from using the territory of
one state to destabilize another, the eradication of arms trafficking, and
the prohibition of any interference in the affairs of another country. The
treaty contained the intention to address "national reconciliation" within
countries suffering from internal strife—a clear reference to El Salvador.†

---

*The Reagan administration unsuccessfully sought to prevent any form of
independent multilateral activity by launching its own Forum for Peace and
Democracy. Ostensibly promoted by Honduras and Costa Rica to unify the
democratically elected governments in the area, this so-called Enders Forum was
widely viewed as a U.S. ploy to isolate Nicaragua and block the first united
efforts of Mexico and Venezuela. The U.S. initiative caused serious tensions
among Latin American nations. Panama, Colombia, Costa Rica, Honduras, El
Salvador, Belize, and the Dominican Republic attended the forum, but both
Mexico and Venezuela declined to participate. Without these two key countries,
the initiative died (*New York Times*, 10 October 1982, p. 26).

†The Contadora Group had initially been unwilling to address the problem of
El Salvador, viewing it as an internal issue rather than a problem between
governments. But realizing that a regional settlement was impossible without
dealing with this conflict, it abandoned its hands-off policy and publicly offered
to help the new Duarte government begin negotiations with Salvadoran rebels.

This had an immediate effect upon that country because it set the stage for President Duarte's first dialogue with the guerrillas at La Palma in October 1984. But these negotiations broke down one month later due to pressure from the right and the military, opposition from the Reagan administration, and the refusal of the FMLN to lay down its arms to take part in elections without prior participation in a provisional government that would set new laws and reorganize the military.

The outlook for resolving the Nicaragua conflict was more optimistic. The compromise offered by the Contadora treaty was clear: the survival of the Sandinista regime would be guaranteed through provisions that would terminate contra activity and lead to the withdrawal of U.S. bases in Honduras. In return, Nicaragua's ability to aid the FDR-FMLN against El Salvador's government or to forge military alliances with the socialist bloc would be clearly circumscribed. The treaty included provisions for amnesty for political dissidents, impartial elections under international auspices, and the termination of support for groups fighting to overthrow Central American governments—the key demands raised by the Reagan administration to justify its efforts to dislodge the Sandinista regime. The implementation of this tradeoff would be subject to verification by neutral parties in order to ensure long-term compliance.

The Reagan administration scuttled Contadora at the very moment when successful peace negotiations seemed imminent, however. In September 1984 the Nicaraguan government unexpectedly announced its unconditional acceptance of a Contadora draft treaty. The Reagan administration, stunned by Nicaragua's actions and unwilling to negotiate, encouraged its Central American allies (the so-called Tegucigalpa Group) to block progress on accommodation. Although a consensus to accept the treaty previously had been reached among all five Central American countries, U.S. pressure led to new objections from Honduras, El Salvador, and Costa Rica regarding the timing for the withdrawal of foreign military advisers, the closing of military bases, arms and troop reductions, the verification process, and the signing of a protocol with the Soviet Union.*

---

*The United States encouraged its allies in Central America to protest the idea of a protocol that would have the Soviet Union and the United States agree in writing not to interfere with the implementation of the Contadora agreement. In the U.S. view, this admitted a political role for the Soviets and Cubans in Central America, thus the very signature of these countries was not acceptable. In addition to having objections over the timing of the withdrawal of foreign advisers, the United States objected to provisions that would bar U.S. military exercises in the

These objections effectively halted the diplomatic momentum of Contadora. As a background paper to the National Security Council later boasted, "We have effectively blocked Contadora Group efforts to impose a second draft of a revised Contadora Act."[13]*

That the Reagan administration was able to use its Central American allies so effectively pointed to a fatal flaw in Contadora: its influence was limited by the fact that it did not directly incorporate the governments of Central America themselves. While Contadora was able to capture the moral high ground by becoming the symbol for regional peace, negotiate a diminution of tensions in key moments, and produce a viable if imperfect treaty, its attempts to find a political solution to the conflicts in Central America were repeatedly undermined by the ability of the United States to utilize its Central American allies as obstacles to negotiations. When the Tegucigalpa Group rejected the third and final version of the Contadora treaty in June 1986, arguing that its provisions were inadequate and that a peace agreement required the prior democratization of Nicaragua, and when the U.S. House of Representatives reversed position by voting $100 million in aid to the contras, Contadora began to fade into the background. Even a last ditch effort by the United Nations and the OAS failed to revitalize it.†

---

region as well as U.S. bases. (See International Policy Report, "Contadora: A Text for Peace," November 1984, and *Oakland Tribune*, 9 November 1984.)

*The Reagan administration had shown this intention from the beginning. Immediately following the formation of Contadora, with its publicly proclaimed platform of disarmament and nonintervention, the United States initiated the Big Pine I exercises in Honduras which brought the first mass landing of U.S. troops to the area. In July 1983, when the presidents of the Contadora countries called for a prohibition on the installation of all foreign bases in the region, the Reagan administration began to construct eight bases in Honduras.

†In the wake of the Iran/Contra scandal of 1986, the Contadora Group made a new push for a settlement. Meeting with the support group, eight Latin American countries declared aid to the contras illegal and invited Javier Perez de Cuellar and João Baena Soares, heads of the United Nations and OAS respectively, to intervene in the Central American conflict. They too failed to break new ground. (See "Contadora, U.S. on Separate Bids," *Latin American Weekly Report*, no. 3 [January 1987]: 3, and William Stockton, "U.N. Chief Pessimistic After Latin Peace Trip," *New York Times*, 22 January 1987, p. 7.)

THE ARIAS PEACE PLAN

At this point the Contadora initiative was superseded by the diplomatic efforts of Costa Rican President Oscar Arias. Encouraged by the weakness of the Reagan administration in the midst of the fast-breaking Iran/Contra scandal and agreeing with Guatemalan President Vinicio Cerezo that Central America should become the protagonist of its own history, Arias put forward a formal plan for peace in San Jose on 15 February 1987.[14] This was eventually signed on 7 August 1987 by the presidents of each Central American country. Arias's plan effectively removed the responsibility for designing a peace process from Latin American regional powers and placed it directly on the Central American countries themselves. While publicly saying only that the four-year-old Contadora process seemed incapable of finding a mutually acceptable solution to the conflict in Nicaragua, Central Americans met the replacement of Contadora with relief, privately complaining of interference in their internal affairs.* Costa Rica, as the continent's oldest democracy, had never recognized the moral authority of Contadora in the first place, arguing that the authoritarian regimes of Panama and Mexico were in an awkward position to demand democratization in the region.

That President Arias should step into leadership in the peace process was no accident. His transformation from a supporter of the contra aid effort to a Noble Peace Prize winner who became the symbol of a political settlement in Central America can be traced largely to the difficult domestic conditions stemming directly from the militarization and economic devastation of Central America. Thus he moved from being a leader in the Tegucigalpa Group to a more neutral arbiter between Nicaragua and the United States. As president of Costa Rica, Arias had to confront the impact of the contra war: the militarization of his country which was potentially a threat to its own democratic institutions,† the lawlessness of roaming bands of contra rebels in the north,

*Carlos José Gutierrez, Costa Rica's Minister of Foreign Relations, describes Contadora meetings where the ministers of Mexico, Panama, Colombia, and Venezuela talked behind closed doors, while those of Guatemala, El Salvador, Honduras, Costa Rica, and Nicaragua "experienced the humiliation of waiting for the instructions regarding Central America that should be carried out" (Guido Fernandez, *El desafio de la paz in Centroamerica* [San Jose: Editorial CR, 1989], p. 71).

†The United States pressured Costa Rica, which has no standing army, to militarize. Although the government of Luis Alberto Monge prior to Arias

the presence of over 125,000 Nicaraguan refugees (about 5 percent of Costa Rica's population) which strained social services, and the flight of foreign investment and tourism, which were badly needed in the mist of a growing economic crisis.* Buffered by a widely shared belief that the contra war, far from protecting Costa Rica from Nicaraguan aggression, actually threatened its vital interests, Arias returned Costa Rica to its official position of neutrality, expelled contra bases from the country, and actively pushed a negotiated settlement for the region.[15]

Similar dynamics pushed other Central American countries to create some distance from U.S. policy and lean toward a political solution to the region's two main conflicts. By 1986 the tremendous military buildup had begun to worry government officials and civilian leaders in Honduras, El Salvador, and Guatemala, who increasingly expressed strong misgivings about the prospect of dealing with vastly strengthened armies in their countries. This was especially true as the military weakness of the contras was demonstrated throughout 1986–87 and as the Iran/Contra scandal revealed the fragility of long-term U.S. support in the region.† The buildup gave the military enhanced control over civilian government because aid was funneled directly to local armies and police, thus threatening the ultimate viability of civilian rule. It was seen as a dangerous phenomenon that could eventually threaten the entire social fabric of the region. Fear over the growth of militaries was coupled with

---

rejected the most blatant forms of military cooperation, it strengthened the Public Security Forces with increased levels of U.S. military assistance and training (which jumped from $1.2 million in 1982 to $4.6 million in 1983), formed its first rapid deployment counterinsurgency battalion, and established a reserve force called the Organization for National Emergencies. (See Maxwell S. Peltz, "Costa Rica and the Reagan Administration: Sparring with a Giant," Senior Honors Thesis, Stanford University, May 1989.) Militarization in turn encouraged the growth of extremist right-wing movements, including fifteen different paramilitary organizations (*Central America Report* 13, 17 [9 May 1986]: 134).

*These problems affected Arias's February 1986 electoral campaign as well. Arias was forced to cut a deal with a faction of his party strongly opposed to President Monge's policy of militarization and collaboration with the U.S. contra war effort, and he narrowly won the election by portraying his principal rival as the "war candidate."

†As a Honduran official remarked, "[The military doesn't] overthrow us because it is not in its interest right now and because the United States has told them not to. But what the United States is basically doing here is paying our army not to have a coup. Who knows what will happen when you are no longer here to stop them?" (*New York Times*, 19 April 1987).

a preoccupation over the presence of an uncontrollable irregular army—the contras—on the borders of Honduras and Costa Rica. When their military weakness was revealed, officials of both countries worried that the contras would degenerate into armed bands threatening the citizens of their host countries.*

Worries over the prospects for economic recovery also fueled this new momentum for a negotiated settlement. By 1987 a growing number of Central Americans realized that it would be impossible to attract foreign capital or tourism or even revitalize plunging exports as long as the war continued. Even in Honduras and El Salvador, where massive amounts of U.S. aid had provided an important bulwark against economic collapse, the reliability of this aid over the long run was increasingly called into question after the Iran/Contra scandal. Furthermore, militarization increased the economic power of the military; in each country the armed forces controlled its own bank as well as farms, private companies, and lucrative government agencies, thereby heightening the growing competition for scarce resources.† In this context, there was widespread agreement with President Arias's statement that "the economic development I want for my country is incompatible with war. . . . That is why I favor a peaceful negotiated solution."[16]

This new sentiment, plus an especially favorable conjuncture, led to the signing of the Arias Peace Plan.** The new treaty was like Contadora in that it did not address the root causes of conflict—misery

*Residents on the borders of both countries reported that roaming bands of contra rebels engaged in kidnapping and robbery, and they formed community organizations to demand protection from their governments (interviews in Honduras and Costa Rica with government officials, October 1985; *Central America Report* 12, 42 [1 November 1985]).

†In Honduras the army runs the merchant marine, the immigration bureau, and the phone company. In El Salvador corrupt officers own large estates, while the military as an institution controls shopping malls, resorts, fishing exports, and urban and rural properties. (See Joel Millman, "El Salvador's Army: A Force Unto Itself," *New York Times Magazine*, 10 December 1989, and *Los Angeles Times*, 2 September 1990.)

**The signing of the treaty coincided with the demise of the contra option in the United States as a result of the Iran/Contra scandal, public divisions within the contra movement itself, and important military victories against them by the Sandinistas. These events prompted the Speaker of the House of Representatives, Jim Wright, to negotiate directly with President Reagan to produce a peace plan aimed at resolving the conflict with Nicaragua. The presentation of the Reagan-Wright plan, which the Reagan administration subsequently disavowed, at the exact moment of the Central American presidents' meeting gave these presidents and repression—but was instead designed to untangle Central America from the East-West conflict. It differed in fundamental ways, however. Designed by the Central Americans themselves, it put the primary focus on democratization rather than demilitarization per se as a means of eventually demobilizing the region. Because both the United States and Central American militaries had refused to accept Contadora's efforts to limit the size of national armies, weapons flows, foreign military advisers, and presence of U.S. bases, the Arias Plan instead concentrated on the holding of elections, amnesty, cease-fires, and reciprocal nonaggression pacts—conditions which would be more difficult to oppose. In addition, all signators committed themselves to the freedom to organize politically, the lifting of states of siege, the abolition of legal measures that hamper political freedom, the end to all outside aid to rebel groups, the respect for human rights, and the seeking of negotiated settlements to internal conflicts. These conditions were premised on the assumption that all existing governments, including that of the Sandinistas, were legitimately elected. The content of the peace agreement was left deliberately vague in places, to be worked out later among the foreign ministers of all five countries.[17]

The Esquipulas II treaty marked a watershed for the conflict in Nicaragua in several respects. First, it provided the opportunity for the Sandinista government to make concessions to other Central American governments and not to the Reagan administration, thereby permitting facesaving and a more flexible negotiating stance. Second, it pulled the rug out from under Reagan administration attempts to keep the contra option alive. Within six months of the treaty's signing, the Sandinistas agreed to establish a National Reconciliation Commission, entered into dialogue with opposition politicians, permitted the reopening of the opposition daily *La Prensa*, and decreed a unilateral cease-fire. At the same time, military aid to the contras was definitively ended by the U.S. Congress, who, having sought unsuccessfully for a formula to stop the unpopular contra policy in the past, eagerly embraced the Arias treaty. Although the timetable established by Esquipulas II was seldom met and there were frequent complaints over the lack of enforceability of the

---

the impression that they would have to choose between a treaty of their own making or one imposed by the United States. In effect, the presentation of the Reagan-Wright draft gave the go-ahead to Honduras, the surrogate of the United States, to support the Arias proposal to stop contra aid before the complete democratization of Nicaragua. Thus it formed the framework that made the signing of Esquipulas II possible (Fernandez, p. 143).

accord, eventually a broad amnesty and new electoral laws followed. Even the opposition's commitment to participate in the 1990 elections was attributed to accords orchestrated by the five Central American presidents.*

Esquipulas II was a failure in other respects, however. Although ostensibly aimed at all Central American countries except Costa Rica, its basic concern was to balance Nicaragua's security needs against the rest of the region's need to moderate the Sandinistas.† The treaty failed to address adequately the problem of internal political reconciliation in Guatemala and El Salvador, and consequently rebels in those two countries resisted calls for an end to fighting. Esquipulas II appeared to have some impact on El Salvador, but this was short-lived. After the accords were adopted, the government let lapse a state-of-siege law, declared a general amnesty, permitted an estimated 4,000 refugees to return to guerrilla-controlled zones, and allowed civilian opposition leaders to open offices in San Salvador. The two sides met in San Salvador, where President Duarte insisted that the rebels disarm and accept amnesty under the terms of the Central American peace accord. The FMLN, militarily stronger than ever before, reiterated its demands to restructure the armed forces, establish a provisional government, and hold new elections. Once again, the dialogue collapsed.

The next breakthrough in negotiations occurred outside the framework of the Arias Peace Plan. On 23 January 1989, the FMLN put forward a proposal, signed by all five guerrilla commanders, which dropped its insistence on power-sharing before elections, promised a cease-fire, and recognized the legitimacy of the electoral process. This resulted in some progress toward a settlement, when eight political parties (including the Alianza Republicana Nacionalista [ARENA] and the Christian Democrats) had their first meeting with the FMLN since the outbreak of the war. Although the FMLN later dropped its demand to be integrated into

*The opposition's agreement to participate in elections is credited to a meeting between Central American presidents in February 1990, when the Esquipulas IV accords were signed. These accords obligated the FSLN government to make important concessions to the opposition in exchange for its participation. In addition, they set a specific timetable for the electoral campaign and for the demobilization of the contras. (See *Envio*, Summer 1989, p. 21.)

†Thus other countries were able to systematically violate the accord with few repercussions. The most conspicuous failure to carry out the accord was the refusal of Honduras to stop assisting the Nicaraguan contra rebels until the change in administration in the United States after the 1988 elections (*New York Times*, 10 January 1988).

the Salvadoran armed forces and instead agreed to lay down its arms in exchange for a reduction of the armed forces to their 1978 pre–civil war level, its call for a six-month delay in the March 1989 elections to permit its participation was rejected by Duarte, and the prospects for a settlement faltered once again. They received a brief boost in an August 1989 summit in Tela, Honduras, when the Central American presidents called on the parties in El Salvador to enter into a dialogue to achieve national reconciliation and end hostilities in keeping with similar efforts in Nicaragua, but the collapse of subsequent talks in San José, Costa Rica, followed by a series of political assassinations, led to a November 1989 FMLN offensive and the most intense fighting of the war.[18]*

Esquipulas II was not successful in dealing with the conflict in El Salvador because, like the Contadora proposals, its bargaining framework attributed a false symmetry to the conflicts in Nicaragua and El Salvador. Central America's smallest country was in the midst of an authentic civil war rather than a proxy war fought on behalf of one of the superpowers. Regional actors were reluctant to intervene in what they saw as an especially intractable internal matter, and they initially believed that resolving the Nicaraguan conflict alone could bring about substantial demilitarization and economic recovery. It soon became clear that neither would be forthcoming without some resolution of El Salvador's domestic strife. Unable to propose viable solutions to the Salvadoran conflict for over a decade and believing that the need for a special regional forum had been eliminated by the resolution of the contra problem, they called upon the United Nations to reinitiate dialogue between the government and the FMLN. In the new atmosphere created by the winding down of the Cold War, they welcomed a 4 April 1990 announcement of Perez de Cuellar that he would oversee peace negotiations in that country "to end the armed conflict through political means as speedily as possible, promote the democratization of the country, guarantee unrestricted respect for human rights and reunify Salvadoran society."[19] The current involvement of the United Nations in

---

*At the San José talks the FMLN proposed that a cease-fire be part of a comprehensive settlement. The government would agree to juridical reform, to purge and professionalize the armed forces, to prosecute persons involved in human rights abuses and the murder of Archbishop Oscar Arnulfo Romero, and to maintain the 1980 land and banking reforms. The government proposed an immediate cease-fire, to be monitored by regional observers, which would be followed by the incorporation of the FMLN into political life and a review of the electoral and juridical systems.

attempting to bring about a negotiated settlement is the direct result of this regional petition.

THE LIMITATIONS OF THE END OF THE COLD WAR

How will the end of the Cold War affect the future of Central America? The diminution of superpower rivalry, at least in the short run, establishes the apparent supremacy of capitalism and democracy, discredits socialist models, and marks the end of significant Soviet or Cuban aid to the isthmus. What impact will these changes have on the prospects for reaching the fundamental pacts and compromises that can serve as the basis for social peace? Evidence from the past indicates that the effects of these changes in the international arena will be less than might be anticipated on the region. Because these conflicts were never rooted in the Cold War, they are unlikely to be resolved by its termination. Nor does this latest manifestation of U.S. hegemony in the hemisphere, with its consequent diffusion of U.S.-based development models, represent anything new for the countries of Central America. This is not to argue that the winding down of the Cold War will have little impact in the long run but rather to emphasize its somewhat limited consequences.

Ironically the effects of the winding down of the Cold War may be felt least in Nicaragua, where Cold War scenarios have been most dramatically played out. While the FSLN leadership is certainly disheartened by the collapse of the Eastern bloc and the enormous problems facing Cuba, it had already distanced itself from socialist models of development from the beginning of the revolution. The collapse of any form of international socialist option merely reinforces a lesson already learned. If anything, it may have positive consequences because it frees the FSLN to continue its search for alternative models without being confined by the shackles of previous socialist dogmas.

Moreover, it cannot be said that the new international situation produced the fragile democratization that now exists in Nicaragua. Both the Sandinista government and the opposition significantly moderated their positions beginning in 1987—prior to the dramatic events of 1989 in Europe. Thus these events confirm a process already well under way. The changes in the actions and perceptions of both sides were due to a combination of factors: the severe blows delivered to the contras by the Sandinista army in 1987 and 1988 which marked their demise as a counterrevolutionary movement, the weakening of the U.S. role by the Iran/Contra scandal (exemplified by the February 1988 rejection of military aid to the contras), the shift from the Reagan to the Bush administration, the profound crisis of the Nicaraguan economy, widespread war weariness in Nicaragua, and external pressure stemming primarily from Esquipulas II but also from the West Europeans. These circumstances, and not changes in superpower relations, were the primary factors transforming the attitudes and actions of Nicaragua.

By 1989 all but the most hardline factions in the Nicaraguan conflict had moderated their past positions. Opposition leaders, once dedicated to the government's overthrow, believed that the Sandinistas had changed.* The opposition itself, formerly dedicated to eradicating every trace of Sandinismo, also became more tolerant. By early 1989 opposition leaders could say, "We accept the existence of the FSLN, with its security forces and its mass organizations and its armed forces."[20] While events in Eastern Europe probably hastened the demise of notions like the vanguard party among FSLN followers and gave increased security to private-sector interests, their impact on the holding of elections or their ultimate outcome was less significant than internal economic factors. Nor have they significantly bolstered Nicaragua's weak right wing, as evidenced by the increasing political isolation of the Consejo Superior de la Empresa Privada (COSEP), the leading capitalist association, as well as the unwillingness of the government of Violetta Chamorro to roll back the social gains of the Sandinista revolution.

Equally ironically the winding down of the Cold War may have its greatest effect in El Salvador, where it has been least relevant. What has been most remarkable about the right and the left in El Salvador, especially when compared to Nicaragua, is their relative autonomy from external actors. All of the guerrilla organizations currently united in the FMLN are products of the turbulent struggles within the Communist Party, but (as noted) there has always been an important degree of distance from and suspicion of Havana and especially the

---

*As former vice-presidential candidate and anti-Sandinista Constantino Pereira explained, "Of course [the FSLN] has changed. . . . Three or four years ago the FSLN realized that the Marxist-Leninist project and democratic centralism are impossible in Nicaragua. They don't work in Nicaragua . . . for historical reasons, including the fact that the U.S. is not going to permit a development like Cuba" (interview with Pereira by Steve Levitsky, cited in Steve Levitsky, "Domination and Democratization in Revolutionary Nicaragua," Senior Honors Thesis, Stanford University, May 1990, p. 137).

Soviet Union.* The right, represented by the military and ARENA, demonstrates a similar level of suspicion of the United States, despite the influx of more than $1 billion in U.S. aid aimed at purchasing its compliance.† This autonomy has meant that both forces have been the fundamental determinants of the war, regardless of the intrusion of outside actors, and have successfully defied the attempts of others to shape their behavior.

There is an important difference between the right and the left in this respect, however. The left has gradually moderated its stance, responding primarily to the widely recognized military stalemate between the FMLN and the government, though the influence of other Latin American countries has also played a role.** This moderation was most notable in the FMLN's new negotiating stance, announced in January 1989, prior to the dramatic events that would soon shape Europe. Making significant concessions since the first negotiations in 1984, the FMLN

---

*In 1970 Salvador Cayetano Carpio, a former secretary-general of the Communist Party, resigned and established the first underground cell of the Fuerzas Populares de Liberación (FPL). This was followed by another split in which ex-party members, Christian Democratic Party dissidents, students, and religious activists joined to form the Ejército Revolucionario del Pueblo (ERP). Two more organizations, the Fuerzas Armadas de Resistencia Nacional (FARN) and the Partido Revolucionario de Trabajadores Centroamericanos (PRTC), split from the ERP. The Communist Party did not form its own guerrilla organization, the FAL, until sometime after 1977. These groups were to unite the FMLN.

†Although both the Duarte and Cristiani governments would have been unable to survive without U.S. support, the traditions of *tanda* (graduation class) loyalty and military primacy over civil authority have made officers and the ultra-right especially resistant to attempts by American advisers to "democratize" and professionalize them. A 1988 Harvard University study by four U.S. lieutenant colonels concluded, "Attempts to supplant the ethos of the Salvadoran officer corps with a more professional model and to develop noncommissioned officers produced little, despite the expenditure of prodigious resources" (A. J. Bacevich, Manes D. Hallums, Richard H. White, and Thomas F. Young, *American Military Policy in Small Wars: The Case of El Salvador* [Washington, D.C.: Institute for Foreign Policy Analysis, 1988], p. vii).

**The FMLN offensive in November 1989 confirmed the reality of the stalemate to even the most skeptical observers. The FMLN demonstrated that it has grown stronger, is well armed, and has the capability of launching a full-scale simultaneous military operation in all major cities of El Salvador, including the capital, which had long been considered a stronghold of the army. But the offensive also demonstrated that the FMLN is still incapable of defeating the army or provoking a general insurrection. (See General Maxwell R. Thurman, Hearing of the Senate Armed Services Committee, 8 February 1990.)

dropped its long-standing demands for power-sharing, an integration of rebel with government military forces, and the abolition of the 1983 constitution. It recognized elections as the legitimate path to power.* The right has not shown a similar degree of flexibility. Though moderates in the government, the ruling party, and the business community have come to support a negotiated settlement as the only way to bring peace, hardliners on the right still support nothing short of a negotiated surrender by the FMLN. Convinced that the United States will not let them lose the war and unwilling to meet the chief demands of the FMLN—which include the restructuring and reduction of the army, the reform of the judicial system to end immunity for human rights abuses, and full guarantees for democratic liberties—they have resisted concessions which would end their immunity in UN-sponsored talks.

Despite the historic autonomy of Salvadoran domestic forces, however, the end of the Cold War could have a significant impact on the resolution of the conflict. In the short run, to the extent that it undermines the U.S. rationale for waging war against the FMLN, it contributes to a possible decisive shift in the willingness of the U.S. Congress to provide aid to the Salvadoran government. This is already evident in a recent decision of the House of Representatives to cut military aid substantially in protest over the lack of judicial progress in the murder of six Jesuit priests in November 1989. A congressional cut or withdrawal of U.S. aid, which has served as a major incentive for the army and the government to resist negotiations, would be a severe blow to the right and would eventually enhance the prospects for a settlement.

Furthermore, the diminution of Cold War tensions reinforces the prospects for concerted international pressure to resolve the Salvadoran civil war. Although domestic political forces have resisted the influence of individual superpowers and multilateral Latin American diplomacy to this point, they have yet to experience the *combined* impact of both great powers and regional actors pushing for the same outcome—a likely scenario for the future. Given the commitment of the newly consensual United Nations to mediate the conflict and move negotiations back into

---

*As Salvador Samayoa, member of the FMLN's negotiating team, noted, "There is simply no single political force that could impose its own agenda on the nation, or on the other political forces. . . . In El Salvador, political pluralism is necessary; regardless of our wishes there would have to be some provision for it. We do wish to have pluralism, but even if we didn't, pluralism would have to exist because there are a variety of political forces and they have real weight and power" (cited in Terry Karl, "Negotiations or Total War: Interview with Salvador Samayoa," *World Policy Journal*, Spring 1989, p. 349).

a formal international organization, members of the Security Council should be more easily united behind a negotiated settlement. Moreover, the long regional negotiating process marked by Contadora and the Arias Plan has created some incentives to reach an accord. By creating a new sense of community among Central American leaders and diminishing the hostility between countries if not within them, it has begun to pave the way for the economic and political integration of these countries, providing still further pressures on El Salvador to end its war.* Although hardliners on the right will undoubtedly continue to resist a settlement in the short run, the combination of international insistence plus regional incentives could be difficult for domestic actors to defy over a protracted period.

The winding down of the Cold War cannot, however, resolve the original problems that gave rise to revolution in Nicaragua and civil war in El Salvador. The apparent "victory" of the United States has renewed the emphasis on private-sector-led growth and trickle-down for the peasantry in the region, but it is precisely these policies that led to widespread unrest in the first place, as the benefits of growth went to established elites rather than poor masses. Militaries, which were the other main cause of conflict, are stronger than ever before, and projected cutbacks in U.S. aid should not be enough to shrink them back to their prewar levels.† Meanwhile, the extreme militarization, economic crisis, and social disintegration that now stamp the region after a decade of war leave it ripe for continued emigration, further environmental devastation, the strengthening of nondemocratic forces on both sides, and

---

*The diminution of hostilities was immediately evident after the signing of Esquipulas II and was manifested in Nicaragua's withdrawal of its World Court suit against Costa Rica, as well as in better relations between the leaders of the region. As Sam Dillon and Andres Oppenheimer have written, "Central America's five presidents—whose communication once consisted largely of public insults volleyed through the press—now chat frequently by phone about their differences" (*Miami Herald*, 1 November 1987). Central American governments have begun to discuss the possibility of a common monetary unit and have agreed to inaugurate a Central American parliament, which will begin locating in November 1991 (see *Excelsior*, 2 September 1990).

†Aid to Honduras has dropped drastically from a peak of $81 million in 1986 to $21 million in 1990, but the Honduran army is resisting cutbacks. In regional talks on arms limits, Guatemala and El Salvador recently argued that they could make no cutbacks because they were fighting internal wars. Even if some dent is made in the numbers of the military, the issue of military dominance will remain.

the expansion of the drug trade.* If Central American militaries are not demobilized as part of a resolution to the region's current crisis, they are likely to continue to intervene in the future, as they have in the past, against any collective expressions of discontent, placing forces of the democratic center and left in extremely vulnerable positions. In the post–Cold War era of the future, this could leave the United States still confronting the same uncomfortable choice it now faces in El Salvador: whether to maintain support for its "traditional friends and allies" against peasant-based movements fighting for economic and political rights or to withdraw its backing from the abusive, corrupt, and increasingly drug-ridden militaries of its own creation.

NOTES

1. Cited in Richard Millet, "Central American Paralysis," *Foreign Policy* 39 (Summer 1980): 101. Also see Ernest R. May, *The Making of the Monroe Doctrine* (Cambridge: Harvard University Press, 1975).

2. See Abraham Lowenthal, "Rediscovering Latin America," *Foreign Affairs* 69, 4 (Fall 1990: 35.

3. Jeane Kirkpatrick, "U.S. Security and Latin America," *Commentary* (January 1981): 50.

4. "Eventually," President Ronald Reagan warned, "we will have to confront the reality of a Soviet military beachhead inside our defense perimeters—about 500 miles from Mexico" ("Why Democracy Matters in Central America," address delivered on 24 June 1986, U.S. Department of State, Bureau of Public Affairs, *Current Policy*, no. 850).

5. On the Reagan Doctrine, see George Shultz, "America and the Struggle for Freedom," address before the Commonwealth Club of San Francisco, 22 February 1985, *State Department Current Policy*, no. 659, and William Bode, "The Reagan Doctrine in Outline," *Strategic Review*, Winter 1986.

6. These studies are cited in Carmen Deere and Martin Diskin, "Rural Poverty in El Salvador: Dimensions, Causes and Trends," pp. 8–9. From research project "Rural Poverty in Central America: Dimensions and Causes." Geneva: International Labour Organization, June 1983.

7. This label is taken from Enrique Baloyra-Herp, "Reactionary Despotism in Central America," *Journal of Latin American Studies* 15, pp. 295–319.

*There is now substantial evidence that the drug trade has moved into Honduras, Guatemala, and El Salvador and is linked to the military.

8. There is a large amount of literature on the economic and political roots of the conflict in Central America. See, for example, Victor Bulmer-Thomas, *The Political Economy of Central America Since 1920* (Cambridge: Cambridge University Press, 1987); William Durham, *Scarcity and Survival in Central America: Ecological Origins of the Soccer War* (Stanford: Stanford University Press, 1979); Robert Williams, *Export Agriculture and the Crisis in Central America* (Chapel Hill: University of North Carolina Press, 1986); and Charles Brockett, *Land, Power and Poverty: Agrarian Transformation and Political Conflict in Central America* (Boston: Unwin Hyman, 1988).

9. As Robert Leiken notes, "It is the organizations that stand at the greatest distance from the Soviet Union which control nearly two-thirds of the fighting force of the FMLN" ("The Salvadoran Left," in *Central America: Anatomy of Conflict*, R. Leiken, ed. [New York: Pergamon Press, 1984], p. 112).

10. *New York Times*, 18 May 1982.

11. "Documentos relacionados con la gestion del grupo Contadora," compiled for the author by the Subsecretaria de Planeación y Asuntos Culturales, Mexico City, 1983.

12. In UN Secretary General Javier Perez de Cuellar's words, "Since Cuba is not a member of the OAS and Nicaragua has no competence in this organism, obviously the OAS is not the appropriate forum to resolve the situation in Central America" (*El Día*, 19 April 1983).

13. *Washington Post*, 6 November 1984.

14. *Los Angeles Times*, 19 February 1988.

15. As early as the summer of 1985, many of Costa Rica's outstanding public figures—including former presidents Figueres, Oduber, Trejos, and Carazo—were calling for a dialogue with Nicaragua and greater prudence in the militarization of the country (*Central America Report* 12, 32 [23 August 1985]: 253–54).

16. *Washington Post*, 1 February 1987.

17. *Miami Herald*, 20 September 1987; *New York Times*, 8 August 1987.

18. For a description of new peace proposals and the events leading up to this offensive, see Terry Karl, "Negotiations or Total War," *World Policy Journal*, Spring 1989, pp. 321–27. On more recent prospects of negotiations, see Tom Gibb and Frank Smyth, "El Salvador: Is Peace Possible?," Washington Office on Latin America, April 1990.

19. Press communique issued by the office of the UN Secretary General, 4 April 1990.

20. *La Cronica*, 14 December 1989, cited in Levitsky, p. 146.

MIDDLE EAST

AMERICAN MIDDLE EAST POLICY AFTER
THE COLD WAR

William B. Quandt

Iraq's invasion of Kuwait on 2 August 1990 set the stage for the first regional crisis of the post–Cold War era. The American response, massive in scale and single-minded in purpose, strongly suggested that some new norms of international relations are taking hold. For many Americans, the lesson of the crisis seemed to be that the specter of Vietnam was now banished for good: America could go to war and the public would support the President enthusiastically. But could the Gulf crisis, surrounded by so many unusual circumstances—blatant aggression, an easily demonized adversary, an apparently ruthless and powerful foe, a threat to oil resources, concern for Israeli security, a fear that inaction would mean that Iraq might acquire nuclear weapons—be seen as a harbinger of things to come, or was it a one-time exception to the pattern of politics in the post–Cold War era? The answer seems to be that the Gulf crisis is more likely to be the exception than the rule.

In this essay, the Gulf crisis will serve as one point of reference for assessing how the United States is likely to defend its interests in the Middle East in coming years. The other issue to be analyzed will be the Arab-Israeli conflict and American policy on how best to pursue the "peace process," as it is euphemistically called.

PRELIMINARY LESSONS FROM THE GULF CRISIS

Whatever else one may conclude from the American reaction to the Gulf crisis, one thing is clear: the United States is still committed to playing a major role abroad in order to defend its national interests. Isolationist impulses did not dominate the debate over policy, although some voices were raised asking why the United States should send so many troops, at so much cost, to defend oil resources that are of primary interest to Europe and Japan.

Conservatives such as George Will, Patrick Buchanan, Rowland Evans, Edward Luttwak, and Robert Tucker all questioned the wisdom of President Bush's strong commitment to the Gulf—a "strategic swamp," in the words of one—but these views were more than offset by conservative calls for the equivalent of a *jihad*—bombing Baghdad, occupying Iraq, toppling Saddam Hussein's regime—coming from commentators such as William Safire, Charles Krauthammer, A. M. Rosenthal, and the editorial writer of the *Wall Street Journal*.

If isolationism was a muted response to the Gulf crisis, so was jingoistic unilateralism. Prior to the outbreak of war, American opinion was almost evenly divided between hawks and doves, and most Americans supported the idea of operating under the umbrella of United Nations resolutions. For many, it was reassuring that, in this crisis, the United States had partners who would share some of the risks and costs—if not too much of the responsibility for the key decisions.

The end of the Cold War and the decline of Soviet power may make Pax Americana seem possible, but such a costly and exposed international posture does not seem to be supported by the majority of the public. The President will find public support, even on the left, for the use of force in specific circumstances, especially if diplomatic alternatives have been exhausted and a modicum of international support can be mustered. Echoes of the Vietnam era remain in the disenchantment with the idea of long, inconclusive, and bloody wars, but the public will support a quick, decisive use of force, even if costs are fairly high.

President Bush chose a kind of American-led internationalism that suits his telephone-style diplomacy. He consulted, he nudged, he cajoled, he met—but he did not wait passively for others to take the lead. He tried to strike a balance between a multilateralist policy, with the well-known constraints that such an approach entailed, without implying that the United States would surrender its freedom of decision if military action were required. Let us look more carefully at the pattern of consultations established during the first phase of the crisis.

At the very outset, Secretary of State James Baker met with his Soviet counterpart to display a common front in opposition to the Iraqi invasion of Kuwait. A year earlier, such agreement would have been unthinkable; now it seemed almost commonplace. Indeed, Soviet spokesmen publicly supported the American decision to send forces to Saudi Arabia. Bush and Soviet President Gorbachev met in Helsinki in September 1990 to reiterate their opposition to Iraq's annexation of Kuwait and to point out that "additional steps" might be taken if sanctions prove to be ineffective.

For the first time in years, the United States was able to conduct military operations in the Middle East without having to worry about how the Soviet Union might react. The risk of U.S.-Soviet confrontation was, quite simply, gone. American officials even said that they would have welcomed Soviet military involvement in the confrontation with Iraq. The end of the risk of escalation of regional tensions to superpower conflict is one of the most obvious gains from the end of the Cold War.

Next to consulting with the Soviets, Bush devoted considerable time and effort to enlisting the support of the Europeans and the Japanese. There were sound reasons for doing so. Some of the Europeans, especially Britain and France, had the capability to contribute to the military buildup in the Gulf. Others, such as Germany and Japan, could be expected to help defray some of the costs of the exercise. All had been asked to participate in the sanctions against Iraq.

Inevitably, there was a fair amount of grumbling about burden-sharing, and the United States revealed its essential weakness by having to ask for financial support from those whose economies are more robust than its own. Despite these undercurrents, the conduct of the allies was a plus. Compared to their behavior in other "out of area" crises, the NATO allies showed a fairly high degree of solidarity.

A further international dimension of the Bush policy was the prominent role given to the United Nations. A series of UN resolutions was passed which provided the framework of legitimacy within which American policy was carried out. Iraq's invasion and annexation of Kuwait were soundly condemned, sanctions were voted, the limited use of force to carry out the sanctions was approved, Iraq was called upon to release hostages unconditionally, and, finally, Resolution 678 authorized the use of "all necessary means" to expel Iraqi forces from Kuwait. It is quite conceivable that the United Nations will be strengthened by this crisis, and UN peacekeeping forces will be an element of the post-crisis security structure in the Gulf.

Finally, the Bush administration made a special effort to enlist regional allies in the confrontation with Iraq. Saudi Arabia, as the country most immediately threatened by Iraq's move into Kuwait, dropped its normal reticence concerning foreign troops on its soil and will be hosting hundreds of thousands of American and other troops. Egypt was also a key partner for the United States in the crisis and worked hard to forge a degree of Arab consensus (some twelve or thirteen of the twenty-one members of the Arab League) behind the policy of opposing Iraq. All of the smaller Gulf emirates—Kuwait, Qatar, the United Arab Emirates, Bahrain, and Oman—also made some contribution to the common effort. Syria was also part of the anti-Iraq coalition, with possibly interesting implications for the future. Finally, Turkey acted as a good NATO ally and regional partner. Egypt and Turkey, in particular, expected some compensation for their efforts. The administration showed a willingness to respond positively by urging Congress to write off nearly $7 billion in Egyptian military debt. Taken together, these dimensions of the American response demonstrated an impressive commitment to a multilateral, internationalist approach to the crisis.

WHY SUCH A STRONG AMERICAN REACTION IN THE GULF?

In past regional crises, one of the motivations for American action was usually to check the spread of Soviet influence. A whole series of "doctrines"—Truman, Eisenhower, Nixon, Carter, and Reagan—were directly or indirectly applicable to the Middle East. In each case, the theme of these doctrines was how best to contain Soviet expansionism—by economic and military assistance, by regional alliances, by strengthening regional surrogates, by sending American forces, or by supporting anti-Soviet resistance movements. But the Gulf crisis, unlike every other Middle East crisis since Suez in 1956, involved no threat at all of Soviet intervention. Why, then, the strong reaction?

One obvious answer is oil. The Gulf region contains about two-thirds of all the known oil reserves in the world. Were these reserves to come under the control of a hostile power, American interests could obviously be affected. But when oil prices soared in the 1970s, sending the Western economies into a tailspin, no one seriously suggested sending an American expeditionary force to occupy the oil fields. Was it really likely that Iraq's occupation of Kuwait would be more detrimental to the world economy than the oil shocks of the 1970s? Did the United States, in short, go to war in the Gulf to keep the price of oil at $20 per barrel, or $25, or $30? Was this what President Bush meant when he said the American "way of life" was at stake in the Gulf crisis?

Oil was surely a major factor in the Gulf crisis, but the United States would not have sent troops if the Organization of Petroleum-Exporting Countries (OPEC) had raised prices to $25 or $30 per barrel. As in the past, it would have adjusted, waiting for the market to bring prices back down.

down. But Iraq's occupation of Kuwait, and its ability then to dictate OPEC policy by controlling Saudi and other Gulf decisions, would have meant that the "oil weapon," along with billions of petrodollars, would have been in the hands of a leader who had shown little regard for the norms of international behavior—witness his decision to invade Iran in 1980, his use of poison gas (including against his own Kurdish citizens), his ambitious military buildup (including chemical weapons and a nuclear program), and his open call to use the oil weapon against the West. Clearly, the balance of power in the Gulf, and in the Middle East more broadly, would have been affected, setting the stage, inevitably, for future wars. In particular, Washington feared a war later in the 1990s between Iraq and Israel, both of whom, by then, would be armed with nuclear weapons.

Oil was primarily of concern because it could be used to transform and threaten the regional political order, not simply because a somewhat higher tax could be imposed on oil consumers. This was the same motivation that had led the United States to the 1988 decision to reflag Kuwaiti tankers in order to deter a major Iranian threat. It was this concern with Iraq's ability to destabilize the region that led some to the conclusion that nothing short of crippling Iraq's military potential should be the goal of American policy.

Early on in the crisis, the President implied that Iraq's invasion of Kuwait was like Hitler's reoccupation of the Rhineland—a blatant violation of international norms that should be stopped in order to prevent further acts of aggression. This image suggested that Saddam Hussein was a Hitler-like figure who sought to expand his power beyond Kuwait into the rest of the Arabian Peninsula, and perhaps even further into Jordan and Syria as well. Such an analogy was a powerful argument against the notion of appeasement, or compromise, but was it accurate? Saddam Hussein may well have some of the same drive for power that has characterized other dictators, including Hitler, and he has certainly shown a ruthlessness and disregard for human life that is chilling. But Iraq is not Germany, and has far less capacity to expand beyond its frontiers; after all, it gained very little territory in eight years of war with Iran.

The ease of the Iraqi conquest of Kuwait—an operation that took only a matter of hours—was by no means proof of the invincibility of the Iraqi army. True, Saudi Arabia alone would have been hard pressed to fight off the Iraqis, but the rapid introduction of outside forces quickly reduced the danger of further Iraqi advances. For the defense of Saudi Arabia, considerably fewer American troops would have sufficed.

Clearly, then, more was at stake than the protection of Saudi oil fields. Indeed, the most frequently mentioned objectives of American policy were the withdrawal of Iraqi forces from Kuwait and the restoration of the legitimate Kuwaiti government. Some trivialized this goal by implying that the United States was prepared to go to war for the sake of a few oil-rich sheiks. Some went further and noted that Iraq had certain legitimate grievances against the Kuwaitis, and that in any case the borders of Kuwait were a product of British colonialism and had no real legitimacy in the eyes of most Iraqis, and of many other Arabs as well.

Such discussion missed the broader point of American policy in this crisis. A primary objective seemed to be to establish new (or reestablish old) rules of the game for the post–Cold War era. Many observers had noted that one likely consequence of the end of the Cold War was an increase in regional conflict. As both superpowers pulled back from some of their global commitments, it was argued, restraints that had previously kept local conflicts in check would fade. A more disorderly world was in the offing. Strong regional powers would devour their weaker neighbors, while the superpowers stood idly by, no longer seeing their vital interests at stake and no longer driven by their rivalry of just a few years ago.

An alternative to this view of growing world disorder—a particularly worrisome scenario in the Middle East because of the enormous stockpiles of modern weapons—was that the end of the Cold War might open the way for a collective security regime, much like that originally envisioned by the United Nations. True, local conflicts would continue, but the major powers of the world would band together to prevent or contain acts of overt aggression. Economic, diplomatic, and military pressures would be mobilized by a broad spectrum of nations operating under the umbrella of the United Nations, if possible.

With this model in mind—once dismissed as idealistic, but now seemingly within reach—it would have been important for the United States to respond in much the same way if the crisis had occurred elsewhere, far from the oil fields of the Gulf. For example, if Ethiopia were to have invaded and annexed Somalia, and then mobilized 150,000 troops on the Kenya border and called for the overthrow of the regime in Nairobi, would Washington have turned a blind eye? Certainly not. At a minimum, UN sanctions would have been voted, arms would have been rushed to Kenya, and perhaps some troops would have been dispatched as well. True, the scale and intensity of the response would have been less than in the Gulf crisis, but some of the same desire to write a new set of rules for the post–Cold War world would have motivated American policymakers to react forcefully. Add to this volatile mix the possibility that the aggressor state would be holding Americans as hostages, that it had chemical weapons at hand and was known to have an embryonic nuclear program, and one can begin to imagine a large-scale American response. In short, the combination of tangible interests and important principles were the key to understanding American behavior in the Gulf crisis. But the principles should not be short-changed, as they often are by cynics.

A POST-CRISIS SECURITY REGIME FOR THE REGION

Secretary of State James Baker, whose absence from the circle of decision-makers during the first weeks of the crisis was much noted, emerged in early September to begin to articulate the need for a post-crisis security structure for the region. His comments gave rise to speculation about a permanent American military presence in the area, a NATO-like alliance in the Middle East (shades of the ill-fated Baghdad Pact?), and a substantial increase in arms transfers to some countries in the region, especially Saudi Arabia, Egypt, and (by way of compensation) Israel. According to some sources, the Kuwaiti government-in-exile was offering the Americans permanent bases in its country after the Iraqis are forced to withdraw.

Most Middle East experts were appalled by the idea of a large, permanent American garrison in the Gulf. Such a presence, it was thought, would provide fuel for the growing Islamic movements, would undermine the legitimacy of those regimes which relied on it, and would ultimately be unsustainable. Some even felt that the Soviet Union, heretofore so cooperative in the crisis, would balk at the idea of a permanent American base in Saudi Arabia. Some of America's allies might react negatively upon seeing the United States so obviously in control of the world's oil tap. Would the Japanese, for example, feel that in future trade negotiations Washington might use the "oil weapon," at least implicitly? Would an American OPEC be viewed with greater enthusiasm than the existing OPEC?

In light of the massive defeat of Iraq in the Gulf crisis—at least half of its military power was destroyed, its unconventional weaponry and surface-to-surface missiles were eliminated, and its modern infrastructure was shattered—it no longer seems to be an unmanageable task to contain Iraqi power. Still, efforts will have to be made to prevent Iraq from once again acquiring an offensive capability. This was one goal of the Bush administration's arms control initiative that was announced in May 1991.

Even a weak Iraq could pose some threat to the Gulf. Therefore a peacekeeping force in Kuwait seems desirable, as do steps designed to enhance Saudi defense. Saudi capabilities, especially for antitank warfare, could be enhanced. More importantly, the enormous quantities of American equipment transported to Saudi Arabia could be left behind as "pre-positioned" hardware available for joint Saudi-American use in future crises. Finally, some Arab forces might be encouraged to remain, especially Egyptian and Syrian troops. This would help cement the Saudi-Egyptian-Syrian alliance that would be an important building block in the post-crisis regional security system. Saudi Arabia could be encouraged to share some of its oil wealth with these two Arab neighbors, which would have the desired effect of distributing some of its wealth to poorer countries.

Three other countries in the region are likely to play some part in the new order. Turkey is an obvious candidate. It has a large army, a common border with Iraq, and considerable leverage because of its geostrategic position and its control over the flow of oil from Iraq by pipeline, and even over the flow of water to Iraq (and Syria). Israel has an obvious interest in seeing Iraqi power contained, if not destroyed, but the United States wisely decided not to involve Israel in its anti-Iraq campaign. Still, Israeli intelligence assets are presumably of value, and Israeli power may act as a deterrent against future Iraqi designs on Jordan. Finally, Iran is a natural counterweight to Iraq, but in the past few years it has been too weak to play that role. As time passes, however, one should assume that Iran will regain its economic and military potential, and that this will help to balance Iraqi power. In short, this second grouping of regional powers—Turkey, Israel, and Iran—all have the ability and incentive to contribute informally to the post-crisis security structure, even if the leading roles will be played by Egypt, Saudi Arabia, and international forces.

This leaves the American role somewhat unclear. Certainly an offshore presence will be retained. The Central Command has proved itself in this crisis and will continue to be generously funded. Advisers and technicians will stay on the ground in Saudi Arabia in conjunction with pre-positioned equipment, and greater investment will be made in sealift and airlift capabilities to prepare for future crises. But how many combat troops will remain, and for how long, and where?

Assuming that a post-crisis security structure can be put in place, can it be sustained and can it be used, along with the United Nations, to pursue other regional objectives such as arms control and an Arab-Israeli peace? For the moment, such an ambitious plan may seem beyond reach, but it should certainly be in the minds of those who are trying to build a stable structure of peace in the Middle East.

THE ARAB-ISRAELI CONFLICT

If the Gulf crisis has been dealt with through American-led multilateral diplomacy, the same can certainly not be said of the long-festering Arab-Israeli dispute. For most of the past twenty years, the United States has acted unilaterally, if at all, in seeking to promote Arab-Israeli peace negotiations. In fact, for much of this period, the mere idea of including the Soviet Union as a partner in peacemaking was seen as anathema.

The reasons for America's go-it-alone style in dealing with the Arab-Israeli dispute have been several. First, the United States has not usually seen eye-to-eye with its European allies, to say nothing of the Soviet Union, with respect to the Arab-Israeli conflict. To state matters bluntly, the United States has shown more concern for Israel's point of view, whereas most others in the international community have tilted toward an Arab perspective on the conflict. Thus multilateralism would quite likely have meant that the United States would be stuck as Israel's advocate rather than being in the role of potential mediator between Israel and an Arab partner.

A second American reason for eschewing multilateral diplomacy on the Arab-Israeli conflict was the belief that the issues were so complex that a comprehensive solution was impossible. Only a step-by-step approach, as practiced between 1973 and 1975 by Secretary of State Henry Kissinger, held much hope of producing results. Thus, the United States generally preferred to focus on one front at a time—starting with Egypt, then turning to Jordan, and finally the Palestinians—all the while leaving the pro-Soviet Syrians on the sidelines.

The comparative success of this approach on the Egyptian-Israeli front, resulting in the American-sponsored peace treaty of 1979, reinforced the view in Washington that the United States, because of its potential influence with Israel, was uniquely qualified to be a mediator in subsequent phases of the peace process. Whenever questions arose about bringing in the Soviets, or convening an international conference, the response in official Washington was cool, largely on the grounds that this would make the Israelis more intransigent and would add nothing of value to the diplomatic process.

During most of 1989 and early 1990, the Bush administration adopted a cautious, unilateralist approach to Arab-Israeli peacemaking. The first objective was to persuade the Israeli government, already confronting the challenge of the Palestinian *intifada* (uprising), to come up with a proposal for breaking the stalemate on the diplomatic front. This the Israelis did, calling for elections to be held in the West Bank and Gaza to choose representatives with whom Israel would then negotiate the "self-government" arrangements foreseen in the Camp David Accords.

The next step in the American strategy was to repackage this proposal and to try to persuade the Palestinians to agree to meet directly with Israelis to discuss the proposal. The belief at this stage was that the meeting, by itself, would begin to transform the conflict and was a symbolically worthy objective, even if agreement was not in sight on substantive matters. By late 1989, Egypt had been brought into the discussions as a kind of front man for the Palestinians, even though the United States maintained its own direct dialogue with the Palestine Liberation Organization (PLO).

On several occasions, the question arose of whether or not the Soviet Union might play some role in the diplomatic effort. Generally, the American answer was negative. The Soviets, it was said, had not yet demonstrated enough new thinking on Arab-Israeli diplomacy. They were still shipping sophisticated weapons to such countries as Syria and Libya, and they had not yet reestablished diplomatic relations with Israel. Nonetheless, it was acknowledged in Washington that the Soviets were, on balance, using their influence with the PLO to encourage a moderate line. By early 1990, the idea had even caught on that Israeli-Palestinian talks might take place in Cairo, with observers present from both the United States and the Soviet Union.

But before any of these formulas could be put to the test, domestic Israeli politics brought things to a standstill. A prolonged governmental crisis, both within the Likud party and between Likud and Labor, finally led to the collapse of the coalition government in March. Labor made an effort to form a narrow government without Likud, which briefly raised hopes in Washington, but then abandoned the effort when it was clear that they did not have enough votes in the Knesset. Eventually a narrow Likud-led coalition was formed. Before its new policies could even be put to the test, a Palestinian faction of the PLO, under the command of Abul Abbas, carried out an unsuccessful raid near Tel Aviv. PLO chairman Yasir Arafat refused to condemn the attack, and by late June the United States had suspended its dialogue with the PLO. The peace process was clearly at a standstill, if not entirely dead. The outbreak of the Gulf crisis in August was the final nail in the coffin, if one was needed.

How might an Arab-Israeli peace effort be resumed in the aftermath of the Gulf crisis? Many things will have changed, but one may be the same: the position of the government of Israel. The current Israeli government has stated that it will not negotiate the return of territory for peace, along the lines of the Egyptian-Israeli model. In Likud's interpretation, UN Resolution 242 does not require any further Israeli withdrawals from any of the territories occupied in 1967. Indeed, East Jerusalem has been annexed and is therefore non-negotiable. Israeli law has been extended to the Golan Heights, a step just short of formal annexation. And Prime Minister Shamir has ruled out ceding control over any of the West Bank. This leaves various autonomy schemes and local self-government as the extent of negotiable items on the Israeli agenda with the Palestinians, and perhaps some form of arms control as a topic for discussion with the neighboring Arab states. Shamir has further said that Israel will have nothing to do with the PLO, and will even refuse to meet with Palestinians who reside in Jerusalem or who are currently outside the occupied territories, even if these individuals have no affiliation with the PLO. The hardness of these positions was leading to a possible argument between Israel and the United States on the eve of the Iraqi invasion of Kuwait. Tensions resurfaced when the Bush administration tried to convene a regional peace conference in the late spring of 1991.

The new Bush initiative took several Gulf-related developments into account. On the regional scene, Egypt and Saudi Arabia emerged from the crisis as the major Arab partners of the United States. Syria also enjoyed a better reputation in Washington than heretofore. The PLO and Jordan, by contrast, were at odds with this Arab grouping, and with the United States as well. (Still, Jordan could count on a degree of understanding, at least from President Bush, for its ambivalent position during the crisis; the PLO could not.) These shifts in alignment suggested that Egypt and Syria will be the key players in a future peace process, with some degree of Saudi support. The PLO, at best, would be on the sidelines. Jordan, whatever its role, would certainly not be out in front of the other Arab partners of the United States if the peace process does get under way. In short, Bush envisaged a more Syria-oriented diplomatic effort than anything since 1974.

On the international front, the crisis in the Gulf changed the environment for Arab-Israeli peacemaking. The United Nations, for example, appeared to be a much more credible forum than it had in the past. The key to this change, of course, lay with Soviet policy. As a result, the United States was more willing to bring the Soviets into an active role in Arab-Israeli diplomacy, especially if they could help to persuade the Syrians to begin negotiations. A regional conference could open the way for Israel and Syria to start peace talks. But Israel cannot talk only to Syria. Jordan and the Palestinians will also have to be brought into the negotiations, possibly in a joint delegation.

Israel, of course, remains reluctant to enter an international conference if the deck seems too heavily stacked against its interests. If talks are to take place with Syria, Israel, inevitably, will be under pressure to give up some or all of the Golan Heights. Syria would also be under pressure to agree to leave the area demilitarized. In today's international climate, it seems possible to imagine that the region would be put under a UN force, including contingents from the United States, the Soviet Union, Israel, and Syria, at least in an initial phase.

In short, if the United States succeeds in reviving Arab-Israeli diplomacy, the context will likely be more multilateral, relying on a larger role for the Soviet Union and the United Nations. Arms control would feature centrally in any such effort. The goal would be to try to bring about a comprehensive settlement, including Syria, Jordan, and the Palestinians. Lebanon would also be a beneficiary of such an approach.

Since Israel is likely to object, there will be many who will ask why the United States should make the effort. One answer is that Islamic movements may gain strength in the aftermath of the Gulf war. If they succeed in setting the agenda for negotiations with Israel in the Arab world, the conflict really will become insoluble, and even the Egyptian-Israeli peace could fall apart. So one argument for negotiating with the existing state structures, and with the mainstream of Palestinian nationalism, is to preempt this Islamic tendency toward defining the conflict with Israel in religious terms. A second reason is to bolster the standing in the region, and at home, of those regimes that aligned themselves with the United States in the Gulf crisis.

It will take serious discussions with the Israelis to get them to overcome their suspicions, but several positive elements could be added to the balance sheet. Israel could certainly expect the Soviets to establish full diplomatic relations and to continue allowing Soviet Jews to emigrate if negotiations do begin. In addition, the United States and the Soviet Union are ready to accommodate the Israeli preference for beginning the peace process with the Arab states and Palestinians who are not openly affiliated with the PLO. That should help allay some Israeli concerns. In addition, the major powers could put arms control on the agenda of a peace conference, which should have some appeal to Israelis.

Finally, a word about the domestic politics of adopting an activist policy toward Arab-Israeli peacemaking. There will always be some voices that will warn against a major American effort to revive the peace process. Some will do so out of concern for Israel. Others will be reflecting an isolationist impulse not to get involved in other people's affairs. But many other friends of Israel, and many Israelis themselves, will see the merits of trying to defuse the other explosive conflict in the region before it is too late. The end of the Cold War will make it easier to mobilize broad international support behind a negotiated settlement. And the Gulf war will exist as a reminder of how dangerous and volatile the region can be. If an Arab-Israeli settlement can help to strengthen the new security environment in the region, most Americans will support a major effort by their government. Even Congress will go along, provided the price tag is not too high. In short, the President will have a wide range of options available if he chooses to act on behalf of Arab-Israeli peace, including the option of cooperating with the Soviet Union.

COULD MIDDLE EAST CRISES SPOIL DETENTE?

Once before, in October 1973, moves toward improved U.S.-Soviet relations were set back by a Middle East crisis. Could it happen again? History will surely not repeat itself. No stage-three nuclear alert is likely to be called because of a Middle East crisis.

But some outcomes of Middle East crises might still have an impact, even if slight, on U.S.-Soviet relations. Much depends, of course, on the Soviets themselves, and on President Gorbachev and whether he survives the multiple problems confronting his country.

What if the United States sought to maintain a large military base in Saudi Arabia or Kuwait after the Gulf crisis? And what if Iran turned to the Soviet Union for large quantities of arms, and the Soviets agreed to sell to them? Would the superpowers be back on a collision course?

Probably not, but there would certainly be some strains in the relation-ship. The extraordinary amity of the Malta to Helsinki summits might not last, and some on both sides might call for a harder line.

On balance, however, U.S.-Soviet detente now seems so much more deeply rooted, and the danger of military confrontation is so remote, that regional crises seem unlikely to be major determinants of how the relationship evolves. This, it seems to me, is more convincing evidence that the Cold War is over. The Gulf war showed, in addition, that the United States has a remarkable opportunity for leadership as part of an international coalition that includes the Soviet Union and works through the United Nations. If this pattern continues, both the Gulf situation and the Arab-Israeli conflict will be addressed by American officials in ways that only a few years ago seemed impossible.

THE SOVIET UNION AND THE ARAB-ISRAELI CONFLICT

Galia Golan

The Soviet Union cannot be considered to be in any way responsible for the origins of the Arab-Israeli conflict or its early development. Indeed Moscow sought to please both sides in the emerging struggle in 1947, finally coming down on the side of the Jews during the 1948 war.[1] Soviet motivation then, as later, was primarily anti-Western—i.e., removal of the British from the region—and support for the Jews was a vehicle for accomplishing this in the case of Palestine. Once this was accomplished, however, Stalin lost interest, reverting to a basically neutral position regarding the conflict. The temporary support for Israel (and India) notwithstanding, there was little room for Third World states in Stalin's Zhdanovist approach.[2] Thus, even the 1952 revolution in Egypt left the Soviet leader unmoved. Arabs as well as Israelis were perceived as bourgeois nationalists and essentially pro-Western in orientation. Only the death of Stalin and the advent of a new foreign policy under Malenkov, and then Khrushchev, opened the way to an appreciation of the value for Moscow of the ongoing conflict in the Middle East.

When the post-Stalin leadership extended the Cold War to the Third World arena, the Arab-Israeli conflict became the central vehicle for penetration of the Arab world and expansion of Soviet influence there. It was not the only vehicle; Moscow could and did use inter-Arab rivalries, notably Egypt's competition with Iraq, to combat Western advances. It was, however, the Arab-Israeli dispute which provided the broadest and most durable basis for involvement. Soviet-bloc arms and training, combined with political backing, to Egypt and Syria (and from the 1970s, the Palestine Liberation Organization—PLO), helped Moscow polarize the area into one of "Soviet-supported Arabs" versus "American-supported Israel." Even though it was not entirely accurate, such a

---

This paper was prepared before the Iraqi invasion of Kuwait. For the effect of the Gulf crisis on the Arab-Israeli conflict, see my chapter "The Test of 'New Thinking': The Soviet Union and the Gulf Crisis" below.

characterization could be used against Washington—the identification of the United States with Israel aiding the Soviets in their penetration. The Soviets' ideological linkage of Israel with Western imperialism also had its attractions for various Arab regimes or factions, such as the Ba'ath in Syria or Iraq at various times or Nasserite pan-Arabists. This attraction was not, on the whole, sufficient to cement the Soviet relationship with the Arabs, however. Indeed, ideology was more often an impediment to these relationships. It was Soviet military and economic aid which made the difference, and the realm in which this was most needed was the conflict with Israel.*

For Moscow the purpose of its moves into the Arab world was not to encourage or perpetuate the conflict as such; this was more a by-product than a goal. The Soviets probably had no more nor less disdain for the social democratic regime in Jerusalem than for the nationalist or quasi-socialist regimes of the Arab world, traditional anti-Semitism not-withstanding. They had no intrinsic interest in supporting Arab destruc-tion of the state of Israel. Moscow's hostility to Israel was based on the same factor which made the Arabs attractive: its place in the East-West competition. Moscow could find auxiliary purposes or interests in the Arab world, perhaps of an economic nature, and did have a traditional interest at least in the northern tier of the Middle East—that is, those countries on its southern border and controlling passage to and from the Black Sea. Its primary interest in the region was dictated by the East-West competition, be it in the political, ideological, or increasingly central strategic-military sphere. Even a Soviet interest in Middle Eastern oil was guided more by the desire to control oil supplies to the West than to gain access for themselves (in view of their own vast oil reserves).

The Arabs were well aware of the primacy of the East-West com-petition in Soviet Middle East interests and policy. Nasser, for example, exploited this skillfully, playing off the superpowers against each other at various times. But this was also a source of tension between Moscow and its Arab partners from virtually the beginning of their relationships in the 1950s. The Arab interest lay in the conflict with Israel, and the value of the Soviet Union in their eyes was linked, if not solely then mainly, to this. When these priorities conflicted, it was the Arab interest which was to suffer, as Egypt, for example, learned as early as 1956.[3] Thus the Soviets armed and prepared the Arabs for war against Israel,

*The Soviets provided aid to regimes such as the Baghdad regime for other conflicts, such as the war against the Kurds, cementing the relationship in that way.

but sought to restrain them from actually going to war because of the risks in the superpower sphere. Moreover, in time of war, Soviet aid was limited by concerns over confrontation with the United States, barring, therefore, direct Soviet military intervention.* This type of contradiction was apparent in other situations as well, such as matters of low-level tension, willingness to negotiate, and so forth. Moscow's efforts to please the Arabs, often in order to maintain influence in a zero-sum–game relationship with the United States, adversely affected broader Soviet interests vis-à-vis the United States. Conversely, efforts to forge a cooperative relationship with the United States in the period of detente adversely affected relations with the Arabs, contributing, for example, to Sadat's expulsion of Soviet military advisers in 1972.

On the whole, however, the Arab-Israeli conflict served Soviet interests so well that the common wisdom, at least in the 1960s and 1970s, if not after, was that Moscow would not welcome, much less assist in achieving, resolution of the conflict. Yet the Soviets may well have had second thoughts about the continuation of the conflict after the Yom Kippur War.[4] By this time their strategic-military competition was shifting to the Indian Ocean area, while the growing importance of economic considerations in their Third World relationships was moving them in the direction of the oil-rich Gulf states.[5] Perhaps of greater significance, the risks of the Arab-Israeli conflict had become more threatening, as the American nuclear alert (Defcon 3) and near superpower confrontation of 1973 had demonstrated. Indeed the war itself repeated the 1967 lesson to Moscow that it had little control over its Arab clients. Even the increased Syrian and Egyptian dependence upon the Soviet Union in the period between the two wars, and the use of arms blackmail by Moscow against Egypt, as well as attempts at persuasion on both Syria and Egypt, could not deter the two countries from going to war in October 1973.[6] Arab independence vis-à-vis Moscow had presumably been augmented by the wealth created in the energy crisis and shared, in the form of assistance, by the oil-rich states with the confrontation states. Soviet influence was further eroded by the inroads made by Washington into the region following the war, threatening Moscow's assets as well.

Thus risks were up, particularly with the increased American involvement, while returns were diminishing, at a time when Soviet

---

*As in the case of Suez, so too in 1967 there were complaints over Soviet refusal to send aid during the Six-Day War. Even the aid which was airlifted in during the Yom Kippur War was deemed insufficient by the Arabs, who accused Moscow of pressing for cease-fires, against the wishes of Egypt and Syria, because of fear of confrontation with the Americans.

priorities may have been shifting even within the region from the confrontation states to the states of the Persian Gulf and Indian Ocean periphery. Resolution of the conflict might, therefore, stem the negative trend apparent in Soviet-Arab relations and provide a more stable basis for the Soviet military and political presence. This could be achieved if Moscow were a party to such a resolution, both in bringing about a settlement and as co-guarantor. A formal, international agreement might afford the Soviet presence greater legitimacy and stability than the already demonstrably unreliable, ostensible Arab dependence based upon an ongoing conflict. Arms sales, when payments had been forthcoming, constituted an economic interest for the Soviets in the conflict, but a settlement did not rule out continuation of such sales. Arms agreements which presumably would come with a settlement might place limits on both superpowers and actually relieve concerns over the dangerous direction the arms race in the region had begun to take, including the pressures upon the Soviets to provide their clients with more and newer weapons.

A case could be made, therefore, for the conclusion that a learning process had taken place on the part of the Soviet Union, together with shifting priorities, even within the "old thinking" of the Brezhnev period. The result was what George Breslauer has called a policy of collaborative competition with the United States.[7] Moscow sought cooperative action with the United States in order to prevent the Americans from gaining or increasing an advantage. Its objective, in seeking to be a party to a settlement, was not disengagement from the competition in the region, but rather prevention of a *Pax Americana* and exclusion from the region. In this sense, the Soviets sought to cooperate with the United States in order better to compete with it.

At the same time, the Soviets did appear to be seeking a means of reducing the risks of this competition. There were even signs that they might be going in the direction of disengagement, or at least reduction of their involvement. In the second half of the 1970s, an extensive debate had developed in Soviet theoretical writings dealing with the Third World. This debate included party and military as well as academic writers (in any case the academic writers were from the institutes, which themselves were in close contact with the party).[8] They raised serious doubts as to the wisdom and potential of Soviet involvement in the Third World, including involvement in regional conflicts and support for national liberation struggles. They questioned the ideological (volunteeristic) approach which had produced the push for vanguard

Marxist-Leninist parties in the Third World; indeed they questioned the value of the very few so-called socialist or socialist-oriented regimes which had emerged. They argued that, given the world economy, most Third World states had or would of necessity link up with the capitalist economy, and that Soviet involvement was not only futile but costly and possibly risky to the interests of Soviet society. There was what could be called a "Soviet-Union-first" approach, which advocated a much more modest investment abroad, including but not only in the realm of power projection and the "external function" of Soviet armed forces.

By 1981 some of the ideas generated by this debate found their way into leadership speeches and possibly actual policy. Andropov had long been of the new persuasion, at least on certain aspects of Third World policy, and Brezhnev gave the first hints of a new approach when he delivered his "rules of conduct" speech in April 1981.[9] This was followed in September 1982 by a speech calling on both East and West to refrain from activity in the Third World, and then he called in his top military people in October to explain to them the facts of Soviet economic life, implying apparently the need for a more restrained policy.[10] Andropov, in power, openly expressed his doubts about the Third World and called for a revision of the party's foreign policy program, advocating a Soviet-Union-first approach based on many of the ideas espoused by Soviet theoreticians in the earlier debate.[11]

It is not clear just how much was initiated, beyond words, in the brief Andropov period. In the Middle East, Andropov actually undertook a massive military supply effort to Syria, presumably in compensation for Moscow's virtually total inactivity during the Lebanon war. But he also continued the already apparent reduced power projection role of the navy in the region.[12] There were certainly verbal signs of a realization that past policies had failed. These may have been generated by the defections to the West of previous Soviet Third World allies, such as Egypt,* or by the serious problems in the Soviet economy, which led to certain cutbacks in military procurement in the late 1970s, or by the extended and increasingly futile involvement in Afghanistan coupled with the failure of detente and the advent of a conservative administration in Washington. Reduced Soviet capabilities, along with an absence

*This had in fact led to a reassessment of Soviet Third World policy in 1972, resulting in the at least partial return of the ideological approach—i.e., encouragement of Marxist-Leninist parties building stronger organizational and ideological structures in the Third World. In the Middle East this policy took more the form of trying to create a bloc of radical states, but both this and the overall policy was deemed a failure by the end of the 1970s.

of foreign policy successes and the ever-increasing costs of East-West competition, clearly strengthened the appeal of the theoreticians' arguments.

This, then, was the background for "new thinking." The situation was difficult and cried out for change. One could easily see all the practical reasons for a new policy, and it is indeed possible to explain the advent of "new thinking" in terms of the inevitable exigencies of the Soviet situation in general foreign policy and, specifically, with reference to the Middle East and the conflict there. Certainly the problems were known, and the ideas for solution or at least change were around. Yet "new thinking" represents a revolution—not a continuation or modification of past policies. Like every revolution, there were practical reasons and ripened conditions for change; there were also harbingers of the new ideas. It took a revolution, however—or in the Soviet case, a new leadership—to abandon the old attempts at solution or tentative modification. Thus "new thinking" goes well beyond the modest theoretical formulations of the gestation period, and, I would argue, it was propelled by more than the purely practical exigencies of the hour. The latter had produced detente, in its time, in order to allow Moscow to compete with the West at the global level in a safer, less costly manner, and a Soviet interest in a settlement of the Arab-Israeli conflict in order to prevent exclusion by the Americans at the regional level. At the global and regional level, the name of the game was still competition.

"New thinking" operates on an entirely different set of premises and is directed to a new set of goals. That is, generated possibly by practical considerations, which were no less obvious to previous Soviet regimes, Gorbachev's solutions to the same problems are based on a different conceptual approach and different theoretical underpinnings. "New thinking" eschews competition, not only because of a conviction that the Soviets cannot win, but also out of a conviction that it is not necessary to win. By positing an interdependent world and the removal of ideology, Gorbachev has eliminated the rationale and potential for the zero-sum-game approach. In so doing he has also provided the basis for a new attitude to regional conflict and a different role for the Soviet armed forces, emanating from a new military doctrine.

The doctrine of reasonable defensive sufficiency and the accompanying reduction, if not elimination, of power projection would take the Soviet armed forces out of regional conflicts. This represents explicit abandonment of the Clausewitzian approach in what is a call for political solutions to regional conflict. In an interdependent world, attempts at military solutions or even the existence of regional conflicts threatens global security.[13] Beyond the idea of escalation, which is not a new concern, conflict at the regional level also threatens superpower relations. The new element here is the Soviet admission that its own involvement in regional conflicts may impede progress at the superpower level.[14] Brezhnev's old "divisibility of detente" has been explicitly discarded. Such concrete things as the effects of regional developments on the maintenance of arms agreements between the United States and the Soviet Union are now seriously considered.

Moscow has developed the idea of taking the superpowers out of regional conflict. If this were done, regional conflicts would be greatly restricted in scope and danger, and their persistence possibly checked. For without the superpowers' aid and encouragement, the parties involved would find it increasingly difficult to pursue conflict. Moreover, removal of the superpowers would reduce conflicts to their local, presumably more easily handled, causes, subject to resolution on the basis of a balance of interests or "national reconciliation," depending on the type of conflict involved. The end of the zero-sum–game East-West competition renders such a withdrawal possible, removing also the power of the local actors to exploit that competition in their pursuit of conflict. The superpowers might assist, individually or collectively, in the resolution of the conflict, but they could no longer be pitted against each other in order to perpetuate it.[15]

There are contradictions, or at least dilemmas, in the new approach, and to some degree the Soviets' themselves are willing to acknowledge some of them. The first and most obvious one is the contradiction between the withdrawal from regional conflict and the maintenance of the Soviet Union's status as a great power. Both popular opinion and elite attitudes, according to a study conducted of Soviet foreign policy elites, favor the withdrawal and a reduction of Soviet involvement in Third World endeavors.[16] Yet they also strongly oppose loss of the country's prestige and great power status in the world. Second, there is the more concrete problem of seeking political solutions and disengaging so as to reduce the military potential of conflicts when the Soviet economy is in need of hard currency earnings from arms sales. Soviet officials have increasingly acknowledged this second problem, and it has been proposed for discussion in the Supreme Soviet as well as being a topic of public debate.[17] It is possible, however, that the arms question is a military-political rather than economic issue. Recent discussion suggests that hard currency earnings from arms sales to the Third World were never great, such supplies on the whole having wound up being "foreign aid" because most clients were unable to pay.[18] Those advocating continuation of the supplies may be found, therefore, not so much among economists as from the military—that is, those concerned with maintaining the Soviet Union's superpower status and positions abroad. Whatever the source, neither dilemma should be underestimated in appraising the course of Gorbachev's foreign policies, particularly when the Soviet leader is faced with declining popularity and low morale domestically. The increasing importance of Russian nationalist elements, as well as of the deteriorating economic situation, must also enter these calculations as political pluralism begins to take root in Soviet society.

"New thinking," with all the above attributes and dilemmas, *is* being applied to the Arab-Israeli conflict as well as to other regional conflicts.[19] This can be seen in the Soviet attitude toward the conflict itself, the parties involved, the type of settlement sought, and the means for bringing about a settlement. If the zero-sum game is obsolete, and ideology has been removed from foreign policy, then the Arab-Israeli conflict, like many others, loses much of its appeal for the Soviet Union. It was already losing its value as a vehicle for Soviet competition with the West, or at least as a productive vehicle. With the end of the competition, there is little political or strategic gain to be sought. What remains of Soviet interests in the region may be obtainable without the conflict, for these are defensive interests more directly associated with the northern tier of Middle Eastern states bordering on the Soviet Union. Under a doctrine of defensive sufficiency rather than power projection, protection of the southern border, including protection from the disruptive spread of Islamic fundamentalism among the restive Moslem ethnic groups of Central Asia, gains ascendancy.

While the conflict loses its importance with the redefinition of Soviet national interests, its continuation may even prove detrimental to these interests. Removal of the superpowers' direct involvement and commitment to their respective clients might reduce the risks of confrontation. Yet the ongoing conflict produces risks of another kind and serious pressures on Moscow (as well as on Washington). The arms race in the region has taken an alarming turn in the direction of non-conventional weapons and the development of systems which can threaten states beyond the region. The presence of intermediate range missiles, the development of ABM capabilities, and the spread of nuclear, chemical, and biological warfare potential could place the efficacy of the superpowers' agreements in doubt.[20]

Moreover, the Soviet response to the arms race—that is, its willingness to continue to supply ever more advanced weapons, including aircraft, to Syria, for example—has become something of a litmus test (one of several) for *perestroika*-"new thinking" in the eyes of the United States. Yet significant cutbacks in the supply of arms, particularly limiting supplies to what Moscow considers "reasonable defensive sufficiency" rather than the "strategic parity" demanded by Damascus in time of continuing conflict with Israel, has created strains in Soviet-Arab relations.[21] In fact this is but one source of the strains in Soviet relations with the Arabs which have been producing pressures on the Soviet leadership.[22] Unlike the past, however, Moscow cannot accommodate these pressures with a "divisibility of detente" type position. Nonetheless, despite the fact that the elimination of the zero-sum approach should obviate the need to accommodate their clients for fear of their bolting to the Americans, Moscow is unwilling to ignore them and completely abandon its influence. This unwillingness is presumably generated by the already mentioned dilemma: the urge, if not for empire, then at least for maintenance of great power status.

There is also a domestic reason Moscow cannot simply ignore Arab pressures. In the new circumstances within the Soviet Union, there is something of a "pro-Arab lobby."[23] These are people who argue for loyalty to Moscow's past allies and friends—the Arabs—in Soviet Middle East policy, and oppose any Soviet step which could weaken the Arabs and/or benefit Israel. The people associated with this position appear to be the "Arabists," be they within the party's International Department (ID), the more important (today) Foreign Ministry, the research institutes, or the press. The ID's top Middle East expert Yurii Griadunov, for example, was one such person, recently transferred to Jordan as Soviet ambassador.[24] Vladimir Poliakov, until recently head of the Middle East Department of the Foreign Ministry, has spoken out for loyalty to Moscow's Arab friends, and it is rumored that Aleksandr Dzasokhov, head of the Supreme Soviet's Foreign Affairs Committee (former ambassador to Syria), is also of this breed of old Arabists.[25] A similar type, Vitalii Naumkhin, can be found at the Oriental Institute, which is under the conservative leadership of Mikhail Kapitsa.[26] And journalists such as Karen Geivandov and Igor Beliaev, old Middle East hands, together with Aleksandr Smirnov (deputy head of the Middle East section) at Novosti (the overseas news service) have been slow to abandon their defense of Arab claims, including occasionally even support for Palestinian terrorist acts.[27]

While some force may be given their arguments by Soviet Moslems, greater influence may be attached to the contribution of anti-Zionists—namely, the Public Committee Against Zionism and the Public Committee Against Resumption of Diplomatic Relations with Israel. These committees are composed of or often allied with persons belonging to anti-Semitic groups such as Pamiat' and Russian nationalists. Their basically negative approach has the net effect of promoting Arab interests; indeed their arguments often take the form of championing the Arabs against "Jewish racism."[28] Domestically they are associated with the conservative, anti-perestroika camp, as positions on the Arab-Israeli conflict have come symbolically to connote domestic political positions. Thus their voices could be expected to augment those concerned with the maintenance of the Soviet Union's position as a great power in the world and those more pragmatically anxious over economic losses from cutbacks in arms sales, as well as those identifiable as military discontents.

Facing these groups are the newly formed proponents of the application of "new thinking" to the Middle East. Some of them have formed the Public Committee for Renewal of Diplomatic Relations with Israel. This committee, which is composed of many non-Jews as well as Jews, has sought to counter the anti-Zionists and anti-Semites. Just as these last are identified with an anti-perestroika position, so the proponents of renewed relations are seen as the defenders of "new thinking." A leading advocate of this position has been the outspoken journalist Aleksandr Bovin, joined by senior Middle East specialists Vladimir Nosenko and Sergei Rogov, as well as Sergei Bychal, aide to ID chief Valentin Fallin, responsible (among other things) for the Middle East.[29] According to accusations voiced at an anti-Zionist demonstration, Evgenii Primakov and, above him, Aleksandr Yakovlev are the main architects of the new policy toward the conflict.[30] Indeed, inasmuch as these two are largely associated with the theoretical underpinnings of "new thinking," and Primakov himself is a Middle Eastern specialist who as early as 1972 had expressed a different Soviet position on the conflict, they may well be the leaders primarily responsible for the application of "new thinking" to the Arab-Israeli conflict.[31] Primakov, however, is a Middle East specialist who retains a certain loyalty to Moscow's Arab allies. Shevardnadze shared at least Yakovlev's views, as evidenced not only in his comments in meetings with Western representatives, but also by such things as his replacement of Poliakov as head of the Middle Eastern Department and his reliance upon Sergei Terasenko, head of the Foreign Ministry's Planning Division.[32]

As a result of the debate and counter-pressures, however, the Arab-Israeli conflict has become something of a domestic issue, unlike most other regional conflicts. In this sense, perestroika may be producing a situation similar to the well-known phenomenon in Washington, with a local lobby and domestic interest groups rendering this a sticky domestic problem. In view of the fact that the opposition has made this into a point of perestroika (even Yeltsin has taken it up from the other angle, pushing for better relations with Israel and a crackdown on domestic anti-Semitism as steps of more radical reform),[33] Gorbachev may well have an added, domestic interest in seeing an end to this conflict. While this may indirectly operate as added impetus for finding a solution, some of these same factors—namely, the pro-Arab or anti-Israel pressures—are also the very factors which restrain such an impetus, operating against Soviet disengagement and an end to the conflict. At the very least, they are compelling elements which must be taken into consideration.

Such constraints notwithstanding, one of the first signs of the application of "new thinking" to the Arab-Israeli conflict was the change in Moscow's approach to Israel. Any genuine effort for a settlement had to involve Israel, and with the end of the zero-sum–game competition and the de-ideologization of foreign policy, there was no longer a rationale for an anti-Israel position. Gorbachev publicly announced (in the presence of visiting Syrian President Assad) Moscow's new policy of normalization of relations with Israel.[34] The announcement actually followed moves already initiated to deal directly with Israel, rather than unofficially or through the United States. Direct and official channels for communication were opened, and relations were developed in a variety of areas, including the exchange of consular missions, with political officers, on a more or less permanent basis; cultural, academic, and sports exchanges; commercial talks; tourism; and even visits to the Soviet Union by ministers of the government of Israel.[35]

Israeli cooperation in the apprehension and return of Soviet hijackers, followed by Israeli aid to Armenian earthquake victims, greatly accelerated the pace of normalization. Indeed normalization reached a level not far from the resumption of full diplomatic relations by 1989, when Shevardnadze included talks with Israeli Foreign Minister Moshe Arens (in Cairo) during his first trip to the region.[36] A symbolic culmination was reached in September 1989 when the Soviets finally abandoned their customary support for the annual Arab bid to have Israel's credentials revoked at the United Nations.[37]

While full diplomatic relations have not been resumed, presumably because of the Arab and domestic pressures mentioned above, Soviet conditions for such a renewal have been greatly reduced.[38] These conditions had often fluctuated in the past, becoming particularly demanding when the pre-Gorbachev leadership perceived little chance of actually becoming a party to Middle East negotiations. In the Gorbachev period there has been a return to a minimalist Soviet demand simply for progress in the peace process, with only brief deviations from the line that Israeli agreement to even preliminary peace talks (for example, with the Palestinians in Cairo as proposed by the Americans) would be sufficient.

To persuade Jerusalem that Moscow has altered its attitude, hostile propaganda has generally been replaced by more objective, sometimes even favorable, reporting on Israel in the government and party media. The existence of *glasnost* means that unfavorable reporting can still be found, particularly in the Russian nationalist papers and journals.[39] Yet even Zionism has received an occasional positive reference, for the first time since the inception of Bolshevism. Several Soviet Middle East specialists, including a Foreign Ministry official, have spoken of the multifaceted nature of Zionism which includes (they claim) a positive, social-democratic stream.[40] Also in part to convince Israel—but also because of American pressures and the dynamics of perestroika, both of which led to a virtually total liberalization in the realm of human rights—Gorbachev undertook the improvement and freeing of Jewish life within the Soviet Union while gradually permitting the increasingly free emigration of Soviet Jews. According to *Pravda*, some 100,000 Soviet Jews left in 1989, and in the first half of 1990 over 60,000 had arrived in Israel.[41]

The massive immigration of Soviet Jews into Israel became the focal point of Arab criticism of the new Soviet approach to the Middle East. Undoubtedly concerned about the specific contribution the immigration would make to Israel's determination and ability to remain in the occupied territories and prevent the creation of a Palestinian state there, the Arab states seemed to be concentrating their stored up anger over a whole range of issues when they took Moscow to task on emigration.[42] Syrian concerns, for example, have gone well beyond this issue because Soviet disengagement from the conflict means significantly less Soviet willingness to provide either the military or political backing for Damascus to pursue the conflict indefinitely. Although the Soviets had long been unwilling to support a Syrian offensive against Israel, or directly intervene militarily in hostilities, the new policy means cutbacks in support even in the absence of hostilities. Quantities of arms supplied have been reduced by as much as 50 percent over the past five years, certain types of weapons have been withheld (SS-23 missiles, specifically), and a Soviet reassessment of the Syrians' credits (for an approximately $16.5 billion bill) have raised Syrian concern over the meaning of the "reasonable defensive sufficiency" promised by Moscow.[43]

The deeper concern of Damascus is that the domestic priorities of perestroika, and with this the weakening of Soviet economic capabilities and military-political power in the world, may lead to the long term loss of the Soviet Union as an effective ally and protector. The crumbling of the Soviet empire and of communism itself in Eastern Europe also spells a weakening of Syria's external support. Moreover, these developments have not only made it more difficult for Damascus to pursue the conflict (or in Syrian eyes, maintain its position vis-à-vis Israel), but they have also been accompanied by direct Soviet urgings to moderate its positions and forego the conflict. Pressure along these lines has been the by-product, if not the point, of Moscow's new positions regarding Israel (and the PLO), which further complicate Syria's pursuit of the conflict. They have been perceived as part of a Soviet move to collaborate with the United States at the expense of Arab interests.[44]

While the Soviet-Syrian relationship has been significantly affected by the change in Soviet policy toward the conflict, this relationship has not been abandoned. There had long been serious disagreement between the two over Moscow's refusal even in the past to provide Damascus with "strategic parity" vis-à-vis Israel, over Syria's move into Lebanon, over the split with the PLO, over the idea of a negotiated settlement with Israel, and numerous other issues. The present problems strike a sharper chord, perhaps, because of the deeper, more long-term (what the Soviets would call strategic) rather than tactical nature of the differences between the two countries as a result of "new thinking." Yet Soviet disengagement from the conflict does not mean disengagement from Syria. Although it is clearly seeking to place the relationship on a new basis, Moscow appears to be unwilling to abandon its great power status or role, provided this can be maintained at minimal economic and political cost.

The change in Soviet thinking on regional conflict in general, and on the Arab-Israeli conflict in particular, has clearly affected the Soviet-PLO relationship as well. This relationship, too, had never been a smooth one, serious differences of opinion having marked Soviet-PLO exchanges for years. Moscow had pressed the Palestinians even more than the

Syrians in the past to moderate their positions so as to become acceptable actors on the international scene, only gradually finding a common ground for support of most PLO objectives. As was the case generally in Soviet relations with national liberation movements, Moscow's interest in the movement had been of a highly tactical nature. Indeed Soviet support for the PLO had increasingly become a function of the Soviet-American competition, as Moscow exploited the Palestinian issue for what was perceived to be the Achilles heel of American policy in the Middle East.[45] This tactical or instrumental approach placed its limits on Soviet support or involvement with the movement, even as it dictated greater attention than Moscow might otherwise have accorded the group.

The PLO could, therefore, expect a substantial change in the Soviet attitude on two accounts under "new thinking." At the more general level, an end to the zero-sum-game approach and the de-ideologization of foreign policy spelled a reduction of support for national liberation movements, including also support rendered the conduct of armed struggle and terrorism. In this specific case, the fact that Soviet support for the PLO was directly related to the competition with the United States even within the context of the Soviet interest in the regional conflict, which interest itself was linked to the superpower competition, there was little hope that support would continue. In theory, at least, disengagement from the Arab-Israeli conflict would mean disengagement from the Palestinians altogether. Yet the interest in resolution of the conflict has led Moscow to maintain, rather than abandon, its involvement with the Palestinian issue, presumably out of a conviction that a lasting settlement would probably be impossible without resolution of this issue.

The nature of the relationship has changed, however. Instead of a basically supportive or cooperative approach, albeit punctuated by disagreements and problems, the Soviets now subjected the PLO to demands and pressures for alteration of the movement's policies. Methodologically this has been symbolized by the shift under perestroika from the party's sympathetic international department emissaries to the more business-like Foreign Ministry officials. Substantively this was first evidenced by Gorbachev's public admonitions to Arafat and pressures on PLO officials Nayif Hawatmeh and George Habash to acknowledge Israel's need for security—that is, the idea of a balance of interests between that of the Palestinians for self-determination and that of Israel for security.[46] They pressed for official PLO acceptance of Israel's right to exist (Security Council Resolution 242) and, also, for compliance with the Americans' demand for an end to the use of terror, so as to qualify for participation in the peace process.

Without abandoning their support for the idea of a Palestinian state, the Soviets have focussed less on this objective than on the need for realistic proposals to engage Israel in negotiations. Moscow opposed the PLO plan to declare a state and withheld recognition for over a year after it was declared at the 1988 meeting of the Palestine National Council.[47] The Soviets preferred to leave future options open, along the lines of the more vague self-determination formula, rather than repel the Israelis with a *fait accompli* and further complicate the situation.[48] The PLO was not only distressed by this response but actually suffered from obstructionist moves on the part of the Soviet Union when the latter cooperated with the United States in preventing Palestinian admission as a state to either the United Nations or the World Health Organization in 1989.[49]

Moscow has been only slightly less negative on the issue of Jewish emigration. The Palestinians are the ones potentially to suffer the most from the massive Soviet Jewish emigration to Israel, and they have made their distress clearly known to the Soviet authorities. Despite the fact that Palestinian complaints have been taken up by most Arab states and domestic Soviet opponents to the Soviet rapprochement with Israel, the most Moscow has been willing to do is to deny emigrant use of the new direct USSR-Israel flights. It has also joined the campaign of countries, including the United States, to demand assurances from Israel that the emigrants would not be settled in the occupied territories. Gorbachev did threaten delays, even suspension of the emigration, if Israel did not comply.[50] It seems unlikely, however, that the threat was more than a gesture, in view of the costs which would most likely ensue in the area of U.S.-Soviet relations and, particularly, trade.

Beyond an unwillingness to sacrifice Soviet-American relations for the benefit of the Palestinians, which is not a new phenomenon, Gorbachev's attitude toward PLO behavior has been significantly affected by the removal of the competition with the United States in the conflict. As early as 1988, but even more so since 1989, the Soviet Union has, on the whole, encouraged the PLO to respond positively and/or make the necessary compromises with regard to the various peace plans proposed, regardless of their source.[51] Indeed this may be one of the most telling signs of Soviet renunciation of its competition with the United States in the conflict. The absence of Soviet opposition—indeed Soviet encouragement of the U.S.-PLO dialogue and PLO cooperation with such things as the Baker Plan for Israeli-Palestinian talks in Cairo—stands in sharp contrast to former Soviet fears of American successes. When Arafat entered into an agreement in 1985 with King Hussein for the purpose of opening a path for the Americans and the Reagan Plan, Moscow eventually responded with a rupture in relations with Arafat, cooperation in efforts to unseat the leader (although not to split the movement formally), and suspension of aid and training to Arafat's Fatah forces until the Arafat-Hussein agreement was abrogated. By 1988 the policy had changed; the Soviets welcomed the opening of the U.S.-PLO dialogue (some even say they facilitated it), and they continuously found something positive to say about virtually every proposal proffered by the Americans (as well as the Egyptians and even the Israelis).[52] When the dialogue was suspended by Washington in response to a June 1990 terrorist attempt on Israeli beaches by the group under PLO executive member Abul Abbas, the Soviets expressed regret. They even indirectly justified the U.S. action in a letter sent to Arafat, in which they reportedly advised the PLO against operations such as Abul Abbas's terrorist attempt.[53]

The change in Soviet policy toward the PLO is indicative of the overall change which has occurred in Moscow's attitude toward the desired settlement of the Arab-Israeli conflict and the means of achieving such a settlement. The nature of the accord envisaged by the Soviets— that is, Israeli withdrawal and resolution of the Palestinian problem within the territories evacuated by Israel, together with guarantees for the security of all concerned—would not appear to have undergone substantial change. What has changed is the way in which Moscow officially refers to it. Rather than demanding or even spelling out these components of a settlement, as had been the case in the past,[54] Soviet officials have stated both publicly and privately to all those involved that they do not have a fixed position or formula for a settlement and that anything acceptable to the parties to the conflict will be acceptable to them.[55] Openness and flexibility are the key words in the Soviets' approach to the nature of a settlement today. As we have seen, this has meant a certain deemphasis on Palestinian statehood, referring rather to the more vague idea of "self determination," and then without any specific mention of borders, Jerusalem, or the refugees. In fact, the only details Soviet leaders have offered are proposals for security arrangements which were introduced by Shevardnadze in Cairo in early 1989. At the time these appeared to be designed to allay Israeli concerns—that is, an attempt directly to address Israel's security interests.

Shevardnadze spoke of the creation of a regional military-risk reduction center, mutual inspections and on-site monitoring, demilitarizations and troop reductions (thinning out of military presence along borders or disengagement lines), mutual and international verifications, nuclear and chemical disarmament of the whole region, and commitments against terrorism.[56] In the spring of 1990 Shevardnadze's proposals began to be presented as a contribution to the process of reaching a settlement as well as to the substance of an eventual accord. The same ideas were raised during Assad's visit to Moscow at the end of April and then again in conversations with Israelis and later between Shevardnadze and Baker.[57]

Clarifications and additions such as non-proliferation of missiles and missile technology, controls on the development of non-conventional weapons, limitations on arms deliveries (beginning with those of the United States and the Soviet Union) or UN registration of arms sales data, prior notification of exercises, and Mubarak's earlier proposals for a Middle Eastern zone free of weapons of mass destruction have all been floated.[58] To the Israelis the ideas have been presented as a basis for bilateral talks between Israeli and Soviet experts, intended both as confidence-building measures and as ideas for future security. To the Americans they have been presented as a basis for a regional security conference, to include all the states in the region and the superpowers, preferably (from the Soviets' and presumably the Arabs' point of view) under the UN Security Council.[59]

The motivation for these proposals, as revived and expanded in 1990, may have been growing concern—even alarm—over the regional arms race, particularly in the realm of non-conventional weapons and missiles. The nature of the weapons, coupled with the proximity of the region, may be creating a greater Soviet interest in seeing a resolution of this conflict than conflicts in other regions—for example, the Angolan or Cambodian conflicts. By the same token, these same factors may account for Moscow's continued pursuit of participation in the achievement of a settlement in this region, despite the end of the zero-sum-game competition with the United States. The continued insistence upon what Gorbachev has called "internationalization" of the settlement may simply reflect both the popular and traditional Soviet will to maintain great power status.[60] Even if this is the case, the security issue could provide the vehicle, if not the reason, for such participation.

The Soviets claim that a regional security conference or the proposed bilateral talks with Israel could run simultaneously with, rather than supersede or replace, the peace process presently orchestrated by the United States. They also claim that an international conference is still the ultimate vehicle of choice. In view of continued U.S. and Israeli opposition to an international conference, the Soviets have completely altered, and opened, their concept of such a conference.[61] They explained, for example, that the plenary sessions would not have veto power over agreements reached in bilateral sessions, and that they would serve mainly to propose solutions to problems unresolved in the bilateral meetings. The Soviets also proposed shifting the focus of talks to the UN Security Council, or at least preliminary talks among the permanent members of the Security Council, suggesting preliminary multilateral and bilateral forums. None of these ideas has met with a positive response and, therefore, have received less and less treatment by the Soviets. Although the United Nations is still referred to as the sponsor if not the venue of talks, the Soviets appear increasingly to accept the American-sponsored plans for negotiations.[62] At the summit in Washington, Gorbachev accepted the idea of American-Soviet consultations (he referred to the Shultz Plan consultations by way of example) as sufficient acknowledgment of Soviet participation, deemphasizing the idea of an international conference.[63] Regional security talks would have the advantage, however, of providing Moscow with a much more legitimate, central role—accustoming both Israel and the United States to constructive Soviet participation—while dealing with and defusing the more dangerous aspects of the ongoing conflict.

There is little reason to believe that the Soviet leadership is absolutely bound to the regional security proposals over any other set of options for resolving the Middle East conflict. Since the beginning of "new thinking," they have been more or less groping for new ideas, and the security talks are the first serious concrete procedural ideas that have been offered with a chance for acceptance. Yet almost by definition, "new thinking" leaves the door open for other ideas and a flexible approach both on procedure and substance. Moreover, the basic decisions to pursue resolution of the Arab-Israeli conflict have been taken, even if questioned by some at home and abroad. From this point of view, constraints such as domestic opposition and low morale, together with Arab pressures, and above all the urge to remain a great power may be operative, perhaps even more so with regard to the Arab-Israeli conflict than other conflicts. Nonetheless, these constraints appear to be less weighty than the goals of international stability, border security, economic renewal, and superpower cooperation. It is a question of priorities, and it may well be that the achievement of these goals will become increasingly and more urgently dependent upon resolution of this conflict, as regional issues move into center stage between the two superpowers.

NOTES

1. For this period, see Yaacov Ro'i, *Soviet Decision-making in Practice*, (New Brunswick: Transaction Books, 1980), or Galia Golan, *Soviet Policies in the Middle East Since World War II* (Cambridge: Cambridge University Press, 1990), ch. 2.

2. Uri Bialer (*Between East and West: Israel's Foreign Policy Orientation 1948-1956* [New York: Cambridge University Press, 1990]) argues that Soviet support for Israel continued even into the 1950s, but Ro'i's evidence of sharp deterioration in Soviet-Israeli relations as early as the end of 1948 is more convincing. In either case, the Soviets did not shift to the Arabs and seek to exploit the Arab-Israeli conflict until after Stalin's death.

3. Soviet inaction throughout the critical period of the Suez war was criticized by Nasser, who said that Soviet concern over confrontation with the United States had paralyzed the Kremlin. Sadat later said that this was an object lesson for him for future relations with Moscow. For details, see Ilan Troen and Moshe Shemesh, *The Suez-Sinai Crisis: A Retrospective* (London: Frank Cass, 1989).

4. For a fuller discussion of the Soviet attitude toward a settlement under Brezhnev, see Galia Golan: *Yom Kippur and After: The Soviet Union and the Middle East Crisis* (Cambridge: Cambridge University Press, 1977), ch. 1, and "Soviet Policy in the 1980s: The Middle East," *Adelphi Paper*, No. 152, (London: IISS, 1979).

5. Gur Ofer, "Economic Aspects of Soviet Involvement in the Middle East," in *The Limits to Power*, ed. Yaacov Ro'i (London: Croom Helm, 1979), pp. 67–95.

6. On this topic, see Golan, *Yom Kippur and After* (note 4).

7. George Breslauer, "Soviet Policy in the Middle East, 1967-1972: Unalterable Antagonism or Collaborative Competition?," in *Managing U.S.-Soviet Rivalry*, ed. A. George (Boulder: Westview, 1983), pp. 65–103.

8. For extensive accounts of these debates, see Galia Golan, *The Soviet Union and National Liberation Movements in the Third World* (London: Hyman and Unwin, 1988), and Jerry Hough, *The Struggle for the Third World* (Washington, D.C.: Brookings Institution, 1986).

9. TASS, 27 April 1981.

10. TASS, 20 September and 27 October 1982.

11. *Pravda*, 23 November 1982, 16 and 17 June 1983.

12. Francis Fukuyama, "Soviet Military Power in the Middle East, or Whatever Became of Power Projection?" in *The Soviet-American Competition in the Middle*

East, eds. Steve Spiegel, Mark Heller, and Jacob Goldberg (Lexington: Lexington Books, 1988), p. 179.

13. Party secretary Vadim Medvedev elaborated on much of this in "Velikii Oktiabr i sovremenni mir," *Kommunist*, no. 2, January 1988, pp. 3–18; see also Sergei Rogov, "The Interaction of the USSR and U.S. Interests," *SSHA: Ekonomika, Politika, Ideologiia*, no. 8, 1988, pp. 3–13, and Georgii Kunadze, "On the Defensive Sufficiency of the USSR Military Potential," *Mirovaia ekonomika i mezhdunarodniye otnosheniia*, no. 10, 1989, pp. 68–83.

14. See, for example, Andrei Kozyrev, "Confidence and the Balance of Interests," *International Affairs*, no. 11, 1988, p. 8, or Richard Ovinnikov,"The Main Components of a Stable World," *International Affairs*, no. 6, 1988, p. 16.

15. See Rogov, "Interaction" (note 13); Kunadze, "Defensive Sufficiency" (note 13); and Andrei Kolosovskii: "Regional Conflicts and Global Security," *Mirovaia ekonomika i mezhdunarodniye otnosheniia*, no. 6, 1988, pp. 32–41, and "Risk Zones in the Third World," *International Affairs*, no. 8, 1989, pp. 38–49; Andrei Kolosov, "Reappraisal of USSR Third World Policy," *International Affairs*, no. 4, 1990, pp. 34–42.

16. Andrei Melville, Alexandre Nikitin, and Philip Stewart, "Prospects for a New U.S.-Soviet Relationship: Perceptions of the Soviet Foreign Policy Community"; Marjorie Mayrock Center for Soviet and East European Research, Hebrew University of Jerusalem, November 1989; Research Paper no. 72.

17. In an interview in *Izvestiia*, 26 June 1990, Deputy Foreign Minister Vladimir Petrovskii enthusiastically endorsed the idea of a Supreme Soviet discussion of the issue.

18. General Western estimates that arms sales accounted for roughly 20 percent of Soviet hard currency earnings appear to have been grossly exaggerated in view of the failure of most clients to pay. Andrei Kolosov, described only as a political analyst, wrote: "The claim that arms deliveries yield us enormous hard-currency profits seems, at this juncture, nothing more than a myth. Of course, individual transactions are profitable, but they have long been cancelled out by all sorts of debts and gratuitous deliveries" ("Reappraisal of USSR Third World Policy" [note 15] p. 40). Thus, while the debate in the Soviet Union refers to economic interests in arms exports, the real issue may be one of power versus change. See, for example, Yurii Kornilov, *Izvestiia*, 31 January 1990, or comments on statistics published in *Izvestiia*, 1 March 1990; Andrei Kolosovskii (Assistant Deputy Foreign Minister and possibly the same person as the above Andrei Kolosov): "Risk Zones" (note 15), pp. 44–45, and "Regional Conflicts" (note 15), pp. 32–41; A. V. Kozyrev in *Izvestiia*, 21 February 1990; Georgii Arbatov, "The Country's Army or the Army's Country?," *Ogonoek*, no. 5, 1990; Petr Litavrin, "The Issue of Arms Trade Limitation," *SSHA: Ekonomika, Politika, Ideologiia*, no. 1, 20 December 1989, pp. 13–20. Speaking of the 90 billion ruble debt owed the Soviet Union, Evgenii Kiselev quoted Admiral Grishin, Deputy Minister for Foreign Economic Relations, to the effect that revelation of the debt owed the Soviets for arms deliveries would cause "another outburst of emotion among the public" and "an information bomb" (Moscow television, "120 Minutes," 7 August

1990). A rebuttal by the military in this debate claimed that Soviet sales constituted a necessary 15 percent of hard currency earnings (Major-General G. Kirilenko in *Krasnaia zvezda*, 21 March 1990).

19. Gorbachev called for linkage of the superpower rapprochement and resolution of regional conflict in *Pravda*, 2 June 1988, and the Politburo was reported to have approved the application of "new political thinking" to the Middle East in April 1988 (*Pravda*, 15 April 1988).

20. Shevardnadze referred to this in his speech in Cairo, TASS, 23 February 1989.

21. See, John Hannah, *At Arms Length: Soviet-Syrian Relations in the Gorbachev Era*, Washington Institute Policy Paper No. 18, Washington, D.C., 1989.

22. See Soviet mention: USSR Foreign Ministry, "The Foreign and Diplomatic Activity of the USSR," *International Affairs*, no. 1, 1990, p. 93.

23. Term used in an *Izvestiia* (18 November 1989) answer to a reader's complaints about such a lobby.

24. See, for example, his comments in *Petra-JNA* (Amman), 28 June 1990, and *al-Ra'y*, 29 June 1990 (FBIS-NES-90-126, 29 June 1990, pp. 30–31).

25. See discussion, "The USSR and the Third World," *International Affairs*, no. 12, 1988, p. 138. Deputy Foreign Minister Yuli Vorontsov, recently named ambassador to the United Nations, is also rumored to be opposed to the new position on the conflict, although as the deputy foreign minister who had responsibility for the Middle East, he favored improved relations with Israel.

26. See Naumkhin interview in *al-Sharq al-Awsat* (London), 8 July 1990 (FBIS-SOV-90-134, 12 July 1990, pp. 17–18).

27. Geivandov, for example, in *Izvestiia*, 30 March 1988, 18 December 1988, and 9 February 1989; Beliaev on Soviet radio, 4 December 1988 and 5 March 1989, or in "Middle East Versions," *International Affairs*, no. 6, 1988, pp. 55, 63, 79; Smirnov in *al-Anba* (Kuwait), 27 May 1988; *Izvestiia*, 6 September 1989; and *al-Majallah* (London), 20 February 1990 (FBIS-SOV-90-033, 16 February 1990, pp. 24–25).

28. See, for example, E. Evseev in *Krasnaia zvezda*, 30 January 1990, or the "Letter of the Writers of Russia," published in *Moskovskii literator* and *Literaturnaia Rossiia*, 2 March 1990, as reported in *The Soviet Union and the Middle East*, Marjorie Mayrock Center for Soviet and East European Research, vol. XV, no. 3, 1990, pp. 13–14.

29. Tatiana Karasova, head of the Israel desk in the otherwise conservative Oriental Institute, is also a member of the committee.

30. This appeared in an anti-Semitic tract which accused Yakovlev (by implication mistakenly taken for a Jew) of promoting Jews (specifically, Primakov and Arbatov) to positions of power and of pressuring Gorbachev to renew relations with Israel. The demonstration was sponsored by the Union of Soviet National Organizations early in 1990 (KUNA [Kuwait] in English, 18 February 1990

[FBIS-SOV-90-034, 20 February 1990, p. 31]). The new Soviet ambassador to Washington, and later Shevardnadze's successor, Aleksandr Bessmertnykh, may also be one of the early proponents of the new policy.

31. See V. V. Zhurkin and E. M. Primakov, *Mezhdunarodnye konflikty* (Moscow: Mezhdunarodnye Otnosheniia, 1972), although Primakov appears to be vacillating somewhat, favoring continued support for the Arab states.

32. Beirut domestic radio, 29 June 1990 (FBIS-NES-90-127, 2 July 1990, p. 29). Poliakov was named ambassador to Cairo.

33. In response to provocative questions from an Arab journalist in Moscow, *Jerusalem Post*, 3 June 1990.)

34. *Pravda*, 25 April 1987.

35. The early stages were quite restrained on the Soviets' part, refusing reciprocity, for example, for Israelis to come to the Soviet Union either in a consular mission or any other capacity, while Soviet officials and groups were sent to Israel. By early 1988, however, even this reticence disappeared.

36. At this time deputy director-general of the Israeli Foreign Ministry Yeshayahu Anug said that Israel and the Soviet Union were engaged in "de facto normalization without calling it that" (*Jerusalem Post*, 23 February 1989).

37. The Soviet delegation abstained for the first time.

38. There has been a public debate on the issue of resumed relations, triggered by an article by Aleksandr Bovin in *Izvestiia*, 26 August 1989, strongly advocating renewal of relations. A negative response was written by Aleksandr Zotov (*Izvestiia*, 22 September 1989), who is considered a new thinker very much associated with the idea of rapprochement with Israel. His surprising position may have been prompted by an effort to improve his image in the eyes of Syria, where he is serving as ambassador. After a number of negative responses from Arab writers, Bovin published a summary of letters sent to the paper in response to the debate; he said that the letters were 9 to 1 in favor of renewed relations with Israel (*Izvestiia*, 25 January 1990).

39. See, for example, *Sovetskaia Rossiya, Leningradskaia pravda,* or *Moskovskaia pravda*. Another source of anti-Israel reporting has been the army daily, *Krasnaia zvezda*, which has published comments by TASS's consistently anti-Israel political commentator Aleksandr Balebanov, as well as the openly anti-Semitic and anti-Zionist writer E. Evseev (chairman of the Committee Against Resumption of Diplomatic Relations with Israel until his death in 1990).

40. D. Makarov, "Diplomacy Without Diplomatic Relations," *Argumenty i fakty*, no. 49, 3–9 December 1988, pp. 5–6 (interview with Vladimir Nosenko, who was then at the Oriental Institute and subsequently moved to *IMEMO*, FBIS-SOV-88-233, 5 December 1988, p. 27); Sergei Rogov and Vladimir Nosenko, "Chto skazal 'A' i chto skazal 'B'," *Sovetskaia kultura*, 9 February 1989; and Soviet Minister to Britain, Aleksandr Golitsyn, quoted in *Davar* (Israel), 23 November 1989, delivering a speech in London in place of Gennadi Terasov.

41. *Pravda*, 22 July 1990; *Mideast Mirror*, 24 July 1990.

42. Journalist and Middle East specialist Andrei Ostal'skii suggested this in *Izvestiia*, 8 March 1990.

43. Hannah, *Soviet-Syrian Relations* (note 21); *New York Times*, 28 August 1988. The number of Soviet military advisers in Syria has also been reduced.

44. These concerns were alluded to, if not explicitly mentioned, for example, in KUNA, 18 February 1990; Moscow international service in Arabic, 3 June 1990 (FBIS-SOV-90-107, 4 June 1990, pp. 43–44); *al-Sharq al-Awsat*, 8 July 1990 (FBIS-SOV-90-134, 12 July 1990, pp. 17–18); and during Assad's visit to Moscow (*Pravda*, 29 April 1990).

45. See Galia Golan: *The Soviet Union and the Palestine Liberation Movement: An Uneasy Alliance* (New York: Praeger, 1980), or "The Soviet Union and the PLO," in *Soviet Strategy in the Middle East*, ed. George Breslauer (London: Unwin and Hyman, 1990).

46. TASS, 9 April 1988; *Pravda*, 10 September and 12 October 1988; *al-Hawadess* (London), 21 October 1988 (interview with Deputy Foreign Minister Petrovskii); *Le Quotidien de Paris*, 13 October 1988 (interview with Poliakov); Moscow domestic radio International Observers' Roundtable, 23 October 1988 (FBIS-SOV-90-206, 25 October 1988, p. 5); *Sovetskaia Rossiia*, 26 October 1988; *al-Anba*, 19 September 1988 and 7 January 1989 (Terasov); *al-Ittihad* (Abu Dhabi), 18 January 1989 (quoting Soviet Foreign Ministry official on Soviet role); and *Izvestiia*, 30 April 1989 (Abu Mazen).

47. Official Soviet recognition came with the opening of a Palestinian Embassy in Moscow in January 1990, the timing of which was clearly intended to offset the visit to Moscow the same week by Israeli Minister of Science Ezer Weizman.

48. This has been explicitly indicated by Soviet experts in talks with Western counterparts (quotation not for attribution: "We have stopped placing emphasis on the necessity of establishing a Palestinian state. The Soviet Union now simply speaks of self-determination").

49. Reuters Information Services, Washington, 7 December 1989, carried State Department and Israeli embassy praise of Moscow's cooperation.

50. At the close of his summit with Bush in June (Moscow television, 3 June 1990 [FBIS-SOV-90-108, 5 June 1990, p. 21]. Going further than the United States, the Soviets called for a UN Security Council resolution "to appeal to the Israeli government not to permit acts capable of changing the demographic structure of the territories" in violation of the Geneva Convention (*Izvestiia*, 13 February 1990, on a press conference by First Deputy Foreign Minister Yuri Vorontsov—now Soviet UN ambassador). Even as they claimed defensively to the Arabs that Soviet laws (not yet passed) forbade interference with the freedom to emigrate, a number of Soviet officials said that the smooth exit of Soviet Jews might in fact be impaired or suspended if Israel did not provide solid assurances regarding their settlement in the territories.

51. There was only one apparent exception in the late fall of 1989, when Moscow briefly counselled the PLO to withhold agreement to American proposals; they subsequently reversed this, however.

52. See Foreign Ministry statement, *Pravda*, 18 December 1988, or *Pravda*, 20 December 1988, and *Izvestiia*, 18 December 1988.

53. Amman domestic service in Arabic, 7 July 1990 (FBIS-NES-90-131, 9 July 1990, p. 1). In public they explicitly denied any justification for the American suspension of the dialogue: TASS, 22 June 1990, claimed the PLO leadership denied any connection with the operation. For a discussion of changes in Soviet policy regarding the PLO's use of terrorism, see Galia Golan, *Gorbachev's New Thinking on Terrorism* (New York: Praeger, 1990).

54. See Soviet plans of 1970s, and particularly 1982 and 1984.

55. For example, in the talks with Peres in Rome, April 1987, or Brutents' interview in Kuwait, KUNA, 3 June 1988 (FBIS-SOV-88-108, 6 June 1988, p. 50), or Gorbachev to Arafat, TASS, 9 April 1988. Indeed, a call-sign of "old thinkers," or opponents to the new policies, is usage of the old three-pronged formula, which is totally absent from official statements and leadership pronouncements under Gorbachev. See, for example, Yurii Griadunov after he presented his credentials as Soviet ambassador to Jordan, *Petra-INA*, (Amman), in Arabic, 28 June 1990 (FBIS-NES-90-126, 29 June 1990, p. 30), or Oriental Institute deputy head and Middle East expert Vitalii Naumkhin, *al-Sharq al-Awsat* (London), 8 July 1990 (FBIS-SOV-90-134, 12 July 1990, pp. 17–18).

56. TASS, 23 February 1989.

57. *Izvestiia*, 29 April 1990.

58. Petrovskii in *Izvestiia*, 26 June 1990; Sergei Rogov in a speech in Jerusalem, 13 June 1990; Terasov in conversations in Washington in July 1990.

59. *Haaretz*, 27 July 1990, presented the conference idea as American in origin, initiated at the Pentagon and now supported by the State Department. According to this article, Egypt claimed to have Jordanian support for the Egyptian idea of two regional conferences—one on chemical weaponry and one on nuclear weapons—and believed it could get Syrian and Iraqi agreement. *Al Hamishmar*, 25 July 1990, reported Egyptian claims to have obtained Iraqi agreement to an Egyptian-Israeli conference for discussion of regional chemical disarmament proposals which would be submitted to the rest of the states in the region, followed by a joint committee to discuss nuclear disarmament.

60. Gorbachev's meeting with U.S. congressmen, Moscow television, 2 June 1990 (FBIS-SOV-90-107, 4 June 1990, p. 30).

61. For example, Shevardnadze, *Izvestiia*, 24 February 1989.

62. TASS, 10 February 1990, joint communique on Baker-Shevardnadze talks.

63. Gorbachev to U.S. congressmen, Moscow television, 2 June 1990.

MIDDLE EAST POLITICS IN THE POST–COLD WAR ERA

Shibley Telhami

Assessing the impact of change in the USSR and East Europe on Middle East politics is obviously dependent on how one interprets this change. If one believes that we are now witnessing a fundamental transformation of the international system in the direction of effective consensus and multilateralism, or that we are seeing the victory of democracy over authoritarianism, the implications for the Middle East can appear promising. Since there are few theoretical or historical reasons to succumb to such romantic notions, I subscribe to a simple realist interpretation of world events: what we are witnessing today is triggered by a major shift in the distribution of world power.

The dramatic events of 1989 will be debated for a long time, and I do not here intend to assess the various competing explanations of them. Rather, I will articulate one interpretation that has both theoretical foundations and verifiable historical relevance. Given this interpretation, I will then assess the impact of these events on Middle East politics.

A. SUPERPOWER POLICIES IN THE MIDDLE EAST: THE IMPACT OF CHANGE IN THE DISTRIBUTION OF ECONOMIC AND MILITARY POWER

While superpower policies in the Middle East have not always been motivated by the competition between the superpowers, incremental changes in the distribution of military and economic power between them have had a discernible impact on those policies.[1] Aware of the relevance of this competition for regional politics, regional actors have often manipulated the competition to their advantage. For example, describing Egypt's strategy after its defeat by Israel in 1967, Egyptian journalist and former presidential advisor Mohammed Heikal wrote:

As a result of the '67 war, the balance at the local level tilted strongly in favor of the Israelis, so the only option to Egypt was to lift the conflict onto the higher, international level, where the balance was more equal, until the time when Egypt was in a position to match Israel's strength with her own.[2]

Later, Egyptian President Anwar Sadat, despairing over the impasse in the negotiations with Israel and the United States, expressed serious fears about the emerging detente between the United States and the USSR:

Detente, sealed between the Russians and the Americans in Moscow at the May 20 summit, is now the dominant strategy of the Soviet Union. . . . But detente means that small powers like us will be crushed. The Soviet Union does not want us to go to war.[3]

Reflecting a similar logic, a symposium held at the Center for Political and Strategic Studies at *Al-Ahram* in May 1972 concluded that Egypt

should realize that the superpowers accorded very low priority to the Middle East problems and that detente would distract their attention from the Middle East even more. Egypt had to shape its policy so as to force the superpowers to become more involved in solving the conflict in the Middle East.[4]

By now, it is conventional wisdom that this reasoning led Egypt and Syria to launch the 1973 war against Israeli forces in order to compel the superpowers to intervene, even though the chances of military success were not very bright. The question, however, is whether the relative influence of the superpowers can be systematically assessed. Realist literature has generally focussed on the implications of the distribution of power for the stability of the international system or the stability of international regimes, but it has not sufficiently separated economic power from military power, and regional power from global power, and it has not suggested particular policy implications for various parts of the world.

Figures 1 and 2 summarize the proposed hypotheses about expected superpower tendencies, given the distribution of both economic and military power between the superpowers at the global level and in the Middle East.

These explanatory variables (the distributions of economic and military capabilities) are clearly consistent with structural-realist assumptions. Moreover, a case has been made for their empirical explanatory power by outlining their historical impact on Soviet-American competition in the Middle East since World War II;[5] the historical patterns of Soviet and American policies in the Middle East appeared to correspond well to the tendencies anticipated by Figures 1 and 2.

Figure 1

Superpower Inclinations toward the Third World Given Relative Economic and Military Capabilities

MILITARY CAPABILITIES

<table>
<tr><td colspan="2" rowspan="2"></td><td>Relatively Strong</td><td>Relatively Weak</td></tr>
<tr><td>1</td><td>2</td></tr>
<tr>
<td rowspan="2">ECONOMIC CAPABILITIES</td>
<td>Relatively Strong</td>
<td>

• Demanding of allies
• Erosion of influence not tolerated even if opponent does not directly gain
Examples:
U.S. either/or policy in 1950s
USSR in late 1960s
</td>
<td>

• Accommodating stance: offer help to other states without too many demands
• Be satisfied with erosion of opponent's power, even without direct gains
Example:
USSR mid-1950s to early 1960s
</td>
</tr>
<tr>
<td>Relatively Weak</td>
<td>

3
• Careful and selective commitments
• Some erosion of influence tolerated
Example:
USSR in 1970s and 1980s
</td>
<td>

4
• Minimal means of influence
• Focus on home front buildup
• Subordination of regional issues; do what is needed for internal strength and projection of power
Example:
USSR mid-1940s to mid-1950s
</td>
</tr>
</table>

NOTE: It is worth noting that the interpretation of Soviet policy in the context of detente is seen here as a function of relative economic disparity. In this sense, Soviet inclination toward detente with the United States is itself viewed as a dependent variable. This, of course, does not mean that detente itself, aside from economic disparity, does not account for *some* deviations from these expected policies.

Figure 2

Superpower Inclinations toward the Third World Given Relative Global and Regional Strength

RELATIVE GLOBAL STRENGTH

<table>
<tr><td colspan="2" rowspan="2"></td><td>Relatively Strong</td><td>Relatively Weak</td></tr>
<tr><td>1</td><td>2</td></tr>
<tr>
<td rowspan="2">RELATIVE REGIONAL STRENGTH</td>
<td>Relatively Strong</td>
<td>

• Demanding of allies
• Seek formal relations
Examples:
USSR in late 1960s
U.S. in 1950s, late 1970s and 1980s
</td>
<td>

• Positive control of allies
• Fear of erosion of power
Example:
Britain in mid-1950s[a]
</td>
</tr>
<tr>
<td>Relatively Weak</td>
<td>

3
• Selective alliances
• Not too demanding of allies to make up for regional weakness
Example:
U.S. in late 1960s, early 1970s[b]
</td>
<td>

4
• Satisfied with erosion of opponent's influence
• Generous, non-selective aid to potential defectors from opponent's camp
• Not too demanding of friends
Example:
USSR in mid-1950s to mid-1960s
</td>
</tr>
</table>

[a] Britain was no longer a superpower but still had ambitions at that point.

[b] Although the United States possessed strategic parity with the Soviet Union in the late 1960s, it had some regional disadvantages emanating from increased Soviet presence in the Middle East, and from the planned withdrawal of British troops from the Persian Gulf. As a result, the United States was less demanding of its allies, especially given its limited options in light of the prevailing domestic mood which, following the Vietnam experience, opposed military intervention.

In this scheme, the current state of power distribution fits an extreme case of Figure 1, Cell 3—so extreme that classifying the Soviet Union as a superpower on a par with the United States may be an exaggeration driven by custom and the lingering American interest in this classification. New economic studies reveal the extent of Soviet economic decline between the late 1970s and the late 1980s. It is now clear, for example, that old estimates of Soviet GNP were highly exaggerated. The extent of the exaggeration will be debated for some time, but some estimates put Soviet GNP somewhere between 50 and 70 percent of the Central Intelligence Agency (CIA) estimates.[6] This would put the Soviet Union on a par with West Germany, far behind Japan. Over the decade of the 1980s, one study argues, there was an actual, but small, *decline* in Soviet GDP.[7] Given approximately a 10 percent rise in the Soviet population over the same period, Soviet per capita GNP declined significantly, ranking somewhere between 60th and 70th among all states, putting the Soviet Union on a par with Paraguay. Taking into account that Soviet military expenditures may have accounted for approximately 25–30 percent of GDP (the CIA's old estimates had it at 15 percent), the actual decline in income for Soviet citizens was even greater. Even if the truth about the Soviet economy lay somewhere between the CIA estimates and these new figures, it is easy to see that the economic decline of the Soviet Union was severe. Maintaining military parity with the United States, while successful, did not come cheaply.

Based on the tendencies shown in the matrices above, one would expect the Soviet Union now to be extremely selective in its support for its allies, and to concentrate mostly on the home front. As for the United States, there will likely be less willingness to tolerate those who do not completely support U.S. objectives in the region, as manifested in U.S. policy toward Jordan in the current Gulf crisis, prompting Crown Prince Hassan to complain that the United States will not allow anyone to sit on the fence: one is either pro-American or anti-American.[8] And no matter how hard the United States is striving to portray the anti-Iraq efforts in the Kuwait crisis as an international effort driven by principle, even supportive world leaders, speaking in a hopeful UN General Assembly, talk of supporting the "U.S. policy," not the "international consensus," hoping to score brownie points with a winning power.[9]

It goes without saying, however, that these general tendencies based solely on the distribution of military and economic power tell only part of the story; an examination of Soviet and U.S. policy objectives in the post–Cold War era is necessary for a fuller understanding of the impact of global change on Middle East politics.

B. REGIONAL PERCEPTIONS OF GLOBAL CHANGE

Regional perceptions of the end of the Cold War were generally consistent in at least five Arab communities: Egypt, Syria, Iraq, Jordan, and the West Bank.[10] The basic interpretation of global change posits the shift in Soviet foreign policy as emanating from the economic decline of the Soviet Union, leaving the United States in a dominant role globally. This theme is clearly expressed in a remarkable speech given by Iraqi President Saddam Hussein at the Amman conference of the Arab Cooperation Council, joining Jordan, Yemen, Egypt, and Iraq, on 24 February 1990—a speech which generated much debate and thinking in the Arab world. Expressing serious concern about the impact of global change, Hussein put it this way:

> Among the results of World War II: the Zionist state has become a reality, and the original owners of the land, the Palestinians, have become refugees. While the imperialist Western world helped the expansionist scheme and aggression of the Zionist entity in 1967, the communist bloc sided with the Arabs in the concept of balance of interests in the context of the global competition between the two blocs, and sought to secure footholds for the East Bloc against the Western interests in the Arab homeland. The East Bloc, led by the USSR, supported the Arabs' rights, including their rights in the Arab-Zionist conflict. The global policy continued on the basis of the existence of the two poles that were balanced in terms of force. They are the two superpowers, the United States and the USSR.
>
> And suddenly, the situation changed in a dramatic way. The USSR turned to tackle its domestic problems after relinquishing the process of continuous conflict and its slogans. The USSR shifted from the balanced position with the United States in a practical manner, although it has not acknowledged this officially so far. . . . It has become clear to everyone that the United States has emerged in a superior position in international politics. This superiority will be demonstrated in the U.S. readiness to play such a role. . . . [11]

This vision of Soviet decline and American dominance was shared by political leaders and analysts in other Arab states. Even the Syrians, who officially expressed confidence about the Soviet ability and willingness to provide them with support, privately expressed concern. One high-level Syrian official put it this way:

> I can give you our official line that we do not expect any change in Soviet support as a result of recent change, but I would not be telling you the full truth. Today it is hard to ignore the facts: the U.S. has emerged in a superior position, and that's bound to affect Soviet policy.[12]

The Arab vision appeared consistent about the global tendencies in light of the Soviet decline: the international community will not permit the emergence of a single hegemon, and a new balancing power to the United States is bound to emerge. Saddam Hussein put it this way:

> We believe that the world can fill the vacuum resulting from recent changes and find a new balance in the global arena by developing new perspectives and reducing or adding to this or that force. The forces that laid the ground for filling the vacuum and for the emergence of the two superpowers, the U.S. and the USSR, after World War II, at the expense of France, Britain, and Germany, can develop new forces, which we expect will be in Europe and Japan. America will lose its power just as quickly as it gained it by frightening Europe, Japan, and other countries through the continuous hinting at the danger of the USSR and communism. The United States will lose its power as the fierce competition for gaining the upper hand between the two superpowers and their allies recedes.[13]

The view that Western Europe and maybe Japan will eventually provide the new counterweight to the United States in the international community was widely shared by political leaders and analysts in Jordan, Egypt, Syria, and the West Bank. But most of those interviewed also agreed with Hussein's assessment that, before a new balance emerges, there will be a "transitional period" of perhaps five years during which the United States will dominate global politics:

> However, we believe that the U.S. will continue to depart from the restrictions that govern the rest of the world throughout the next five years until new forces of balance are formed. Moreover, the undisciplined and irresponsible behavior will engender hostility and grudges if it embarks on rejected stupidities.[14]

One indication of the negative impact of U.S. dominance, for most Arabs, was the Soviet decision to allow massive Jewish immigration to Israel, and not to question the large U.S. presence in the Persian Gulf:

One might cite recurrent statements by U.S. officials about their intention to keep their fleets in the Gulf for an unlimited period of time, and their support for the unprecedented exodus of Soviet Jews to Palestinian territory, neither of which would have been possible solely under the cover of the human rights slogan had not the Americans put pressure on the Soviets, exploiting the latter's special circumstances so as to incorporate the issue into their bilateral agreements with the Soviets.[15]

The dominance of the United States is perceived to be largely negative for the Arabs. This view was shared by those who traditionally supported the United States and those who had opposed it, the basic assumption being that the United States simply could not be "won over" by the Arabs, no matter how closely their interests matched, because of U.S. domestic politics. Whereas Anwar Sadat, for example, thought that he could successfully compete with Israel for strategic alliance with the United States,[16] the general Arab mood, including that in Egypt, was that American foreign policy is simply hostage to the "Zionist lobby."[17] Most agreed with Saddam Hussein's assessment that, while "we are not out to antagonize or incite public opinion against the United States," the U.S. support for Israel may result in Israeli regional dominance:

> Given the relative erosion of the role of the Soviet Union as the key champion of the Arabs in the context of the Arab-Zionist conflict and globally, and given that the influence of the Zionist lobby on U.S. policies is as powerful as ever, the Arabs must take into account that there is a real possibility that Israel might embark on new stupidities within the five-year span I have mentioned. This might take place as a result of direct or tacit U.S. encouragement.[18]

Most Arabs thus expressed fear that, in the short term, during the transitional period, the new global environment works against them. But almost all were also optimistic about the long-term impact of change, seeing in it the eventual emergence of strong Arab-European relations that would replace the Soviet-Arab alliance on an even more solid basis. The key to Arab conclusions in this regard are several assumptions:[19]

1. U.S. and European interests in the Middle East are not identical. Now that communism is no longer a threat, these differences are bound to surface.
2. European economic interests and Arab interests are interdependent.

3. In the post–Cold War era, economic power will be more relevant to alliances and policies than military power.

In the short term, most Arabs interviewed expressed serious, even desperate, concerns. The sentiment was summarized this way:

> The sense of despair, the belief that Israel is expansionist and does not want peace, and the rising tide of anti-Americanism have created a situation where war is more likely than at any time since 1973. In important ways, the current situation combines some of the dangerous aspects of the 1950s, 1960s, and 1970s: the anti-Americanism at the popular level is approaching the anti-British sentiments of the 1950s; Arab frustrations, their feeling that the U.S. seems to think that they have no alternative to the status quo, could lead to a desperate explosion. . . . And the talk of collective Arab defence, coupled with the emerging role of Iraq, could lead to a series of escalations that would result in an unintended war, as in 1967.[20]

Still, Arab leaders, while sharing the regional sentiment along the lines expressed above, exhibited different attitudes about what steps they should take. The Jordanians and the Palestinians were highly desperate, almost fatalistic, about an impending disaster (which helps explain why they were willing to align themselves even with Saddam Hussein); the Iraqis expressed defiance and intention to mobilize Arab resources to reverse the tide; the governments of Egypt and Syria, however, while expressing concerns, appeared more patient and reconciled to facing hard times, with the attitude of trying to make the best of a bad situation.*

Change and Democratization in the Middle East. Although some optimists in the West had expressed the hope that the events in the Soviet Union and Eastern Europe would trigger a process of democratization in the Middle East, or at least rising expectations of greater political freedom, such optimism was misplaced. Two primary factors account for the absence of positive linkage between the two regions. The first is that the changes in Eastern Europe and the Soviet Union were seen largely through their perceived negative impact on the region (increased Soviet Jewish emigration to Israel and declining support for Arab causes). The

---

*In my report to Congressman Lee Hamilton, I concluded that "the Syrians appear interested in improving relations with the U.S. I think that there are several reasons for this: Soviet advice in this regard; Syria's pleasure in capitalizing on U.S. hostility toward Syria's rival, Iraq; and the apparent attempt to open up economically."

second is that the failures of the political systems in Eastern Europe were seen as failures of the *communist* system, which most Arabs opposed in any case. This interpretation is also common in Arab states that have been considered friends of the Soviet Union, such as Iraq[21] and Syria.[22]

The political liberalization which was initiated in Jordan through relatively free parliamentary elections, followed by more modest Syrian plans, were not seen as being linked to events in Eastern Europe. The general assessment was that the Jordanian elections were a direct result of the riots of April 1989 protesting tough economic measures. Jordanian analysts argue that, besides the economic factor, Jordanians were inspired by the Palestinian uprising and the perceived heroism of the people in South Lebanon.[23] The demonstrations were especially threatening to King Hussein since they took place in almost exclusively Jordanian, not Palestinian, communities. There was a sense that, had the Palestine Liberation Organization (PLO) not advised its supporters in Jordan against joining the demonstrations, King Hussein would have been in serious trouble.[24] Expecting more difficult economic times ahead, complicated by the fear emanating from Soviet Jewish emigration to Israel, the king sought to defuse the situation and spread the blame by holding elections. In short, the elections were not directly linked to the events in Eastern Europe.

C. THE IMPACT OF CHANGE ON AMERICAN POLICY IN THE MIDDLE EAST

To the extent that global change leaves the United States in a dominant position in world affairs, understanding American foreign policy becomes critical. A central question is how American objectives in the Middle East will be reshaped in the post–Cold War era. One obvious outcome of global change is that Soviet containment in the region will no longer be a priority. Instead, securing the flow of oil to the West will become the primary issue for U.S. policy. How best to serve this American objective becomes a more straightforward proposition in the absence of the Soviet element.

Nonetheless, the debate will no doubt intensify in the coming months about the role for Israel in this Western objective. Israeli Foreign Minister Moshe Arens was asked whether or not he was concerned that the end of the Cold War will diminish the need for Israel as a strategic ally for the United States, thus leading to the erosion of American support, especially given the congressional sentiment to cut foreign aid.[25] Mr. Arens replied that, to the contrary, Israel will now be even more important strategically. Citing data that show Middle East oil becoming more vital to the West in the next decade, he suggested that Israel will be more needed than ever in securing the flow of oil.

This Israeli optimism has given way to serious concern in light of the Gulf crisis. However sincere the rhetoric about international law may be, the massive U.S. intervention in the Gulf would not have occurred if oil was not an issue. But, as the Israeli press now regularly notes, Israel is not perceived to be useful in defending this primary American objective in the region. More significantly, Arab states like Saudi Arabia, Egypt, and even Syria are critical to the success of the American efforts; their strategic utility, long in question, has become obvious.

The emergence of serious strategic cooperation between the United States and Arab states is particularly threatening to long-held Israeli objectives. Israel has sought to prevent strong strategic relations between the United States and the Arab states ever since coming into existence, always perceiving such relations as a threat to U.S. support for Israel.[26] This competition for alliance with the United States provided a dominant dynamic in the Camp David negotiations.[27]

But, despite elements of truth in this interpretation of U.S. interests in the region in the post–Cold War era, Israeli pessimism (and Arab optimism) in this regard are not completely justified. For, rhetoric aside, the U.S. commitment to Israel has never been predicated on the assumption of strategic utility. The U.S. commitment to Israel must be posited as an independent component of U.S. policy in the Middle East which sometimes conflicts with, at other times enhances, the strategic interests of the United States. American foreign policy in the Middle East, especially in an era of few international constraints, is heavily dependent on domestic dynamics, and those dynamics, generally favoring Israel, are not likely to change dramatically in this new era.

Nor is it likely that a shift in American public opinion less favorable to Israel will dramatically alter U.S. support, as a recent survey of American public opinion indicates.[28] The conclusion was based on the assumption that the opinion of the general public on the Arab-Israeli conflict is usually not significantly relevant to the formation of American policy on that issue. If public opinion matters at all, it is primarily the opinion of the "issue public" that has policy consequences—i. e., the opinion of that segment of the American public that ranks the issue very high in its priorities. Unlike the issue public, Americans who do not rank a given issue very high in their priorities are not likely to vote, to make campaign contributions, or to write letters expressing their opinion on that issue. The survey confirmed this assumption.

On the other hand, the positions of the issue public are usually based on some *a priori* commitment and are thus less dependent on changing events. They do not necessarily react to events in the same way as the general public. For example, it was found that while slightly more people among the non-issue public became more sympathetic to the Palestinians than became more sympathetic to Israel, the opposite was true within the issue public, which could be accounted for by a more pro-Israeli tilt within the issue public, which, at a time of crisis and perceived threat to U.S. support of Israel, tends to overcompensate. There was no reason to expect those facts of American public opinion to change dramatically in the new era.

The issue-public hypothesis of American politics can be extended beyond public opinion to decision-making institutions, like the U.S. Congress.[29] For example, one can correlate those members of Congress who rank the Arab-Israeli conflict high in their priorities with those members who tend to become members of congressional committees that are relevant to policy toward that conflict, and to those members who tend to attend committee meetings when this conflict is discussed. The views of the members of the issue public could then be correlated with congressional positions on the Arab-Israeli conflict. Applying a similar approach to bureaucracies in the executive branch would probably yield similar results.

The point of the above is that the nature of U.S. domestic politics and the makeup of the different constituencies result in policies that are independent from both the argument of strategic utility and the general public opinion. This, however, is not to say the latter are completely irrelevant for American foreign policy in the Middle East.

Under most circumstances, the opinion of the issue public is significantly more relevant to the formation of policy than the opinion of the non-issue public. But there are two qualifiers to this conclusion. The first is that the issue-public opinion, no matter how stable, is bound to be somewhat influenced by the views of the majority. The results indicating a close fit between the two on substantive issues suggest that this may be the case. The second qualifier is more complex: the opinion of the non-issue public (usually constituting the majority of the general public) becomes critical in crisis situations that elevate the importance of the issue for most Americans, as indicated in Figure 3 below.

Figure 3

Influence of Issue and General Publics
in U.S. Policymaking

ISSUE PUBLIC

		Preferences *Match*	*Preferences* *Do Not Match*
GENERAL PUBLIC	*High Importance Issues*	Issue public prevails	General public prevails
	Low Importance Issues	Issue public prevails	Issue public prevails

This matrix indicates that the only case in which the preferences of an issue public do not prevail is when those preferences do not match those of the general public (which includes both the issue and the non-issue publics) *and* the given issue becomes of high personal and national priority for the general public. On the face of it, this hypothesis seems trivial: in essence, the general public is transformed into an issue public during crisis situations. But a closer examination reveals that there are important differences.

First, the opinions of the issue public are not identical with those of the non-issue public, even when the issue is elevated in the priorities of the entire population; as noted earlier, the opinions of the issue public tend to be stable and less influenced by crisis situations. Therefore, one still needs to separate the two even in crisis situations when studying the impact of opinion on decisions.

Second, although crises over an issue tend to elevate the importance of an issue to the general public, the opinion of the general public is not always immediately affected; there is usually a temporal lag between events and opinions. Thus prior opinion can sustain a policy through a crisis, even if one can expect that public opinion will change if the crisis is sustained. For example, the 1973 Arab-Israeli war, and the accompanying Arab oil embargo, elevated the national and personal importance of the Arab-Israeli conflict for the general public. But the prior general public opinion was sympathetic to Israel because the Arabs initiated the war, had the Soviets as allies, and launched an embargo that was viewed as a form of blackmail—this despite one's objective expectation that U.S. support of Israel conflicted with the U.S. interest in oil. But public opinion does not change overnight to match objective reality. Therefore, prior opinion can be critical in crisis situations, which are usually outlived by the lag. One can assume, therefore, that in crisis situations the prior opinion of the general public becomes extremely relevant. But even here, to the extent that the non-issue public is usually neutral on the issue, the opinion of the issue public could be critical in determining the policy options.

In contrast to the 1973 Arab oil embargo, consider the recent trends in the general public opinion toward the Israeli-Palestinian conflict, which indicate a shift favoring the Palestinians. In this case, however, the importance of this issue was not elevated to the top for most Americans since vital U.S. interests were not at stake. In this case, we expect the issue public to have a central role in shaping policy. General public opinion alone, without elevated issue-importance will have little impact, but elevated issue-importance will not result in behavioral change if not accompanied by opinion change. Only when there are both—a severe conflict between the opinions of the issue and the non-issue publics and significant elevation in the importance of an issue to the general public—will the relevance of an issue public be reduced.

This indicates that Middle East crisis situations pose the most serious threat to the influence of the issue public because it is only in those situations that other issues become highly relevant. Typically, therefore, the issue public will try to prevent any major shifts in U.S. policy before the crisis is defused. As in the case of the 1973 war and the Arab oil embargo, the pro-Israeli issue public will advocate no movement toward resolving the Arab-Israeli conflict before the current crisis is resolved. Once the crisis is over, the usual domestic political considerations will become dominant once again in shaping U.S. Middle East policy.

Still, one can wonder whether American priorities in the post–Cold War era will be altered in a way that expands the Arab-Israeli issue public. Now that Iraq's invasion of Kuwait has been reversed, is it reasonable to expect that the United States will be inclined to go along with the typical international consensus on the Arab-Israeli conflict?

Whether one is an idealist in interpreting the emerging consensus as an end in itself, or a cynic, seeing the forging of this consensus as the doing of a hegemon asserting itself in forging a new post–Cold War regime intended to make the most efficient use of its new preeminent role, the short-term impact on American policy will be the same: the United States cannot quickly abandon what it has so successfully been able to build. The result will be, as President Bush put it in a speech to the United Nations, that new opportunities will emerge to resolve the Arab-Israeli conflict,[30] with wide-ranging support from other Americans who may not want to see the consensus quickly disappear. Moreover, as happened in the 1973 crisis, the threat to American interests in the Middle East highlights the tension between the U.S. commitment to Israel, on the one hand, and other U.S. interests, on the other, *so long as the Arab-Israeli conflict remains unresolved.* For it is clear that while Saddam Hussein's ambitions were unrelated to the conflict with Israel, his reading of Arab public frustration with the absence of movement in resolving this conflict may have led him to believe that he could get away with the occupation of Kuwait without major Arab opposition. Even after the occupation of Kuwait, Hussein retained leverage with Arab public opinion through his rhetorical link to the Palestinian issue.

All this suggests that some movement on the Arab-Israeli front, led by the United States, is likely now that the immediate Gulf crisis has been resolved. Still, given the patterns of American politics in the absence of crises, the usual domestic dynamics will remain intact, guaranteeing that American policy in the Middle East will not be altered substantially.

D. SOVIET POLICY IN THE MIDDLE EAST IN THE POST–COLD WAR ERA

Whether or not the Soviet Union can legitimately be seen as a superpower on a par with the United States, both the USSR and the United States will have an interest in pretending that this remains the case. Even with its diminished economic capabilities, entailing reduced and selective commitments to old allies, the Soviet Union will continue to provide some support to Syria. President Assad's visit to the Soviet Union last spring secured the flow of military aid to Syria in the immediate future, according to both Syrian and Soviet officials.³¹ However, there are differences between the old and new Soviet commitments to Syria:

1. As one Western diplomat put it, the Soviet decision to supply Syria with the weapons it requested is no longer dependent solely on the political leadership, which then simply asks the bureaucracy to comply; rather, the political leadership now forwards the request to other governmental agencies to study economic and military feasibility.³² A positive reply is no longer automatic. While this arrangement does not appear to have altered the pattern of Soviet supplies so far, it makes the Syrians uncomfortable.

2. One important component of Syrian reliance on Soviet support has been the near certainty that, if Syria engages in war, the Soviets will resupply the Syrians, if not come to their help. There is no longer such certainty in Syrian thinking.

3. The terms of military aid to Syria have become more constrained by the Soviet need for hard currency. Already, bilateral Syrian-Soviet meetings place Syrian debts high on the agenda.

4. In the past few years, the Syrians have been engaged in a campaign to attain strategic "parity" with Israel. Today, the Soviets say that they cannot support this objective; instead, they advocate "defensive sufficiency." The two concepts are not as different as they first seem because both entail a Syrian deterrence capability, predicated on a survivable second-strike capability that would make an Israeli attack on Syria unacceptably high. The primary difference is that Syrian planning for strategic parity always included a limited ground-offensive component intended for taking the initiative to regain the Golan Heights; "defensive sufficiency" apparently rules this component out.³³

5. One consequence of Iraq's defeat may be a stronger Soviet commitment to Syria intended to appease the Soviet military, who have expressed displeasure at the defeat of an old ally.

6. Aside from its bilateral relations with Syria, the USSR will actively seek to prevent an Arab-Israeli war since such a war could seriously strain Soviet-American relations and upset Soviet priorities. Increasing political pressure on Syria is likely to ensue in that direction.

But despite the economic difficulties of the Soviet Union and the reshuffling of Soviet priorities, the key element of Soviet leverage in the

Middle East remains—i.e., the capacity to supply sophisticated weapons. Although the Soviets have been advocating regional arms-control regimes in the Middle East, both regional realities and Soviet need for hard currency will compel them to maintain, if not accelerate, their sales of arms to the region.

It will become clear to the Soviets before long that their primary need for cash will not be satisfied by the new relationship with the United States and the West. Indeed, it was partly this realization that led Saddam Hussein to conclude that the substantial Arab investments in the West could be "diverted to the USSR and East European countries. It may prove even more profitable than investment in the West, which has grown saturated with its national resources. Such a course of action may yield inestimable benefits for the Arabs and their national causes."[34] The Soviets will soon reconcile themselves to the fact that the sale of sophisticated weapons remains their most viable source of hard currency. Driven by this motive, however, the *pattern* of Soviet weapons supply is likely to change: sales will shift toward the sources of money.

The new acceptability of the Soviet Union to the conservative governments of the Persian Gulf, as evidenced in the normalization of diplomatic relations, coupled with the increasing insecurity of the Gulf states in light of the Iraq-Kuwait crisis, will open new opportunities. The current crisis will cost states in the region a great deal, while at the same time pushing them to buy large quantities of weapons. They will look for the greatest "bang for the dollar" they can get, which the Soviets will seek to exploit. But the poor performance of Soviet weapons in the Gulf war, and the sense of gratitude by Gulf states to the United States, will probably mean that the Soviets will not make short-term gains in the Gulf.

Even Israel may see opportunities in the Soviet predicament, especially if it senses strategic cooperation between the United States and the Arab states. One Israeli military analyst has already made a novel proposal. Noting, for example, that the Soviet MiG-29 fighter aircraft are "every bit" as good as their American counterparts at less than half the cost, he sees an opening for Israel: Israel could enter into a joint venture with the Soviet Union by supplying these aircraft with more sophisticated electronics, then marketing them internationally to compete with U.S. aircraft. He claims that Israeli-Soviet discussions on a similar joint venture in the civil aircraft area are already underway.

This Israeli scenario is somewhat far-fetched, but global and regional changes will undoubtedly open the way for new Soviet policy patterns, especially in the supply of weapons area, which after all has always been the key to their influence in the region.

E. REGIONAL POLITICS IN THE POST–COLD WAR ERA

While the end of the Cold War and the current Gulf crisis will almost certainly change Middle East alliances, there are historical patterns of relations among states in the region that are likely to endure. Understanding these patterns is essential for a full assessment of the likely impact of recent events on Middle East politics.

Several hypotheses about inter-state relations in the Middle East have been shown to hold over time:

1. Despite the strong popular sentiment against the presence of foreign troops in the region, Middle Eastern states, like other small states, have generally preferred dependence on outside superpowers over dependence on regional powers. There are several reasons for this. First, every small state is dependent on superpowers regardless of its circumstances. Second, because of its obvious superiority in power and resources, a commitment from a superpower is generally more stable and rewarding than one from a regional power. Third, the extent of regional independence partly determines their independence in their relations with the superpowers: the more regionally independent a state is (or the more dominant it is regionally), the more attractive it becomes to the superpowers, and the more influence it will wield with them. Examples of this abound.[35] The recent Saudi reliance on the United States, while highly risky at the popular level, is not an aberration.

2. Despite the strong pan-Arab and Islamic sentiment among the Arab population, inter-Arab relations have almost always been characterized by competition for leadership among the Arab states, dominated by Egypt, Iraq, Syria, and, more recently, Saudi Arabia. Several factors account for this competition:

   A. Despite the dominance of statism, all Arab governments share similar and fundamental elements of legitimacy emanating from Arab and Islamic popular dispositions. This means that the stability of every regime in the Arab world is partly dependent on what happens in the other Arab states on issues that psychologically link Arabs and Muslims.

B. As I have argued elsewhere, states are generally affected by their immediate environment; consequently, whatever their objectives may be, they desire at a minimum a stable and predictable environment, and at a maximum they seek to have the ability to shape that environment.[36] It follows from this that the more unstable the immediate environment is, the more a particular state will be inclined to shape it, and whenever major changes in the environment appear likely, the tendency to play a leading role manifests itself more clearly. Of states that exist in an unstable environment, the ones that possess the capability to play a leading role—i.e., the states that have relative advantages in size and resources—are more likely to be inclined to dominate the shaping of the environment.

C. Given A and B, Arab states feel dependent on the environment even without fear of inter-state war because of the interdependence of the legitimacy of Arab governments. It is not surprising, therefore, that the closer competing states are in ideology, the fiercer the competition. The conflict between Iraq and Syria—two Ba'athist states—is one example. A more telling example is the competition between Egypt and Iraq in 1961. The regime of Abd al-Kareem Qasim of Iraq was as anti-British as that of Nasser's Egypt, advocating similar pan-Arab ideals. Qasim, however, unwilling to subordinate himself to Nasser, quickly became Egypt's most targeted opponent, with Nasser adamantly opposing Qasim's plan to control Kuwait following British withdrawal—a plan consistent with Nasser's pan-Arab ideals. So sharp was Egypt's opposition to the incorporation of Kuwait that it was willing to reconcile its differences with its ideological opponent Saudi Arabia and risk the dissolution of its union with Syria. More embarrassingly, Egypt found itself unable to oppose the deployment of British troops in Kuwait to defend against potential Iraqi attacks.

D. The central symbolic issue for Arab and Islamic legitimacy has been, and will most likely remain, the Palestinian question. Whether or not the PLO's political role diminishes following the resolution of the Gulf crisis, and whatever happens to the PLO's relations with Arab governments, the centrality of the Palestinian issue will remain because of its link to this legitimacy. Because of the importance of this issue, states vying for leadership in the Arab world must provide some leverage in favor of the Palestinians if they are to succeed. In the 1950s and 1960s, Egypt's leadership was predicated on its ability to use military leverage; the Camp David

Accords brought an end to that. The recent increase in Egyptian influence was predicated on Egypt's promise to use its leverage with Washington and Israel to deliver a peaceful settlement that favors Palestinian rights; the apparent demise of the peace process during the past year has diminished Egyptian influence and enhanced Iraq's, which now claims to wield military leverage on behalf of the Palestinians. The Syrians also understand this rule. One Syrian official, who was advocating closer relations with the United States, told me that Syria now believes that its diminished regional influence derives from an inadequate effort to project its championship of the Palestinian cause.[37] The Saudis too have always recognized that funding the PLO has provided them significant political leverage.

Given these general principles of Arab politics, it is easy to see how Egypt would choose to oppose the Iraqi invasion of Kuwait. An Iraqi success in dominating Gulf politics would leave Egypt highly vulnerable. Already, following the Arab summit in Baghdad in late May 1990, Egyptian officials were expressing serious concerns about the rising influence of Saddam Hussein, who scored a major victory by his masterly handling of the summit meetings, which were televised (and closely watched) in every Arab state.[38] Egyptians were particularly dismayed that Yasir Arafat, who had spent a great deal of time in Cairo while hopes for Palestinian-Israeli negotiations were alive, was now spending much of his time in Baghdad. This was clearly a sign of declining influence for Egypt.

3. Israeli policy toward the Arab states has had two enduring assumptions: divisions in the Arab world are welcome, and Arab-American strategic relations are threatening to Israel. While those components served Israel well in the first two decades of its existence, I have argued that they no longer hold, and that proceeding on their basis is counter-productive for Israel.[39] The Iraqi invasion of Kuwait brought these points home: there are common interests between Israel and some Arab states which many Arab actors recognize. Israel could eventually become part of regional security arrangements, forging alliances with some Arab states. One Saudi intellectual, for example, wrote an unprecedented article in an Egyptian newspaper suggesting that other Arab states should follow Egypt's model in forging peace with Israel. But while the coincidence of interests is clear to many, carrying through with such plans is prevented by one unchanging obstacle—the illegitimacy of Israel in the

Arab popular mind, which is inextricably linked to the unfulfilled rights of the Palestinians.

4. Despite the Israeli public arguments about Israel's utility in defending Western oil interests, it has been recognized that these interests cannot be defended without relying on some states of the Gulf. To the extent that Israel fears Arab-American relations, the historical Israeli preference has been for Iran to play this role. But even if Iran can be restored to playing a dominant role or, at a minimum, that of a balancing state, the nature of the legitimacy of the post-Shah government in Iran guarantees that Israeli-Iranian relations cannot be normalized so long as the Palestinian issue remains unresolved: Islamic legitimacy is as linked to the question of Palestine as is Arab legitimacy. This may lead some to flirt with the idea of designing a new role for Turkey in Middle East politics: now that the Soviet threat has diminished, Turkey may be equally interested in finding a new strategic role that keeps Western aid coming.

CONCLUSION

Now that the Gulf crisis is over, Egypt, Syria, and Saudi Arabia will probably reassess their pre-crisis assessment that the United States, because of its domestic politics, cannot forge close strategic ties with Arab states. Coupled with the other factors outlined above, there will be new movement to resolve the Arab-Israeli conflict. As soon as the issue becomes the Arab-Israeli conflict, however, the tension in U.S.-Arab relations will reemerge. There will not be sufficient economic benefits from the relationship with the United States to alleviate the serious socioeconomic conditions in most Arab states. In the short term, to the extent that the Arabs will have few other alternatives, regional despair will give way to massive political upheavals across the Middle East.

Through their effective security forces and monopoly of the media, most Arab governments will survive, but only by being even more repressive. Repression will lead to increased Islamic political activism: in the absence of legal-political organizations, the populace will turn to available social structures—in this case, the mosques.

In the end, the post–Cold War, post–Gulf war era in the Middle East will not be one of stability, freedom, and democracy. And all this will be ascribed to some inherently unstable and unpredictable characteristics of

Middle Eastern culture and religion, a judgment which flies in the fact of facts: the longevity of Arab governments from Morocco to Iraq, and the relative absence of militarized and effective opposition to central authorities despite persistent economic and political hardships, testify to a puzzling stability of Middle Eastern culture. The region's troubles are not cultural and religious, but political and economic, of the sort that any serious student of politics can understand.

NOTES ·

1. Shibley Telhami, *Power and Leadership in International Bargaining: The Path to the Camp David Accords* (New York: Columbia University Press, 1990).

2. Mohammed Heikal, *The Sphinx and the Commissar: The Rise and Fall of Soviet Influence in the Middle East* (New York: Harper & Row, 1978), p. 243.

3. Saad El Shazly, *The Crossing of the Suez* (San Francisco: American Mideast Research, 1980), p. 175.

4. Ismail Fahmy, *Negotiating for Peace in the Middle East* (Baltimore: Johns Hopkins University Press, 1983), pp. 6–7.

5. *Ibid.*, ch. 3.

6. The estimates used in this study were given by G. I. Khanin in a presentation to the Fourth World Congress of Soviet and East European Studies, Harrogate, England, 24 July 1990.

7. *Ibid.*

8. *Washington Post*, 20 September 1990.

9. See, for example, the speech by the President of Colombia, 1 October 1990.

10. This evaluation is based on my visit to the region in May–June 1990. During that visit I met with dozens of officials and others.

11. FBIS-NES-90-039, 27 February 1990.

12 Interview in Damascus, 1 June 1990.

13. See note 11.

14. *Ibid.*

15. *Ibid.*

16. See Telhami, *Power and Leadership*, ch. 3.

17. This view was expressed by several former Egyptian diplomats and other political leaders in Cairo in June 1990.

18. See note 11.

19. These assumptions represent a summary of the points of consensus among most of the several dozen Arab officials, intellectuals, and opposition leaders whom I interviewed in Egypt, Jordan, Syria, Iraq, and the West Bank, 25 May–15 June 1990.

20. Report to U.S. Representative Lee Hamilton, 30 June 1990.

21. See note 11.

22. This interpretation was given to me by several Syrian officials on 2 June 1990 in Damascus. These officials also argued that "Syria has always been more democratic than the communist states."

23. Interview with Jordanian political scientist.

24. This view was expressed by Jordanian analysts as well as PLO Chairman Yasir Arafat during my meeting with him on 5 June 1990.

25. Personal interview, Jerusalem, 10 June 1990.

26. "Israeli Foreign Policy: A Static Strategy in a Changing World," *Middle East Journal*, Summer 1990.

27. Telhami, *Power and Leadership*.

28. See "Public Attitudes and American Policy Toward the Arab-Israeli Conflict," paper presented at the annual conference of the International Association of Political Psychology, Tel-Aviv, Israel, June 1989.

29. Preliminary results of a study of this question being conducted in Congress are positive.

30. President Bush's speech to the United Nations General Assembly, 1 October 1990.

31. These results were confirmed by the Soviet Ambassador to Syria as well as Syrian officials in interviews conducted on 1–3 June 1990.

32. Interview in Damascus, 1 June 1990.

33. Interview with a Western diplomat in Syria, 2 June 1990.

34. See note 11.

35. For a full articulation of this view, with examples, see Telhami, *Power and Leadership*, pp. 85–90.

36. *Ibid.*, pp. 87–88.

37. Interview in Damascus, 1 June 1990.

38. In my report on my Middle East visit, which took place during and after the summit, I noted that Saddam Hussein, never a popular man in most of the Arab world, had suddenly become popular.

39. "Israeli Foreign Policy" (see note 26).

THE TEST OF "NEW THINKING": THE SOVIET UNION AND THE GULF CRISIS

Galia Golan

From the advent of Gorbachev to power in 1985 and the gradual elucidation of his "new thinking" for Soviet foreign policy, there were a number of so-called tests. Skepticism both at home and abroad ran high, not only with regard to Gorbachev's sincerity, but also, in time, with regard to his ability to reverse past Soviet positions, to put the new rhetoric into practice, and to define a national interest for the troubled—and crumbling—Soviet Union. The INF Treaty was considered by many as proof of both the sincerity and validity of "new thinking"; Moscow made concessions regarded as inconceivable by his predecessors. The big test became withdrawal from Afghanistan. Somewhat slower to come, this extraordinary reversal—with its admission not only that the communist superpower could not win in this backward, border outpost of Marxism, but also that the entire venture had been a mistake—persuaded most skeptics in the West that there was indeed a new policy in the Kremlin. There were still some in the West who attributed it purely to practical considerations born of the particular situation, with no bearing on Moscow's continued long-term interest in world domination; some even claimed the Soviets had not really left Afghanistan. Soviet policy toward the Angolan war and Namibia, the Cambodian conflict, the naval base in Camranh Bay, Central America, the Sino-Soviet dispute, the dismantling of communism in Eastern Europe—all these became signposts of the authenticity of "new thinking."

Yet even as Gorbachev passed these tests, there were those who claimed that "new thinking" did not apply to the Third World, or at least not to the Middle East—the proximity and geostrategic importance of which rendered the region somehow different.[1] More significantly, "new thinking" remained to be tested with regard to the outbreak of a new regional conflict which fit most if not all of the parameters of a major East-West challenge: military confrontation between a progressive Arab state, allied by treaty with the Soviet Union, and the United States, protecting conservative, pro-Western regimes and Western oil interests. Even as it provided a further (perhaps for some, unnecessary) test of "new thinking," the crisis which erupted on 2 August 1990 with Iraq's invasion of Kuwait also produced the first case study of regional crisis in what was considered the post–Cold War era.

While such an "era" was by no means static, and the Soviet Union itself was in a stage of transition, Soviet policy and behavior in the Gulf crisis promised to demonstrate not only the proscriptions and applications of "new thinking" to a crisis situation, but also Gorbachev's perception of the Soviet role in the world today. The precedence of global, particularly Soviet-American, relations over regional considerations—in itself nothing new—assumed new contours and meaning in the absence of ideology and zero-sum–game competition. And regional considerations themselves were redefined as a new national interest began to take shape. The domestic Soviet decision-making process, still in evolution, was of a new order, while *perestroika* and *glasnost* created an entirely new domestic environment for Soviet policymaking. In addition to the impact and interplay of all of these factors upon Soviet behavior in the Gulf crisis, the ramifications of Soviet policy—for and within the domestic environment, as well as for regional and global relations—were sure to have a great bearing upon future policies and even, possibly, the shape of the post-Cold War world.

"NEW THINKING" AND REGIONAL CRISIS

While "new thinking" applied to ongoing or prolonged conflicts, the theory did not explicitly address the outbreak of new conflict or crisis control, aside from the demand for political solutions to the exclusion of military measures. It did, however, call for reference to international law and, in particular, recourse to international bodies for resolution of conflict. Both interdependence and the end of competition led to the idea of collective security—not of the twentieth-century alliance or bloc-versus-alliance or bloc type, but rather a new model. In almost utopian terms, this model was not supposed to be one wherein the two superpowers policed the world together, or of the North—that is, today's industrialized powers—maintaining order over (or in) the South—that is, regional order. While "new thinking" did have something of this element of paternalistic care by the advanced nations over the less developed Third World, the model advocated was that of the United Nations and other collective bodies in which the powers could now cooperate to keep every country in line with international law and the norms of international behavior. This was, of course, the original meaning of collective security, attainable—and obligatory—now because of the interdependent nature of problems in the world today, be they environmental, economic, military, or other (terrorism, drugs).

The prevention of regional crises was also to be subject to a collective approach, beginning in fact with regional measures, with or without the world community in the form of the United Nations or other international bodies. In the Middle East this was to mean, according to proposals raised just prior to the outbreak of the Gulf crisis, the creation of a military risk-reduction center to introduce and monitor a number of security measures for the whole region. These were to include limitations on arms deliveries to the countries of the region, control on the transfer of technology (particularly in the realm of non-conventional weaponry), nuclear and chemical disarmament, troop reductions and demilitarized zones, prior notification of exercises, international inspection and verification procedures, commitments against terrorism, and other similar measures.[2]

As the major arms suppliers, the Soviet Union and the United States would be the principal initiators and presumably supervisors of such arrangements, but the United Nations was to provide the overall framework and necessary mechanisms.[3]

SOVIET BEHAVIOR IN THE CRISIS

Born of the new theoretical approach, the above security proposals were prompted in part by growing Soviet concern over the arms race in the Middle East, including the appearance of intermediate-range missiles and non-conventional capabilities. Iraq was one of the states which worried the Soviets, both because of its developing nuclear potential and its use of chemical warfare against the Kurds and Iran, in addition to the Iraqi conversion of Soviet-made missiles to intermediate-range weapons.

Saddam Hussein's bellicose statements in the spring of 1990 suggested that he was making a bid for power as the leading Arab force in the region. This type of regional threat—that is, the dangers of regional conflicts—was part of what appeared to Moscow, and probably Washington, to be the next item on the superpowers' agenda now that the bilateral East-West conflict was a thing of the past. While higher priority was given to the ongoing conflicts—Afghanistan, Cambodia, Israeli-

Arab (probably in that order)—regional security issues were to be discussed by the superpowers' foreign ministers.

It was during the Shevardnadze-Baker meeting in Irkutsk that the Iraqi invasion of Kuwait occurred. In a sense the stage was set for the unprecedented cooperation which was to characterize the superpowers' behavior during the crisis. Thus the early stages of the crisis saw a joint Soviet-American statement, issued in Russia, as well as a Soviet government statement condemning the invasion and calling for the "swift and unconditional withdrawal" of Iraqi forces plus the restoration and protection of Kuwaiti "sovereignty, national independence and territorial integrity."[4] In their joint statement, the final demand included restoration of Kuwait's "legitimate authorities," obviously an American insertion which was not, however, to prove to be a difference of particular significance.[5]

Moscow immediately suspended arms deliveries to Iraq, joining Baker in a call for all countries to follow suit.[6] It also supported the UN Security Council resolutions condemning Iraq and initiating sanctions and then an embargo. Moscow extended praise to the Arab Summit decision to send forces to join the Americans in Saudi Arabia, without exhibiting any sign of concern over the potential implications of the startling cooperation between Soviet ally Syria and the United States.[7] The Soviet Union persisted in its condemnation of Iraq, refusing to assume any role which might imply neutrality even as it maintained political contacts with the Iraqi government. Conducting virtually daily consultations with the Americans (usually between the two foreign ministers), the Soviet government refrained from criticizing any American move, avoiding even propagandistic exploitation of the crisis against the United States.

One could provide practical, even cynical, explanations for the Soviets' cooperative behavior. Preoccupied with an overwhelming number of domestic problems, they had neither the will nor the means to become involved in a conflict overseas; dependent upon Western economic assistance, they did not want to jeopardize their new relationships with the industrialized capitalist nations. An explanation proposed by one Western journalist claimed that Moscow had hopes for investments from the moderate, pro-Western Arab states, including Kuwait. And not a few commentators, in the Soviet Union as well, suggested that Moscow even welcomed the crisis because of the resultant rise in oil prices to the benefit of Soviet energy exports for sorely needed hard currency.[8] Some estimates claimed the Soviets would earn as much as $7.5 billion from the price rises.[9] To this could be added explanations to the effect that the Soviets had already shifted from the more radical states like Iraq in favor of better trading partners and better sources of regional stability, such as the moderate Arab states and Israel. Conversely, it could be said that nothing had changed: Moscow had suspended arms deliveries to Iraq when that state invaded Iran in 1980, while the Soviet Union had always considered a direct threat to Saudi Arabia to be a red line for the United States, barring any Soviet intervention when America's vital interests were involved.

The Soviet position in the Gulf crisis, including active cooperation with the United States and participation in sanctions against Iraq, went well beyond anything like merely refraining from intervening where America's vital interests were concerned, or like temporarily suspending direct arms deliveries while continuing indirect supplies through East European proxies, as was the case in 1980. Although it is true that the Soviet government was tied up with domestic crises, under "old thinking" one could have made the case for a Soviet interest in an outside diversion, even if only a propagandistic one against Western imperialists in such circumstances.

Even the economic argument, which probably did motivate a desire to maintain a positive image in the eyes of the West and particularly the United States, is not wholly satisfactory. Although less important than the hoped for economic benefits from the West, there were losses to the Soviet economy from its participation in the embargo on Iraq. Past Iraqi debts to the Soviet Union, said to be anywhere from $5 to $20 billion, were most unlikely to be paid, while there was the loss from what would have been ongoing projects and commercial deals, the most important of which were the tripartite oil deals Moscow had with Baghdad.[10] Iraqi oil imported to the Soviet Union was reexported to Bulgaria, Rumania, and India; losses of this trade would amount to the loss of 2 billion rubles in goods for the Soviet market, according to K.F. Katushev, Soviet Minister for Foreign Economic Relations.[11] Deputy Foreign Minister Belonogov, denying that Iraq was in debt to the Soviet Union, gave the parliamentary Committee on International Affairs the following breakdown in dollars: a projected loss of over $800 million in 1990, of which $520 million would result from oil not supplied by Iraq for reexport to India, Bulgaria, Rumania, and other countries, plus $290 million in the form of goods and services not supplied the Soviet Union.[12] To this was to be added $115 million worth of goods and $700 million of financial resources from Kuwait. The last referred mainly to the loss of a subsidy promised by Kuwait for the development of oil extraction in Siberia.[13] Finally, Soviet economists added indirect losses to the Soviet Union as a result of the crisis, such as increased difficulties in obtaining Western credits, increased payments on the foreign debt, higher prices for foreign equipment, and reduced repayment of Soviet credits from Third World countries.[14]

With regard to revenues from increased oil prices, the Soviet oil industry was in no position to benefit from the possible boom. According to *Izvestiia*, oil extraction had fallen in the Soviet Union, with production declining by 3 percent in 1989 as compared with 1988; oil exports declined by 17 million tons, with oil deliveries to the West expected to fall from the 1988 figure of 54 million tons to 25 million projected for 1990.[15] In July 1990 oil deliveries to Eastern Europe were rescheduled and reduced because of difficulties in meeting Soviet domestic energy needs. Following the outbreak of the Gulf crisis, they were further reduced because of the loss of 10.7 million tons owed Moscow by Iraq.[16]

Admittedly there were practical factors involved in Moscow's position today, just as there were practical aspects of "new thinking" itself. But the explanations for Soviet behavior in this crisis must be sought in "new thinking," and the new national interest it sought to elaborate. This national interest was indeed dictated, at least in part, by diminishing economic (though not the still awesome military) capabilities. It was, however, intended primarily to put Soviet domestic needs first while seeking acceptance in the international order of nations as a "normal" country—that is, a responsible, trustworthy participant in a legally bound community of nations. In a sense Gorbachev viewed the world order in terms similar to the society he was trying to achieve by domestic perestroika: restructuring along pluralistic, democratic lines wherein the rule of law and the legitimate play of interests would be respected and provide a stability and security previously sought through force and coercion. Thus, in the Gulf crisis, it was his intention to demonstrate that the Soviet Union was part of the rational, law-abiding world order, and that Moscow was serious when it declared its intention to abandon foreign adventures, power projection, ideological competition, brinkmanship, subversion, and the like.

The problem was that this was not an easy matter. There were contradictions and dilemmas in the practice, just as there were contradictions and dilemmas in "new thinking" itself. The first was the use of military force. A linchpin of "new thinking" was political rather than military means for the resolution of conflict. This was not the old condemnation of military force when applied by the West; it was full admission that the Soviet use of force or support for military action was counterproductive as well as domestically unpopular. Call it "post-Afghanistan syndrome" or morality or pragmatism, the Soviet leadership would have been hard put to justify participation in a military action abroad. That is why, from its very first statement on the Gulf conflict and in all subsequent comments, the Soviet government abstained from threats of military action, calling for peaceful resolution of the conflict—even with the demand for Iraqi withdrawal and the return of Kuwaiti sovereignty.

It was this opposition to military action which led the Soviets to delay the acceptance of Resolution 665 and later 678 in the UN Security Council. Moscow was apparently willing to approve the UN authorization of the use of force to implement the embargo on Iraq only once it received assurances from the United States that ample opportunity would be allowed for the embargo to in fact work, hopefully eliminating the need for force at any stage. It was only at the end of September that Shevardnadze was willing to condone—indeed virtually threaten—the use of force, in his speech to the UN General Assembly, should the tightened embargo prove ineffective.[17] This position was reiterated in early November when Baker made his tour of the anti-Iraqi coalition states in search for support of military action.[18] Once again, in early December, the Soviet Union supported still another Security Council resolution authorizing the use of force (Resolution 678, which set the 15 January deadline for Iraqi withdrawal). On this resolution too, the Soviets delayed the final decision in an attempt to give Saddam more time, but their agreement in principle to the use of force was maintained. Earlier in the crisis there had been hints that Moscow might contribute to the American military buildup in the region if this were part of an international force under the United Nations.[19] The suggestion was for activation of the UN Military Staff Committee. Whether the Soviet Union would then join such a force was not confirmed until the end of September, when Moscow revealed its altered position on the use of force. The change itself may well have been in keeping with a timetable promised President Bush in the September summit.

The suggestion to activate the Military Staff Committee was eventually dropped, probably because Moscow did not want to contribute forces of any kind (although senior staff officers from the permanent members of the Security Council reportedly did meet a number of times during the crisis).[20] The proposal itself, however, was indicative of something broader than Soviet interests in dealing with the military aspect of the crisis. The whole approach to regional conflict under Gorbachev had to be multilateral and internationally sanctioned, legally and practically. This too was stated from the very first Soviet response to the crisis, with its call for action by regional multilateral or international bodies, such as the Arab League and the Islamic Conference, as well as the United Nations.

It was probably true that Moscow preferred an "Arab" solution to the crisis so as to avoid having to choose sides within the Arab world or be accused of shirking responsibilities. In the past, during Arab-Israeli wars, particularly the Lebanon war, the Soviets called for joint Arab action so as to avoid the need or demand for Soviet intervention. Also in the past, Soviet appeals for UN action were often "red herrings" designed to block American interests and delay or obstruct genuine resolution or actions. Yet in the Gulf crisis, the call for internationalization was not accompanied by anti-American politicking or propaganda; there was no official effort to obstruct or even criticize American actions or block Syrian cooperation with the United States, for example. Nor was there any Soviet violation of the embargo or softening of position vis-à-vis Iraq so as to try to play both sides or hedge its bets. The appeal for a UN framework appears to have been a genuine attempt to activate a neutral, supranational approach to the enforcement of world norms— necessary to create the kind of world stability viewed by Moscow as essential to its own as well as others' security and prosperity.

There may have been additional motivation for the Soviet appeal for a UN umbrella. When the Soviet Union, under Gorbachev's "new thinking," abandoned bipolarity, the intention was to usher in an era of multilateral internationalism or a multipolar world. What emerged instead, at least as evidenced by the Gulf crisis, was a unipolar one under the United States. Without acting necessarily against Soviet interests or wishes, the Americans, by their massive military buildup in the Gulf, created a number of problems for Moscow. With memories of the Cold War still fresh, particularly in the minds of the military, such a strong American presence close to Soviet borders raised instinctive alarm. Moreover, the United States gave the appearance of acting under a type of "old thinking" by pouring in power and resisting a UN framework on the ground, giving special importance to the assurances apparently accorded Gorbachev by President Bush in the September summit that American forces would not remain permanently in the region.

Nonetheless, these acts highlighted a dilemma already apparent in "new thinking": the Soviet desire if not compulsion to refrain from foreign entanglements without, however, becoming a second-rate power—that is, accommodating the traditional Russian aspiration to great power status. American "unipolarity" demonstrated Moscow's near irrelevance in a crisis gripping Europe, the United States, and the entire Middle East; at the least it exposed the grave asymmetry between American and Soviet power. This matter had an important domestic side to it, which we shall discuss below, but together with the other concerns it may further explain Soviet interest in internationalization. Within the UN framework, this asymmetry would have been obfuscated; multipolarity could be achieved.

Aside from the effort to achieve collective action, and probably genuine concern that developments in the Gulf might lead to war, the Soviet leadership played only a minor role in the crisis. Most importantly, presumably, for the United States, Gorbachev continued to back American policy and maintain a united front. This may, in fact, be all that Washington requested; President Bush told reporters that he was not asking the Soviets to share the burden of the Gulf deployment or to mediate.[21] The Soviets undertook the evacuation of dependents of their citizens working in Iraq and all 880 Soviet citizens in Kuwait. In the fall, roughly 2,500 Soviet citizens were evacuated from the total of 7,830 originally in Iraq and Kuwait.[22] Following a KGB report on restrictions placed on Soviet citizens remaining in Iraq (5,000 in number), Moscow sought Iraqi permission to evacuate this personnel as well, and most were out by mid-January.[23] In September Gorbachev told visiting U.S. senators that 193 military specialists were being left in Iraq until the expiration of their contracts—in non-operational jobs—so as not to endanger the lives of the remaining several thousand Soviet citizens in Iraq (mainly economic and technical advisers working in the oil industries).[24] By the end of December approximately only fifty military specialists were left.[25] President Bush would appear to have accepted Gorbachev's explanations during the September summit, but the Soviet press itself was not satisfied, and the matter was actually raised in a session of the Supreme Soviet. Moscow did, however, order all government ministries and departments to implement the embargo and to halt ongoing relations with Baghdad, excluding presumably the offices responsible for the personnel still in Iraq. The Soviet government also conveyed "technical information" to the United States embassy in Moscow with regard to Soviet weapons and equipment previously provided Iraq.[26]

At the political level, Moscow rejected the role of mediator, but nonetheless undertook an effort to persuade Saddam Hussein to withdraw from Kuwait. Aside from a genuine interest in resolution of the crisis without war, the Soviets had an additional interest in appearing to be able to play an important role in this international crisis, without, however, implying the neutrality the role of mediator carried with it. Thus, after sending two messages to Saddam Hussein, which, according to deputy Foreign Minister Belonogov, failed to soften Iraq's position, Gorbachev sent a special government envoy, Mikhail Sytenko, to Iraq and several Arab countries (including Syria, Egypt, Libya, and Jordan plus the PLO).[27] Later, a more important emissary, Presidential Council member and Middle East expert Evgenii Primakov was sent, twice, to Baghdad as "special Presidential representative." To avoid the appearance of mediating, Primakov's initial talks with Saddam were officially described as designed to obtain permission for the evacuation of Soviet personnel from Iraq.[28] Nonetheless, Primakov traveled to Amman, Cairo, Rome, Paris, and Washington after these talks and returned to Iraq at the end of October in what was clearly admitted to be an effort to find a solution to the crisis (which Primakov described as an effort of the entire international community).[29] Despite some optimistic comments along the way, Primakov's talks, which apparently included a proposal for some sort of inter-Arab peace initiative (presented by Gorbachev to Mitterrand at approximately the same time) proved a failure.[30] So too did talks conducted by Igor Belousov and Foreign Ministry Middle East Department head Vasilii Kolotusha with Saddam and Tariq Azziz, Iraqi Deputy Prime Minister and Foreign Minister, in Baghdad at the end of December.[31]

Both before and after these efforts there were talks in Moscow with Iraqi officials. On 20 August Iraqi Deputy Prime Minister Sa'dun Hammadi came to Moscow, and just prior to the September summit Tariq Azziz met in Moscow with Gorbachev.[32] Azziz came again at the end of November, just prior to the passage of the crucial UN Security Council resolution (678) which set the 15 January deadline for Iraqi withdrawal. Following the talks with Hammadi, Shevardnadze told an interviewer that there were some "noteworthy elements" in proposals made by Saddam Hussein. But subsequent official clarifications indicated that the fact that the Soviet Union was willing to at least study any proposal made, particularly with regard to the creation of a multinational force to protect Saudi Arabia, did not constitute a change in the Soviet position vis-à-vis Iraq.[33] Indeed, Gorbachev's political adviser Nikolai Shishlin told an Arab interviewer that Saddam Hussein's proposals were not a "serious initiative," but rather were designed "to split the Arab world" and spread "erroneous ideas."[34]

The Iraqi initiative referred to was Saddam Hussein's 12 August proposal to withdraw from Kuwait in favor of an Arab multinational force for Saudi Arabia and Syrian withdrawal from Lebanon, along with an Israeli withdrawal from all occupied territories. As clarified by the Foreign Ministry and Shishlin, the Soviet government did not accept Saddam's idea of "linkage" for Iraqi withdrawal. Nor did it even acknowledge, much less support, Palestinian claims that the Arab-Israeli conflict constituted a source of the present crisis, as Soviet leaders would have done in the pre-Gorbachev era.[35] Linkage did creep into the Soviet-French communique when French Foreign Minister Roland Dumas visited Moscow at the end of August, but this was apparently at the request of France, for it did not appear in any of the communiques with similar visitors from Yemen or Egypt, for example, nor in talks with the Japanese or the Turks, nor in public statements by Gorbachev or other Soviet leaders.[36] Even on the eve of the Soviet-U.S. summit, Foreign Ministry spokesman Gennadii Gerasimov explicitly ruled out linkage.[37]

Yet also on the eve of the summit, in a major foreign policy speech delivered by Shevardnadze to the Asia-Pacific Conference in Vladivostok, the Soviet Foreign Minister previewed a linkage which was indeed to be raised at the summit. Referring indirectly to Saddam Hussein's proposals, Shevardnadze said that there was a growing awareness that "a complex set of problems involving the Arab-Israeli conflict, the fate of the Palestinians, and the tragedy in Lebanon awaits its resolution in the Middle East. Indeed we are faced with several highly complex *interlocking* problems that have many critical undertones" (my emphasis).[38] Invoking the dangers of the arms buildup in the Middle East, he renewed Moscow's call for an international conference with the claim that Israeli agreement to such a conference "could exert a positive influence on the overall situation in the Middle East and on efforts to defuse the crisis in the Persian Gulf." He promised a fresh Soviet look at Soviet-Israeli relations if Israel were to comply—that is, the standard Soviet offer to renew diplomatic relations if Israel would agree to a conference. Shevardnadze stopped short of directly linking settlement of all the issues, as Saddam had done, but he warned that efforts for the resolution of one should not be deferred while seeking resolution of the other.

Further foreshadowing positions which would be raised at the summit, Shevardnadze added another warning. He asserted that pursuit of a peaceful solution to the Gulf crisis, as advocated by Moscow, "should in no way imply that the aggressor has nothing to fear, for it runs the risk of finding itself totally isolated from the rest of the world." He closed this portion of his speech with the assertion that the Soviet Union was convinced that sanctions would work, adding that the Soviet-American meeting which was about to take place would "mark a major milestone on the road toward resolving the crisis in the Persian Gulf."

Just what that milestone was was never revealed, but the U.S. government was apparently satisfied with the outcome of the summit. Gorbachev did indeed raise the issue of the Arab-Israeli conflict and an international conference, receiving apparently a long-sought concession from Bush: American agreement to Soviet participation in the Arab-Israeli peace process. In exchange, presumably, Washington received assurances that Moscow would remain closely allied with the United States with regard to the Gulf crisis. It is difficult to know if any *quid pro quo* arrangements were made, but the Soviets also received assurances that U.S. forces would not remain permanently in the Gulf, while Moscow, possibly, agreed to join a UN military force and condone a nonpolitical solution at the necessary time, which commitments were finally expressed publicly at the UN General Assembly session at the end of September. While linkage was in a sense allowed, in the area of continued Soviet-American cooperation, it was not accepted in the meaning applied by Saddam. The joint communique spoke of settling the present crisis and then of making security arrangements for the region, adding that all "remaining conflicts in the Middle East and Gulf" should be resolved.[39] Thus, viewing linkage only in sequential terms, Gorbachev did not permit anything to impede a basically unified Soviet-American position. His own inclinations, whether out of concern for Moscow's Arab allies or genuine conviction, or in response to domestic pressures, prompted Gorbachev to take a slightly different position on linkage in the post-summit press conference. In answer to a question from a Palestinian journalist, Gorbachev allowed that there was a link between the two conflicts "because the failure to find a solution in the Middle East at large also has a bearing on the acuteness of the particular conflict we have been talking about," referring presumably to the regional arms buildup and/or chronic instability and tension within the region prior to the Gulf crisis.[40] Nonetheless, only sequential linkage was advocated in official statements such as Shevardnadze's report to the Supreme Soviet in December or the Foreign Ministry's statement to *Sovetskaia Rossiya* at the same time.[41]

DOMESTIC RESPONSE—EVIDENCE OF "NEW THINKING"

The Gulf crisis was not only the first test of "new thinking" in the post-Cold War era, but also the first test of the connection between domestic perestroika and foreign policy in a time of major international crisis. The domestic side of "new thinking" was supposed to be the exposure of foreign policy-making to public debate and parliamentary control. Decisions in foreign policy were thus to be responsive to the domestic interests and demands of a pluralistic, open society. It is not entirely certain that any democratic society could formulate its foreign policy in a time of international crisis in this manner, even assuming that perestroika had already reached its full implementation. Nonetheless, with the help of glasnost, there was an extraordinary difference between domestic reaction and behavior in this crisis and that which had characterized the Soviet Union in pre-Gorbachev days.

While there had always been differences of opinion and even conflicting groups or bureaucracies seeking to influence policy, in the past they had had to operate almost clandestinely, detectable only to the most perceptive interpreter of signs and codes. The most typical if not characteristic phenomenon of the domestic response to the Gulf crisis was the open and lively debate in the Soviet media, alongside objective, impartial reporting, punctuated by interviews and press conferences, complaints and criticism, and the raising of controversial issues relating to future as well as past policies. "Old thinkers" were as much in evidence as "new thinkers," but the stage appeared to be open to all. Moreover, *Pravda* no longer represented the final word or best clue to leadership decisions; government and party were no longer one and the same.

One of the most important issues to be raised was that of Soviet arms sales. The debate on this issue had already begun roughly a year before the Gulf crisis, but the new events—in particular, the fact that the Soviet Union had been the main arms supplier to Iraq—added fuel and rancor to this debate.[42] The argument had all the signs of "new thinking," with Iraq merely serving as an example or trigger. Arms sales were criticized because (1) the supply of arms served to encourage and perpetuate conflicts; (2) dealing in instruments of destruction was immoral; (3) arms could fall into undesirable hands or be used for nefarious purposes; and (4) global as well as regional and local security could be threatened.

The core of the argument, however, was the contradiction such sales presented within "new thinking"—that is, the concrete clash between, on the one hand, the principle that foreign policy serve domestic interests, which in this case meant the acquisition of sorely needed hard currency by arms sales, and, on the other hand, the tenets which called for political solutions to international problems and reduction of the military potential of conflicts. This inner contradiction was resolved to some degree by the assertion that arms sales did not in fact bring in hard currency because the recipient countries rarely paid their debts. Thus the whole Soviet military sales program was described as one big giveaway.[43] A rebuttal by the military argued that Soviet arms sales constituted a necessary 15 percent of all hard currency earnings (Western experts generally estimated 20 percent).[44]

Official figures on this previously taboo subject were unavailable (which fact was also criticized by Soviet commentators).[45] Speaking of what he claimed to be the 90 billion ruble debt owed the Soviet Union, Admiral Grishin, Deputy Minister for Foreign Economic Relations, was quoted to the effect that revelation of that part of the debt owed the Soviets for arms deliveries would cause "another outburst of emotion among the public" and be "an information bomb."[46] This startling statement was quoted on Soviet television in response to a comment by a Soviet analyst, Andre Kokoshin (deputy director of the USA-Canada Institute) that the Iraqi invasion of Kuwait "has once again thrown light on the need for a very serious and profound reconsideration of our obligations to the Third World."

A frequent political commentator on Soviet radio, Igor Fesunenko, put it more colorfully:

This situation has revealed the absurdity and unnaturalness of our frequent, so-called aid, especially military aid to Third World countries. This paternalism of ours, this feeding by us of frequently odious dictatorial regimes, which call themselves anti-imperialist and progressive, and on this basis alone we send weapons, money, food, anything there. . . . More than once I have seen how this is done in deeds, how weapons are thrown about, in whose hands they end up—it is a terrible picture from every point of view. It is not just a matter of huge profits, because Angola, Ethiopia, Mozambique, Cuba, Cambodia, Vietnam, and many other countries will never return even a small part of the expenditures on weaponry which we have supplied them.[47]

He called for parliamentary controls on such supplies—an idea raised in previous discussion and supported, for example, by Deputy

Foreign Minister Vladimir Petrovskii.[48] An international register of arms transfers, also previously proposed, was advocated by Major General Vadim Makarevskii, indicating that the military, at least, was not united in its defense of this trade. Makarevskii added the original point that Soviet security was now threatened by the "South"—those "to whom the Soviet Union has sold and continues to sell (or to be more precise, has given and continues to give as presents) state-of-the-art devastating weapons."[49]

It was not only the issue of military relations that was to be reconsidered. The crisis prompted a number of critical examinations of overall Soviet policy in the region. One critic, taking up the theme of the dangers of such weapons in the Third World, explained that they got there in the course of the Soviet-American confrontation. The East-West competition was continued in the Third World even during periods of superpower detente for financial purposes as well as political:

> Weapons deliveries were for the USSR the chief means of penetrating developing countries. The search for "allies" throughout the world resulted in the Soviet Union being drawn indirectly (and, in a number of cases, directly too) into many conflict situations. It was to justify that policy that the concept of giving aid to "national liberation movements" and "anti-imperialist states" was invented. The splendid stucco moldings of ideological exclamations concealed a traditional globalist approach which was not commensurate with the financial, economic, and political possibilities. The partners became accustomed to the fact that they frequently did not have to pay for aid from Moscow, which contributed still further to the drop in our prestige.[50]

An article in *Novoye vremia* went further, reviewing the whole of Soviet policy in the Middle East. Beginning with Stalin's support of the creation of Israel because he wanted an "anti-British stronghold in the Middle East," the article explained that Moscow later considered the Arab states as the "genuine anti-imperialist and particularly anti-American force in the region" at the expense of ideological principles:

> CPSU leaders often renounced their principles for the sake of concord with newly acquired friends. Al-Nadir cracks down on Communists? So what? Sudan's al-Numayri slaughters Communists? He will have his weapons anyway! Communists fleeing from Iraq call Saddam Husayn a fascist? Saddam shoots those Communists who had no time to escape? It does not really matter. The main thing is the President is a stalwart fighter against imperialism and Zionism.

Thus he called for a reconsideration of Soviet interests in the region and a thorough revision of policy there, particularly arms deliveries, in view of the fact that confrontation with the West was no longer in the Soviet national interest.[51]

Writing of the contribution the superpower rivalry made to the conflicts with the region, Andrei Olitskii in *Moskovskie novosti* called for a serious look at a "delicate" matter not previously raised in the Soviet Union: the internal contradictions of Soviet policy in the region. He spoke of the myths in Soviet policy, the exaggeration of the anti-imperialist nature of regimes in the Middle East and the ideological stereotyping of them. Olitskii also spoke of the often unexpected, destabilizing effect Soviet aid—especially military aid—had on the region:

Our leaders found themselves hostages to the fatherland's peacemaking activity, and they hardly imagined that Libya would use Soviet weapons for a war of conquest against Chad, Syria—for the conduct of combat operations against Lebanon's civilian population, South Yemen's revolutionaries—for a bloody civil conflict, and Iraq—for the annexation of Kuwait. Did any of them realize that many of the so-called anti-imperialist regimes in the "Third World" (Libya, Syria, Iraq, and many African countries) are in fact dictatorial, and that some of our friends and allies are in fact dealing not so much in politics as in politicking, adopt a parasitical attitude toward our aid, and—in the event of changing circumstances—could suddenly execute a 180 degree turn, as has already happened on several occasions?[52]

Senior *Izvestiia* commentator Aleksandr Bovin joined this demand for reevaluation, pointing specifically to Iraq as one of the "friends" with whom the Soviet Union had "tied its hands too tightly" in the past when it supported "radical, left-wing 'anti-imperialist' regimes, particularly if their leaders learned to pronounce the word 'socialism.'"[53] Bovin noted Moscow's silence when Iraq invaded Iran, and, in a radio discussion with Shishlin, he spoke of Iraq's use of chemical warfare against the Kurds. In this discussion Shishlin was quite explicit in his description of the nefarious regime of Saddam Hussein, which he said continuously waged "a battle within his own environment," maintaining "an atmosphere of terror and repression . . . against its own citizens, first and foremost Communists," who were cruelly exterminated and against the Kurds, among whom "a sea of blood was shed."[54]

These are but a few of the many condemnations and revelations concerning Iraq which appeared in Soviet media, including comparisons of Saddam to Hitler similar to those in the Western press, and condemnation of the taking of Western hostages.[55] There was, in addition, a scathing article on Iraq that appeared in *Argumenty i fakty* two months before the crisis, which included all the above plus a much more explicit description of the tyranny of Saddam Hussein and the evils of the Iraqi Ba'ath regime. Written by two Soviet Orientalists, it also contained a scathing criticism of the support for Iraq accorded by the Soviet leadership, for whom

> the real state of affairs in Iraq, even after the execution of the communists, which began soon, was of no great importance . . . compared with the opportunity to "add on" one more country to the "steadily expanding sphere of influence and dissemination of world socialism." In foreign policy, as in domestic policy, the stagnant bureaucratic regime could not get along without false reporting and keeping up appearances.

At the time of publication (June 1990), however, the editors saw fit to add an "afterword" defending in part the Iraqi regime and dissociating the paper from a "certain one-sided approach" of the authors, although the editors did advocate open expression of opinions and criticism of official foreign policy organs if the latter deserved it.[56]

Without any caveats, following the outbreak of the crisis and official condemnation of Saddam, *Izvestiia* · political observer Stanislav Kondrashov also made the direct link with domestic Soviet policy. Speaking of the past, he noted that

> in its rivalry with the capitalist world, the Soviet Union was seeking allies among the developing states, proclaiming itself as an example of a better and more democratic society, and enticing the Third World onto a noncapitalist, socialist path . . . but it is obvious now that our example did not carry weight either in East Europe or, for example, in the Arab world for the chief reason that it had not given us ourselves, the Soviet people, a free and prosperous life. The large Soviet aid to states in the East and the South cannot be cancelled out. Something else also cannot fail to be seen: *How many times this aid helped to build on different soil the same thing as in our country—antidemocratic, authoritarian systems.* How many dictators we helped to become firmly established in power and how much money we threw to the wind *because we were not accountable to our own people.*[57]

This comment was accompanied by others critical of domestic decision-making on these issues. *Moscow News*, for example, carried a lengthy article by Sergei Volovets not only criticizing the supply of Soviet arms to countries like Iraq, Syria, and Ethiopia, which endangered peace and stability in their regions, but also questioning the government's claim that there were no military "advisers" in Iraq but only 193 "experts." He said that a Foreign Ministry briefing on 6 August revealed that 1,000 Soviet servicemen were in Iraq. "Where," he asked, "have the remaining 800 military experts disappeared to?" He challenged more than the figures, however. He questioned whether the Soviet supply of arms and experts served Soviet national interests or were merely the result of "the excessive influence of the military-industrial complex in our society, the momentum of the giant machine once started and, only thirdly, due to the interests of narrow groups who wish for a lengthy stay abroad in order to advise others."[58] He therefore called for parliamentary control beyond departmental interests.

A *New Times* article allowed that the necessary parliamentary control promised little with regard to the military, given the present composition of the parliamentary Committee on Defense and State Security. This article was particularly critical of the role of the military, including their decisions to dispatch military advisers as well as arms to the Third World. Specifically questioning the decision not to recall the specialists from Iraq, the author, Petr Gladkov, rejected the explanations provided by the Soviet General Staff, proclaiming, "I still have no trust in our military" in view of their previous lies over the supply of missiles to Iraq and the like. Moreover, he added that he did not believe the military's claim that there were no such advisers in Iraq today (only "specialists").[59]

Even stronger, however, was the comment by Olitskii in *Moskovskie novosti* that he was "alarmed" by the fact that the persons who had participated—and committed numerous errors—in the formation of Soviet policy in the region for the past few decades were still influencing the mechanism of political decision-making.[60] One can only guess if he meant Karen Brutents, still carrying responsibility for Middle Eastern affairs as first deputy head of the party's international department, or possibly Evgenii Primakov, long-time leading Middle Eastern expert who was a member of the Presidential Council at the time, or other, conservative "Arabists" still at the Foreign Ministry and the Oriental Institute of the Academy of Sciences.

There were additional challenges of this type—that is, from the "left," or the basically democratic trend—even with regard to policies adopted during the crisis itself. The failure to withdraw even the "193 specialists" was criticized, for example by political observer Fesunenko. He said that he had received an "evasive" answer when he telephoned a high-ranking Foreign Ministry official to find out why the specialists were not being evacuated along with the women and children.[61] Some combined criticism on this issue with criticism of the government's decision to comply with the Iraqi demand for the closure of embassies in Kuwait.[62] Aside from commentators' remarks, a joint statement was put out by the Soviet Peace Committee, the Soviet Committee for Peace, Disarmament, and Ecological Security on the Seas and Oceans, the Soviet Peace Fund, and the Soviet Association for the Law of the Sea, calling among other things for review of the question of the Soviet specialists in Iraq and abrogation of the Friendship and Cooperation treaty with Baghdad.[63] Public opinion too called for the return of the specialists. According to Soviet broadcasts abroad, the Soviet public "has been increasingly critical of the fact that Soviet specialists continue to work in Iraq."[64]

Most significantly, there was a sometimes direct, sometimes indirect voice calling for greater Soviet action. Galina Sidorova, in a *Novoye vremia* article, asked why the Soviet Union was on the sidelines in this crisis, advocating, at least by implication, Soviet military action, albeit through the United Nations.[65] Journalist and Middle East specialist Igor Beliaev took this a step further in asking rhetorically why Moscow should not consider participating in the naval patrols of the Gulf and provide aircraft for the transfer of troops and military equipment to the front zone, or even dispatch soldiers to join the very likely military action against Iraq.[66] Others spoke at least of Soviet volunteers, but the implication was that Shevardnadze need not have limited Soviet participation to the case only of a United Nations force.

These may or may not have been the sentiments behind those in the media who justified and defended America's military deployment in the Gulf. Bovin, for example, opposed the sending of Soviet troops because of the critical situation inside the country and the post-Afghanistan syndrome, but he called for support for an American military action should such action take place.[67] The fact that there were such defenders of the American position was significant in itself. As important a political consultant as Shishlin, who also opposed the dispatch of Soviet troops even as volunteers, told an Arab interviewer that, in his personal opinion, "the steps taken by Washington were a response to the cause of the Gulf crisis. It [the United States] has taken defensive, not offensive, measures. And I believe that it is Iraq's policy—not the U.S. policy or the West's—

that is the offensive one."[68] This was also the thrust of his comments, defending the United States (and even Israel's interest in avoiding war) in Soviet radio discussions.[69] In one of these discussions, Bovin was somewhat critical of the United States' moving without a UN military framework, but in *Izvestiia* just two days before Bovin had defended America's unilateral moves with the comment that the

> community of states is only just learning to work together in protect-
> ing international law and the new world order that is taking shape.
> The corresponding UN mechanisms have not yet grown strong. And
> *it is difficult in this case to criticize the Americans for getting on with it,*
> *for not waiting for the UN "rear" to catch up and take responsibility. They*
> *are taking a risk of course. All the more reason for wishing them success.*[70]

And a week later he wrote in response to Arab criticism that, without idealizing the United States, the Soviet Union understood that

> in this situation the United States is obviously committed to stopping
> the aggression and punishing the aggressor. . . . I do not think the
> Soviet Union is exactly delighted about the massive U.S. military
> presence in Saudi Arabia either. But what alternative is there? . . . In
> fact, the Americans were summoned by the Arabs themselves. So who
> is the offending party? Whom do you criticize? . . . [S]upport for Iraqi
> policy, criticism of the United Nations, anti-American demonstrations
> and attacks on the USSR prevent Baghdad from making a self-critical
> appraisal of the situation and objectively, contrary to the will of the
> supporters and the demonstrators, diminish the prospects for peace
> and bring war closer.[71]

Bovin's comments came in response to accusations in Arab publications that Soviet and American agreement indicated a retreat by the
Soviet Union and loss of its great power status. Such accusations most
likely touched a sensitive nerve, given the traditional tension in Russia
between respect and contempt for the Western world and historical
yearnings for great power status. Indeed, this was perhaps the core issue
in the debate over Soviet policy in the Gulf crisis: the place of the Soviet
Union and, the other side of the coin, evaluation of the Americans'
position. The respected Third World specialist Georgii Mirsky put matters bluntly. Assessing Soviet alternatives, he told a French interviewer
that Moscow could not have disagreed with the United States on this
issue of international law and order without risking the loss of "the trust
earned in the West." Yet to send Soviet troops would alienate the Arab

world. More frankly, he invoked the "post-Afghanistan syndrome," adding that Soviet troops only just out of Afghanistan were now tackling the problems in the Caucasus. "All we need now is the Gulf!" He concluded:

> To be frank, we are less and less interested in the Near East. It was a parade ground, an ideal place for destabilizing the West, an area for spreading ideology. But with the bankruptcy of socialism and the rapprochement with the West, the Near East is becoming less important. We no longer play a superpower role there. We are no longer a superpower.[72]

Izvestiia journalists Koryavin and Kondrashov put the matter a bit more regretfully, contrasting America's power with Moscow's weakness. The Soviet Union could no longer rely on the Warsaw Pact, even for formal support, as the United States could on NATO, Kondrashov pointed out, and the Arabs paid no heed to Moscow's call to "counter aggression only within the UN framework," demonstrating their "sober regard for which side has the real advantage in strength." The United States accorded the region greater priority, and, Kondrashov reminded his readers, "the multifaceted internal crisis in the Soviet Union . . . makes us lie down on the bottom, so to speak, conforming to our modest available potential."[73] Somewhat less directly, Koryavin too spoke of Soviet weakness, noting that "It is said that the United States is in a leading position today, without any competition. We are no longer living in the sixties, when there were thousands of Soviet military personnel in Egypt. The United States is the sole real force in the region."[74]

Wistful rather than critical, these journalists sought to justify a role nonetheless for Moscow, claiming that it could at least act as a restraining balance to the United States in the explosive situation developing. An open debate between two analysts from the USA and Canada Institute took place on this issue in a Soviet foreign broadcast.[75] Petr Glatkov accused Andrei Kortunov of "old thinking" for explaining the differences in the Soviet and American positions in "Cold War" terms. Kortunov said that the United States, unlike the Soviet Union, would prefer to see Saddam overthrown rather than strike a deal because a Saddam still in power would be "one of the most persistent anti-American leaders in the region." The commentator Sergei Goryachev and Kortunov in turn suggested Glatkov was being a bit "idealistic" for arguing that it was not a matter of the superpowers but of the international community and the United Nations to determine the outcome. Asserting Moscow's continued strength, both said that UN decisions were valid only because the Soviet Union and the United States stood behind them; the United Nations would be paralyzed without agreement between the two, implying that the Soviet Union still had a controlling voice.

DOMESTIC RESPONSE—SIGNS OF OLD FEARS OR LOYALTIES

Perhaps unintentionally, this exchange gave expression to the frustrations felt by some regarding Moscow's new weakness and even regarding "new thinking." It was most likely "old thinking," for example, which motivated one member of the Supreme Soviet Committee on International Affairs, Gennadii Yanaiev—who just happened to be the CPSU Politburo member responsible for international affairs (which fact was not mentioned in the press accounts of his comments).[76] Yanaiev complained that there had been only a "flabby response" from Moscow to attempts abroad to cast aspersions on Soviet intentions. This was actually the other side of the debate, in which displays of "old thinking" were particularly apparent in negative references to the United States, including, as distinct from the government's position, some agreement with Saddam's arguments or at least linkage with regard to the Palestinian issue and an anti-Israel position. These implicitly or explicitly critical views could be heard from military and party circles as well as from "Arabists"—that is, academics and journalists who had spent most of their careers dealing with the Arab world. There may also have been some correlation between Russian nationalist-anti-Semitic sentiment and a critical approach to Soviet policy in the Gulf crisis.[77] In time, the opposition of these different groups to the Soviet policy, combined with their underlying grievances with "new thinking" and perestroika, gained sufficient strength to precipitate the resignation of Shevardnadze, as we shall see below.

The problem, as expressed in comments by the military, concerned not what was seen as the justified Soviet condemnation of the Iraqi invasion of Kuwait, but rather the exaggerated military response of the United States. Thus Soviet behavior in one respect was not questioned, but discomfort with the growing American military presence was clearly expressed in what could be interpreted as veiled criticism of Moscow's tolerance, even cooperation, with this buildup. *Krasnaia zvezda* became the champion of peaceful solutions and diplomacy, one article even quoting *Ecclesiastes* that "wisdom is better than martial weapons."[78] The Soviet army daily warned of "hotheads" and "hawks" in the United States who might attempt a preventive strike against Iraq, answering aggression with aggression.[79] More critical, however, were a number of commentaries which claimed that U.S. military circles were using the crisis as an excuse to create a permanent American military presence in the Gulf, either out of traditional hawkishness or as a substitute for forces in Europe, which were rapidly losing their legitimacy.

Major A. Skryl'nik raised the question as to just why the United States was introducing so many troops into Saudi Arabia, answering that the Pentagon might be intending not only to repulse Iraq's probable invasion of that country and organize a naval blockade of Iraq, but also "to demonstrate to public opinion the enduring importance of U.S. military might and the U.S. role as ruler of the destinies of countries and peoples." He cited American Secretary of Defense Cheney on the need to reorient U.S. military strategy and spending toward participation in regional conflicts and the protection of U.S. interests far beyond its borders. Cheney, in this account, therefore stressed that in addition to the preservation of the U.S. nuclear deterrent capacity, forward-based forces in Europe and the Pacific should also be maintained, together with the strengthening of America's role as a leading sea power. Skryl'nik concluded, in what could be interpreted as a warning to "new thinkers" who would reduce Soviet military strength and power projection mission, that "the stereotypes of the past and reliance on force are still valued across the ocean."[80]

A variation on the same theme was evident in a *Krasnaia zvezda* commentary which saw the crisis as the savior ("as if by magic") of American military "hawks."[81] Now these circles could forestall planned defense budget cuts ("How can a reduction in the Pentagon's expenditures even be mentioned now that tens of thousands of American boys are being sent across the ocean in order to 'defend Saudi Arabia' and also take the opportunity to punish Iraq?"). The article claimed that now the Pentagon was dusting off previously postponed plans such as "the construction of the B-2 Stealth bomber, the C-17 military transport plane, the multi-role V-22 and Osprey aircraft." In addition, the United States now acquired the military bases it had been trying to obtain in Saudi Arabia for forty years. Thus, in countering the Iraqi invasion, one must be careful not only of the danger that the United States could "go too far and provoke a bloody flare-up in the Middle East instead of preventing it," but also one must be careful "not to foul our own nest, as the saying goes, the home of all mankind."

Warsaw Pact Chief of Staff Vladimir Lubov elaborated still further on this theme. Exhibiting a full dose of "old thinking" and a good deal of dissatisfaction, Lubov spoke of the "great responsibility of politicians for the decisions they make" in view of the problems created by Saddam's act.[82] The "problems" referred to, as cited by a Moscow radio discussion, were as follows:

> If, as they intend, the United States were to put 250,000 soldiers into Saudi Arabia, with NATO member Turkey next door, and then move into Iraq—and this option likewise should not be wholly excluded—then an unbroken arc could be formed between NATO's eastern flank and Saudi Arabia, and this would radically alter the strategic balance in the region.

Moreover, the proximity of Iraq (200 kilometers) to the borders of Georgia, Armenia, and Azerbaijan would give the United States "the possibility of exerting pressure on the development of events in that area." And finally, the placement of such a large force in the Middle East would torpedo the Vienna talks on force reductions because it would strengthen NATO's right flank, not accounted for in the Vienna talks but sharply altering the balance of forces. Therefore, the Soviet Union must take all this into consideration when forming its policy regarding the Gulf crisis.

Although the new person in charge of the Middle East in the party central committee's international department, Vladimir Zenchev, displayed no disagreement with the positions taken by the government, including support for American actions,[83] the party daily, *Pravda*, echoed some of the same ideas as those of the military. One commentary employed some of the same terms and ideas when it pointed to the opportunity that the crisis presented the Americans as "an unexpected gift" in the form of the possibility of "deployment of U.S. armed forces on the territory of Saudi Arabia and the United Arab Emirates, the enlistment of Arab subunits in combined forces with the Americans to oppose an Arab country, and the involvement in its actions in the Persian Gulf of the ships of West European countries that with a few exceptions previously opposed the use of their forces beyond the NATO region."[84] The commentary, by *Pravda*'s political observer Gennadii Vasiliev, claimed that although this was ostensibly an international force facing Iraq, it was in fact an American-Iraqi conflict in which the United States, "acting under the banner of defending the victim of aggression," was in fact pursuing its real interests: "oil, strategic considerations, and the consolidation and expansion of the U.S. military presence in the region."

A similarly anti-American item was filed by the paper's Cairo correspondent. Contrary to the Soviet message sent the Cairo summit congratulating them on their decisions, the Arabs were criticized for inviting the Americans into Saudi Arabia.[85] The article spoke of the doubts of even some "pro-American regimes . . . about the selflessness of future U.S. plans for staying in the region," quoting an Egyptian scholar to the effect that Washington would not limit itself to punishing the aggressor. It then cited Egyptian comments that the divisions within the Arab world could provide a pretext for "independent actions by the West without taking into account Arab opinion." The same article also presented the PLO and Jordanian positions in a relatively positive light. Without mentioning their abstention from the Arab summit condemnation of Iraq, the party daily spoke favorably of the efforts by King Hussein and Arafat to find a peaceful solution to the crisis; Libya, Algeria, and Yemen, all of which initially supported Iraq, were cited almost positively as having "put forward their proposals to settle the crisis."

This account, more typical of Cold War than of "new thinking," found an echo in another *Pravda* commentary, also characterized by anti-American sentiment.[86] Written by Vladimir Beliakov, this piece went still further by linking the Gulf crisis with the Arab-Israeli conflict, which had been the custom in pre-Gorbachev days. This was done not in the way proposed by Saddam—indeed Beliakov explicitly rejected binding the solution of one conflict with that of another because of the complexity of the problems involved (although in a later defense of linkage, he said even the solutions might be linked).[87] His linkage was primarily to liken Iraq to Israel—the aggressor occupying an Arab neighbor—and he characterized the United States as that power which for twenty-three years had been "propping up Israel and its policy of aggression and expansion." He implied that the United States was making a tragic error in trying to force Saddam to retreat, risking what appeared to be an inevitable explosion with untold consequences. His conclusion was that the Soviet Union, as "a state enjoying authority among the sides to the conflict," should initiate a political solution somewhat along the lines proposed by Saddam—that is, an Iraqi withdrawal from Kuwait in exchange for an American withdrawal from Saudi Arabia in favor of a pan-Arab force under UN supervision. He offered the proposal as "someone who has studied the problem of the Near East for two decades," but it also appeared to be a bid for a Soviet role, not only as a great power, but as one better suited than the United States to understand and deal with the region.

These *Pravda* articles appeared to reflect something of the Arabists' discomfort with the way Moscow was conducting its policies and with the whole course of the crisis. Indeed another Arabist long associated with *Pravda* in the past, deputy head of the Africa Institute Alexei Vasiliev, exhibited similar discomfort, if not with official Soviet policy, then with the domestic response.[88] Condemning "self-flagellation over our past," he chastised some Soviet media "that are wallowing in their newly acquired piety and calling the USSR's revenue from increased oil prices 'cynical' or any weapons sales 'immoral.'" Concerned, however, with the reaction of the Arab world, Vasiliev was particularly critical of the United States, comparing Iraq's invasion with U.S. moves into Panama and Grenada. Even justifying America's motives, which the author did not wholly, the consequences of the U.S. buildup were likely to be detrimental even to these goals themselves. Thus he compared the move to the Soviet intervention in Afghanistan as a case where troops had been invited in by the local government, "and we know what happened there." At the same time, he too compared Iraq to Israel, arguing that more Palestinians had perished in the *intifadah* than Kuwaitis in the Iraqi invasion. He found still more critical words for Israel, attacking its policy in general and suggesting that Israel might even strike a deal with Saddam Hussein for the creation of a Palestinian state in Jordan. He was closer to the mark when he said that Iran might strike a deal with Iraq, but he also offered some words of sympathy for the pro-Iraqi position adopted by the Palestinians.[89] On a note quite similar to the previous *Pravda* article, Vasiliev concluded with a call for a Soviet initiative, given Moscow's credibility in the Arab world, but he also struck an ominous note when he said that "by no means everyone in Moscow itself believes that cooperation and mutual understanding with the United States implies full and unconditional support for all Washington's actions."

Another senior Arabist, Igor Beliaev, also criticized both the United States, for not adhering to Soviet advice in handling the crisis, and domestic Soviet reaction which was critical of Moscow's past Middle Eastern policies, particularly the arms supplies to the region. "Hastening to disagree with this approach," Beliaev argued that past military cooperation, especially with Egypt, had enabled the Soviet Union to enter the Middle East, a step which had been "necessary" to protect the Soviet Union's southern border and aiding in the defense of newly independent Arab states. Justifying Moscow's past role as a balance to the Americans in the region, Beliaev added that today the Soviet Union had all the more reason to take an interest in the area "close to our southern borders," implying perhaps the connection with disorders in the southern Soviet republics, particularly the Moslem ones.[90]

Signs that conservative-nationalist Russian elements shared the Arabists' and perhaps party and military dissatisfaction with Moscow's positions could be seen in the reporting of *Sovetskaia Rossiya*. As with all the other critics, the paper disclaimed any justification of Saddam's acts, adding a "but."[91] This was directed at the Americans, who were denounced for having neither the right nor the legitimacy for their military buildup in the Gulf, in view of their past record and their refusal to work through the United Nations. Indeed, it was argued, the moves by the United States merely served to strengthen anti-Western sentiment in the Arab world and, with this, pro-Iraqi sentiment, as evidenced by popular demonstrations in some countries. Moreover, the purpose of what was basically portrayed as a foolhardy American buildup was said to be "the desire to control the world's largest oil deposits . . . [and] defend its own strategic interests and the interests of its allies in the region—mainly Israel" by means of a permanent military presence. Although occasionally eschewing linkage, the paper nonetheless argued that the alleged application of universal norms to Iraq should be applied to Israel as well: "the action of laws, including international laws, should be universal and not selective," and it quoted Arab sentiment justifying such linkage.[92] *Sovetskaia Rossiya* also published a lengthy interview with PLO Ambassador to Moscow Nabil 'Amir, which criticized the Soviet media as well as the United States and Israel, adding the claim that the "region's problems [Palestine, Lebanon, the Gulf] are interconnected."[93]

DECISION-MAKING

The variety and intensity of the debate within the Soviet media were themselves a part of perestroika, while the debate apparently reflected public opinion on the issues involved. For example, a poll conducted by the Soviet Center for the Study of Public Opinion found that 38 percent of its respondents believed to some extent that the Soviet Union as a supplier of arms to Iraq shared some of the responsibility for the invasion of Kuwait, as distinct from 24 percent that believed there was no Soviet responsibility involved. Some 47 percent approved of Soviet policy in the crisis; only 7 percent said they did not approve.[94] The fact that this and other such polls were conducted during a crisis was extraordinary in itself; it was one more piece of evidence of "new thinking."

Public control or input regarding foreign policy was to be conducted not only through the media, but also through the elected organs of the society—that is, the Soviet Parliament. To some degree this may have been the case when 400 Soviet deputies, of the group of Communists called "Soyuz," issued a statement on the crisis. They opposed the Soviet agreement announced by Shevardnadze to participate if a UN force were created for the Gulf.[95] While this sentiment may have reflected public opinion (a poll indicated only 8 percent of the public favored sending even naval contingents),[96] the motivation may not have been the same, for "Soyuz" was a group described by TASS as "dedicated to the preservation of a strong Soviet Union"—that is, a nationalist position which viewed "new thinking" and particularly the cooperation with the United States as detrimental to Soviet prestige and strength in the world.

The institutional framework more directly involved, at least theoretically, was the International Affairs Committee of the Supreme Soviet of the Soviet Union. This committee did debate the crisis following a presentation by Deputy Foreign Minister Belonogov, who was the ministry's chief person dealing with the Gulf conflict. Belonogov elucidated the economic losses to the Soviet Union in its compliance with the sanctions; he also revealed that the United States had given Moscow prior notification of its decision to dispatch troops to the Gulf.

The ensuing committee discussion, according to Soviet press accounts, heard samples of both sides of the public debate. The concerns of the military over the American buildup in the region were expressed by Warsaw Pact chief Lubov.[97] What were presumably the concerns of the CPSU to what it apparently viewed as an overly accommodating stance on the part of the government were expressed by Politburo member Yanaiev in his comments on the "flabby response" to outside aspersions cast on Soviet intentions.[98] And even the hints from the Arabists found expression in comments noting the lack of unity in the Arab world regarding Iraq "the aggressor."[99] From the other side, it heard criticism of the removal of Soviet diplomats from Kuwait, accompanied by demands for the withdrawal of all Soviet military personnel from Iraq and abrogation of the Soviet-Iraqi Friendship and Cooperation Treaty.[100] The issue of arms supplies and overall Middle East policy were not mentioned by the press accounts, but they must have been raised.

The statement issued by the committee reflected most of these conflicting positions, citing both the importance of restraining the United States from the use of force (calling for a solution through the United Nations) and the need to review the advisability of recalling the specialists once their dependents were evacuated from Iraq. The statement also reiterated that removal of embassy personnel from Kuwait did not mean recognition of Iraq's annexation of the country. It expressed support for the government's position demanding the "complete and immediate withdrawal of Iraqi troops from Kuwait, the complete restoration of its sovereignty [*sic*], national independence, and territorial integrity"; it also condemned Iraq's taking of foreign hostages.[101]

The committee also heard criticism of the Foreign Ministry for its failure to provide information and analyses of events with regard to Soviet state interests. The fact of this criticism was reported only by *Izvestiia*, which itself was critical of the fact that Belonogov's presentation to Parliament had contained nothing which had not already been available in the press.[102] The paper repeated this complaint later, not only with regard to information provided the Parliament and the public, but also the failure of the Supreme Soviet itself to conduct a thorough debate of policy in the crisis. Criticizing the committee's perfunctory discussion and approval of the government's policy, *Izvestiia* correspondent Skosyrev bemoaned the fact that foreign policy remained in the hands of "the top people in the state, the Foreign Ministry and other powerful departments," despite the numerous demands for parliamentary control over the formation of state policy.[103]

Voicing similar criticism, Bovin argued that many "doubts and questions" would disappear if "our super-departments—Foreign Ministry and Defense Ministry—were to behave less coyly, if they were clearly to explain and describe the motivation behind their decisions and their positions."[104] Also in *Izvestiia*, Kondrashov presented a more nuanced picture of infighting between the two ministries. On the question of the military specialists, he said that in private discussions with "senior staff members" of the Foreign Ministry, opposition to the specialists remaining in Iraq was expressed on moral grounds. Defense Ministry people reportedly said that the decision must be made by the political leadership, but the Foreign Ministry people argued that the recommendation for withdrawal must come from the military inasmuch as the personnel belonged to them.[105]

From these comments it could be seen that just who or what organs were critical in the foreign policy decision-making process under perestroika, in a crisis situation, were not entirely clear. Whereas it was explained that the party had transferred most of its foreign policy duties to the Foreign Ministry, as the "ruling party" it aspired to maintain its "responsibility for the elaboration of the Soviet Union's foreign policy strategy."[106] According to one military spokesman, neither the military nor the party was responsible for decisions regarding, for example, arms sales. Lt. General Nikutich told *Izvestiia* that such decisions, once taken by the Politburo and the Council of Ministers, were now taken by the President and the Council of Ministers.[107] While the latter did set up an interdepartmental committee to organize the evacuation of Soviet citizens from Kuwait and Iraq, there was no information released on the jurisdiction, authority, level of participants, or *modus operandi* of this committee. Nor was there any mention of any other interdepartmental body or task force created to handle the crisis.

Virtually no mention was made of the Presidential Council's role in the crisis. One report (gleaned, it was commented, only from "a great many phone calls"), explained that the Council was still in the formation stage, the implication being that it would be "another few months" until the council assumed its function as a "national security council" modeled after Washington.[108] In any case, according to an interview with Aleksandr Yakovlev (probably written before the Gulf crisis), he and the council were to have only advisory capacity, interpreting events and advising the President, with no decision-making powers.[109] An interview with Valentin Fallin, head of the CPSU International Department, was a tiny bit more explicit. He explained that operational matters were in the hands of the Foreign Ministry (as distinct from the past, when the party Politburo "had to approve virtually every verbal note"), while problems of "a broad state level" were the domain of the Presidential Council. He implied that the party's role was to express the public mood on those matters "protruding beyond the framework of interstate relations." While this was not entirely comprehensible, Fallin did explain that each of the three bodies would provide its own, presumably different, analyses and proposals to the President.[110] In November, however, the surprising announcement came that the Presidential Council was to be disbanded. While this apparently had more significant implications for domestic policy, it also left open the question of the creation of a national security council or some other advisory body for foreign policy.

Equally confusing and potentially even more significant, if not actually explosive, was the distinction that appeared between the Supreme Soviet of the Soviet Union and that of the Russian Republic (RSFSR). A few weeks after the debate in the International Affairs Committee of the Soviet Parliament, the analogous committee of the Russian Republic, chaired by Vladimir Lukin (a very forward-looking and long-standing "new thinker"), also debated Soviet policy in the Gulf. Unlike the Soviet Parliament, however, the Committee of the RSFSR Parliament did not approve the government's policy, but rather called for the recall of all Soviet specialists in Iraq, including the military experts, abrogation of the Soviet-Iraqi treaty, and cessation of the training of Iraqi military personnel in the Soviet Union.[111] The central Soviet media avoided all mention of these decisions or even the fact of the committee's debate, undoubtedly hoping to avoid the potentially explosive implications of serious, oppositional involvement of a republic in the foreign policy of the Soviet Union.[112] RSFSR President Yeltsin himself refrained from any public disagreement with the central government's Gulf policy, but the appointments of such outspoken foreign policy "new thinkers" as Lukin to chair the committee and Andrei Kozyrev as RSFSR Foreign Minister suggested that a new problem of jurisdiction and decision-making even for foreign policy might be added to the increasingly untenable Soviet federal system.

RAMIFICATIONS OF THE CRISIS FOR SOVIET POLICY

Despite all of the domestic debate and discussion, the Gulf crisis was not the primary subject of interest within the Soviet Union, given the plethora of domestic economic, ethnic, and political problems. Greater attention was understandably accorded the Gorbachev-Yeltsin conflict, the nationality issue, and the new economic plans, even as the international crisis unfolded. Yet some aspects of the domestic side of Soviet foreign policy were likely to be affected by the Gulf crisis. There could be few complaints over the freedom for public expression of differing views, but the media's dissatisfaction over the lack of information supplied by the foreign policy-making bodies could lead to a reappraisal of government communications. Press conferences and briefings may have been deemed by the government sufficient innovations (introduced by glasnost over the past few years), but the media clearly sought greater substance to these new channels, as well as more direct access to information. Presumably what was required was greater official responsiveness and accountability to public opinion. These could come through the International Affairs Committee of the Parliament, but this organ itself would have to be granted greater status and authority. Foreign policy was not one of the areas accorded particular attention within the Soviet Parliament from its creation under perestroika. There was the possibility, therefore, that the varied domestic response to the Gulf crisis would prompt Soviet lawmakers to allot this realm increased attention while, perhaps, demanding a greater role in the foreign policy decision-making process. At the same time, the apparently anomalous role of the parliamentary committees of the various republics and of the republics' foreign ministries, which began to emerge in this crisis, could become the subject of constitutional consideration, prompting further adjustment of the Soviet federal system.

The foreign policy decision-making process itself could undergo some adjustment. A reappraisal might be the consequence of the clash, or at least independent functioning and bureaucratic autarky of the various branches of the Soviet government which became apparent during the crisis. The previously theoretical discussions on the differences in interests between economic, military and foreign policy organs were given concretization through the issue of Iraq's Soviet-supplied weapons, the matter of payments (or lack of payments), and the problem of the Soviet military specialists in Iraq. Just who should be responsible for what decision concerning these matters, during or without the advent of a crisis, remained to be regularized. In particular, the role of the military establishment and ministerial responsibility overall were likely to be examined more scrupulously and procedures established. In this realm too, the matter of parliamentary control by the Committee on Defense and State Security as well as the International Affairs Committee might be affected.

With the elimination of the only partially formed Presidential Council, it was difficult to know what organs, if any, were likely to be created to advise the President on foreign policy, as distinct from the Foreign Ministry and the party or other ministries. Indeed, aside from the fact that the party was no longer the central player or highest authority, little else became clear in the course of the Gulf crisis regarding the decision-making process in a crisis situation. This may have been due less to lack of information than to the absence of clear procedures and role delineations. While not limited to foreign policy alone, this lacuna in Gorbachev's administration became apparent in the course of the crisis and could have, therefore, prompted consideration of operational if not constitutional correction.

There were early signs of the ramifications of the crisis on Soviet policy at the regional level. Deputy Foreign Minister Belonogov told an interviewer that "In light of recent developments, our entire concept of military cooperation with the countries of the Middle East has to be revised and conclusions drawn."[113] This could have serious consequences for Moscow's ally Syria (and Libya). The Soviets had already triggered some concern in Damascus over Moscow's refusal to provide arms beyond what the Soviets considered "reasonable defensive sufficiency."

More serious cuts in arms concessions were now a real possibility, although it was also likely those in Moscow advocating arms sales for economic reasons—in the event that payment were assured—would win out over those opposed on moral or political grounds.

However, the division within the Arab world, with some of Moscow's major clients supporting Iraq, prompted not only a Soviet review of relations, but also a counter-response on the part of the Arabs themselves. Many in the Arab world had already been concerned over what they perceived as a weakening of the Soviets' world position and therefore its potential, as well as willingness, to act as a major supporter. It was not surprising, therefore, that PLO executive member Abdallah Hourani responded to Soviet policy in the crisis by characterizing Moscow's behavior as "an attempt to please the Zionist movement and obtain American money." Indicating what was probably the response of others as well, Hourani concluded, "It is no longer possible to regard Moscow as a friend and ally of world forces of liberation, including the Arab world and the Palestinian people and cause."[114] Unwilling to go quite that far, the Palestinian embassy in Moscow issued a statement which limited its criticism to the Soviet press, but visits by PLO officials Abu Mayzin, Yasser abd Rabbu, Nayif Hawatmeh, and later George Habash were probably designed to stem the deterioration occurring in relations.[115]

Gorbachev himself admitted to an Arab journalist that "it may already seem to some that there has been a decline in our common prestige or in that of somebody's country." Without by implication minimizing the harm that might accrue to Soviet-Arab relations, he said that the problems would be resolved favorably if Moscow's policy in the crisis proved successful.[116] That he was not too concerned about the Arab reaction was evidenced by the upgrading of Soviet-Israeli relations he initiated during the crisis. Gorbachev took the unprecedented step of receiving two ministers of the Israeli government in September, and then raised official relations between the two countries to consular level following a meeting between Shevardnadze and Israeli Prime Minister Shamir in Washington.[117]

Actually some positive results of Soviet policy became apparent even during the crisis. Not only was there a significant warming of Soviet-Egyptian relations, which had been improving steadily prior to the crisis in any case, but there was also the opening of diplomatic relations with Saudi Arabia. This step had been sought for some time by Moscow, expected after the withdrawal from Afghanistan, and finally accorded by Riyadh as a token of appreciation for Soviet cooperation in the crisis. The Saudi move brought a boost to the Soviets' standing in the Gulf region itself (including the opening of relations with Bahrain as well), which was a net gain for Moscow. By the end of December this was to include a $4 billion credit from the Kuwaiti government, Saudi Arabia, and the United Arab Emirates.[118] Political gains were also registered in Soviet-Iranian relations, as the Soviets increasingly engaged Teheran in their peacemaking efforts. This included trips to Iran by both Belonogov and Primakov, presumably in order to preserve some distinction between the Soviet Union and the United States in the eyes of Iran. Such a distinction was of particular importance inasmuch as Soviet-Iranian relations held significant economic potential for the Soviet Union, as well as security value, in view of the long Soviet-Iranian border and its connection with events inside the troubled southern republics.[119]

Another positive result in the region for Soviet policy was the American agreement at the September summit to permit Soviet participation in the Arab-Israeli peace process—an agreement reiterated in the communique after the Soviet-U.S. foreign ministers' meeting in Washington at the end of January and rendered quite explicit by Secretary Baker in his testimony to the U.S. Congress at the beginning of February 1991. While Moscow may have had to provide a regional *quid pro quo*—possibly that was the impetus for renewal of consular relations with Israel—this was clearly one of the rewards for cooperating with the United States in the Gulf crisis. Thus the Gulf crisis promised to have significant repercussions for the Arab-Israeli conflict. While neither the United States nor the Soviet Union accepted Saddam's proposed linkage, the logical response of both superpowers to the dangers raised by Iraq's power play was to seek removal of the dangers and sources of instability in the region as a whole.[120] In particular, Saddam's threats to use chemical warfare emphasized the need to bring about some controls on arms development and transfers, if not to resolve the situation—that is, the Arab-Israeli conflict—which propelled the regional arms race. A direct result of the crisis promised to be, therefore, greater priority and pressure on the part of both superpowers, possibly in concert, for the achievement of a settlement in the Arab-Israeli conflict.[121]

At a global as well as regional level, the Soviet-American cooperation in a crisis situation cleared the way for future collaboration. Soviet behavior in the crisis may have significantly contributed to building trust and sensitizing both domestic and international elites and populations to the phenomenon of superpower cooperation. Assuming that the United

States did not seek to place a permanent military force in the Gulf, and that "new thinking" remained in force, one might conclude that the cooperation would eliminate a good deal of the skepticism previously evident in both countries and outside. Some Soviet commentators said during the crisis that Saddam might not have acted as he did had he known that the Soviet Union would cooperate with the United States rather than support Iraq in an "anti-imperialist" struggle. Here then was proof of the tenet in "new thinking" that regional conflict without super-power competition could be significantly altered. At least resolution of such conflicts, if they were to break out, would proceed differently.

Another possible result of the crisis could be the creation of mechanisms, be they bilateral or collective, regional or global, for the institutionalization of cooperation and the preservation of security. Soviet Foreign Ministry official Kozyrev proposed, during the crisis, a new look at the potential of UN forces—on a permanent basis—now that the Cold War was over.[122] He suggested the creation of a "permanently functioning national readiness center" to train Soviet and foreign nationals for international duty abroad based on the experience of UN forces in the past. At the same time, he urged the Soviet Union to provide greater support, as well as participation, in existing UN forces. Whether the specific proposals would gain serious consideration or not, Kozyrev's ideas may have been an indication of added backing for the United Nations created by the crisis. An irony of the Gulf crisis was, in fact, that both supporters and opponents (from the military) of "new thinking" were to invoke the United Nations—the latter in order to curb the Americans, the former to support them as well as part of the pre-crisis tenets of "new thinking" which called for collective security.

Other ideas, not necessarily new, were proposed by Shevardnadze in the course of the crisis. For example, he asked the United Nations to add to its agenda discussion of restrictions on international sales and supplies of conventional weapons based on the principle of shifting from "over-armament" to "reasonable defensive sufficiency." To this was added limitations on the proliferation of "the most destructive and destabilizing means of making war." Restrictions would be applied by a multilateral regime governing non-proliferation of certain types of missiles and missile technology and certain types of weapons, in addition to the creation of an international registry of arms sales and supplies. Regional approaches were to be considered as well as self-regulation and mutual controls for parties to regional conflicts as part of the political settlements worked out.[123]

While these and other details in the proposal were subsequently repeated by Shevardnadze for the Asian-Pacific region, they also resembled those offered both Israel and the United States in earlier talks on the Arab-Israeli conflict.[124] These ideas were likely to receive a greater degree of urgency and backing from the Soviet Union as a result of the Gulf crisis. They were apparently raised in the Bush-Gorbachev summit, and it may well be that the most immediate result of the Gulf crisis would be a Soviet proposal for a regional security conference in the Middle East. Presumably this would not be intended as a substitute for peace talks to resolve the Arab-Israeli issue, but both superpowers as well as the regional actors could be expected to consider security arrangements the more pressing topic in view of Saddam's behavior.

EPILOGUE

A final question to be asked in considering the repercussions of the Gulf crisis is: Did the crisis hurt or harm Gorbachev and "new thinking"? The answer to this is not entirely clear even following the outbreak of hostilities in January 1991. Up until December it appeared that the Soviet public was satisfied that the Soviet Union was not involving itself in another overseas venture. This plus the stature gained by acceptance in and cooperation with the international community, plus hoped for economic dividends or assistance expected in return, appeared to strengthen Gorbachev's position and that of his policies. Yet there was also the strengthening of those who bemoaned Moscow's apparent irrelevance and therefore loss of stature, or others who feared the policy would put the Soviet Union in a bad position for the future (in the Third World) in the event that perestroika failed—or, as the military would put it, in the event that America continued its Cold War tendencies. The opposition of the military, for example, to cooperation with the United States in this instance coincided with the post-Afghanistan public sentiment against the dispatch of Soviet fighting men overseas. And it was just this sentiment which was exploited by the military and conservative forces as they strove for dominance at the end of the year. The anti-perestroika alliance employed false accusations regarding Soviet intentions to send troops to the Gulf in a campaign against Shevardnadze.[125] In a sense, these forces were thus able to play demagogically on the post-Afghanistan emotions of a public already angry over the deprivations and chaos attributed to perestroika. In view of the mounting criticism and what appeared to be rising conservative influence over Gorbachev,

Shevardnadze resigned as Foreign Minister on 20 December. Soviet policy in the Gulf crisis was perhaps the final element necessary to coalesce the various elements already dissatisfied with Gorbachev's policies such as the arms agreements with the United States, the loss of Eastern Europe, the decline of Soviet power and prestige, the abandonment of positions and allies in the Third World (including the change toward the Arabs and Israel), and so on. In this way the Gulf crisis played a role in the temporary retreat from perestroika which became evident from December 1990 onwards.

If, therefore, in the first stage "new thinking" appeared to be strengthened by Moscow's participation in the world alliance regarding the Gulf, later, after December, "new thinking" appeared to be seriously threatened by this very position. Once the military-conservative opposition to perestroika gained in influence, in part because of the Gulf policy, it appeared to be only a matter of time before their power regarding domestic issues such as the nationality question, law and order, and economic reforms would be extended to foreign policy matters. Indeed it seemed almost inevitable that foreign policy would be affected inasmuch as key components of this opposition were the military and the party, both of which strongly objected to many if not all of the elements of "new thinking."

Shevardnadze's replacement by career diplomat Bessmertnykh was in fact a positive sign promising the continuation of his Middle East policies, which had been supported by Bessmertnykh in the past.[126] But the new Foreign Minister lacked the authority and power of Shevardnadze, especially against the rising power of party conservatives such as Yanaiev, the Politburo member responsible for international affairs who was named Vice-President, and Aleksandr Dzasochov, party secretary for ideology. While these two party people gained a greater say in foreign policy, conduct of the Gulf policy fell increasingly into the hands of Middle East expert Evgenii Primakov. Although a supporter of "new thinking," Primakov had nevertheless come into conflict with Shevardnadze as early as October regarding what he saw as the need to pursue a more independent policy in the Middle East (vis-à-vis the United States) for the protection of future Soviet interests in the Gulf. It was Primakov who undertook a number of initiatives to prevent and later to end the war against Saddam, culminating in the last-minute "Gorbachev proposals" for a cease-fire prior to the ground war.

Signs of the change came during Bessmertnykh's talks with Baker in Washington at the end of January, when the new Soviet Foreign

Minister cautioned the Americans against destroying Iraq rather than concentrating on the withdrawal of Iraq from Kuwait.[127] This was followed by what appeared to be a bid for a cease-fire launched by Gorbachev. He issued a statement which called for Iraqi withdrawal from Kuwait and condemned Iraq's effort to provoke Israel into the battle but also spoke of what Gorbachev said appeared to be moves by the coalition forces that went beyond the mandate accorded by the Security Council.[128] This statement followed just a few days after a decision by the Communist Party Central Committee calling on Gorbachev to "take the necessary steps" to bring about an end to the bloodshed.[129] It was accompanied by the dispatch of Primakov to Baghdad on 12 February 1991 with what turned out to be a Soviet plan for a cease-fire and Iraqi withdrawal from Kuwait. Primakov's plan was subsequently refined in talks with Tariq Azziz in Moscow 21–22 February, calling for a cease-fire to be followed forty-eight hours later by an end of the sanctions against Iraq and an Iraqi withdrawal from Kuwait over a period of three weeks.

At the same time, there were increasing rumors of the continued presence of Soviet military advisers in Iraq (despite official Soviet denials), of continued Soviet military aid to the country, and even a report that Iraqi planes shifted to Iran had been transferred to Soviet air bases in Afghanistan for maintenance.[130] While these were for the most part only rumors, they may also have been signs of the increased influence of military circles in Moscow either conducting their own "foreign policy" or forcing Gorbachev's hand in the interests of preserving Soviet positions in the Middle East (that is, a policy commensurate more with power projection than with "new thinking").

The cease-fire initiative was obviously a last-ditch attempt to head off the planned ground offensive which Gorbachev had urged the Americans to postpone. It represented, however, the supreme effort by the besieged Soviet leader to placate the conservative forces in Moscow, primarily his military, without seriously damaging relations with Washington. While his interest in preserving the relationship with the United States was not fully shared by the military, Gorbachev may have believed that the arrangements for Iraqi withdrawal would be open to further negotiation by the coalition and that support from some West European countries such as France would minimize damage to Soviet-U.S. relations. That Gorbachev was engaged in a juggling act to please domestic opponents in hopes of resuming his own policies was demonstrated by the full cooperation accorded by the Soviets in the events which followed. The United States virtually ignored the Soviet plan, the ground war was commenced, and the Soviets joined with the coalition at the Security Council in the dictating of terms to Baghdad for a cease-fire and compliance with all the Security Council resolutions.

Thus, although the ominous specter of the Cold War seemed to appear briefly, Gorbachev would appear to have placated his opponents and even succeeded in preserving good relations with Washington. This was evidenced not only in Secretary of State Baker's comments that the Soviet-American relationship had passed a critical test, but also by the fact that the Soviet leader was able to return to his cooperative posture not only with regard to resolution of the Gulf War, but also in matters connected with the Arab-Israeli conflict. Gorbachev's warning, presumably to his conservative opponents, about the fragility of the relationship with Washington, combined with several expressions of flexibility and openness with regard to suggested methods (other than an international conference) for negotiations to resolve the Arab-Israeli conflict, suggest that "new thinking" survived the Gulf War.[131] Nonetheless, not only opponents but even supporters of perestroika may now demand at least some adjustment in the direction of greater Soviet independence in the implementation of the cooperative aspects of the policy.

NOTES

1. Aleksandr Bovin, *Izvestiia*, 26 August 1989 and 25 January 1990; Andrei Kolosovskii (Assistant Deputy Foreign Minister): "Risk Zones in the Third World," *International Affairs* 8 (1989): 44–45, or *Christian Science Monitor*, 9 August 1990.

2. TASS, 23 February 1989; *Izvestiia*, 29 April 1990. (Shevardnadze speeches).

3. The proposal was not fully formed; among those who presented it to the United States and to Israel, there were differences in emphasis regarding the role of the United Nations versus that of the two superpowers, but discussions had not proceeded beyond the most tentative stages.

4. Moscow radio, 2 August 1990 (*New York Times*, 3 August 1990). (All references to Soviet radio and television may be found in FBIS-SOV.)

5. *Izvestiia*, 5 August 1990 (joint statement and press conference at Vukunovo II Airport, Moscow). Subsequent Soviet statements spoke of restoring Kuwaiti sovereignty, but Shevardnadze's pre-summit speech and the joint statement issued after the September summit once again spoke of restoring Kuwait's legitimate government (*Washington Post*, 10 September 1990).

6. *Ibid.*

7. Gorbachev sent a message to President Mubarak and other Arab leaders who participated in the Cairo summit expressing "satisfaction over the desire, displayed by the Arab leaders, to make an energetic contribution to the settlement of the dangerous crisis that emerged in the Persian Gulf" (Soviet Foreign Ministry statement, 11 August 1990).

8. See for example, *New York Times,* 8 August 1990; *Washington Post,* 3 August 1990; *Izvestiia,* 7 August 1990 (Stanislav Kondrashov).

9. *Rabochaia tribuna,* 12 August 1990.

10. Experts' estimates on Soviet television (29 December 1990) put the debt at $10 billion.

11. *Sovetskaia Rossiya,* 26 August 1990.

12. TASS, 30 August 1990. According to a member of TASS's editorial board, Vitalii Chutseyev, Western experts claimed Iraq had about $6 billion worth of military equipment at its disposal. According to Chutseyev, this equipment had not yet been paid for; it was due to be paid for at the rate of $1 billion a year by deliveries of oil. Lt. Gen. Vladimir Nikitiuk, chief of the Main Directorate of the Soviet Chiefs of Staff, also said that "Iraq has fully compensated our country for the expenses it incurred in making these [weapons and military equipment] deliveries" (*Sztandar Mlodych* [Poland], 2 August–31 September 1990).

13. *Sovetskaia Rossiya,* 26 August 1990. In December the Kuwaiti government, together with Saudi Arabia and the United Arab Emirates, granted Moscow a $4 billion credit, presumably above and beyond the promised subsidy, to compensate the Soviets for their support.

14. A. Kondakov, "The Third Oil Shock? Economic Consequences of the Iraqi Aggression in Assessments and Predictions by Specialists," *Ekonomika i zhizn'* 38 (1990): 20.

15. *Izvestiia,* 18 August 1990 (E. Guseynov).

16. Interview with Deputy Minister for Foreign Economic Relations Yevgnii Osadchuk, Moscow world service in English, 28 August 1990.

17. The very tough Shevardnadze speech to the UN General Assembly came as Moscow joined the Security Council decision (Resolution 670) to extend the arms and economic embargo to air traffic. Shevardnadze said: "In the context of recent events, we should remind those who regard aggression as an acceptable form of behavior that the United Nations has the power to suppress acts of aggression. . . . There is ample evidence that this right can be exercised. It will be, if the illegal occupation of Kuwait continues. . . . An act of terrorism has been perpetrated against the emerging new world order. This is a major affront to mankind" (*International Herald-Tribune,* 26 September 1990).

18. *International Herald-Tribune,* 9 November 1990.

19. On 21 August 1990 Soviet Foreign Ministry spokesman Gremitskikh denied Western reports that Moscow was willing to join a military force if it were under the United Nations, explaining that official comments calling for activation of

the United Nations Military Staff Committee had been misinterpreted (TASS, 21 August 1990). Karen Brutents, first deputy chief of the CPSU's International Department, had told an Italian interviewer, however, that he did not rule out Soviet participation in a "multilateral force under UN auspices" (*L'Unita*, 17 August 1990).

20. "Forging a Superpower Alliance," *The Economist*, 1 December 1990.

21. TASS, 2 September 1990, carried comments by President Bush to the effect that the Soviet Union was too strained to be expected to contribute to the burden of the forces sent to the Gulf and would not be asked to contribute. Nor would it be asked, or had it offered, to serve as a mediator.

22. TASS, 2 and 3 September 1990; Moscow television, 4 September 1990; Moscow domestic radio, 31 August 1990 (Deputy Foreign Minister Belonogov). KGB chief Vladimir Kryuchkov told visiting journalists that slightly more than 5,000 Soviet experts remained in Iraq (AP, 19 September 1990).

23. TASS, 19 September 1990. According to TASS, 10 October 1990, some 1,800 such experts requested permission to leave. *Komsomolskaia pravda*, 17 October 1990, carried a report that the body of a Soviet citizen who "died from a blow on the head with a blunt instrument in Iraq" had been flown back to the Soviet Union on 8 October. The following day it was announced that 1,500 civilian specialists were to begin returning home over the next month on twice-weekly Soviet flights. Once the evacuation was completed, by 10 January, some 150 Soviet citizens were expected to remain in Iraq, by choice, according to Soviet Deputy Foreign Minister Petrovskii, but a Soviet television account of 7 January 1991 said that, with the evacuation virtually complete, some 350 people had remained, described as "personnel of establishments operating abroad, and also certain specialists who have expressed a desire to remain in Iraq voluntarily." On 10 February a Soviet spokesman said that none of the military specialists had remained in Iraq (see below for later reports to the contrary).

24. TASS, 5 September 1990. The official figure was later reduced to 150.

25. Soviet Defense Ministry spokesman Valeri Myasnikov and Foreign Ministry spokesman Vitalii Churkin both denied British claims at the end of January that Soviet military advisers were still in Iraq. Myasnikov said the last such "specialist" left on 9 January 1991 (*International Herald-Tribune*, 25 January 1991).

26. General Mikhail Moiseyev, Chief of the General Staff of the Soviet Armed Forces and First Deputy Defense Minister, interview to the *Washington Post* in the *International Herald-Tribune*, 28 September 1990. The Soviet Defense Ministry had earlier denied that quantities or tactical and technological details had been transmitted, but it did say that the defense attaché in Washington had passed on some information to the Pentagon on 19 August (*Sovetskaia Rossiya*, 25 August 1990; TASS, 23 August 1990).

27. *Izvestiia*, 7 August 1990. Sytenko was described by TASS (15 August 1990) as an "authoritative diplomat and a prominent expert on Middle East problems." Gorbachev also sent a personal message to Saddam on the eve of the Security Council session at which the Soviets voted in favor of the use of force to implement the embargo of Iraq (Moscow world service in English, 27 August 1990).

28. TASS, 4 October 1990. Igor Belousov, deputy chairman of the Soviet Council of Ministers, who was in charge of the interdepartmental committee dealing with the evacuation of Soviet personnel from Iraq, did accompany Primakov on his first trip to Iraq in early October, and some success apparently was achieved with regard to the return of Soviet civilian specialists from Iraq.

29. *Al-Sharq al-Awsat* (London), 18 October 1990, and *Middle East International,* 9 November 1990, p. 10.

30. *International Herald-Tribune,* 30 October 1990. Also rumored to be part of the Soviet proposal was a compromise which would leave Iraq with certain oil fields and maritime routes. This was reportedly rejected by both Baghdad and Washington(AFP, 17 October 1990). Belousov and the head of the Foreign Ministry's Middle East Department, Kolotusha, met with Saddam in Baghdad at the end of December, probably to discuss the evacuation of the last of the Soviet citizens from Iraq, and Soviet-Iraqi relations, rather than attempt to resolve the crisis as Primakov had (TASS, 27 December 1990).

31. TASS, 4 January 1991.

32. In addition to talks with Shevardnadze, Hammadi met with Belousov, in charge of the evacuation of Soviet personnel. He also met with Katuschev, who was in charge of foreign economic relations, presumably to discuss the embargo and the fate of Soviet projects and trade with Iraq.

33. *Pravda,* 21 August 1990. See comments by Soviet Foreign Ministry spokesman Yurii Gremitskikh, TASS, 21 August 1990. See also *Izvestiia,* 23 August 1990; TASS, 23 August 1990, citing Foreign Ministry officials and spokesman Gremitskikh.

34. *Al-Sharq al-Awsat,* 19 August 1990.

35. A domestic broadcast even termed "unconvincing" Saddam's anti-imperialist "historical" explanation for his annexation of Kuwait (Moscow domestic radio, 23 August 1990).

36. TASS, 26 August 1990 (France); TASS, 29 August 1990 (Yemen); TASS, 30 August 1990 (Gorbachev to *Paris Match*); Moscow domestic radio, 31 August 1990 (Gorbachev press conference); *Yomiuri Shimbun,* 28 August 1990 (Shevardnadze interview) or Shevardnadze interview appearing the same day as the French communique (*Pravda,* 26 August 1990). Linkage reappeared in the French message telephoned to Moscow on the eve of the summit (TASS, 6 September 1990); it also appeared in a most general and brief way in the report of Sytenko's talk with Arafat in Tunis (TASS, 30 August 1990).

37. Acknowledging the need to apply Security Council resolutions to the Arab-Israeli conflict as well, he said that he "was not sure that the two situations should be linked. The annexation of Kuwait is now on the agenda, and to link the matter with Israeli aggression against occupied territories means putting off the solution of the conflict in question indefinitely" (TASS, 6 September 1990).

38. TASS, 4 September 1990.

39. Text of statement and transcript of press conference, *Washington Post,* 10 September 1990.

40. *New York Times,* 10 September 1990. Primakov reiterated the sequential approach when he told a press conference in Paris that "the world community will not accept any strong linkage of the problems of the Near East," but resolution of the Kuwaiti crisis should "become the impetus for resolving other issues in this region, including the Palestinian." He too spoke of the need to stabilize the region (TASS, 17 October 1990).

41. *Pravda,* 13 December 1990, and *Sovetskaia Rossiya,* 13 December 1990. When, just two weeks before the 15 January deadline, Arafat made a statement in Baghdad which appeared to accept sequential linkage (*New York Times,* 3 January 1991), a similar line was echoed by the PLO ambassador to Moscow in an interview to the sympathetic *Sovetskaia Rossiya* (5 January 1991). Nabil 'Amir said: "We by no means insist on the mechanical linkage of the solution of the region's problems. Primarily it is necessary to settle the Kuwait crisis by peaceful means. But following that it is essential immediately to resolve all other Near Eastern problems in a package."

42. The issue was publicly raised, tentatively and sparingly, as early as 1988 by Foreign Ministry official Andrei Kolosovskii ("Regional Conflicts and Global Security," *Mirovaia ekonomika i mezhdunarodniye otnosheniia* 6 (1988): 32–41), as well as by Viktor Kremeniuk, of the Institute for the Study of the USA and Canada, Alexei Vasiliev, deputy head of the Africa Institute (who, it would appear, later changed his position, as we shall see below), and Oleg Peresypkin, rector of the Foreign Ministry's Diplomatic Institute—the last three in a symposium on "The USSR and the Third World" (*International Affairs* 12 [1988]: 134–45).

43. This was a comment accompanying statistics published in *Izvestiia,* 1 March 1990. Andrei Kolosov, described only as a political analyst, wrote: "The claim that arms deliveries yield us enormous hard-currency profits seems, at this juncture, nothing more than a myth. Of course, individual transactions are profitable, but they have long been cancelled out by all sorts of debts and gratuitous deliveries" ("Reappraisal of USSR Third World Policy," *International Affairs* 4 [1990]: 40). See also Yurii Kornilov, *Izvestiia,* 31 January 1990, or Andrei Kolosovskii (possibly the same person as the above Andrei Kolosov): "Risk Zones" (note 1), and "Regional Conflicts and Global Security," *Mirovaia ekonomika i mezhdunarodniye otnosheniia* 6 (1988): 32–41; A. V. Kozyrev in *Izvestiia,* 21 February 1990; Georgii Arbatov, "The Country's Army or the Army's Country?," *Ogonoek* 5 (1990): 13–20; Petr Litavrin, "The Issue of Arms Trade Limitation," *SSHA: Ekonomika, Politika, Ideologiia* 1 (1989): 13–20. Even Libya was said to still owe $2 billion to Moscow for arms supplies (Moscow domestic radio, 1 September 1990).

44. Major General G. Kirilenko in *Krasnaia zvezda,* 21 March 1990.

45. See, for example, radio commentator and Middle East specialist Evgenii Grachev, Moscow domestic radio, 21 September 1990).

46. Moscow television, "120 Minutes," 7 August 1990.

47. Moscow domestic radio, 25 August 1990. He expressed the same sentiments again on Moscow radio, 1 September 1990.

48. *Izvestiia,* 26 June 1990 interview with Petrovskii.

49. Major General Vadim Makarevskii, "The Threat from the South," *New Times* 34 (1990): 12.

50. D. Yevstafiev, *Komsomolskaia pravda*, 4 September 1990.

51. Leonid Mlechin, "The Friends We Did Not Choose," *New Times* 34 (1990): 6–7.

52. *Moskovskie novosti*, 26 August 1990.

53. *Izvestiia*, 24 August 1990, and "Observers Roundtable," Moscow domestic radio, 26 August 1990.

54. *Ibid.*

55. See, for example, V. Matveyev, *Izvestiia*, 4 September 1990; TASS, 22 August 1990; or Moscow domestic radio, Dmitrii Vol'ski, 19 August 1990, or Igor Mikailov, 30 August 1990.

56. Iuri Georgiev and Iuri Dakhab, "On Iraq Without Any Sterotypes," *Argumenty i fakty* 21 (1990): 6–7. It is interesting that neither this account nor subsequent criticisms mentioned the fact that the Soviet Union actually aided Baghdad in its bloody repression of the Kurds in the 1970s.

57. *Izvestiia*, 15 August 1990. Emphasis added.

58. *Moscow News*, 2 September 1990.

59. Petr Gladkov, "I Do Not Believe You!," *New Times* 36 (1990): 7.

60. *Moskovskie novosti*, 26 August 1990.

61. Moscow domestic radio, 25 August 1990.

62. *Izvestiia*, 5 September 1990 (Bovin), and Galina Sidorova, "The World Closes In," *New Times* 36 (1990): 4–5.

63. TASS, 28 August 1990. Others raised the idea of abrogation of the treaty as well—for example, Iuri Kornilov of TASS on Moscow domestic radio, 6 September 1990; Igor Beliaev, *Literaturnaia gazeta*, 15 October 1990; Kremeniuk on Moscow radio to North America, 22 September 1990; Vadim Kikushkin, Moscow domestic radio, 22 September 1990.

64. Moscow radio in English to North America, 31 August 1990.

65. Sidorova, "World Closes In." Pressure for the Soviet Union to send a military contingent under the United Nations may have been the intention of an article by Foreign Ministry official Andrei Kozyrev (who was shortly thereafter named Russian Foreign Minister and was known for his outspoken "new thinking" on the Soviet Union in regional conflict). He published a long article (surprisingly, in *Krasnaia zvezda*) advocating the use of the United Nations and the creation of permanent peacekeeping forces with the participation and now possible cooperation of both the Soviet Union and the United States (*Krasnaia zvezda*, 14 August 1990).

66. *Literaturnaia gazeta*, 10 October 1990. This was in fact a surprising proposal from Beliaev in view of the quite conservative positions he expressed earlier in the crisis, which we shall see below. Similar ideas were expressed by Alexei Arbatov, limited, however, to the dispatch of volunteers (*Moskovskie novosti*, 14 October 1990).

67. *Izvestiia*, 20 September 1990.

68. *Al-Sharq al-Awsat*, 19 August 1990.

69. Moscow domestic radio, "Observers Roundtable," 26 August 1990, and "Point of View," 18 October 1990.

70. *Izvestiia*, 24 August 1990. Emphasis added.

71. *Izvestiia*, 5 September 1990.

72. *Le Figaro*, 16 August 1990.

73. *Izvestiia*, 15 August 1990. See also Kondrashov in *Izvestiia*, 4 September 1990.

74. *Izvestiia*, 6 September 1990.

75. Moscow radio in English to North America, 24 August 1990.

76. *Pravda*, 31 August 1990. Yanaiev was subsequently named Vice-President, as we shall see below.

77. Each of these has been a more or less identifiable group regarding Soviet policy in the Middle East more generally, and specifically with regard to the Arab-Israeli conflict, since the advent of "new thinking." See Galia Golan: "The Soviet Union and the Arab-Israeli Conflict," in this volume, and "The Soviet-Israeli Rapprochement," Washington Institute for Near East Policy, Washington, D.C.—forthcoming.

78. *Krasnaia zvezda*, 30 August 1990 (Major M. Pogorelyi).

79. *Krasnaia zvezda*, 19 August 1990 (Col. I. Vladimirov); 31 August 1990 (M. Ponomarev).

80. *Krasnaia zvezda*, 17 August 1990 (Major A. Skrylnik). There was even one article which suggested some jealousy of the "brilliant 'Desert Shield' operation" in a discussion of the disillusionment American troops were bound to experience once their "high level of combat readiness [based on] a well-oiled system of training professionals" and high morale encountered the conditions of the desert and the difficult battle, including possibly chemical warfare, threatened by Iraq (*Krasnaia zvezda*, 6 September 1990 [Colonel V. Markushin]). The author also made it clear that American motivation was spurred by "the whiff of lost influence not just anywhere, but in the kingdom of black gold."

81. *Krasnaia zvezda*, 31 August 1990 (M. Ponomarev).

82. Moscow domestic radio, "Observers Roundtable," 2 September 1990.

83. *L'Humanité*, 24 August 1990, contained an interview with Zenchev.

84. *Pravda*, 2 September 1990.

85. *Pravda*, 28 August 1990.

86. *Pravda*, 25 August 1990.

87. See a second defense of linkage and attack on Israel by Beliakov in *Pravda*, 19 October 1990.

88. *Pravda*, 23 August 1990.

89. There was similar sympathy, combined with linkage of the area's problems and strong comments against the United States, in an article by another Arab-ist—or at least more conservative journalist, Karen Geivandov—who has taken exception in the past to the changes in Soviet Middle Eastern policy under "new thinking" (*Izvestiia*, 17 August 1990). The same could be said for TASS analyst Albert Balebanov (see, for example, TASS, 28 August 1990).

90. *Literaturnaia gazeta*, 29 August 1990. As noted above, later in the crisis Beliaev appeared to change his position, adopting a more activist position regarding the crisis which clearly implied sympathy with the U.S. behavior.

91. *Sovetskaia Rossiya*, 22 August 1990 (Iu. Subbotin).

92. See, for example, *Sovetskaia Rossiya*, 19 September 1990.

93. *Sovetskaia Rossiya*, 1 September 1990.

94. Moscow radio in English to Great Britain, 3 September 1990.

95. TASS, 5 October 1990.

96. Moscow television, 2 October 1990.

97. *Izvestiia*, 1 September 1990. A TASS account in English claimed that Lubov said he was expressing his own personal opinion (TASS, 30 August 1990). In a British television interview, USA-Canada Institute deputy head Viktor Kremeniuk minimized military disagreement, dismissing their arguments as an effort to gain a larger defense budget in the coming period (ITV, 3 September 1990).

98. *Pravda*, 31 August 1990, and TASS, 30 August 1990.

99. *Pravda*, 31 August 1990.

100. *Izvestiia*, 1 September 1990.

101. TASS, 30 August 1990.

102. *Izvestiia*, 1 September 1990.

103. *Izvestiia*, 16 September 1990.

104. *Izvestiia*, 5 September 1990.

105. *Izvestiia*, 4 September 1990.

106. *Pravda*, 13 August 1990 (interview with Yanaiev).

107. *Izvestiia*, 16 August 1990.

108. *Izvestiia*, 1 September 1990, following the visit by White House chief of staff John Sununu.

109. *Soyuz* 34 (1990): 4.

110. *Pravda*, 20 August 1990. It was amazing that although this interview took place at the height of the Gulf crisis, no reference was made to the crisis or decision-making at the time.

111. *International Herald-Tribune*, 13 September 1990, and *Post facktum*, September 1990. A few weeks later it was revealed that on 4 September a group of 48 Soviet oil specialists in Iraq had sent a letter to the RSFSR parliament calling for

assistance in helping some 300 Soviet specialists seeking to return to Russia (*Argumenty i fakty*, 5 September–29 October 1990, p. 5). A similar letter was handed to the Soviet ambassador in Baghdad by a different group, representing 400 specialists, on 1 October (*Izvestiia*, 5 October 1990).

112. Only very indirect references were made in the central press—for example, *Izvestiia*, 16 September 1990.

113. Interview with Belonogov in *New Times* 33 (1990): 6.

114. Reuters, 27 September 1990.

115. Radio Peace and Progress in Arabic, 26 September 1990 (Palestinian statement); D. Zgerskiy, interview with Palestinian Ambassador, *New Times* 38 (1990): 6–7; Moscow radio in Arabic, 28 September 1990 (Abu Mazin and Abd Rabbu visits); TASS, 4 January 1991 (a second visit by Abu Mazin), and TASS, 13 December 1990 (Habash visit). There was still another visit during the war during which the Soviets reportedly cautioned the PLO against any action which might exacerbate the situation, meaning, presumably, terrorist acts (Israel television, 31 January 1991). It had been rumored in December that Shevardnadze would meet with Arafat during the Soviet Foreign Minister's 13–14 December stopover in Turkey, but the meeting did not take place, according to some because Arafat declined. The highest level official to meet with PLO representatives in this period was, apparently, deputy Foreign Minister Belonogov.

116. Moscow domestic radio, 31 August 1990.

117. The meeting, the first since the 1967 break between a member of the Soviet government and an Israeli prime minister, took place on 12 December. The Israeli consul in Moscow presented his credentials on 24 December 1990.

118. *Izvestiia*, 24 December 1990.

119. It is not clear just how much cooperation there was between the Soviet Union and Iran during the war with regard to such things as servicing the Soviet aircraft transferred to Iran from Iraq or the future of these aircraft.

120. This response was apparent in the speeches to the UN General Assembly at the end of September.

121. The communique at the end of the Baker-Bessmertnykh talks in January 1991 indicated the continued likelihood of such an effort.

122. *Krasnaia zvezda*, 14 August 1990.

123. *Pravda*, 26 August 1990.

124. TASS, 4 September 1990; *Yomiuri Shimbun*, 28 August 1990 interview.

125. See the above mentioned accusations by "Soyuz" as well as subsequent ones on 3 December (Reuters, 5 December 1990) and various speeches to the Parliament sessions in December.

126. Gorbachev's appointment of the conservative Politburo member Yanaiev to the Vice-Presidency may actually have been a move to prevent Yanaiev's becoming Foreign Minister instead of a professional diplomat loyal to "new thinking" (and expert on American affairs).

127. *International Herald-Tribune*, 28 January 1991.

128. TASS, 4 February 1991.

129. *Pravda*, 4 February 1991.

130. Reuters, 25 January 1991; *Liberation* (Paris), 12 February 1991; *Nouvel Observateur*, 14 February 1991. In response, Bessmertnykh told French Foreign Minister Dumas that only a few dozen Soviet nationals remained in Iraq (*International Herald-Tribune*, 13 February 1991).

131. Soviet domestic radio, 26 February 1991.

CONCLUSION:
THE SUPERPOWERS, INTERNATIONAL ORDER, AND REGIONAL CONFLICT

THE SOVIET UNION AND REGIONAL CONFLICTS IN THE POST–COLD WAR ERA

George W. Breslauer

In his contribution to this volume, Steve Weber has outlined three possible scenarios for superpower relations in the Third World: uncoordinated disengagement, cooperative disengagement, and joint imposition. The purpose of this essay is to examine the potential Soviet receptivity to these scenarios, and its capability to meet the requirements of each. Drawing in part on the findings of the case studies in this volume, and in part on other research about Soviet Third World policy,[1] I will argue that Moscow's current orientations and capabilities will lead it to be most receptive to still another strategy: joint facilitation of political solutions. However, conflicting tendencies within Soviet politics, and destabilization of the Soviet Union, could result in changes in both orientations and capabilities. Those changes could increase receptivity to the other forms of cooperation described by Weber. Or they could lead to a loss of Soviet interest in Third World cooperation altogether.

THE EVOLUTION AND DETERMINANTS OF SOVIET THIRD WORLD POLICY

Soviet policy toward Third World conflicts has evolved significantly in the past twenty years. Under Brezhnev, Moscow was quite willing to seize opportunities to assist "anti-imperialist" forces in distant regions of the globe. Material and military assistance to the Palestine Liberation Organization, Syria, Libya, Cuba, Angola, Ethiopia, the African National Congress, Nicaragua, Afghanistan, and Vietnam increased substantially during the 1970s. The sources of such global, radical activism were many: (1) an ideological heritage that defined such assistance as the historical responsibility of the Soviet leadership,

(2) entrenched interests with a material stake in the pursuit of such policies, and with substantial influence on the policymaking process, (3) a global alliance structure which constantly challenged Soviet leaders to demonstrate their revolutionary credentials, and (4) a nationalistic conception of great power status which impelled Soviet leaders to demonstrate regularly their ability to compete with the United States for influence and allies on a global scale. Hence, when many new opportunities arose in the 1970s for expanding the alliance network, Soviet leaders were quite willing to seize them.

Even during those years of relative optimism, however, Soviet behavior was tempered by ambivalence. That ambivalence derived from conflicting goals and concerns. For one thing, the Brezhnev leadership was divided about the relative importance to attach to competition in the Third World. Some leaders and institutions were more concerned to protect and expand the fragile detentes achieved in the 1970s with the United States and Western Europe: they feared a backlash against detente in response to Soviet competitive gains. For another thing, most Soviet leaders feared the consequences of an escalatory American response to Soviet gains, and therefore preferred a policy of low-risk, incremental escalation of Soviet involvement, with attention to possibilities for de-commitment if necessary, and with an interest in negotiations to keep open the lines of communication.

Nonetheless, Soviet policy was not deflected from its radical activist thrust by these ambivalences and disagreements. Instead, the regime sought to compartmentalize and insulate Third World competition from East-West detente, and to seize opportunities that, in the context of the U.S. "Vietnam syndrome," appeared to present low risk of escalation. Publicly all this was rationalized as proof that the "correlation of forces" was shifting decisively in the direction of socialism, and that the United States was being "realistic" in accommodating itself to the new era.

We know now that Soviet leaders were kidding themselves (though it was not so apparent at the time). The U.S. reaction against detente, coupled with the growing crisis (economic, political, and social) within the Soviet Union, led to a heightened awareness within the Soviet leadership, long before Gorbachev's coming to power, that the old policies were unsustainable. That awareness, however, was not acted upon until Gorbachev's ascension and consolidation of power created the political preconditions for the replacement of personnel in charge of Third World relations, and for new perspectives to be incorporated into policy. The result was that, during 1987–90, Soviet policy in Third World conflicts (as in East-West relations more generally) became concessionary to an unprecedented degree.

The list of accommodations is an impressive one: withdrawal of Soviet troops from Afghanistan; upgrading of Soviet diplomatic, cultural, and economic relations with Israel; a reduction in the military commitment to Syria; pressure on the Cubans and the Angolans to cooperate with U.S. efforts to mediate an end to Cuban and South African involvement in the Angolan civil war; a reduction in the Soviet commitment to Ethiopia; pressure on Vietnam to withdraw from Kampuchea; a reduced commitment to the Sandinista regime in Nicaragua, followed by a willingness to collude with the United States in a process that led the Sandinistas to be voted out of office; a sharp reduction in material assistance to Cuba; and, most dramatically, a tacit alliance with the United States to legitimize a military assault on a former Soviet ally—Iraq.

THE "NEW THINKING": CAUSE OR JUSTIFICATION?

Soviet authorities have justified such accommodative or concessionary behavior by arguing that it is consistent with the "new political thinking" in Moscow. Their claim is that a process of fundamental learning has occurred. Translated into familiar language, their argument goes as follows:

Brezhnev's foreign policies were misguided and proved to be too costly to sustain. It also proved to be impossible to keep Third World competition from damaging or reversing progress in East-West cooperation, and the military risks of escalation in Third World conflicts proved to be far greater than had been anticipated. Still more fundamentally, the experiences of the 1970s proved that "two-camp" thinking, and fixation on the "anti-imperialist" struggle, could do more damage to Soviet national security than they could do good for the larger socialist cause. The correlation of forces had not shifted to the advantage of socialism; if anything, the depths of the Soviet domestic crisis suggested perhaps the opposite. In short, one's thinking about the dynamics of international politics had to change.

We do not know to what extent the new thinking was the cause or the justification for the concessionary policies of 1987–90. Forthcoming memoirs by Eduard Shevardnadze, Yegor Ligachev, and other retired members of the Soviet leadership may shed light on this question. It seems reasonable to propose, however, that the depths of the Soviet domestic crisis created a feeling within the leadership of the need to reevaluate the costs of Soviet commitments in the world. We know that such a foreign policy review had already taken place under Andropov, and that Andropov himself advocated a retrenchment in Soviet Third World policy. These tentative conclusions were broadened under Gorbachev, who would argue that foreign policy ambitions must be subordinated to domestic policy imperatives in order to shift resources, attention, and Western goodwill toward solving the domestic crisis.

Thus, perhaps making a virtue of perceived necessity, the new thinking justified policies that, within the old frame of reference, would have been called capitulationist. In content, the new thinking calls for a philosophical conversion, dropping the optimistic, militarized, two-camp, zero-sum perspective on U.S.-Soviet competition that prevailed earlier in favor of a perspective that (1) treats the world as highly interdependent and fragile, in which two-camp competition has become dangerously counterproductive, and in which the insecurities of one great power will only create insecurities for the other powers, (2) demands multilateral solutions to problems of global and national security, with such international organizations as the United Nations becoming forums for the strengthening of collective security, international law, and conflict resolution, (3) demands the de-ideologization and de-militarization of conflicts, thus rendering them more susceptible to political resolution based upon a "balance of interests," and (4) treats "all-human values" as more important than "class struggle" because the threats of nuclear war, nuclear proliferation, ecological disaster, and other transnational specters (including, now, AIDS, drugs, and terrorism) are of far greater concern to humanity than are the nation- or class-specific benefits to be gained from anti-imperialist struggle.

There are other aspects to new thinking that make it an excellent instrument for justifying retrenchment to audiences raised in a Leninist political culture. Like Leninism, the new philosophy is optimistic and missionary about the ability of the Soviet Union to stand at the head of a moral crusade that defies traditional *realpolitik* and assists in transforming the international order. The means toward that end, and the definition of the relationship between socialism and "imperialism," are fundamentally different from those prescribed by Leninism. But the optimistic, missionary, and progressive qualities of the appeal allow Soviet leaders to generate élan and to emphasize the allegedly positive consequences of concessionary policies.

If the new thinking was the justification, but not the cause of the new policies, it is still possible that the justification came to be internalized among groups of politicians and their constituents. This is a familiar phenomenon in politics more generally. Arguments made frequently enough can come to be believed in their own right. This tendency is further strengthened when the arguments become the basis of legitimacy of a political leadership. And it is still further strengthened when the leaders of a government (in this case, Gorbachev and Shevardnadze) develop comfortable, politically rewarding relationships with their foreign counterparts that are based on the premises of the new thinking. Thus, whereas Gorbachev and Shevardnadze might have embraced the new thinking expediently in the mid-1980s, they may have internalized it by the late 1980s. Finally, the repeated invocation of the new thinking has the effect of mobilizing into political life constituencies that find not only the form but also the content of the new thinking to be appealing on normative and philosophical grounds.

When we inquire into the potential availability of the Soviet Union as a partner of the United States in settling regional conflicts during the post–Cold War era, we cannot rest the case on a philosophical conversion by given leaders. We must also ask whether the material factors that drove the expansionism of the 1970s (and earlier) have changed as well. Specifically, has the internal political structure and external alliance structure changed fundamentally? On this score, the answer must be tentative.

STRUCTURAL DETERMINANTS OF EXPANSIONISM

The process of reform within the USSR has broken the ideological and organizational monopoly of a Communist Party that defined and legitimized that monopoly with reference to an adversarial global mission. Even though the Soviet Union is currently going through a conservative reaction against the centrifugal forces unleashed by *glasnost'* and *perestroika*, it appears highly unlikely that a conservative *restoration*, should it take place, would be based on revitalization of *Leninist* ideology.

Parts of the Soviet military, the military-industrial complex, and the police, however, remain as formidable potential opponents of democratization. Until recently, Gorbachev's policies had systematically deprived them of the overwhelming influence over defense, budgetary, and foreign policy they once enjoyed. Gorbachev's democratization program had transformed the institutional context within which those interests had exercised their political clout. To the extent that further reform succeeds in institutionalizing a democratic political order and a market economy based on consumer sovereignty, the institutional bases for foreign policy expansionism will have been weakened. Of course, democratic regimes can be aggressive and expansionist, and Russian nationalism or patriotism would still be available as a legitimizing ideology for such expansionism. Short of that, Russian nationalism could be invoked by a military-oriented regime to justify a reversion to expansionism. But at present, the likelihood of such a reversion is diminished by both the policy and institutional changes that have taken place, and by the perception on the part of even many would-be expansionists that the domestic crisis must be the top priority.

The external stimuli to expansionism have also changed. While opportunities for anti-imperialist assistance will exist as long as the Third World remains impoverished and oppressed, the pressure on Moscow to demonstrate its revolutionary credentials to allies within the communist world has diminished greatly. Were this simply a product of policy changes in the capitals of communist countries, the abatement of pressure could be defined as perhaps temporary. But a structural change has taken place. The collapse of communism in Eastern Europe, and the discrediting of Leninist ideology in the Soviet Union and elsewhere, means that the Soviet role as main ideological and organizational referent for a world communist movement has disappeared or been thoroughly marginalized. To the extent that Soviet responses to the opportunities of the 1970s were conditioned by expectations attached to that role, the external stimuli for expansionism emanating from within the world communist movement are likely to be very weak for the foreseeable future. During that period of time, the reform process within the USSR will have had further opportunity, if successful, to destroy the internal bases of Soviet expansionism.

As the Soviet government faces the 1990s, however, it must formulate foreign policies for the so-called post–Cold War era. That era has been marked already by a major, perhaps formative, experience: Soviet acquiescence in the U.S.-led war against Iraq. This acquiescence certainly squares with the concessionary pattern of Soviet Third World policy since 1987. But does it preview the future? Is this case of what Steve Weber calls "joint imposition" a model for future U.S.-Soviet relations in the Third World?

The answer cannot be predicted with confidence, in part because the course and outcome of the Persian Gulf war will affect both superpowers' subsequent definitions of what is desirable and feasible in the post–Cold War world. However, even a tentative response must come to terms with the diversity of orientations that remains within the Soviet foreign policy and defense establishments.

LIMITS TO THE NEW THINKING

For some individuals and groupings, the new thinking has been a genuine philosophical conversion. For other individuals and groupings, however, the new thinking is merely a convenient, idealistic way of justifying foreign policies embraced for pragmatic reasons. This is the familiar *peredyshka* ("breathing spell") mentality which we have seen many times in the Soviet past. Given the magnitude of the domestic crisis, these people are willing to be accommodative, and to justify conciliation, because higher priority goals are at risk if one continues in the old way. The normative and philosophical components of their belief systems have not changed.

This "pragmatic" embrace of the new thinking can create coalitions among a great variety of groupings. In some cases, unreconstructed ideologues, who would prefer to prosecute the anti-imperialist struggle, have simply become more realistic about what is currently possible. These people are likely to attempt to draw the line: willing to abandon Nicaragua under duress, for example, they may compensate by demanding that the commitment to defend and assist Cuba be reaffirmed. In other cases, national security planners, whose fears about Soviet border security by far exceed their concern to foster global "mutual security," may be willing to reduce or abandon commitments to geographically distant allies (Angola and Nicaragua, and perhaps even Cuba and Vietnam), but may demand that the line be drawn closer to Soviet borders. They may insist that Afghanistan not "fall" to the Islamic fundamentalists, or that a U.S. military base in Saudi Arabia would constitute an intolerable extension of U.S. global encirclement of the USSR. Still other national security planners may worry deeply about the impact of Islamic fundamentalism in southwest Asia, the Persian Gulf, and the "Fertile Crescent" on stability within Soviet Central Asia. They may view a loss in Afghanistan, a U.S. military destruction of Iraq, or a failure to solve the Palestinian problem as likely to destabilize the entire region, with ominous implications for the ability of the USSR to avoid fragmentation.

In still other cases, individuals who invoke the new thinking to justify retrenchment may simultaneously adhere to values that make them very sensitive to traditional nationalistic concerns—be these "Soviet" or "Russian." In some cases, these are common to all governments—e.g., Soviet nationals trapped or captured abroad, or the loss of Soviet lives in a regional conflict, may reinforce the determination to avenge the affront. Less concrete, however, is the nationalistic impulse that reinforces the current Soviet urge to avoid letting global retrenchment become global abdication or abandonment. Both the tsars and the Soviets have had a desire to be recognized as a great power. This status-seeking has made their diplomats and leaders unusually sensitive to slights and humiliations. While the crudity of their reactions has changed, and while the urge is by now a bit diluted, the basic desire remains. People for whom this is highly salient will be likely to define the limits of concessions in substantive rather than geographic terms— that is, they may be less concerned about *which* allies are the victims of retrenchment and more concerned about the extent to which the Soviet Union is caving into American demands under duress.

Of course, many Soviet policy-influentials possess multiple impulses. Even the converted "new thinkers" are not oblivious to threats to Soviet border security and internal stability, to Soviet humiliation, or to the fate of Soviet citizens abroad. The differences among officials are likely to hinge on the intensity of their attachment to varied normative, philosophical, and empirical beliefs.

I have elsewhere argued that four impulses have shaped the Soviet posture toward the Third World during the past forty years:[2] sectarian activism, ecumenical activism, crisis-prevention, and a neo-isolationist, siege mentality I have dubbed "Russia-first." Under Gorbachev we have witnessed the decisive subordination of sectarian activism, and an absolute strengthening of all three of the other tendencies. Yet the three are frequently in conflict with each other. This conflict has been highlighted and heightened by the ambivalent Soviet reaction to the war in the Persian Gulf.

As Galia Golan's chapters in this volume demonstrate in abundant detail, because of the differential attachment to different values and perspectives within the Soviet elite, the conciliatory foreign policy that Gorbachev has followed in the name of the new thinking is highly controversial. And it follows, therefore, that Gorbachev is faced with a real challenge in trying to sell his foreign policies to audiences comprised of diverse orientations. Thus far he has done well in legitimizing a posture that, among other things, allowed the fall of Eastern Europe, German reunification within NATO, and a military coalition with the United States against a Soviet ally (Iraq). The question for our purposes, then, is: what forms of superpower cooperation, and additional Soviet flexibility, are still "sellable" to a Soviet elite and public comprised of such diverse orientations?

This task is further complicated by tensions between the content of the new thinking and the realities of U.S. politics. The new thinking has appropriately been referred to as a new philosophy of international relations (new for the USSR, that is). Its basic premises are all about the nature of the international order. It posits, for example, an interdependent world in which transnational problems mandate multilateral, de-militarized solutions. This perspective contains both normative and cognitive components; it is attractive to many Soviets precisely because it accords with a traditional Russian and Soviet optimism and messian-ism. But in the real world of international politics, policy advocacy is often governed more by the actor's image of the adversary than by the actor's image of the international order. The Soviets have been no ex-ception. While they have succumbed regularly to optimistic assumptions about the course of history, they have typically justified policies with reference to the "nature of imperialism." Now the new thinking says relatively little about the new nature of U.S. imperialism, except to intone that the constraints of the increasingly interdependent international order will enmesh the United States to the point that "realism" will prevail. Reagan's second term and Bush's first two years generally reinforced the Soviet hope that pragmatists, not crusaders, were prevail-ing in Washington. And this reinforced confidence that by robbing the United States of *its* enemy image (i.e., by convincing American publics that the Soviet Union is a trustworthy partner), Moscow could strengthen the pragmatic impulse in U.S. policymaking.

There were limits to the effectiveness of such a strategy. U.S. prag-matists are students of the realpolitik school of international politics. They do not mirror the idealistic liberal internationalism of the new thinkers in Moscow. Nor do they have to do so, for the United States remains more powerful than the USSR, and more capable of affording an interventionist foreign policy. Hence, tensions were bound to arise, as they have with regard to the U.S. invasion of Panama (see the essay in this volume by Zaitsev), U.S. policy favoring the Khmer Rouge in

Kampuchea (see the essay by Chufrin), and the magnitude of the U.S. military buildup and victory in Saudi Arabia (see the essays by Golan). Each of these manifestations of U.S. interventionism has made it somewhat harder for Gorbachev to sell the idea that the new thinking and Soviet conciliation have forced imperialism to change its spots.

Furthermore, Soviet cooperation with the United States in acts of joint coercive imposition of solutions (as in Iraq) stands in tension with those precepts of the new thinking that demand *political*, not military, solutions to problems. Since the new thinking has been one of the means by which Gorbachev has legitimized his policies and built his authority in Soviet politics, it becomes awkward to be allied with a former adversary who may opt for military over political solutions to problems. In the case of Iraq, that tension has thus far been mitigated by touting the United Nations Security Council as the ultimate legitimator of military action and guarantor of collective security—which is entirely in accord with the idealism of the new thinking. But still, the magnitude of the military wipeout of a former Soviet ally,[3] led largely by the United States, raises questions about the new thinking's claim that military solutions to problems solve nothing. Simultaneously, it raises further questions about a "partnership" with a former adversary that seems not to adhere to basic precepts of the new thinking.

Moreover, Gorbachev's conciliatory foreign policy essentially meant conceding in most cases to the maximal (or near-maximal) American demands on arms control, Eastern Europe, NATO, Iraq, and other issues. At some point it was inevitable that the debate in Moscow would shift from "Have the Americans come around to doing business with us?" to "Are we giving away the store to the Americans?" That is precisely the shift that took place during 1990, and it is likely to accelerate in 1991 in the wake of the U.S. victory over Iraq and the failure of Gorbachev's effort to mediate a less violent and total endgame. Under these circumstances, it is also difficult to sell the notion that the constraints of an interdependent world, strengthened by Soviet conversion to a strategy of reassurance, have changed the Americans fundamentally.

One should not exaggerate this problem, however. On such Third World conflicts as the Arab-Israeli confrontation, Angola, Kampuchea, Central America, and now Iraq, the United States has privately or publicly offered the Soviets side-payments of reassurances that have made it easier for Moscow to accept U.S. terms. Moreover, in some cases, the United States has partially accepted Moscow's demands. A continuing superpower dialogue has been taking place, at both the foreign minister and sub-cabinet levels, that has tempered U.S. realpolitik with acknowledgment of, if not deference to, Soviet national security and prestige concerns, as well as Soviet negotiating positions on some issues.

Nonetheless, the tension in Moscow between the image of the adversary and the new philosophy of international relations is palpable. It is bound to affect Soviet receptivity to different forms and terms of superpower cooperation geared toward conflict resolution in the Third World.

THE ATTRACTIVENESS OF JOINT FACILITATION

One can imagine circumstances under which the Soviet regime would lose interest in cooperating with the United States in the Third World, reverting either to isolationism or to intensified competition. One can also imagine circumstances under which Moscow would embrace joint imposition, cooperative disengagement, or unilateral disengagement. I will discuss below just what those circumstances might be. But first, let me outline the policy that is currently most attractive to the dominant coalition in Moscow, and explain why that policy—joint facilitation of political solutions—has support that spans many of the elite orientations discussed above.

The contributions to this volume converge on the conclusion that, in addition to diminishing the extent of Soviet military involvement in regional crises (unilateral or cooperative disengagement), Moscow has displayed an interest in deescalating these conflicts and in facilitating political resolutions, preferably based on governments of national reconciliation. Is support for these policies limited to the new thinkers? Why has the Soviet government considered such an approach to be in its interest? I would suggest a series of reasons.

First, conflict-mitigation which results in governments of national reconciliation allows the Soviet Union to disengage without abandoning its allies. This accords with a convergent finding of the contributors to this volume: that, in most regions, the Soviets have been sensitive not to allow their retrenchment to result in either abdication of a regional role or abandonment of their allies.

Second, the very process of conflict-resolution entails relatively protracted negotiations, during which the Soviet Union is able to play a political role as partner with the United States (and other powers) in mediating among the parties. This, in turn, allows Moscow to redefine its global interests, and reduce its global commitments, without abdicating its role as a global power (a Soviet aspiration on which the contributors also seem to agree). According to the new thinking, the "new" Soviet Union is not to be isolationist, but rather is to remain a global leader, exercising influence by means other than military intimidation. Thus the new thinking shares with the "old thinking" a commitment to globalism, although the new thinking's version of globalism is closer to liberal internationalism than to either realpolitik or assistance to anti-imperialist struggle. Joint Soviet-American facilitation or mediation of local conflict-resolution can for this reason appeal to a broad spectrum of Soviet policymakers.

Third, Moscow prefers that political solutions to regional problems that are distant from immediate Soviet security concerns (i.e., excluding Afghanistan) be based on multilateral negotiations that draw in as many powers as possible, and that are channelled through, or guaranteed by, the United Nations or other multilateral institutions. Both liberal internationalists and "old thinkers," once agreed on the need for retrenchment, find it appealing to channel settlements through multilateral institutions, though for somewhat different reasons. This approach simultaneously has the advantage of diminishing the bipolar competition, diffusing responsibility for both conflict-resolution and post-settlement guarantees, reducing the chances that the conflict will be settled purely on American terms, and reducing the likelihood that the Soviet Union alone (if at all) will be accused of abandoning its allies.

Fourth, regional conflict-mitigation reduces the likelihood of escalations that could force the USSR into a binary choice: either reengage militarily or see its ally defeated. Since many regional conflicts threatened to reach this condition in the late 1980s, old and new thinkers who were agreed on the need for graceful disengagement would find political settlements (however temporary) to be useful means of gaining a "decent interval" for Soviet disengagement. In the short term at least, such an approach can simultaneously be "sold" as allowing for Soviet military disengagement without forcing Soviet allies to capitulate to their antagonists.

Fifth, diminishing the escalatory potential of regional conflicts simultaneously reduces the threat of East-West nuclear confrontation in regions of high interest to both superpowers, and reduces the chance of a backlash against detente in Western capitals. The prospect of another such backlash haunts Soviet decision-makers, who now realize how dependent they may become on outside assistance to weather their domestic crisis, and who also now realize that the West does not need detente as badly as Moscow does.

Sixth, to the extent that joint facilitation results in somewhat balanced, political solutions to regional conflicts, it softens the "image of the adversary" in Moscow, and thereby allows new thinkers more easily to argue that imperialism has changed its spots.

Seventh, joint facilitation is preferable to joint imposition because it avoids charges from the Third World of superpower "condominium," and because it diminishes the chances that Moscow will be asked by Washington to impose solutions that are disproportionately to Washington's liking. This has been the thrust of Soviet warnings of February 1991 that the United States not take them for granted in escalating its war aims in the Persian Gulf.

The contributions to this volume also demonstrate, however, that Soviet interests in the Third World, even as redefined by the new thinking, are not of equal weight. While the Soviet leadership would like to remain a key player in mediating regional conflict-resolution, it is more willing to "lose" in some places than in others. The polar cases in this regard are Afghanistan and Nicaragua.

Moscow was willing (though not delighted) to abandon the Sandinistas to their fate; it was not willing to abandon Afghanistan, where, even without the Red Army, it continues to spend some $300 million per month to sustain the Kabul regime. At points in between, Cuba and Vietnam have come under Soviet pressure, but they seem to remain of higher priority to the current leadership than are the alliances with Ethiopia and Angola. Syria has been put on notice by Moscow not to expect past levels of military and political support against Israel, while Iraq was largely abandoned by Moscow in light of the U.S. response to Saddam Hussein's invasion of Kuwait. (Nonetheless, Moscow's diplomacy during the Persian Gulf war suggests a concern to continue playing an important political role in the region after the war is concluded.) These issues of prioritization and terms of settlement are bound to be more contentious within the Soviet regime than is the more general commitment to joint facilitation. Hence, it would be folly to predict specifically what terms will prove acceptable to Moscow in specific conflicts.

The upshot of this combined global retrenchment, demilitarization of involvements, and reprioritization of Third World commitments is a Soviet government that has been eager to explore forms and degrees of superpower cooperation that were previously inconceivable. In the case of Nicaragua, Moscow proved willing to engage in unilateral disengagement from a regional crisis. In the case of Iraq, Moscow proved willing to join with the United States to impose solutions against the will of a former Soviet ally. In most cases, however, Moscow's preference was joint superpower facilitation of local reconciliation. That is what is currently being negotiated with respect to Afghanistan, Kampuchea, Angola, and El Salvador. It is also what Moscow has for years been advocating with respect to the Arab-Israeli conflict, although, under Gorbachev, Soviet negotiating terms have become markedly more flexible. And Ethiopia may shortly join this list.

Thus far, Moscow has displayed a strong preference for joint facilitation, though it has acquiesced in both unilateral disengagement and joint imposition. Is this pattern likely to continue?

ALTERNATIVES TO JOINT FACILITATION

The line between joint imposition and joint facilitation is a thin one. Arguably, instances of joint facilitation in Kampuchea and Angola have actually entailed enough subtle, implied, or overt coercion behind the scenes to qualify as joint imposition. If such coercion, jointly applied by the superpowers against the resistance of their clients, is the defining characteristic of joint imposition, then the future tenability of this strategy may hinge on the frequency with which the superpowers can agree on the terms of interim settlements. Thus far, Soviet eagerness to disengage from costly commitments, and to mollify the United States, has led them to accept terms that have been more disadvantageous to their clients than to the U.S. clients. It is conceivable that this pattern will continue in areas that are not contiguous to the USSR. But to the extent that joint imposition becomes a prescription for timid Soviet acquiescence in continuing U.S. efforts to employ military force against would-be regional hegemons in diverse regions, the controversiality of such a policy among elites in Moscow is likely to rise dramatically.

To be sure, the three variants of superpower cooperation are not necessarily mutually exclusive, for they can be employed *sequentially* during the successive stages of a regional conflict-resolution process. For example, unilateral or mutual military disengagement can change the incentives for local actors to continue the military struggle, fostering a stalemate and the start-up of a negotiating process, within which the superpowers could then engage in either joint facilitation or joint imposition. Alternatively, the specter of joint imposition could lead the local actors to begin a process of negotiation that leads to either superpower military disengagement (unilateral or mutual), joint facilitation, or even (but less likely) joint exclusion. Finally, a process of joint facilitation at the early stages of negotiation could result later in a shift to joint imposition or military disengagement if the stalemate lasts for long and the facilitators lose patience. Of course, in all cases, the process of seeking exit from the stalemate can also result in a breakdown of superpower cooperation and a return to competition. At present, that seems unlikely, given the new definition of Soviet interests that prevails in Moscow. The alternative to Soviet acquiescence in unequal concessions to the Americans could be as tepid as a simple refusal to endorse American actions (as Soviet diplomats hinted at in the Persian Gulf war during February 1991). Another alternative could be a resurgence of Soviet competitive expansionism through actual obstruction of American efforts. Or the response could be a reversion to militant isolationism (a Fortress Russia mentality): a withdrawal from globalism entirely.

Were Moscow to opt for either resurgent expansionism or militant isolationism, this would probably be accompanied or preceded by a change of regime in the USSR. Both approaches are so discordant with the reformist thrust of the new thinking that they would not likely be adopted by the present regime. Of course, such a regime change is not to be excluded. The conservative reaction now taking place within the USSR has increased the influence and power of "hard-liners" who, if the situation deteriorates further, could become the harbingers of a more far-reaching backlash. Yet if I were asked to rank the probabilities, I would guess that such an anti-reformist regime would sooner follow a militant isolationist than a militant expansionist foreign policy. The magnitude of Soviet domestic problems would so preoccupy the regime that it would more likely concentrate on internal repression than external expansion.

There is the possibility that external expansion would win out—not as a result of ideological ambitions, but rather (à la Kaiser Wilhelm) as a misguided effort to artificially unify the country through foreign adventures. This is a possibility, but not a high probability, for at least four reasons: (1) the realities of the nuclear age limit the field of opportunities to exploit foreign adventures, (2) the magnitude of the domestic crisis—and especially its ethnic-separatist dimension—is such as to defy mitigation through foreign adventures, (3) the awareness is widespread within the political elite that economic assistance (of some sort) from capitalist states is necessary to bolster domestic stability, and (4) in any case, distant, Third World regional conflicts are not likely to resonate with domestic audiences for purposes of mobilizing patriotic sentiments.

Another possibility is the breakdown of central governmental authority in the USSR to the point that it no longer controls foreign policy. Civil war within the country, or paralysis of the central government's ability to deploy troops abroad, commit the country to a given course of action, and the like, would change the equation substantially. Central governmental paralysis could confound almost any strategy of cooperating with the United States, but especially a strategy of joint imposition.

Continued superpower cooperation of the kind we have been witnessing presupposes, then, that the current constellation of political forces continues to hold power in Moscow, and continues to define the course of foreign policy. It presupposes, that is, that the new thinkers remain in power, that the central government maintains sufficient autonomy to conduct a foreign policy, and that the new thinkers pursue a strategy of cooperation that appeals to diverse orientations within the political elite.

I am not claiming that such an approach is most likely in fact to solve regional conflicts. As a Sovietologist, I lack the expertise to make such judgments about regional dynamics. Steve Weber has presented a framework that leads to the conclusion that only joint imposition and unilateral disengagement constitute stable equilibria within the post– Cold War world order. The specialists on regional dynamics who have contributed to this volume, in turn, seem largely to agree that *conflict-mitigation* could be a consequence of mutual superpower military disengagement from regional conflicts. At a minimum, such military disengagement might reduce the numbers of human casualties. The regional specialists, however, also seem relatively pessimistic that the superpowers could do much to actually *resolve* conflicts. If conflict-resolution means the elimination of the local factors that drive the conflicts, that proposition is almost a truism. But if mutual exhaustion at the regional level leads to a shared aversion to continuing to bear the pain of war, then joint superpower facilitation of political reconciliation could make a difference somewhat greater than is implied by the term conflict-mitigation. In any case, should this prove to be the case, the burden of this essay has been to argue that diverse forces within Soviet politics would push Soviet leaders toward a strong preference for one particular form of superpower cooperation: joint facilitation of political solutions.

NOTES

1. Notably: Jerry F. Hough, *The Struggle for the Third World: Soviet Debates and American Options* (Washington, D.C.: The Brookings Institution, 1986); Galia Golan, *The Soviet Union and National Liberation Movements in the Third World* (Boston: Unwin Hyman, 1988); George Breslauer, *Soviet Strategy in the Middle East* (Boston: Unwin Hyman, 1990); Alvin Rubinstein, *Moscow's Third World Strategy* (Princeton, N.J.: Princeton University Press, 1990).

2. George W. Breslauer: "All Gorbachev's Men," *The National Interest* 12 (Summer 1988): 91–100, and "Learning in Soviet Policy Toward the Arab-Israeli Conflict," in *Learning in U.S. and Soviet Foreign Policy*, eds. George Breslauer and Philip Tetlock (Boulder, Colo.: Westview, 1991).

3. Recall that the Soviet Union still has a "Treaty of Friendship and Cooperation" with the government of Iraq!

THE UNITED STATES, THE SOVIET UNION, AND REGIONAL CONFLICTS AFTER THE COLD WAR

Steve Weber

> The essence of Concerts of Powers . . . is that they have the means and have agreed or can agree upon the procedures by which to enforce peace upon the small and weak countries; but that they have neither the means nor the serious intention to enforce peace upon each other.
>
> —Jacob Viner[1]

INTRODUCTION

The end of the Cold War in Europe has not brought peace to the rest of the world. This is no surprise, because regional conflicts during the Cold War were rarely if ever caused only by superpower involvement. Civil and interstate wars have been frequent outside of Europe during the latter half of the twentieth century, and they would have been so regardless of U.S. and Soviet intervention. Still, the history of many of these conflicts was deeply marked by Cold War competition.

For reasons of power and ideology, and because of a nuclear-induced truce in Europe, the contest between the two superpowers was often dislocated to the Third World and superimposed upon local conflicts. The game, at least that played out between the superpowers, was never entirely zero-sum. Each side sought to make marginal gains on the other through "victories" in the periphery, but neither was willing to accept any substantial risk of nuclear war for that purpose. This shared interest in avoiding nuclear war meant that some form of U.S.-Soviet cooperation in the Third World was possible. Cooperation was never extensive; it was mostly directed at crisis management and prevention and other limited means of assuring that the competition could be carried out without risking escalation.

In retrospect, it seems that the task was relatively easy. The risk of regional conflicts escalating to superpower war was never high, and it did not require very extensive cooperation to reduce it even further. Despite the legacy of misunderstandings and frequent disappointments of efforts to cooperate more extensively, the United States and the Soviet Union never came close to fighting each other in the Third World. The end of the Cold War means that this risk is now less than it ever was, but it does not translate to peace in the Third World. And it does not mean that the great powers of the North are free of interests there.

U.S. and Soviet presence will still be felt in the Third World. The scope and scale of that presence may be diminished somewhat, but, more importantly, its character may change. This essay examines the possibilities for superpower cooperation that lie beyond the "negative" cooperation of the Cold War. What are the incentives for engaging in "positive" cooperation that goes beyond avoiding the shared aversion of nuclear war? What forms might that cooperation take? What will be the impact on regional conflicts and on the U.S.-Soviet relationship itself?

I argue here that we may be entering a period where a great power condominium, a "security regime" led by the United States and the Soviet Union, will set and enforce terms on which smaller states are compelled to settle continuing conflicts among themselves. This will happen not just because the great powers of the North would prefer to see regional conflicts end for moral, ideological, or economic reasons. Instead, we will see a very old tradition of power politics played out in a slightly new guise. Great powers have throughout history made instrumental use of small states in the periphery to suit the needs of more vital interests on the "central front." Regional conflicts in the Third World played this instrumental role for U.S.-Soviet *competition* during the Cold War. I think that the politics of closing down regional conflicts will now play a similarly instrumental role in supporting *cooperation*—cooperation on issues of vital interest that lie outside the periphery.

PRECONDITIONS

The papers in this volume suggest a list of sources of conflict in the Third World—a list that is not much shorter than an exhaustive review of the causes of war. While some of those sources are likely to be less prevalent in the 1990s, others will replace them in importance. The most significant general trends that will probably exacerbate regional tensions are demographic. In what used to be known as the "arc of crisis" or "instability" around the Middle East, there are nineteen predominantly Muslim countries. In fifteen of them, per capita GNP has fallen through the 1980s; in seventeen, more than half the population is under age 25. Countries made up of poor, young people with declining expectations for the future are fertile breeding ground for Islamic fundamentalism and other radical ideologies. Ironically, the growth of democracy, or at least of electoral processes, may aggravate this problem; fundamentalists have recently done very well in elections in Jordan, Tunisia, and Algeria. In Latin America, as Terry Karl's paper points out, the twin trends of economic crisis and democratization may produce similar windfalls for the left.

This is not to say that fundamentalist or leftist governments are necessarily inimical to U.S. or Soviet interests. The problem begins when these states are presented with seductive opportunities for expansion. The majority of interstate borders in the Third World remain illegitimate in the eyes of many of the people who inhabit the states on either side of them. They are also not very defensible. Backed up with universalizing ideologies, states will claim to be fulfilling a historical destiny as they challenge those borders with military force. The deep sources of conflict may be demographic, economic, religious, ideological, or otherwise, but the picture is likely to be a familiar one. Without the Cold War assurance that the superpowers will maintain a balance of power in regional conflicts, the temptations for would-be hegemons to seek territorial gains will probably be decisive. Iraq's invasion of Kuwait, a simple grab for undefended wealth that is the most traditional form of aggression, will not be the last such attempt.

Will powerful states outside the region turn their backs? There are political, economic, and security reasons to say that they will not, and moral arguments to say that they *should* not. Regional conflicts need not take place on top of the world's oil supply in order to engage those reasons and arguments. The spread of advanced military technologies to Third World states makes both even sharper. The Non-Proliferation Treaty and the Missile Technology Control Regime have slowed the proliferation of some technologies, but not all. In the Middle East, Syria, Iran, Iraq, Yemen, Saudi Arabia, Egypt, Libya, and Israel already possess medium-range ballistic missiles. At least three of those countries can fit them with chemical warheads, and at least one with nuclear. It is unlikely that any of these weapons will be used against the U.S. or Soviet homelands, but they will be used elsewhere. The SCUD missiles that fell on Tel Aviv in January 1991 represent the beginning, not the end, of a trend. Unless they expect to insulate themselves politically and economically from similar regional conflicts that will break out, and are willing to accept the moral responsibility of non-action, the great powers of the North will, at a minimum, *want* and, at a maximum, *need* to have some influence over events.

The dilemma for the great powers will continue to be that military force is not always so applicable to the problem of control as has often been hoped. On balance, it will probably become more difficult to intervene effectively in the Third World in the coming decade, as readily available defensive technologies get cheaper relative to the more sophisticated offensive technologies. Argentina's use of an Exocet missile (in the hundred thousand dollar range) to attack a British destroyer (in the multi-million dollar range) is a potent reminder, as is the difficulty the United States had in trying to convince Saddam Hussein to leave Kuwait peacefully. Superiority in air power is more than just the new version of gunboat diplomacy, but it does not by itself move well-defended occupation armies. To make its threat real, the United States had to transport an enormous land army halfway around the world, supply it, protect it, and eventually use it. While technology and overwhelming power produced an easy victory in Iraq, the "Four Day War" will turn out to have been an extraordinary case. Not all despots will be as inept as Saddam Hussein, and not all armies will be as dispirited as his. Others may fight back instead of surrender.

It is military power that remains the final arbiter of who wins and who loses in regional conflicts. The local actors, be they states or rebel groups, understand this simple fact and will act accordingly, after the Cold War as before. Classic balance-of-power politics played out on a regional level is the most likely result. If states cannot supply the needed capability to defend interests on their own, they will seek alliances with others. The central question is what shape those alliances will take.

For more than forty years, the shape of alliances in the Third World has depended to a considerable degree upon the context of U.S.-Soviet involvement. Because these two states still have the largest military resources that could be brought to bear on a regional conflict, that is likely to continue to be the case. The terms of U.S.-Soviet involvement will not be as they were in the past, of course. But the point is simply this: the choices that regional actors face will depend on what the United

States and the Soviet Union do, or choose not to do, in setting a different context for alliances and conflicts in the Third World.

I propose three scenarios as general possibilities. In the first, the United States and Soviet Union race to disengage from regional conflicts, in an effort to cut their losses and marshal declining resources for more important commitments. In the second, the United States and the Soviet Union engage in "cooperative disengagement" after agreeing on terms under which both sides will dissociate themselves from regional conflicts in a gradual and controlled way. In the third, the United States and the Soviet Union act together to shut down regional conflicts by jointly imposing a solution on regional antagonists. In the next sections I will look at the prerequisites for heading down each of these paths, and the possible consequences.

1. UNILATERAL DISENGAGEMENT

It seems likely (and most of the contributors to this volume agree) that we can expect to see both superpowers continue the process of disengaging from at least some Third World conflicts, a process that actually began in the mid-1980s.* Some of the reasons for this reversal were in place before the decisive finale to the Cold War. Both sides found through bitter experience that the gains to be had in the Third World were smaller than they expected and extremely unreliable, while the losses were generally more painful than anticipated. Both sides suffered from tightening economic constraints, as well as further limitations imposed by societies that were increasingly politicized and active vis-à-vis the state on issues concerning the Third World.

The most important reason, however, came from parallel reassessments of the importance of gains and losses in the periphery for each superpower's vital security interests. This reassessment was ruled out, I think, until the ideological crusades that were both motivating and legitimating forces in the 1960s and 1970s for leaders of both states were gone, or at least partially diffused. That condition was met on both sides in the 1980s. President Reagan's rhetorical flourishes about "freedom fighters" aside, the Reagan Doctrine itself was driven mainly by a

---

*There were, of course, earlier efforts at partial disengagement—either global (the Nixon Doctrine) or regional. I refer here to both superpowers' expressed interest in reducing commitments to regional conflicts during the period of renewed U.S.-Soviet detente (from about 1986) and before the collapse of Soviet power in Europe during 1989.

perception of concrete American interests in opposing Soviet proxies and not by an ideological crusade to spread democracy around the world. Soviet activism in the Third World under Brezhnev and his successors was supported by ideologues within the foreign policy establishment, but was also driven primarily by assessments of Soviet state interests and by the expectation that gains in the periphery would cumulate and contribute to an ongoing progressive shift in the correlation of forces between capitalism and socialism.

This declining emphasis on ideology relative to reasons of state as the rationale for involvement in Third World conflicts opened both sides to a deeper reassessment of the costs and benefits of that involvement. By the middle of the 1980s, the balance could not have looked very promising in either Moscow or Washington. Whatever gains a Soviet leader could claim (and there were not many) had to be arrayed against a panoply of costs, including the damage done to superpower detente. In Washington, the Reagan Doctrine had succeeded in making life difficult for some Soviet clients, but had not achieved the goal of "roll-back" against a single communist regime, except when it was supported by the direct use of American combat forces, as in Grenada.

Once the confusing blur of ideology cleared, it became evident to leaders on both sides that the world outside Europe actually worked on principles of balance of power similar to those inside Europe. That is, neither "correlation of forces" nor "domino theory" accurately described politics in the periphery. Instead, it seemed that gains for one superpower in one area (small as they turned out to be) tended in any event to be balanced by gains for the other elsewhere. The incentives to expend valuable resources in Third World conflicts declined apace. By the end of the 1980s, it was possible to imagine the United States and the Soviet Union each racing to wash its hands of these conflicts without much concern for what the other side might do. The preconditions for this kind of disengagement, as the papers in this volume suggest, seem to have been a mutually hurting stalemate where the concerns for who might "win" and who might "lose" in pulling out were diminished—and that would characterize many regional conflicts both at the end of the 1980s and currently.

Can this scenario be sustained? Is it a viable solution to regional conflicts after the Cold War? I think not, because the "solution" is most likely to unravel. The basic problem is that rapid unilateral disengagement is unlikely to lead to the resolution of many regional conflicts. Most of the papers here agree that it would be naive to hope that, with the superpowers gone, local antagonists would find themselves demoralized, exhausted, and willing to make the compromises necessary to bring these wars to a close. Central America may be the easiest test case, as Karl suggests, but even there locally inspired efforts to bring peace have languished in the face of American indifference. Left to their own devices, it is hard to imagine the Afghan rebels giving up their struggle against Najibullah, or vice versa, even if both sides were cut off from superpower aid. The same apparently holds true for Cambodia.

The more optimistic scenario seems to rest on the premise that with the superpowers gone, local arms races would gradually slow down, and eventually the lack of resources to continue fighting wars would force a reconciliation. This is mistaken. Doubtless we would eventually see stocks of U.S. and Soviet-supplied weaponry fall off, but there are plenty of second-tier arms suppliers—Brazil, China, France, etc.—that will be more than happy to take up the slack. If the world economy continues its path toward recession in the first part of the 1990s, they may be positively competing to do so, which means that weapons will be abundantly available at healthy discounts. The weapons suppliers who replace the United States and the Soviet Union will not, in any case, be lacking for customers.

States prefer to spend others' money when it is available (as it was for much of the Cold War), but if they remain insecure, they will spend their own money for weapons. Consider the case of Southeast Asia, where a brisk regional arms race is now brewing. Despite a drastic cut in American military aid from $102.3 million in 1985 to $5.2 million in 1990, the Thai arms budget increased 16 percent in 1990 alone and now stands at $2.1 billion. Malaysia's budget for arms increased 20 percent between 1988 and 1990. Singapore, a rich island state heavily dependent on seaborne trade, is busily purchasing F-16s and missile corvettes armed with Harpoon surface-to-surface missiles to defend sealanes 1,000 miles outside its territory. In 1990 Singapore spent about $2 billion on arms, which is about 6 percent of its GDP and 23 percent of the state budget.[2]

These numbers suggest that arms stocks in the periphery are not likely to decline much as the superpowers retrench. Apart from the obvious security implications, the drain on economic resources needed for development is staggering. In 1986, the developing countries spent about $159 billion on their armed forces, which is about five times what they received in development aid that year. The situation seems to have gotten worse, not better, since, on both sides of the equation.[3]

The effects of economic deprivation are not simply of humanitarian

The effects of economic deprivation are not simply of humanitarian concern when the poor are armed with advanced weaponry. It is naive to expect peace under these circumstances. More likely, we would continue to see arms races, insecurity, and smoldering wars in the periphery that are only partly a legacy of Cold War competition. These conflicts may not engage the Northern powers' interests directly (unless wars affect supplies of vital resources such as oil). However, it is unlikely that these conflicts will smolder forever without some foreign intervention. Weakened states will soon appear as tempting targets for aspiring regional powers that have reason to expand, either for simple ambition or to buttress their security. When it becomes evident that China, India, Iraq, Vietnam, and the like are behaving as if they have been given carte blanche to expand into power vacuums, policymakers in Washington and Moscow will renew their attention. The Soviets may choose to remain out of the picture entirely, or they may have no choice.[4] The United States, however, will not be so tightly constrained. At least in terms of capabilities, we are in a very different position and will have a broader set of options at hand.

That is not to say that a decision to intervene with military force in a Third World conflict has suddenly become an easy one for a U.S. president. The case of Iraq was so convincing that the American people and the coalition allies rarely wavered in support of U.S. policy.* But the victory in Kuwait does nothing to change the underlying constraints of money and public opinion, both domestic and international, that would complicate less clear-cut cases for intervention. Not every aspirant to regional hegemony, as I said, will be as inept as Hussein. It does seem that an American president will be most reluctant to champion the idea of directly involving U.S. troops in the defense of Third World borders as a preferred option, unless control over oil were once again at stake.

Outside the Persian Gulf, and perhaps even within it, U.S. policymakers are more likely to think in terms of establishing regional alliance systems, with the primary responsibility for maintaining the security of the participant states going to local actors. Already, the Bush administration has floated the slogan "A NATO for the Persian Gulf." The rhetoric may seem somewhat strained, but the basic idea appears at first glance

---

*I do not ignore the misgivings of the French, the Soviet Union, the Japanese, and other coalition partners, as well as the vocal antiwar movement in the United States. In retrospect, however, I think what is striking about the Gulf crisis is how *much* agreement there was between these states given their cross-cutting interests, and how popular American military action was at home given the inevitable concerns.

to be sound. Why not construct a multilateral alliance among regional actors, with the United States playing a supportive background role?

The answer to this question is simple and distressing. On a theoretical level, the preconditions for constructing multilateral alliances do not exist in the Third World. Multilateral institutions are good at propounding generalized principles and implementing policies that follow from them, by splitting up the division of labor (not always equitably) among the participant states. Such a principle was present in Europe during the Cold War. The North Atlantic Treaty Organization was built on a general organizing principle shared by all its members: no Soviet invasion of Western Europe, and an attack on one will be treated as an attack on all. The challenge was clear: to defend a well-defined status quo on a precise boundary line. The only real arguments lay in parcelling out the costs.[5]

Outside of Europe, and particularly in Asia, there has been no status quo of this sort. Most of the big wars of the past forty years have been fought in Asia, over disputes about territory, nationalism, resources, religion and ethnicity, and economics. I can see no general organizing principle that could underlie a multilateral security regime to deal with such disputes. The only one that comes to mind as a possible candidate is "no change of borders except by peaceful means." But that dissolves on close examination. Outside Europe, there are few states that would be willing to accept the legitimacy of this principle since borders are generally viewed as arbitrary. Nor would states generally accept the concomitant notion that violence is acceptable so long as it is contained within one country. Outside Europe in 1987, there were thirty-six conflicts that resulted in more than 1,000 deaths per year. Only four of those were being fought across internationally recognized borders; all the others were effectively civil wars.

The collapse of multilateral organizations in the Third World is not just an analytic prediction based on differences in the character of the security threat there. It is also an historical observation. At present, there is no complex system of multilateral institutions in Asia, no common market, and no regional security organizations of any note. The point is that this is not for lack of trying. On the non-communist side, there have been six important security agreements in Asia that involved the United States, all of which were forged in the 1950s. Three of those were multilateral agreements while three were bilateral. The three multilaterals—the Central Treaty Organization (CENTO), the Southeast Asia Treaty Organization (SEATO), and the Australia–New Zealand–United States

(ANZUS) Pact—no longer exist, at least not in multilateral form. What survives, in effect, are four bilateral agreements: U.S.-Japan, U.S.-Korea, U.S.-Philippines, and U.S.-Australia (under the titular label of Anzus).

The history of the Baghdad Pact, later CENTO, is suggestive. While the United States and Britain were trying to engage Arab states in a multilateral anti-Soviet alliance, Egypt's President Nasser claimed a competitive leadership role by offering an alternative platform for Arab unity—the quest against Israel. The competition between Nasser and the Baghdad Pact to define a general organizing principle did more to inflame tensions in the region than to provide any kind of multilateral security.

Turkey and Iraq, charter signatories to the Baghdad Pact in February 1955 (they were later joined by Pakistan and Iran), tried desperately to reassure other Arab states that the alliance did not harm their interests, but to no avail. In March 1955, Egypt, Syria, and Saudi Arabia joined together in a new treaty opposed to the Baghdad Pact. When the British proposed to Jordan that it join the pact at the end of the year, riots in Amman and Jerusalem ended in the sacking of the Turkish consulate and the death of a British military representative. These riots were warmly welcomed in Egypt, Syria, and Saudi Arabia, and may have even been planned or organized abroad. Desperate to preserve his reign, King Hussein of Jordan in January 1956 declared that his country would not join any new treaties, and proceeded to dismiss the British commander of the Arab legion as well as all British officers serving with him.

On 14 July 1958, just as King Faisal of Iraq and his prime minister were leaving Baghdad for a meeting of the Baghdad Pact council in London, they were murdered in an army revolt. The new military government soon withdrew Iraq from the alliance, leaving it moribund. Washington, predictably, stepped into the breach. On 5 March 1959 the United States proceeded to sign bilateral agreements with Turkey, Iran, and Pakistan for mutual cooperation in security and defense. That summer the Baghdad Pact changed its name to CENTO, but for all intents and purposes it ceased to exist as a viable security organization.

A similar story could be told of SEATO. After a series of failures to act, most notably in the Laos crisis of 1961, SEATO was marginalized and marked a "paper tiger" by Thai policymakers, who began seeking a more sturdy security guarantee from the United States.* In early 1962,

---

*These failures were the result of broad disagreements among SEATO members over exactly what the purpose of the alliance was. There was never any clear agreement on a common threat: while the United States saw China as the major

Bangkok got that assurance when the United States announced that it considered its commitment to SEATO to be individual as well as collective. This was a de facto "bilateralization" of the security guarantee between the United States and Thailand, leaving SEATO for all intents and purposes irrelevant.

The move to bilateral security treaties in Asia should be seen as a dependent variable—a *result* of the character of the security threat in that part of the world and not a cause. America's allies and even its adversaries in Asia seem to have had a much better understanding of that point than Americans generally have. It has never been the regional powers who pushed for a local version of NATO or some other multilateral security arrangement.[6]

Most insecure states on the periphery have preferred and will continue to prefer a bilateral deal with the United States to any other means of assuring their security. There are a number of reasons behind that preference, some of which were reinforced by the end of the Cold War. From the perspective of an insecure state in the Third World, the United States looks like the nearly perfect bilateral ally. Militarily it remains without question the dominant actor on the world stage, particularly when it comes to the all-important capability to project power at a distance. Politically it is a fairly reliable and predictable actor whose commitments, once made, are likely to be honored. At the same time, the United States is relatively far away from most of the Third World (save Latin America). It is not likely to be provoking many conflicts that could drag smaller states into wars in which they do not want to be involved. Finally, the United States is not disposed to be tempted to indulge in many imperial or colonial adventures abroad for quite some time. This means that Washington is less likely to turn out to be the kind of friend who stays around too long and ends up helping you, as it were, more than you ever really wanted.

Each of these factors must have entered into King Fahd's calculations when he invited the United States to deploy its forces in Saudi Arabia against Iraq. That a multinational coalition was later assembled does not erase the essence of the deal that was cut in early August 1990: it was essentially a bilateral security guarantee between Washington and Riyadh.

---

risk, and Pakistan joined to counter India, some of the smaller states in the region felt threatened primarily by Japan. And while SEATO was set up explicitly to counter *external* aggression, most of the local actors were more directly worried about internal subversion.

That example will not be lost on other states in the periphery. The fact that the United States has achieved most of its objectives against Iraq and will leave Saudi Arabia more secure than when it arrived is important, because it sends a very clear message to other threatened states. The United States emerges from the Gulf with swelled credibility in terms of both willingness and capability to use force against aggression. That further enhances Washington's attractiveness as an ally. Many states will probably try to bring the United States in to their own security problems on a similarly bilateral basis, but unless they happen to sit on top of resources that are as vital as a quarter of the world's oil reserves, they are not likely to have quite so easy a time of it.

Unfortunately, "success" in the Gulf in this way brings new dilemmas. The United States for its part will not be anxious in the post–Cold War world to involve itself in very many such arrangements. Even if the preferences were in place (which they are not), the resources are lacking. This means that Washington will be compelled to prioritize its commitments as never before and deny many of the pleadings that will follow on King Fahd's. At least some Third World states will be left without a superpower guarantee for regional security and without the promise of gaining one.*

The smaller countries of Southeast Asia, for example, may very well be left wondering who will protect rights of passage through the strategic choke-points of the South China Sea if America is no longer willing to do the job. Fears of such abandonment by the United States have already surfaced directly in Asia. The choices as perceived by the Association of South-East Asian Nations (ASEAN) countries—Indonesia, Malaysia, the Philippines, Singapore, Thailand, and Brunei—are worth noting. Following Washington's announcement of its decision to cut off support for the three-part coalition fighting the Hun Sen government in Cambodia, Secretary of State Baker was at pains to comfort the ASEAN states by saying "You can be assured that the United States will remain wholly engaged as a partner in the Pacific." This promise was taken with a grain of salt. At least as important was the statement of the Japanese foreign

---

*Similar problems would have arisen, and more quickly, if the Gulf crisis had ended less favorably. An America turned isolationist by partial defeat or political humiliation in the Gulf would not have looked like a viable security guarantor for other states. If the United States had accepted a face-saving compromise and left Hussein with his enormous military capability intact, Saudi Arabia, Egypt, and other "front-line" states that cast their lot explicitly with the coalition would have been perceived as having been abandoned to face Saddam on their own.

minister, who reassured his neighbors that Japan would continue to support a powerful American role in the region.[7] This soothed, at least temporarily, the smaller nations' real underlying fear: that they would at some point have no choice but to turn to Tokyo, their former occupying power, for a guarantee of security.

That fear highlights an ominous consequence of American withdrawal. If insecure states are denied the possibility of the alliance with the United States that they would in most cases prefer, they will turn, reluctantly, to other sources of security. The Soviet Union is probably no longer attractive or even available. The more likely deals are with powerful regional states or presumptive "regional superpowers" such as India, Vietnam, Iran, or China. These partners are not unwilling. The Vietnamese, predictably, welcomed Washington's decision to abandon the guerilla coalition in Cambodia, and Prince Sihanouk's son, the commander of his father's army, reluctantly acknowledged that "in the future, to survive, to go on fighting, we will have to accept more aid from China."[8]

That is an outcome to worry about, for a number of reasons. It leads almost inexorably to a regionalization of security relations and probably of economic relations as well. Comparisons to Japan's Greater East-Asian Co-prosperity Sphere and Germany's Mitteleuropa empire, already being made quietly but frequently by leaders of the smaller states, are not entirely misplaced. From the small states' perspective, being left enthralled to the equivalent of Saddam Hussein or to a de facto yen economic bloc is not a desirable outcome. U.S. policymakers should be equally troubled because our ability to penetrate these blocs economically or politically may be quite limited. Finally, and perhaps most ominously, there is potential for the blocs to expand and bump up against each other. In the meantime, there will be competition among aspiring regional powers for control, as more than one nation may try to preside over what the late Zia of Pakistan called a "sweeping strategic realignment." His only problem was that his country was competing with Iran, India, and even Saudi Arabia for the leading role.

Although this story could continue in an increasingly speculative fashion, I will stop here because the analysis is already sufficient to answer the question of whether the unilateral disengagement scenario is a viable and desirable one. I led the scenario through a number of steps to show how unattractive the medium- and long-term consequences of rapid unilateral disengagement might be. Alternative paths from disengagement, particularly the notion of multilateral security alliances that would recapitulate NATO in the Third World, seem likely to unravel. This would by steps leave the United States and many smaller states stuck in a world that looks more dangerous, and potentially *much* more dangerous, than it does today.

What I have left out of the analysis up till now has been a serious appreciation of Moscow's position, particularly in light of Soviet domestic politics. From the stark perspective of international *realpolitik*, it might indeed best suit the Soviet Union to disengage as quickly and as broadly as possible from regional conflicts that continue to drain its scarce resources. That would also be consistent with a basic principle of the "new political thinking"—that foreign policy interests must be subordinated to domestic policy needs. But it would not settle certain problems of domestic politics. There are strong factions within the Soviet elite which continue to support an activist role (albeit at reduced scope and with different methods) in the periphery.[9] Those factions are not confined to the military or to the far right. Although the radical "new thinkers" want Moscow to drop commitments in the Third World, many would still prefer to see the Soviet government engaged in a gradual and cooperative deescalation of regional conflicts rather than a wholesale withdrawal. This might allow the Soviet Union to play a low-cost role in negotiations leading to political resolutions. If the road to peace could thus be made to run through Washington and Moscow (via the United Nations in New York, if possible), the Soviet Union could retrench effectively and conserve precious resources without seeming to abandon its allies wholesale and forfeiting its role as a global power. What are the prospects for this kind of solution?

2. COOPERATIVE DISENGAGEMENT

For want of a better term, I label this scenario "cooperative disengagement." This would find the United States and the Soviet Union, sometimes in conjunction with other interested powers and the United Nations, cooperating to disengage gradually and in a coordinated fashion from regional conflicts. In most cases, the scenario would include what George Breslauer calls "joint facilitation of political solutions."[10] In other words, the United States, the Soviet Union, and other outside powers would join together to mediate the search for a compromise settlement among the local antagonists. Breslauer also describes the many perquisites cooperative disengagement and joint facilitation promises to Moscow. My concern here is different. Can it work?

Looking only at U.S.-Soviet politics, the answer might very well now seem to be Yes. The 1990s are not the 1970s, and both Moscow and Washington seem to have learned some lessons from the miscues of their attempts to cooperate in the Third World during that unfortunate decade. This time there would be no misunderstandings about a "Basic Principles Agreement" or noxiously ambiguous concepts like "peaceful coexistence." Where cooperative disengagement has so far been tried in the last few years, officials on both sides have quite sensibly focused their efforts on delineating, in each individual case, the specifics of what each side could and could not do (or expect the other to do) in support of its friends.* There are further possibilities, such as explicit agreements not to intervene with manpower, strict limits on the support of proxy forces backed up by various monitoring schemes, and even precisely shared terms for establishing a balance of power in military supplies. From the United States-Soviet perspective, this looks to be a reasonable and probably also a sustainable resolution.

But it would not be so from the perspective of the regional antagonists. Would cooperative disengagement by itself hold any substantial prospects for the peaceful settlement of these conflicts? The contributors to this volume almost unanimously think not. Economic constraints would certainly bite harder, but they would bite all sides in roughly equal measure. The intensity of violence might in the short term diminish, but for many of the same reasons that unilateral disengagement seems to fail, the respite in most cases would probably be a temporary one.

Somalia and Ethiopia are notable examples. The United States and the Soviet Union may have settled their affairs in the Horn of Africa through a form of cooperative disengagement, but they left behind a set of brewing conflicts which have one by one exploded. Events that followed in Somalia are less well known than the disasters of Ethiopia. In 1988 the two countries finally signed a peace treaty that would bring to an end eleven years of hostilities over the disputed territory of Ogaden. As part of that treaty, a rebel clan organized as the Somali National Movement returned to its homeland from Ethiopia, still armed with Soviet AK-47 rifles and other modern equipment. In the next two years, at least five additional rebel groups fought bitterly against the government in Mogadishu and among themselves. There have been

---

*Notice, for example, the specificity of deals that were made concerning military supplies in Afghanistan, or the specific terms of the disengagement agreement (including phased timing of Cuban troop withdrawals) in Angola.

thousands of battle casualties, and additional thousands have died of famine and disease. Washington cut off virtually the last of its aid to the Somali government after the president, Siad Barre, ordered his troops to slaughter hundreds of civilians during street demonstrations in July 1989. But the fighting has by no means slowed, and the Libyans are reported to have stepped into the breach as a new supplier of weapons. An American embassy official, asked about the future of the country, can now predict only "more turmoil and instability."[11]

The next question is whether cooperative disengagement teamed with joint facilitative mediation would do any better. Success would seem to rest on the argument that, minus superpower meddling, simple exhaustion at the regional level would make local rivals just willing enough to accept a friendly offer of outside mediation from a U.S.-Soviet consortium (again, possibly configured through the United Nations). That is a hopeful conclusion, but it will most often turn out wrong.

At a minimum, the local roots of the conflict—present before the superpowers ever got involved and usually exacerbated by events in the interim—will still be in place. Mediation does not succeed when the disputing parties find no overlap in their negotiating spaces. Even if there were room to settle civil wars, what of the interstate frictions—as between Costa Rica, Nicaragua, El Salvador, and Guatemala, for example—that would still fester? Finally, and perhaps most importantly, who will institute the land reform measures which many of the contributors to this volume point to as nearly a *sine qua non* of any solution with hopes for long-term stability? Governments that are in a position to negotiate about their preferences have rarely agreed to meaningful land reform; where that has taken place, it has usually been under the threat or the reality of forceful external intervention. Cooperative disengagement with or without facilitative mediation vitiates that threat.

The legacy of superpower involvement complicates mediation still further. Distrust shading into hatred between the local rivals, and between them and their former puppetmasters, is only part of that legacy. So are large stocks of weapons, some of which are concentrated in the hands of irregular military forces composed of individuals who have given up their lives to pursue ideologically impregnated causes. Mediation will not provide an easy answer to the fate of such forces. Rarely will groups like the Contras or the many factions of *mujahidin* be accepted voluntarily as legitimate participants in imagined governments of "national reconciliation." Lacking participation, they may not find offers of repatriation (should they be forthcoming) attractive. At the same time, neighboring states that have served as sanctuaries for guerilla groups will no longer want them. Neither the Hondurans nor the Pakistanis nor the Thais were ever particularly enthusiastic about playing the sanctuary role, and the last thing they want on their territories when the war is "over" is a heavily armed and ostracized paramilitary force with nowhere to turn its anger. Of course, paramilitary forces are not the only potential source of trouble. Many of the states that ring these regional conflicts have over time found it reassuring to increase the size of their regular armies, in part to balance against the presence of guerillas. Large numbers of military forces looking for something to do may not have to look very hard.

Joint facilitative mediation may work in some selected cases. More often, we would expect to see what Selig Harrison suggests to be the future of Afghanistan: balkanization. States left in that condition with large numbers of soldiers loyal to more than one cause are prime candidates for civil war. They are also tempting targets for would-be regional hegemons, as I pointed out earlier. The story of war in Lebanon may turn out to be a prophetic example of what happens when aspiring powers bump up against each other in a struggle for control over balkanized "states." Notice that the potential for escalation between countries like Syria and Israel probably exceeds what was realistic when the outsiders were the United States and the Soviet Union. To prevent lopsided outcomes gained by military force, Washington and Moscow as well might find themselves redirecting aid to the equivalents of Syria and Israel elsewhere in the world. Such conflicts can go on for an extremely long time. Lebanon very well might have been a battleground for as far into the future as one can see: over the course of at least fifteen years, Israel, Syria, and other regional powers made it abundantly clear that they preferred a hemorrhaging conflict to any compromise on basic issues. That war only ended when the crisis over Kuwait handed Syria a unique opportunity, and it ended with the decisive victory of one side. That is instructive.

Cooperative disengagement may look better from the perspective of Washington and Moscow, and it may be particularly appealing to important domestic political constituencies in these countries. But the outcome on the ground, with or without joint mediation, does not promise to look all that different in Indonesia or Malaysia or El Salvador. It would be reckless to get caught up in celebrating a short-term victory for U.S.-Soviet cooperation if that success meant little for the rest of the world, and was predisposed in any case to bring further and probably more severe trouble not far down the line. Another alternative is called for.

3. JOINT IMPOSITION

The third scenario, and the most demanding in terms of the level of U.S.-Soviet cooperation, I label "joint imposition of peace." Here, the United States and the Soviet Union would work together to set the terms for comprehensive or nearly comprehensive settlements of regional conflicts. They would then impose those settlements on recalcitrant local actors, using diplomatic, economic, and, if necessary, military instruments for persuasion and coercion. Note that by joint imposition I do not mean to imply any kind of cartoon picture, such as U.S. and Soviet armies occupying the West Bank of the Jordan and forcing the Israelis and Palestinians to shake hands at gunpoint. I mean, instead, a long-term, high-profile, and expensive commitment to compel compromises among local actors and impose settlements, the terms of which would be dictated primarily by the great powers of the North.*

Given the relative strengths of the countries concerned, and particularly the military balance, joint imposition is probably possible, at least in principle, in a substantial subset of regional conflicts. I do not underestimate the obstacles. Joint imposition would in most cases be expensive, difficult to implement, and hard to enforce. It may present problems from a moral standpoint as well. And it would demand an unprecedented measure of cooperation between Washington and Moscow. Still, the idea should be taken seriously because the major impediments have now gone away. There are also important incentives that I believe will push both Washington and Moscow in this direction over the next few years.

What has happened to the impediments? Through four decades of Cold War competition, the United States and the Soviet Union found it difficult to cooperate even when leaders recognized a set of broadly shared

---

*I see the difference between cooperative disengagement with joint facilitation, and joint imposition, as more than simply a matter of degree. Joint facilitation implies a *reduction* in the level of resources that the Northern powers would commit to settling conflicts in the South. It also implies mediation among local actors, who would remain primarily responsible for developing peace proposals and generating the necessary compromises themselves. Joint imposition implies an *increased* level of commitment, with the Northern powers taking the primary responsibility for developing and implementing proposals, while prodding and if necessary, coercing local actors into accepting compromise terms.

interests. The effort to construct a detente in the Third World during the early 1970s was no exception. Ideology and misunderstandings were both important parts of that story, but neither captures the central reason why this effort collapsed. That reason rests in the traditional logic of great power competition in an anarchic international system. Great powers threaten the interests and ultimately the autonomy of other great powers. Survival rests finally on maintaining a balance of power.

So long as that is the case, each state must worry about the problem of relative gains—the ever-present possibility that if they cooperate, one side will profit more than the other from the collaboration. There were no such relative gains to be had when it came to the simple problem of avoiding escalation to superpower war that might engage nuclear weapons—what I have elsewhere called "negative cooperation." "Positive cooperation," which would have gone beyond simply avoiding nuclear war, was still heavily disfavored. As long as there were relative gains to be had, leaders on both sides were tempted to defect from or cheat on agreements in search of some unilateral advantages. The Third World was often a theater for this kind of interaction. It was also a theater in which leaders demonstrated the credibility of their commitments to defend the state's more vital interests. This was a way of inverting the domino theory: if Washington would spend money and lives to prevent a relative Soviet gain of small magnitude in the periphery, it would presumably risk much more to protect the areas that really mattered to the balance of power.

It is sometimes said that with the Cold War at an end, the relative gains problem between the United States and the Soviet Union has diminished in magnitude. That statement is true in a broad sense, but it confuses cause with effect. To put it straight: the end of the relative gains problem made the end of the Cold War possible. Relative gains went away because the deeper source of the problem—the ever-present threat to a state's autonomy and territorial integrity—was overcome. It was not overcome by exhaustion or by world government, but by the condition of mutual nuclear deterrence. That condition has probably existed in an objective sense for almost thirty years, but it was only recently matched with a set of ideas learned through failed attempts at "nuclear diplomacy" and "brinkmanship" in a series of crises and Cold War confrontations.[12] In other words, leaders in Washington and Moscow came to recognize that the age-old dilemma of states—ensuring the integrity of homeland territory and vital interests—was no longer a dilemma for them. It was that recognition that brought the occupation of Eastern

Europe, the conventional arms race on the continent, and the other facets of jostling for security and relative gains that made up the Cold War to an end. It has also had significant consequences for superpower interaction in the Third World.

In early 1990, I argued that the end of the relative gains problem between the United States and the Soviet Union would produce a superpower security regime stretching out from the central front to a substantial part of the periphery.[13] I suspect that my argument is being borne out by the evidence. The United States and the Soviet Union now seem to want to cooperate across a broad range of issues, from the most ambitious kinds of arms control measures that have put a de facto end to the possibility for an invasion of Europe to finding solutions for Third World conflicts where only a few years ago they were on different sides of the war.

Not only has the Soviet Union given up the role of "spoiler" for U.S.-led initiatives in the Persian Gulf and the Middle East, but quite early in the Kuwait crisis, Moscow essentially threw in its chips with Washington to oppose its former ally Iraq. The United States, for its part, invited the Soviet Union to do so. At their Helsinki meeting in early September, the first U.S.-Soviet summit ever held during a time of world crisis, Presidents Bush and Gorbachev proclaimed that their two states would "be united as long as the crisis exists." For the most part, both states lived up to that vow.

This is not to deny that over the course of the crisis there were important differences, both procedural and substantive, over possible conditions for the use of force. But it would be terribly wrong to miss the forest for the trees. On balance, both Washington and Moscow went to great lengths to bridge the gaps between their sometimes differing interests in an effort to maintain the essence of the alliance. In September, Gorbachev overruled Soviet generals who expressed concern over the massing of U.S. forces in the Gulf, and he ridiculed suggestions that this could harm East-West arms talks.[14] Bush responded by telling American reporters that he had not specifically asked Gorbachev to send Soviet troops to the Gulf but that "if the Soviets decided to do that at the invitation of the Saudis, that would be fine with us."[15] After the summit, administration officials confirmed the sea change in American policy: the United States would now welcome broad, active Soviet participation in all aspects of Mideast diplomacy, ranging from the resolution of the Iraq crisis to a possible international conference on the Arab-Israeli-Palestinian conflict at some point in the future.[16]

This overturned what had long been a cardinal axiom of U.S. policy for the Mideast—to exclude Moscow whenever possible from active participation in the politics of the region. When the United States was *least* constrained to do so by the "realities" of power, when Moscow was in its weakest position relative to Washington, the Bush administration reversed course and brought the Soviets in as partners.

What is striking about the crisis in retrospect is how solid that partnership remained, even as Moscow's erstwhile ally was pressed and finally crushed by American military power. The Soviets agreed to authorize the use of force against Iraq in a dramatic vote at the UN Security Council in November. As the 15 January deadline approached, the failed peace efforts of Gorbachev's special representative Yevgeny Primakov and others were left behind in a clear choice to stand by the coalition forces. With a ground war imminent in mid-February, the Soviets made one last series of efforts to salvage something of their former ally, but when Saddam proved intransigent, Moscow stood by the United States.[17]

No doubt Gorbachev put the United States on notice that the Soviets were concerned about the level of violence, the expansion of coalition goals to include the removal of Saddam, and the uncompromising stance of Washington's cease-fire demands. But on balance, it is remarkable how easily and with how little substantial opposition the Soviets went along.

There must have been many arguments for doing otherwise in Moscow. Apart from their long-standing ties with Saddam and other radical Arab regimes, the Soviets had plain interests in what happened on the ground that ran counter to those of Washington. These were for the most part sacrificed to the greater perceived interest in maintaining U.S.-Soviet solidarity. To do that, Gorbachev probably had to overrule Arabists in his foreign ministry, right-wing politicians criticizing the "final sellout" to the West, and military officials who could not have savored the sight of a largely Soviet-supplied army falling prostrate to the United States, among others. He overruled them all with remarkably small concessions to their concerns. And once the ground war started, Moscow pulled back its peace initiatives and stood firmly with the coalition, supporting the Security Council's final demand on 26 February that Iraq accept all twelve resolutions of the council as a prerequisite for a cease-fire.[18] For their part, Bush administration officials worked to dismiss the Soviet peace initiatives in the week leading up to the ground war as quietly and politely as possible in a clear effort to ameliorate Gorbachev's plight and minimize potential damage to U.S.-Soviet relations. There will be relatively few grudges left over from this course of events.*

The Middle East is the most striking case, but it is not the only part of the world where U.S.-Soviet ventures are moving forward. Both sides have been involved for some time in efforts to resolve the Cambodian conflict, but the tenor of the effort changed when the Soviets began actively to pressure their Vietnamese allies for a withdrawal of their occupation army.[19] In October 1990, Moscow for the first time joined the United States in an effort to bring a cease-fire to El Salvador, and began to press Cuba on cutting arms shipments to the FMLN rebels.[20] In Angola, the United States and the Soviet Union have been working together for several years—first to conduct a staged withdrawal, and then to press the local parties to some kind of peace settlement.

Neil MacFarlane's paper notes that Moscow has probably increased its military assistance to Angola since Gorbachev came to power in 1985, but he suggests that this is not so much to press any kind of unilateral advantage as it is to stimulate a regional settlement. That argument is reinforced by the observation that Moscow at the same time urged its allies in the Angolan government to accommodate Savimbi's guerillas under a cease-fire that would be followed by elections, both monitored by a joint U.S.-Soviet force.[21] Notice that this would make the additional military aid obsolete. It would also entail a longer-term investment of money and political capital in a part of the world that is far from vital in the Soviet calculus of interests. For a state with precious few resources to waste in the midst of what was supposedly a massive strategic retrenchment, that is surprising.

Cooperation of this sort is not trivial. The end of the Cold War makes unprecedented kinds of cooperation possible, but it does not make extensive cooperation easy. There are still disincentives of other kinds, the most obvious being the economic constraints. Why should two powers, one in relative economic decline and the other in absolute, want to get involved in costly efforts to impose peace on regional conflicts that remain peripheral to their vital interests?

---

*There were reports that some high officials in the Bush administration were both annoyed and worried by Moscow's peace initiatives, although those officials never came forward publicly with their arguments. There also seems to have been some concern that Gorbachev's motions were another signal of a growing military influence in Soviet decision-making. But the general tone in Washington seems to have been a sensitive appreciation of the many constraints under which Gorbachev was operating, and a recognition of his broader effort to sustain the essential elements of U.S.-Soviet cooperation in the Gulf crisis.

Interests intrinsic to the Third World are a part of the answer. Both sides want to avoid the unfortunate outcomes that I associated with unilateral and even cooperative disengagement. For Washington, the undesirability of those outcomes may not seem quite so immediate. For Moscow, the issues are usually much closer to home. Southern Africa is roughly equidistant from the Soviet Union and the United States, but the Middle East and the Southeast Asian subcontinent are not. Instability in these parts of the world, and particularly in the fertile crescent, laps at the southern borders of the Soviet Union, where nationalist-ethnic tensions are already high. But these intrinsic interests can only be part of the story, since joint imposition of peace in cooperation with the United States is not an obvious solution to the threat of Islamic fundamentalism dismantling the southern republics. Similarly, intrinsic interests are not enough to explain Moscow's willingness to engage in similar enterprises in Africa.

I suspect that the rest of the explanation lies in a new form of U.S.-Soviet politics. What we are now seeing and will continue to see in the Third World is a repeat of a very old great power politics tradition in a slightly new guise. Throughout history, great powers have made instrumental use of small states, arranging and rearranging relationships in the periphery to suit the needs of the "more important" issues being worked out or fought out on the central front. The Third World played this instrumental role for U.S.-Soviet *competition* during the Cold War. I think that it is beginning to play a similarly instrumental role for *cooperation*.

The United States and the Soviet Union are now interested in making a series of deals with each other in areas of central interest— strategic arms control, a future security system for Europe, economic aid and interaction, etc. Relative gains may no longer be a decisive concern, but that does not replace central authority in the international system. The system is still anarchic, which means there is no central government that can make and enforce rules. More important right now for Moscow and Washington is the fact that there is no international authority to ensure the enforcement of contracts that individual sovereign states choose to make between themselves. Private enforcement is still the rule, and because the same condition of mutual nuclear deterrence that undermined the relative gains dilemma also rules out enforcement by threat in U.S.-Soviet relations, some other mechanism is needed if these two countries are going to be able to make and sustain contracts between themselves. Lacking that, deals that would be in both sides' best interests will not be made for want of a credible promise.

How do states make credible commitments to contract in a world without centralized enforcement? Power, specifically military power, is only one way (although it is certainly the most reliable). Reputation helps, but it is easier in international relations to gain a bad reputation than it is to maintain a good one. A more convincing method is to create a domestic political system that ensures transparency to outsiders.[22] If other states can look inside the state's polity and decision-making system, they can understand the state's interests and how those interests get translated into policy. In that case, the state can make a credible promise that it will fulfill the terms of a contract because others can see that the contract accords with the state's interests. Credibility is further enhanced if the state's legal system respects international treaties as the "supreme law of the land" and makes it difficult or impossible for a government to undermine them arbitrarily or on short notice. All of these factors currently operate in Washington's favor, enhancing its ability to make credible promises to potential partners when it is in its interest to do so.

Unfortunately, none of these strategies is currently available to the Soviet Union. Whether deserved or not, Moscow's reputation for observing international agreements with the West started badly at Yalta and has, if anything, gotten worse over time. Political institutions that could encourage greater transparency of interests are only now coming into being in the Soviet Union; neither their current influence nor their longevity are proven. The legal system is almost irrelevant. Under these conditions, it becomes difficult for a Soviet leader to promise anything to Washington, and it is equally difficult for Washington to believe, even if both sides would in fact prefer to do so.

There is another way to increase the credibility of a commitment which is, fortunately, still available to Moscow—that is, to make *illiquid investments*. Firms do this all the time as a way of making credible commitments in markets that similarly lack central enforcement. That is, they place significant resources in fixed investments in plant or other endeavors, and do so in ways that the resources cannot be recovered or redirected to other purposes.[23]

This is also a common strategy for states. And it may explain why the Soviet Union is now willing to invest economic and political resources in cooperative endeavors aimed at places like Angola or El Salvador. These are similarly illiquid investments which would be lost wholesale if the Soviet Union were to suddenly shift gears and defect on its commitments to the United States. That the Soviets do not have a lot of extra resources to play with at this time increases the potency of the strategy, and the more resources that Moscow invests, the more effective it is likely to be.

That is why joint imposition of peace with all its dilemmas is a real possibility for the 1990s. I propose that what we are seeing and will continue to see is a reversal of the 1970s dynamic, when the failure of cooperation in the Third World worked to undermine more central features of a nascent U.S.-Soviet detente. Successful cooperation in the Third World is now instrumental to contracts on more central issues, and the more extensive the cooperation in the periphery, the larger the payoff elsewhere.

Domestic politics comes back into the picture here. In his paper, George Breslauer rightly stresses the problem of the reciprocal "enemy images" that are part of the legacy of the Cold War. He points out that domestic politics in the Soviet Union could undermine sustained cooperation with the United States even in the light of "new thinking" because the reconceptualization of the international order contained therein does not extend to a reconceptualization of the United States as an actor. Washington faces comparable dilemmas in managing American domestic politics when it comes to making policy for cooperation with the Soviets. The hard right-wing in American politics may be subdued for the moment, but it is sure to reemerge given any substantial opportunity. How can these states alter the enemy images that imperil cooperation?

Joint imposition, precisely because it is so costly, could again be instrumental to these larger goals. Enemy images change slowly, but they are most likely to change when actors make voluntary concessions to each other that are both costly and consistent.[24] Both sides have made such moves over the last few years, most spectacularly by the Soviet Union in arms control and in Europe. There are not many more dramatic concessions to be made in either arena. That makes the Third World an important source of opportunity.

The Soviets have made active use of such chances, even in parts of the Third World where they were not previously willing to make substantial investments. In late December, for example, Moscow essentially sold out its erstwhile friends the Sandinistas by helping the United States to track arms shipments from Nicaragua to the resistance in El Salvador.[25] The Gulf crisis, paradoxically, has presented Washington with chances of its own to prove that its "imperialist spots" have in fact changed. In a series of major policy statements during the fall of 1990, Secretary of State Baker consistently argued that the Bush administration saw the Gulf crisis as setting precedents not only for potential aggressors in the post–Cold War world, but also for the new environment of superpower cooperation. Among the members or pseudo-members of the coalition arrayed against Hussein, he consistently singled out the Soviet Union for praise: "In particular, the Soviet Union has proven a responsible partner, suggesting new possibilities for active superpower cooperation in resolving regional conflicts."[26] Bush went to Helsinki a few days later and, as I noted before, invited Gorbachev into Middle East politics as a partner, reversing a fundamental tenet of American foreign policy and conceding status to the Soviet Union when he was under the least compunction to do so. That is a voluntary and costly concession that is not likely to be lost on the doubters in Moscow.[27] If the United States follows up on that promise with the war at an end, the evidence will be even more convincing.

CONCLUSION

I began this essay with the presumption that the Third World would continue to feel the presence of the United States and the Soviet Union, but that the old superpower politics of Cold War competition in the periphery was at an end. What kind of politics will replace it? Unilateral disengagement and cooperative disengagement did not seem viable alternatives. A third scenario—joint imposition of peace—demands an unprecedented level of U.S.-Soviet cooperation. But the major impediments are gone, and there are substantial incentives for both sides to proceed in that direction. We may be witnessing the evolution of a U.S.-Soviet security regime that will set the terms for peaceful settlements in at least some of the continuing conflicts in the periphery.[28]

Is that morally repugnant in the context of what is possible in international politics? It is worth remembering that great powers have always tried to impose their vision of order on lesser states, and that the weak have frequently gotten bloodied in arguments between great powers over whose vision of order would prevail. If it were left on its own, the Third World would likely continue to be bloodied by conflicts between regional powers, between religious and ethnic groups, between nationalist rivals each seeking their own state. Facing this kind of an alternative, it may be that some solution, almost any solution, would be better than none.

The terms of an imposed solution are not likely to be so burdensome as other terms were in the past. The likely imposers are coming to share a set of ideas about the desirable internal characteristics of governments that will favor democratic or at least representative regimes over totalitarian or authoritarian ones. There is a broad recognition of the rights of self-determination for ethnic-racial groups like the Palestinians. There is an expanding commitment to preventing the proliferation of weapons of mass destruction, and sanctioning countries that try to slip through the cracks. And there is a strongly shared reluctance to use force except when it is absolutely necessary to back each of those things up. The declining relative status of the United States and the Soviet Union as "superpowers" reinforces these trends. If the United States and the Soviet Union are to be the leaders, they will still have to appeal to the Europeans and the Japanese for financial and political support in unprecedented and increasing measure. This will provide a healthy measure of restraint and a greater range of ideas about how to proceed. The result may be more peace and eventually even more prosperity in parts of the Third World even if the peace has at first to be imposed.

NOTES

Thanks to George Breslauer, Eileen Doherty, David Stuligross, and Felicia Wong for extensive comments and criticisms.

1. Jacob Viner, from a speech of 16 November 1945 in the Symposium on Atomic Energy and Its Implications; reprinted as "The Implications of the Atomic Bomb for International Relations," *Proceedings of the American Philosophical Society* 90, January 1946.

2. Steven Erlanger, "Rush for Resources Impels a New Asia Arms Race," *New York Times*, 6 May 1990; *The Economist*, 12 January 1991. For comparison, NATO nations in 1987 spent on average 3.4 percent of GDP on defense.

3. See *World Bank Development Report 1990* (New York: Oxford University Press).

4. George Breslauer discusses both possibilities in his contribution to this volume.

5. At least this was the case after 1949. See my *Multilateralism in NATO: Shaping the Postwar Balance of Power, 1945–1961* (Berkeley: International and Area Studies, 1991).

6. This was true even of what became NATO; see my *Multilateralism in NATO* for details.

7. Reported in *The Economist*, 4 August 1990, p. 25; also in Thomas Friedman, "U.S. Shifts Cambodia Policy," *New York Times*, 19 July 1990. This is probably

also a major reason why Singapore has showed interest in receiving American bases that look ready to be evicted from the Philippines.

8. *Ibid.*

9. George Breslauer builds on this theme in his contribution to this volume and in "All Gorbachev's Men," *The National Interest* 12 (Summer 1988): 91–100.

10. See the contribution by Breslauer.

11. Quoted in Jane Perlez, "Somalia, Abandoned to Its Own Civil War with Other's Weapons," *New York Times*, 6 January 1991.

12. See my "Interactive Learning in U.S.-Soviet Arms Control" in *Learning in US and Soviet Foreign Policy*, eds. George Breslauer and Philip Tetlock (Boulder: Westview, 1991); also "Security After 1989" in *The Future of Nuclear Weapons*, ed. Patrick Garrity (New York: Plenum, 1991).

13. "Realism, Detente, and Nuclear Weapons," *International Organization* 44, Winter 1990.

14. See Gorbachev's response to the comments of General Vladimir Lobov, Commander in Chief of the Warsaw Pact, reported in Leyla Boulton, "Soviet Anxiety at U.S. Military Build-Up," *Financial Times*, 3 September 1990, p. 2. The next day, Soviet Foreign Ministry spokesman Gennady Gerasimov repeated the message and rejected any suggestion that the American buildup might represent an "imperialist" venture aimed against Soviet interests, adding that "the Americans are there [in the Gulf] at the invitation of Saudi Arabia. . . . The Americans appeared there not on their own initiative, but they were provoked into it by Iraqi actions" ("Soviet Union Lines Up with West Against Iraq in Gulf," *Financial Times*, 4 September 1990), p. 1.

15. Bill Keller, "Bush and Gorbachev Vow Unity in Opposing Baghdad," *New York Times*, 10 September 1990.

16. "Bush, Reversing U.S. Policy, Won't Oppose a Soviet Role in Middle East Peace Talks," *New York Times*, 11 September 1990. The Bush-Gorbachev joint statement from Helsinki contained the following lines: "As soon as the objectives mandated by the UN Security Council resolutions mentioned above have been achieved and we have demonstrated that aggression does not pay, the Presidents direct their foreign ministers to work with countries in the region and outside it to develop . . . measures to promote peace and stability. It is essential to work actively to resolve all remaining conflicts in the Middle East and Persian Gulf." Behind those words, according to American officials, was a serious American commitment to involve the Soviet Union as a partner—not merely as a figurehead as had been the case in the short international peace conference of December 1973.

17. On 26 February, Soviet Ambassador to the United Nations Yuli M. Vorontsov reversed his government's previous position—which had called for a cease-fire in exchange only for Iraqi withdrawal from Kuwait. Henceforth, the Soviets would demand an agreement for full Iraqi compliance with all twelve Security Council resolutions at the same time as a cease-fire (Paul Lewis, "Soviet, at UN, Sides with Allies on Setting Terms for Cease-Fire," *New York Times*, 27 February 1991).

18. *Ibid.*

19. Frederick Brown (in this volume) discusses some additional reasons why Moscow chose this course—most notably the linkage established by the Chinese, who demanded a Vietnamese withdrawal from Cambodia as a prerequisite to improving Sino-Soviet relations.

20. Clifford Krauss, "U.S. and Soviets Jointly Urge Settlement in Salvador," *New York Times*, 19 October 1990.

21. This proposal is reported in Clifford Krauss, "U.S. and Soviets Outline a Truce and Vote in Angola," *New York Times*, 2 October 1990. This would replace a cease-fire arranged in 1989 under the mediation of President Mobutu Sese Seko of Zaire. The United States and the Soviet Union were not involved in that agreement: it broke down quickly and led to intensified fighting.

22. Thanks to Peter Cowhey for this idea. See his "Elect Locally, Order Globally"; manuscript for Ford Foundation Project on Multilateralism, December 1990.

23. The well-known "chain-store paradox" in economics is one example. For a more general discussion, see Oliver E. Williamson, *Economic Organization: Firms, Markets, and Policy Control* (New York: New York University Press, 1986).

24. See Deborah Larson's work on the social psychology of attribution errors in international politics, and on the emergence of conventions in U.S.-Soviet relations.

25. Clifford Krauss, "Moscow Promises to Remain Steady in Foreign Affairs," *New York Times*, 29 December 1990, reports that Soviet ambassador to Washington Aleksandr Bessmertnykh, in discussions over El Salvador held in the last week of December with President Bush and Undersecretary of State for Political Affairs Robert M. Kimmitt, "helped prove that SA-14 anti-aircraft missiles deployed not long ago by the Salvadoran guerillas came from Nicaragua, by identifying the serial number on an SA-14 missile casing found near a downed aircraft as that of a missile Moscow donated to the Nicaraguan Army in 1985."

26. "America's Stake in the Persian Gulf Crisis"; prepared statement of Secretary of State Baker before the House Foreign Affairs Committee, 4 September 1990; reprinted as U.S. Department of State *Current Policy*, No. 1297, p 2.

27. Gorbachev seemed to underscore that point when, in response to a question at the joint news conference following the summit, he revealed what he called a "secret" about his conversation with Bush: "In our talks, the President said 'You know, there was a long time when our view was that the Soviet Union had nothing to do in the Middle East . . . and had no business being there.' This was something that we had to talk through during this meeting here in Helsinki, and what was said here is that it's very important for us to cooperate in the Middle East, just as it is on other issues of world politics" (*New York Times*, 10 September 1990).

28. This regime need not be limited to the former superpowers. I suspect it may come to include the European Community as a principal actor at some point in the medium term. For a discussion of some of the prospects, see my "Security after 1989."

INTERNATIONAL AND AREA STUDIES
University of California at Berkeley

2223 Fulton Street, 3rd floor   Berkeley, California 94720

Albert Fishlow, *Dean*

Recent books published by International and Area Studies include:

RESEARCH SERIES

71. *State & Welfare, USA/USSR: Contemporary Policy & Practice.*
Eds. Gail W. Lapidus & Guy E. Swanson. $22.50

72. *The Politics of Debt in Argentina, Brazil, & Mexico.*
Robert R. Kaufman. $9.50

73. *No Longer an American Lake? Alliance Problems in the South Pacific.*
Ed. John Ravenhill. $14.95

74. *Thinking New about Soviet "New Thinking."*
V. Kubálková & A. A. Cruickshank. $11.50

75. *Iberian Identity: Essays on the Nature of Identity in Portugal & Spain.*
Eds. Richard Herr & John H. R. Polt. $17.50

76. *Argentine Unions, the State & the Rise of Perón, 1930–1945.*
Joel Horowitz. $16.95

77. *The New Europe Asserts Itself: A Changing Role in International
Relations.* Eds. Beverly Crawford & Peter W. Schulze. $19.95

78. *The Soviet Sobranie of Laws: Problems of Codification and
Non-Publication.* Eds. Richard Buxbaum & Kathryn Hendley. $16.95

79. *Multilateralism in NATO: Shaping the Postwar Balance of Power,
1945–1961.* Steve Weber. $9.50

INSTITUTE OF INTERNATIONAL STUDIES:

POLICY PAPERS IN INTERNATIONAL AFFAIRS

35. *Large-Scale Foreign Policy Change: The Nixon Doctrine as History
& Portent.* Earl C. Ravenal. $8.50

36. *The Internationalization of Japan's Security Policy: Challenges &
Dilemmas for a Reluctant Power.* Michael G. L'Estrange. $5.95

37. *Why We Need Ideologies in U.S. Foreign Policy: Democratic Politics
& World Order.* Edward H. Alden & Franz Schurmann. $8.50

38. *Vanguard Parties & Revolutionary Change in the Third World: Soviet
Perspectives & Their Implications.* David E. Albright. $9.50

INSTITUTE OF EAST ASIAN STUDIES:

RESEARCH PAPERS AND POLICY STUDIES

33. *U.S.-Thailand Relations in a New International Era.*
Eds. Clark Neher and Wiwat Mungkandi. $20.00

34. *Korea-U.S. Relations in a Changing World.*
Eds. Robert Sutter and Han Sungjoo. $20.00

35. *Japan, ASEAN, and the United States.*
Eds. Harry H. Kendall and Clara Joewono. $20.00

36. *Asia in the 1990s: American and Soviet Perspectives.*
Eds. Robert A. Scalapino and Gennady I. Chufrin. $20.00

KOREA RESEARCH MONOGRAPHS

16. *North Korea in Transition.*
Eds. Chong-Sik Lee and Yoo Se-Hee. $12.00

CHINA RESEARCH MONOGRAPHS

36. *China's Education Reform in the 1980s: Policies, Issues, and Historical Perspectives.* Suzanne Pepper. $12.00

37. *Building a Nation-State: China after Forty Years.*
Ed. Joyce K. Kallgren. $12.00

INDOCHINA RESEARCH MONOGRAPHS

5. *The Bunker Papers: Reports to the President from Vietnam, 1967–1973.*
Ed. Douglas Pike.   (3 vols.) $35.00

**CENTER FOR SLAVIC AND EAST EUROPEAN STUDIES/
BERKELEY-STANFORD PROGRAM IN SOVIET STUDIES**

Analyzing the Gorbachev Era: Working Papers of the Students of the Berkeley-Stanford Program. $8.00

Can Gorbachev's Reforms Succeed?
Ed. George W. Breslauer. $12.95

Steeltown, USSR: Glasnost, Destalinization & Perestroika in the Provinces.
Stephen Kotkin. $6.00